Life-Study of Thessalonians Timothy Titus Philemon

Witness Lee

Living Stream Ministry
Anaheim, California

First Edition, May 1984.

Library of Congress Catalog
Card Number: 84-80725

ISBN 0-87083-134-8 (1 & 2 Thessalonians,
1 & 2 Timothy, Titus, and Philemon)
ISBN 0-87083-126-7 (9 Volume Set of Paul's Epistles)

Published by

Living Stream Ministry
2431 W. La Palma Ave., Anaheim, CA 92801 U.S.A.
P. O. Box 2121, Anaheim, CA 92814 U.S.A.

Printed in the United States of America

02 03 04 05 06 / 11 10 9 8 7 6 5 4 3

1 Thessalonians

CONTENTS

2 Thessalonians

CONTENTS

1 Timothy

CONTENTS

2 Timothy

CONTENTS

Titus

CONTENTS

Philemon

CONTENTS

LIFE-STUDY OF FIRST THESSALONIANS

MESSAGE ONE

INTRODUCTION TO A HOLY LIFE FOR THE CHURCH LIFE

Scripture Reading: 1 Thes. 1:1-3

The two Epistles of Paul to the Thessalonians may be considered the earliest of Paul's writings. Thessalonica was a city of the Roman Empire in the province of Macedonia, north of the province of Achaia. After the Macedonian call, which Paul received on his second journey of ministry, he and his co-worker Silvanus visited first Philippi and then Thessalonica (Acts 16:9-12; 17:1-4). The apostle stayed and worked there for only a short time, probably less than one month (Acts 17:2).

WRITTEN TO NEW BELIEVERS

The two Epistles to the Thessalonians were written in the early days, while Paul was still on his second journey of ministry. In the course of this journey, Paul stayed in Thessalonica for less than a month. According to Acts, Paul worked there for three Sabbaths, for about three weeks, not long after his visit to Philippi. The Epistle to the Philippians, a wonderful book, was written much later, during Paul's imprisonment.

No doubt, when Paul wrote to the Thessalonians, the church in Thessalonica was still very young. I doubt that the believers there had been in the church life for even a full year when these two Epistles were written. Thus, in 1 and 2 Thessalonians we see certain points that are not covered in Paul's other Epistles. Because the church in Thessalonica was so young, Paul's Epistles to the Thessalonians are more or less to those in a childhood stage. Some of what Paul says to the Thessalonians is different from what he says to other churches that were more experienced. It is worthwhile for us to study 1 and 2 Thessalonians in order to know the situation and condition of a young church. By reading these two books we can know the young Christian life and the young church life. If we keep in mind this aspect of the background, we shall be helped in our reading of these Epistles.

The books of 1 and 2 Thessalonians were not written to experienced Christians. They were written to young believers, to those who had been saved for less than a year. Most of them had been typical Gentiles. Therefore, in writing to them, Paul surely viewed them as young believers. These Epistles are very precious, for they render us particular help concerning the young Christian life and church life.

THE ORGANIC UNION

First Thessalonians 1:1 says, "Paul and Silvanus and Timothy to the church of the Thessalonians in God the Father and the Lord Jesus Christ: Grace to you and peace." This Epistle and the second were both addressed to the local church in Thessalonica, composed of all the believers in Christ in that city. Such a local church is of the believers and is in God the Father and the Lord Jesus Christ. This indicates that such a local church is born of God the Father with His life and nature and is united with the Lord Jesus Christ organically in all He is and has done. Hence, it is of men (such as the Thessalonians), yet in God and in the Lord organically. Such an organic union in the divine life and nature is the vital base for the believers to live a holy life for the church life, which is the theme of the two Epistles.

In his opening word to the Thessalonians Paul speaks in a plain manner. He does not say, as in Romans 1:1, that he is "a slave of Christ Jesus, a called apostle, separated to the gospel of God"; neither does he say, as in Ephesians 1:1, that he is an "apostle of Christ Jesus through the will of God." The opening of Romans and Ephesians is more complicated than that of 1 Thessalonians. Because this Epistle was written to young believers, in 1:1 Paul simply says, "Paul and Silvanus and Timothy to the church of the Thessalonians."

It is a particular characteristic of Paul's writing to emphasize the organic union of the believers with the Triune God. In fact, the emphasis on the organic union with Christ is an outstanding feature of Paul's writings. In his Epistles Paul again and again speaks of being in Christ, in the Triune God. Although 1:1 is written in a simple way, it nevertheless includes Paul's characteristic reference to the organic union. In this verse Paul speaks of the church of the Thessalonians *in* God the Father and the Lord Jesus Christ. The preposition "in" here is very important; it indicates that the church is in the Triune God. The church is composed of human beings, but they, the believers, are in the Triune God. On the one hand, the church in Thessalonica was of the Thessalonians; on the other hand, this church was in God the Father.

A LIFE [redacted]D THE FATHER

Paul does not merely say that the church is in God; he says that the church is in God the Father. Unless God is our Father, we cannot be in Him. We were not created in God; however, we were regenerated, born again, in Him. We were created outside of God. This means that in creation we did not have any organic union with God or any life relationship with Him. Instead, there was only the relationship between the creature and the Creator. As a result of creation, we are God's creatures, and He is our Creator. Hence, there is a relationship of creation, but no relationship in life. God's life was not created into our natural being. As God's creatures, we did not have the life of God. We had only our created life, our natural human life.

When we were regenerated, born of God, our life relationship with God began. This rebirth brought us into the organic union with the Triune God. At the time of our regeneration, our rebirth, we obtained God's life. Now God is not merely our Creator, our God; He is our Father, the One who has begotten us. God is no longer merely our Creator—He is also our Begetter, for He has begotten us with His life. Therefore, He is God our Father.

[redacted]

Through regeneration the Thessalonian believers had become sons of God. According to the book of Romans, the church is a composition of sons of God. It is impossible for sinners to be components of the church. Sinners can be members of a secular organization, but they cannot be components of the church of the living God. Such a church is composed only of sons of God.

We have been predestinated by the Father to be His sons. As Ephesians 1:5 says, we have been predestinated unto sonship. At a certain time, God called us and moved us inwardly. Then we repented, believed in the Son of God, Jesus Christ, and received Him. By receiving Christ, we were reborn and became sons of God. Now that we are sons of God, we are the components of the church, the Body of Christ. Because we, as sons of God, are the members of Christ, 1:1 says not only that the church is in God the Father, but also that the church is in the Lord Jesus Christ.

CALLING ON THE LORD JESUS

It is very significant that in 1:1 Paul inserts the title Father after God and the title Lord before Jesus Christ. It is not sufficient to speak either of God or of Jesus Christ. Rather, we need to say that God is our Father and that Jesus Christ is our Lord. If Jesus Christ is not our Lord, then we have nothing to do with Him in a practical way. But when Jesus Christ becomes our Lord, this means that we are in Him, organically united to Him.

When we call on the name of the Lord Jesus, we should not just say "Jesus"; we should say, "Lord Jesus." To call on Him only by saying "Jesus" is to call somewhat ignorantly. The Lord, however, is merciful, and He sympathizes with us. He still responds when we call "Jesus" instead of "Lord Jesus," for He realizes that actually we are calling on Him as Lord. Nevertheless, we need the proper knowledge of calling on the Lord. Instead of saying, "Jesus, I love You," it is better to say, "Lord Jesus, I love You." How sweet it is to call on the Lord in this way!

Some Christians like to say, "Praise God!" But in the New Testament the emphasis is on praising God the Father. We need to realize that for us today God is our Father and Jesus is our Lord. According to 1 Corinthians 12:3, when we say, "Lord Jesus," we are in the Spirit. This indicates that the Spirit honors the proper calling on the Lord Jesus. Many of us can testify that when we call, "Lord Jesus," we sense the anointing of the Spirit within. The same is true of saying, "Abba, Father." If we merely call on God, Elohim, we do not have much anointing. But when we cry, "Abba, Father," we experience the anointing. This is not a matter of terminology; it is a reality in our experience.

THE CHURCH IN GOD THE FATHER AND THE LORD JESUS CHRIST

We need to be impressed with the fact that the church is in God the Father and the Lord Jesus Christ. To say "the Lord Jesus Christ" implies a great deal. First, it implies that Jesus Christ is our Lord. Second, it implies that He is our Savior, for the name Jesus means Jehovah the Savior. Third, it implies that Christ, God's anointed One, is bringing us into the riches of God and is accomplishing everything with us for God. Therefore, to say "the Lord Jesus Christ" is to utter something all-inclusive.

When Paul says that the church is in God the Father and the Lord Jesus Christ, he indicates that we have been born of God and have been brought into the organic union with Christ. What is the church? The church is a group of human beings who have been born of God and who have been brought into the organic union with Christ.

WORK OF FAITH

In verses 2 and 3 Paul goes on to say, "We give thanks to God always concerning you all, making mention of you in our prayers, remembering unceasingly your work of faith, and labor of love, and endurance of hope of our Lord Jesus Christ, before our God and Father." Here we see that when Paul prays for the church he gives thanks to God for three matters: for the work of faith, the labor of love, and the endurance of hope. Faith here indicates the nature and strength of the work. Our work is our faith. This means that the nature and strength of our Christian work is faith. The strength with which we work and the nature of our work should both be faith. Our Christian work should be of the nature of faith, not of the nature of human knowledge, ability, or power.

LABOR OF LOVE

We need to understand the difference between work and labor. Work may be something which is not very deep and which may not be very difficult. Labor, however, is both deeper and harder than work. When we are doing a work that is difficult to accomplish, that is a labor. This labor should be of love. Love is the motivation and the characteristic of our Christian labor. This means that love is the expression. Our Christian work eventually becomes a labor, something that is deeper and more difficult. For this labor, faith alone is not adequate; we also need love, a love that is lasting.

Raising children is a good illustration of a labor of love. Mothers know that caring for a child is a labor, not merely a work. After giving birth, a new mother will have a tender love for her infant. For a while she will work happily to care for the child. Eventually, however, that work will become a labor that presses and exhausts her. How good it is that the Lord has created within this young mother a mother's love for her child! Without such a love, she would not be able to bear the burden of caring for her child over the years. This love motivates her to care for her child. It is also the characteristic, the expression, of her labor. This illustrates that in the Christian life first we have a work of faith and then this work becomes a labor of love.

ENDURANCE OF HOPE

From the work of faith and the labor of love we go on to the endurance of hope. Hope is the source of endurance. All mothers know that caring for children requires endurance. It takes endurance for a mother to bear all the troubles that come with raising children.

In the church life as well as in the family life we all need endurance. We must be trained, educated, first to work, then to labor, and eventually to endure. An apostle is one who endures. As long as he has endurance, he is qualified to be an apostle. In 2 Corinthians we can see the endurance of the Apostle Paul. Such endurance is the topstone of our work. Elders, endurance is the topstone of the eldership. Likewise, in the work of shepherding others, endurance is crucial. If we would be successful in shepherding the saints, we must exercise endurance. Endurance involves suffering, not enjoyment. Shepherding always involves an amount of suffering.

In 1:3 Paul speaks of the endurance of hope of our Lord Jesus Christ. This endurance comes from the hope in the Lord's coming, or from the hope in the coming Lord. Hope is the source of endurance.

THE STRUCTURE OF THE CHRISTIAN LIFE

The faith, the love, and the hope in 1:3 depict the structure of the genuine Christian life, constructed with these elements. Faith receives the divine things (John 1:12) and realizes the spiritual and unseen things (Heb. 11:1). Hope reaps and partakes of the things realized by faith (Rom. 8:24-25). Love enjoys the things received and realized by faith and partaken of by hope for nourishing ourselves, building up others, and expressing God. Such a life originates not from the ability of the believer's natural being, but from the infusion of what God is, in whom they believe. It is carried out by their sacrificial love toward their loving Lord, who loved them and gave Himself for them, and toward His members, whom He has redeemed through His death in love. This life lasts and stands unchanging by the sustaining power of the hope that looks for their beloved Lord, who promised that He would come to take them to Himself. Such a life is the content of this Epistle.

I hope that from 1 and 2 Thessalonians we shall all see something that is helpful to young believers. We need to help the new ones to grow in faith, in love, and in hope, in particular, in the work of faith, in the labor of love, and in the endurance of hope.

It is marvelous that the Thessalonian believers could live such a life through the apostle's short ministry of less than one month. This encourages us to preach, in full assurance of faith, the complete gospel to typical unbelievers and minister the deeper truths concerning the Christian life to new converts. Do not hold the concept that, as you preach the full gospel, others will not be able to understand what you are saying. First we must believe for others. Then they themselves will believe. If we do not believe what we are preaching, others will never believe it. Thus, we must believe that those who hear us will be able to understand, receive, and accept the full gospel. Likewise, we must go on to minister the deeper truths of the Christian life to new believers. May we all learn to preach something deeper than what we think others are able to understand.

In the two Epistles to the young church in Thessalonica, the genuine Christian life for the proper church life is revealed in a simple and brief way. It is a life of three dimensions in the light of the Lord's coming back: faith as the beginning, the foundation; love as the process, the structure; and hope as the consummation, the topstone. Faith is toward God (1:8); love is toward the saints (3:12; 4:9-10); and hope is in the Lord's coming (2:19). The first Epistle is for encouragement and comfort; the second is for correction and balance. The believers should live, walk, and work by faith and love in the hope of the Lord's coming back. But we should not have the wrong concept that the Lord will come immediately, so that we need not do anything for the long run.

THE CONSUMMATION OF THE CHRISTIAN LIFE FOR THE CHURCH LIFE

These two Epistles may be considered the consummation of the Christian life for the church life. They conclude the section of the Apostle Paul's writings that begins with the book of Romans. Although these two Epistles are for the young Christian life and church life, they may also be regarded as the consummation of the Christian life for the church life.

According to the sequence of the New Testament writings, we have Romans, 1 and 2 Corinthians, Galatians, Ephesians, Philippians, Colossians, and 1 and 2 Thessalonians. These nine Epistles may be considered a group. The consummation and conclusion of this group of nine Epistles are 1 and 2 Thessalonians.

In this message we have covered two basic points: first, that the church is composed of human beings in God the Father and in the Lord Jesus Christ, those who have the life of God and who are in the organic union with Christ; second, that the church life is the Christian life constructed of the work of faith, the labor of love, and the endurance of hope in the coming Lord. May we all be deeply impressed with these two points. We need to see that the church is the composition of human beings who are in God the Father with life and who are organically in the Lord Jesus Christ. We also need to see that the Christian life for the church life is constructed of the work of faith, the labor of love, and the endurance of hope. In forthcoming messages we shall see more concerning this work of faith, labor of love, and endurance of hope.

LIFE-STUDY OF FIRST THESSALONIANS

MESSAGE TWO

CHARACTERISTICS OF A HOLY LIFE FOR THE CHURCH LIFE

Scripture Reading: 1 Thes. 1:4-10

The more we read the book of 1 Thessalonians, the more we realize that it truly was written to young believers. In this Epistle Paul is speaking to new believers.

SELECTED BY GOD

In 1:4 he says, "Knowing, brothers beloved by God, your selection." Selection refers to God's choosing before the foundation of the world for His eternal purpose (Eph. 1:4). The apostles knew that the brothers beloved by God were chosen in such a manner by God for the fulfillment of His heart's desire. The apostles knew that the Thessalonians were included among God's selected people, His chosen ones. Their selection had been made manifest to such an extent that the apostles had the assurance that the Thessalonian believers had been selected by God.

The fact that the Thessalonians had been selected by God was manifested by their reaction to the gospel. How do we know that we have been selected? We know this by the way we respond to the gospel. If a person rejects the gospel, that is a sign that he has not been selected by God. But if he accepts the gospel willingly in a positive way, that acceptance is a sign, an indicator, that he surely has been selected by God.

God selected us in eternity, before the foundation of the world. But in time He comes to us in the preaching of the gospel. Now it is a matter of our reaction. If our reaction is positive, that is a positive sign, a sign that we have been selected. But if our reaction is negative, that is a negative sign, a sign that we have not been selected. The apostles knew that the Thessalonians had been selected by God because of their ready and willing acceptance of the gospel in a very positive way.

No doubt, Paul's word in 1:4 concerning selection is directed to young believers. New Christians need to be helped to know that they have been selected by God. The foundation of our salvation was not laid in this age; rather, it was laid in eternity past. Based upon His selection, God saves us. Furthermore, with God's selection as the foundation, the Spirit moves us to believe in Christ. The move of the Spirit in this way is based upon the foundation of selection laid in eternity. We should try to help new believers realize God's selection as the eternal foundation of their salvation. We all need to see that in eternity past we were selected by God and that our being in the church today is a sign of this eternal selection. Therefore, in 1:4 Paul could say, "Knowing, brothers beloved by God, your selection."

PREACHING IN POWER, IN THE HOLY SPIRIT, AND IN MUCH ASSURANCE

In verse 5 Paul continues, "Because our gospel did not come to you in word only, but also in power, and in the Holy Spirit, and in much assurance, even as you know what kind of men we were among you for your sake." The apostles not only preached the gospel; they lived it. Their ministering of the gospel was not only by word, but also by a life which displays the power of God, a life in the Holy Spirit and in the assurance of their faith. They were the model of the glad tidings they spread.

We all should learn that to preach the gospel we must preach in power, in the Holy Spirit, and in much assurance. As we preach the gospel, we need to have the assurance that it is a saving gospel. The gospel we preach is able to save others. Before sinners can believe in the gospel, we ourselves must believe it. We must believe that the gospel is able to save sinners. When we preach the gospel, we should look away from those in the audience who may be opposing our message. Looking at them may cause our faith to diminish. Instead of looking at the faces of opposers, look at the gospel. The expression on the faces of the opposing ones is a lie. We must have the assurance that the gospel we are preaching can save even these opposers.

In verse 5 power, the Holy Spirit, and much assurance are linked to the words "what kind of men we were among you for your sake." It may seem to us that Paul's writing here is not logical, and we may wonder how the two parts of this verse fit together. This verse reveals that if we would preach the gospel in power, in the Holy Spirit, and in much assurance, we must have a life to match this kind of gospel preaching. Our manner of life must match the power, the Holy Spirit, and the assurance.

A careless person, one who does not live Christ, cannot preach the gospel in power, in the Holy Spirit, and in much assurance. To preach the gospel in this way, we must first live Christ and have a manner of life to match the power, the Holy Spirit, and the assurance. In other words, the power, the Holy Spirit, and the assurance require a certain manner of life. If we do not have the proper living, we shall not have the power, the Holy Spirit, and the assurance in our gospel preaching, for our manner of life will not match these characteristics.

IMITATORS OF THE APOSTLES AND THE LORD

In verse 6 Paul goes on to say, "And you became imitators of us and of the Lord, having accepted the word in much affliction with joy of the Holy Spirit." Since the preachers were the model of the gospel, the believers became their imitators. This then led the believers to follow the Lord, taking Him as their model (Matt. 11:29).

First the Thessalonians as new believers became imitators of the apostles, and then they became imitators of the Lord. This indicates that we need to be a pattern, a model, for others. The believers do not see the Lord first; they see us first. If we are not a proper pattern or model, it will be difficult for others to see the Lord. Because we are the

Lord's representatives, we need to be a proper pattern. Then others can imitate the Lord by imitating us. This means that through us they imitate Him.

In verses 7 and 8 Paul says, "So that you became a pattern to all those who believe in Macedonia and in Achaia. For from you the word of the Lord has sounded out, not only in Macedonia and Achaia, but in every place your faith toward God has gone out, so that we have no need to speak anything." Here we see that the imitators of the apostles became a pattern to all other believers. They imitated the pattern and then they became a pattern to the believers in the Roman provinces of Macedonia and Achaia.

THE ORIGINATION OF A HOLY LIFE FOR THE CHURCH LIFE

The book of 1 Thessalonians is concerned with a holy life for the church life. In 1:1-3 we have the structure of this life. This structure includes the work of faith, the labor of love, and the endurance of hope. This means that a holy life for the church life is constructed of faith's work, love's labor, and hope's endurance. In 1:4-10 we have the origination of this holy life for the church life. This life originates through the preaching of the word and the acceptance of the word that is preached. Thus, we need to help new believers by presenting them the word of God in power, in the Holy Spirit, and in much assurance, matched by our manner of life. Then the new believers will accept this word and follow us to follow the Lord, thereby becoming a pattern for other believers. This is the way a holy life for the church life originates.

THREE CHARACTERISTICS OF THE CHRISTIAN LIFE

In verses 9 and 10 we have the details of such a life: "For they themselves report concerning us what manner of entrance we had to you, and how you turned to God from idols to serve a living and true God, and to wait for His Son from the heavens, Whom He raised from among the dead—Jesus, Who delivers us from the wrath which is coming." In these verses we have three details as the contents of a holy life for the church life: turning to God from idols, serving a living and true God, and waiting for His Son from the heavens. To turn to God from idols, to serve a living and true God, and to wait for His Son from the heavens are the three basic substances of the Christian life viewed from another angle. To turn to God from idols is not only to turn away from false gods, with the Devil and demons behind them, but also to turn away from all things other than God. This is by faith infused into the new converts through hearing the word of the gospel. To serve a living and true God is to serve the very God who is triune—the Father, the Son, and the Spirit—processed to be the believers' life and life supply for their enjoyment. They should experience Him not only as the object of worship, but also as the all-inclusive Supplier who lives in them. This is done by love produced within them by the sweet taste of the rich supply of the Father through the Son in the Spirit. To wait for the Son of God from the heavens is to look for the One who has passed through incarnation, human living, and crucifixion, has entered into resurrection and ascended to the heavens, and who will come back to receive His believers into glory. This is the hope that strengthens the believers to stand steadfastly in their faith.

Turning to God from Idols

The first characteristic of the Christian life is that we turn to God from idols. Some people claim to be atheists. They say that they do not believe in God or worship Him. Actually, every human being worships something. Everyone has a spirit, a spiritual stomach. In our physical stomach we are hungry for food, and in our spiritual stomach we are hungry for God. We would not have a physical stomach if it were not necessary for us to eat in order to live. Our spirit, our spiritual stomach, is for worshipping God, contacting Him, receiving Him, and containing Him. Both our physical stomach and our spiritual stomach were created by God.

During the day we must eat a number of times to satisfy the hunger of our physical stomach. In the same way, everyone worships something in order to satisfy the hunger in his spiritual stomach, the spirit. For this reason, all people worship something. Whether we worship a false god or the true God is another question. The point we are making here is that everyone, including atheists, worships something. Whether the food we eat is proper or improper food, we all eat some kind of food. In the same principle, everyone worships something, even if it is a false god.

Do you know what atheists worship? They worship themselves, for they are their own god. In Philippians 3:19 Paul speaks of those whose god is their belly. Others worship education, fame, or position, all of which are idols. God alone is the proper object of worship. Any person, matter, or thing that we worship other than God is an idol.

In my youth I had the impression that Americans did not have any idols. There were many idols in China, but my concept was that the United States was a land free of idols. But when I came to this country as an older person, I realized that there are idols everywhere. The idols in China were outward, but the idols in the United States are hidden, concealed. In their intense love of pleasure and entertainment, many in this country are worshipping idols. It is true to say that the United States is a land of entertainment. When many pursue certain forms of worldly amusement, they act without restraint, seeming even to forget their own names. In this way, their pursuit of entertainment becomes the worship of idols. The Lord's Day was ordained by God for His people to worship Him. But what do most people do on this day of the week? In one way or other, they worship idols. How many genuine worshippers are there of the true God? Surely many more people worship idols today than worship the true God.

We usually think that the goal of the gospel is to turn people from sin to God. But Paul's preaching of the gospel turned people also from idols to God. It is not sufficient merely to turn others to God from sin. If our preaching of the gospel only does this, our preaching is weak and inadequate. The stronger preaching of the gospel turns people both from sin and from idols. It is somewhat easy to turn others to God from sin, but it is much more difficult to turn them to God from idols.

Do you know what is the beginning of the Christian life? The beginning of the Christian life consists in turning to God from idols. When we turn from idols, we also turn from sin, for sin lurks behind idols. In today's entertainments and amusements there is a great deal of sin. Those who do not worship idols may not sin. But whenever someone is worshipping an idol, it is impossible for that person not to sin.

Idols are actually parts of the Devil. They are demons. Behind every idol there is at least one demon. This means that there are demons behind the scene of today's entertainments, amusements, and pleasures. Therefore, the Christian life must be a life that begins with turning to God from idols.

Many of us still need a further turn from certain idols unto God. If you want something other than God Himself, that thing is an idol. Anything other than God that draws our attention or anything that distracts us from God is an idol. Any who are distracted in this way need a further turn to God from their idols. The Christian life must have the turning to God from idols as its first characteristic. The Christian life is a life without idols.

Serving a Living and True God

In verse 9 Paul speaks also of serving a living and true God. Literally the Greek word rendered serve means to serve as a slave. The living and true God is in contrast to the dead and false idols. In this verse the word living is mentioned before the word true. It is rather easy to serve a true God; it is not so easy to serve a living God. Nevertheless, we need to serve a living God. God must be living to us and in us in our daily life. He should be living in our speech, in our behavior, and in every aspect of our daily life.

How can we prove that God is living? We prove it by our daily life. If God were not living, our daily life would be very different from what it is. Our present living is a testimony that the God whom we serve is living. He is living in us, and He controls us, directs us, and deals with us. He will not let us go. Rather, in many matters He corrects us and adjusts us. The fact that God controls us and directs us, even in small things such as our thoughts and motives, is a proof that He is living. Furthermore, it is by our daily walk that we can prove to our relatives, neighbors, and friends that our God is living.

We live under the control, direction, and correction of a living God. An idol, however, does not direct or correct anyone. In the presence of an idol someone can gamble or steal without being corrected at all. But we cannot do such things before a living God. For example, if God is living in us, He would never allow us to tell a lie. If our God is living, we cannot lie in His presence. Serving a living God is the second characteristic of the Christian life. We must live a life which bears the testimony that the God we worship and serve is living in the details of our daily life.

Years ago, when I was in Manila, I learned that certain people could steal and then immediately go into a cathedral to worship. Some repented of their thefts and then immediately went out to steal once again. Some robbed others even in the cathedral. Surely such people do not worship a living God. On the contrary, the god they worship has no life.

What about your God? Is He a living God to you? The proper Christian life should bear a testimony that God is living. The reason we do not do or say certain things should be that God is living in us. The God whom we worship and serve is living not only in the heavens, but also in us. We have turned to God from idols to serve a living and true God. No doubt, when God is living to us in our experience, He is also true.

Waiting for the Son of God

A third characteristic of our Christian life is that we are waiting for God's Son from the heavens. As Christians, we must live a life that declares to others that our hope is not on this earth or in this age. Instead, our hope is in the coming Lord, and our future is in Him. On this earth we do not have any destiny, destination, or future. Our future, our destiny, and our destination are altogether focused on the Lord who is coming. He will be our hope, our future, and our destination. We are going to the Lord, and our destiny is to meet Him. Worldly people, on the contrary, have the kind of living that gives others the impression that their future is on earth and that their hope, destiny, and destination are all in the present. Although their future is thoroughly related to this age, our future is not. Because we are waiting for the Son of God from the heavens, our future is focused on Him. We have no hope on this earth and no destiny in this age.

Genuine Christians do not have any idols, they live a life that testifies that their God is living, and they declare by their living that they have no hope on this earth, but only in the coming One. We should not have anything other than God, our God should be living in our daily life, and we should declare that we are waiting for the coming of the Son of God from the heavens. I hope that those who are working with new converts and young believers will render them help concerning these things from 1 Thessalonians. Furthermore, even some of us who have been in the recovery for years still need to be helped to make up things lacking in the Christian life. Some of us may still be clinging to certain idols, to things other than God Himself. Moreover, our daily life may not testify that the God whom we serve is living, for we still may do many things without His direction, control, or adjustment. If this is our situation, then we have a negative testimony that our God is not very living to us day by day. If He is living to us, we shall surely be under His control and correction. If our God is living, He will correct us and not allow us to be careless in our living. Many of us may also lack a waiting spirit, a spirit waiting for the Lord's coming back. Our living may not declare or testify that we are waiting for the Lord's coming. We may lack this kind of atmosphere in our living. May we all see from 1 Thessalonians that a proper Christian life for the church life is a life without idols, a life that testifies that our God is living, and a life waiting for the Lord's coming back.

LIFE-STUDY OF FIRST THESSALONIANS

MESSAGE THREE

THE LIVING GOD AND THE WORK OF FAITH

Scripture Reading: 1 Thes. 1:1-10

For the most part, Christians understand and interpret the Bible in a natural way. This may be the case in reading 1 and 2 Thessalonians. We have pointed out that these Epistles were written by Paul in an elementary way to new believers, to those who had been in the Lord probably for less than a year. When I was very young, I was told that the books to the Thessalonians are very precious, and I began to pay close attention to them. However, my understanding of these Epistles was natural. As I look back on the past, I realize that I interpreted these books in a very natural way. We all need to see the difference between understanding the Word in a natural way and understanding it in a spiritual way.

THE CHURCH IN THE TRIUNE GOD

Although 1 and 2 Thessalonians were written to new believers, in these books a number of profound terms are used. Both 1 and 2 Thessalonians begin in almost exactly the same way: "Paul and Sylvanus and Timothy to the church of the Thessalonians in God the Father and the Lord Jesus Christ." Of the many Epistles written by Paul, only these two have this expression, the church in God the Father and the Lord Jesus Christ. Instead of taking this expression for granted, we should seek to find out what it means. If we check in this way, we shall learn that it is a very profound matter to say that the church is in God. This thought cannot be found in the Old Testament. God never told His people, the children of Israel, that they were in God. But in the New Testament there are two Epistles that tell us that the church is in God. We need to learn the real significance of the church being in God. What a great matter that the church is in God!

In 1 Corinthians Paul says that the church is in Corinth. He also speaks of the churches in Macedonia. Both in 1 and 2 Thessalonians the location of the church is not a city—it is God. Furthermore, the church is in the Triune God. This is indicated by the fact that Paul says "in God the Father and the Lord Jesus Christ." The object of the preposition "in" is both God the Father and the Lord Jesus Christ. The Father and the Son are two and yet are one. For the church to be in God the Father and the Lord Jesus Christ means that the church is in the Triune God.

The God revealed in the New Testament is not merely God the Creator; He is God the Father and our Lord Jesus Christ. He has passed through the process of incarnation, human living, crucifixion, and resurrection. The name Jesus indicates incarnation, and the title Christ, resurrection. If God had not become incarnate, how could He be Jesus? If He did not enter into resurrection, how could He be Christ? The God who has passed through incarnation and resurrection is now in our spirit to be our life. The church is an entity in such a God, even the Triune God.

Although the church in Thessalonica was a new church, the Thessalonians nevertheless had to realize that the church is in God. Those in this young church needed to see that the church is in the Triune God, in the very God who is our Father and our Lord. The books of 1 and 2 Thessalonians were written not to individuals, but to the church in the Triune God. This is the reason we speak of a holy life for the church life. These two Epistles are addressed to the church, and the church is in the processed Triune God.

THE STRUCTURE OF A HOLY LIFE

In 1:3 Paul says, "Remembering unceasingly your work of faith, and labor of love, and endurance of hope of our Lord Jesus Christ, before our God and Father." The work of faith, the labor of love, and the endurance of hope are all great and profound terms. However, we may take for granted that we understand what the work of faith is. Actually, we may not be able to give an adequate definition of faith. What is faith, and what is the work of faith? Some would say, "The Thessalonians believed in God, and because of their faith they did a work for God. This is the work of faith." However, this is a natural understanding of the work of faith. The actual meaning of this expression is different from what is in our natural way of understanding.

During the training on 1 Timothy we sang a chorus based on 1 Timothy 3:15 and 16:

> The church is the house of the living God,
> The church is the pillar and base of the truth;
> And great is the mystery of godliness—
> That God was manifested in the flesh.

Even a child can sing these words strongly and clearly. However, a child would not be able to tell you what it means to say that the church is the house of the living God or the pillar and base of the truth. Neither could a child say what is the mystery of godliness, God manifest in the flesh. A child may sing of such profound things without having any understanding of them. In principle, we may be exactly the same in our reading of the Bible. We may say the words "the church of the Thessalonians in God the Father and the Lord Jesus Christ" without having any understanding of what they mean. Likewise, we may have only a natural understanding of the structure of the holy life for the church life, a structure consisting of the three elements of the work of faith, the labor of love, and the endurance of hope. We may know these matters in a natural way, not according to the way Paul used them.

In 1:9 and 10 Paul says, "For they themselves report concerning us what manner of entrance we had to you, and how you turned to God from idols to serve a living and true God, and to wait for His Son from the heavens, Whom He raised from among the dead—Jesus, Who delivers us from the wrath which is coming." We may think that we know what it means to turn from idols, to serve a living and true God, and to wait for His Son from the heavens. Actually, we may not know the proper meaning of these things.

In 4:7 Paul says that God has called us in sanctification. We also may assume that we understand the term sanctification. Actually, we do not have very much understanding of what sanctification is. Here Paul does not say that God has called us in holiness; he says that He has called us in sanctification. There is an important difference between holiness and sanctification.

First Thessalonians 5:23 says, "And the God of peace Himself sanctify you wholly, and may your spirit and soul and body be preserved complete, without blame, at the coming of our Lord Jesus Christ." We may read this verse without knowing the true significance of the words "sanctify you wholly." In like manner, we may not know what it means for our spirit and soul and body to be preserved complete. We may read this verse again and again thinking that we understand it, when actually we may not understand it at all.

First Thessalonians emphasizes sanctification. God calls us unto sanctification, and the God of peace sanctifies us wholly. This Epistle emphasizes a sanctified life for the church life. This is the reason we adopt the expression "a holy life for the church life."

MORE PROFOUND TERMS

Second Thessalonians also contains some profound terms. In 2:13 Paul says, "But we ought to thank God always concerning you, brothers beloved by the Lord, because God chose you from the beginning unto salvation in sanctification of the Spirit and belief of the truth." To say that God has chosen us unto salvation in sanctification of the Spirit is to utter something great and profound. Salvation is in sanctification of the Spirit. Such an expression is used only once in the entire New Testament.

In 2 Thessalonians 2:14 Paul goes on to say, "To which also He called you through our gospel unto the obtaining of the glory of our Lord Jesus Christ." The expression "the obtaining of the glory" is also unique, used in the New

Testament only here. Through the gospel God called us unto the obtaining of the glory of our Lord Jesus Christ.

In 2 Thessalonians 2:16 we read another profound expression: "Now our Lord Jesus Christ Himself, and God our Father, Who has loved us and given us eternal encouragement and good hope in grace." Here Paul speaks of eternal encouragement and good hope in grace. These terms are also used only once in the New Testament.

GOD LIVING IN US

Recently in a meeting a sister gave a testimony concerning the living God. She explained that she was in a strange place late at night and that a teenage girl, who had been riding on a bus with her, was very helpful to her. The sister went on to say that this proves that God is living, for He had prepared someone to help her in that situation. In 1:9 Paul speaks of turning to God from idols to serve a living and true God. Do you think that Paul's concept of the living God here is the same as that of the sister who gave this testimony? What does Paul mean by serving a living God? When Paul speaks of the living God, does he mean that God will send someone to help you when you are in trouble? If this is your concept, this indicates that you have a natural understanding of this matter. In many instances the living God did not keep Paul away from trouble and hardship. This would seem to indicate that in the sense of the testimony given by that sister, God was not very living to Paul in his experience. I mention this testimony in order to point out that we need to learn what Paul means when he speaks of serving a living and true God. We should not understand the Bible in a natural way. Rather, we must understand it according to God's revelation.

If we read only 1 Thessalonians, it may be difficult to find out what is Paul's understanding of the living God. But if we read the other books written by Paul, we shall see that for him the living God is the God who is now living in us. We are not serving a God who is merely in the heavens. The God we serve is the One who lives in us. Therefore, to serve a living God means to serve the God who is living in you right now. In the Old Testament the children of Israel served a God who was in the heavens. Solomon prayed to God in heaven. Even in what is called the Lord's prayer, the Lord Jesus says, "Our Father Who is in the heavens" (Matt. 6:9). But now, after the cross and the resurrection, the God whom we serve is no longer merely in the heavens, for He is now living in us. This is revealed clearly in Paul's Epistles (Rom. 8:10; Col. 1:27). We even have a song which says that our God is living and that He is living within us. When Paul says that we serve a living God, he means the God who is living within us and who is one with us.

How do we know that our God is the living God? We know it by the fact that He is living in us. Suppose a brother is about to quarrel with his wife. However, the living God in him does not want to quarrel. Therefore, the brother does not proceed to argue with his wife. In this way he serves a God who is living, a God who not only lives in him, but who also lives with him. By this illustration we see that the living God is living not only objectively but also subjectively.

I am bothered by testimonies which refer to the living God only in an objective way and not in a subjective way. Even those who have been in the Lord for years still testify only that the God they serve is objectively living. It seems that He is not the subjectively living One to these saints. We should be able to testify that the God we are serving today is living within us. What we need is not a testimony about how God sent someone to help us in trouble. We need subjective testimonies concerning the living God in our daily life. For instance, a sister may testify of how she was tempted to look at her husband in a very unpleasant way. But because the living God in her did not agree, she did not show such an unpleasant expression toward her husband. This proves that her God is living and that He is living within her. An idol does not interfere with anyone who is about to lose his temper. But the God whom we serve is living, and He inwardly adjusts us and corrects us.

OBJECTIVE AND SUBJECTIVE FAITH

Let us now go on to consider what faith is and also what the work of faith is. In 3:2 Paul says, "And we sent Timothy, our brother and God's fellow-worker in the gospel of Christ, to establish and encourage you for the sake of your faith." In 3:5 Paul goes on to say, "Because of this, when I also could bear it no longer, I sent to know your faith, lest somehow the tempter had tempted you, and our labor would be in vain." In both of these verses Paul refers to "your faith." Paul was deeply concerned about the Thessalonians' faith. In these verses faith is not only subjective, referring to the saints' believing, but also objective, referring to what they believe in. Objective faith also refers to what we may call our belief. Belief denotes what we believe in. In 1 and 2 Thessalonians it is difficult to tell whether faith is objective or subjective. For the most part, as used in these two Epistles, faith is both objective and subjective.

Faith is related both to a view and to sight. First there is a view, a scene, before us, and then we have the sight to see this view. Spontaneously, we have faith. This means that when we have the view and the sight, we automatically have faith.

Suppose you are preaching the gospel to a group of unbelievers. What you speak to them is not only in word, but also in power, in the Holy Spirit, and in much assurance. You tell them the story of the gospel, relating how God loves them and how He sent His Son to be a man and to die on the cross for them. As you are speaking, you are not merely telling a story—you are presenting a view, a scene. Those to whom you are speaking begin to see this view. They realize something about being a sinner and see that there is a God, Jesus Christ, and the cross. This view portrayed in the preaching of the gospel is God's revelation. As soon as unbelievers see this revelation, spontaneously faith is produced in them, and they believe. They believe in what they see. This is faith. However, not many Christians understand faith in this way.

In order to have more faith, stronger, broader, and greater faith, we need more view. A broader faith depends on a broader view. An increased view gives us increased sight, and increased sight results in increased faith. Thus, the extent of our faith depends on our sight, and the scope of our sight depends on the measure of our view. This is why we need to know more of the Holy Word and hear more messages. Both the Word and messages help to give us a broader view. Then we shall have greater sight, which produces a greater faith.

BROUGHT INTO THE ORGANIC UNION

This kind of faith on the one hand brings God into us, and on the other hand it brings us into God. In other words, such faith always produces an organic union.

We may use photography as an illustration of how, through faith, God is brought into us, and we are brought into the organic union with Him. When you take a photograph with a camera, you press the shutter. Then light brings a particular scene into the camera to reach the film. In this way the scene, the view, is impressed onto the film. In the same principle, faith brings God into our spirit, which can be compared to the film. Before faith is produced in us, our spirit is blank. But after faith is produced, God is brought into our spirit. Now our spirit is no longer blank. Instead, something of God Himself has been impressed into our spirit. God is brought into our spirit, and we are brought into God. Spontaneously, there is an organic union between us and God.

FAITH WORKING

To be sure, a certain kind of work will issue out of such faith. Genuine faith is never in vain. It is living. It brings God into us, it brings us into God, and it makes God and us one. This living faith works in a particular way. This is what Paul means by the work of faith.

SPIRITUAL UNDERSTANDING AND DIVINE REVELATION

This word concerning the living God and the work of

faith may help you to see the difference between the natural way and the spiritual way of understanding the

Word of God. In reading 1 Thessalonians, a precious book written to new believers, we must be on the alert not to understand any part of this Epistle in a natural way. If we have a natural understanding of this book, we shall be hindered in our reading of it. Therefore, we need to pray, "Lord, I don't want to understand anything in the Bible, especially any terms in 1 Thessalonians, in a natural way. Lord, keep me always in the spirit, and show me the real significance of the profound terms in this book."

It would be helpful if you keep in mind certain important terms used by Paul in 1 Thessalonians. In particular, remember that the church is in God the Father and our Lord Jesus Christ. Also remember the work of faith, the labor of love, the endurance of hope, and the turning to God from idols to serve a living and true God and to wait for His Son from the heavens. If you keep these terms in mind, eventually light will come and, gradually, you will have the proper spiritual understanding. Otherwise, you may understand the entire first chapter of 1 Thessalonians in a natural way, in a way that is absolutely not according to the divine revelation. Only when we have the proper spiritual understanding can we receive the divine revelation. The divine revelation in 1 Thessalonians 1 goes along with the spiritual understanding of Paul's writing.

LIFE-STUDY OF FIRST THESSALONIANS

MESSAGE FOUR

SOME BASIC MATTERS

Scripture Reading: 1 Thes. 1:1-10

In reading or studying any part of the Bible, it is always necessary to find out what was in the spirit of the writer. Once we know the writer's spirit, we can learn his purpose, intention, goal, and aim. In order to learn what was the burden in Paul's spirit in 1 Thessalonians 1, we need to consider some basic matters in this chapter as indicated by the words Paul uses and by the way this chapter is constructed. This means that Paul's spirit here is related to certain basic words he uses. Any chapter of the Bible is constructed of specific words that refer to basic elements. Let us now consider some basic matters in 1 Thessalonians 1 expressed in the words chosen by the Apostle Paul.

THE TRIUNE GOD

In chapter one of 1 Thessalonians the Triune God is revealed. First, we have the Father. In 1:1 Paul says that the church is in God the Father, and in verse 3 he again refers to "our God and Father." In verse 10 Paul speaks concerning the Son: "And to wait for His Son from the heavens." Furthermore, Paul mentions the Holy Spirit in verse 5, where he says that the gospel came to the Thessalonians in the Holy Spirit, and also in verse 6, where he says that the Thessalonians accepted the word with joy of the Holy Spirit. In this chapter we have the Triune God—the Father, the Son, and the Holy Spirit.

At the time of Paul, any typical Jew would have been offended by the expression "His Son." This was offensive to Jews because they believed in the true God, but did not realize that He has a Son. To a certain extent, the Jews believed that God has a Spirit. However, they did not have the understanding that the Spirit is the same in rank as God Himself. Rather, they believed only that God has a Spirit and that this Spirit is subordinate to Him. According to Jewish belief concerning God, God is unique and yet this unique God has a Spirit. The Jews certainly did not believe that God has a Son; neither did they believe that both the Son of God and the Spirit of God are on the same rank as God. This is altogether contrary to the Jewish concept. Hence, for Paul to speak of the Father, His Son, and the Holy Spirit is to utter something very basic.

In chapter one Paul not only speaks of the Son of God, but also speaks of Jesus Christ. The Son of God is Jesus, and this Jesus is Christ. The name Jesus refers basically to the manhood of the Son of God, to the Son of God as a man. Through incarnation the Son of God became a man named Jesus. This name is an equivalent to the Hebrew word for Joshua, a name which means either Jehovah our Savior or Jehovah our salvation. The name of Jesus, therefore, is rich in its implications.

Like everyone else, Jesus, the Son of God, has a history. We know that He was born in Jewish territory, lived in that region for thirty-three and a half years, and eventually died on the cross. Now when we speak of Jesus, we need to recall His history, His biography.

The Lord Jesus is also the Christ. For the most part, the title Christ denotes that aspect of the Lord's history related to resurrection, whereas the name Jesus denotes that part of His history related to incarnation and human living. Christ, the resurrected One, has been made Lord of all and Head of all. God has made Him Head of the church.

SELECTION, DELIVERANCE, AND TRANSMISSION

If we read 1 Thessalonians 1 carefully, we shall see that even in such a short chapter there are indications of what the Father has done, of what the Son is doing, and of what the Spirit has done and continues to do. In verse 4 Paul speaks concerning selection: "Knowing, brothers beloved by God, your selection." Who selected us? Surely selection was not accomplished by the Son. The Father is the One who selected us. According to verse 10, the Son delivers us. This verse says that the Son "delivers us from the wrath which is coming." I would call your attention to the fact that in this verse the word "delivers" is in the present tense, whereas wrath is spoken of as something which is coming. The deliverance is taking place right now, but the wrath is coming. The point here is that the Son accomplishes the work of deliverance.

Selection is of the Father, and deliverance is of the Son, but what is the work of the Spirit? According to this chapter, the Spirit is for propagating, for imparting. In verse 5 Paul points out to the Thessalonians that the gospel came to them not only in word, but also in power and in the Holy Spirit. In verse 6 he reminds them that they accepted the word with joy of the Holy Spirit. These verses indicate that the Spirit is for transmission.

As Paul was writing 1 Thessalonians 1, deep within he was exercised concerning the Triune God. He was burdened concerning the Father's selection, the Son's deliverance, and the Spirit's transmission. It is very important for us to see this.

THE TRIUNE GOD EMBODIED IN THE WORD

The Triune God is conveyed to us, transmitted to us, through the Word. In verse 6 Paul speaks of accepting the word, and in verse 8, of sounding out the word of the Lord. No doubt in Paul's concept the Triune God today is fully embodied in the Word. The Word may be compared to a battery that contains electricity. As a battery is the embodiment of electricity, so in the spiritual realm the Word of God, a divine battery, is the embodiment of the Triune God. The Father, the Son, and the Spirit are all embodied in the Word. Thus, when we preach the Word, God is conveyed to others. Through the Word the Triune God is transmitted to others.

Paul had spent about three weeks with the Thessalonians. I believe that during those weeks Paul told the Thessalonians how God had selected them in eternity past.

He must also have told them how one day God the Son became incarnate, how He was born in a manger and given the name Jesus. Surely Paul also told the Thessalonian believers how Jesus lived on earth, was crucified, and was resurrected to be the Lord, the Head, and the Christ, how He is now in the heavens, and how He has become the life-giving Spirit. Paul, therefore, preached the Father, the Son, and the Holy Spirit. This was his gospel, the word accepted by the Thessalonians.

BORN OF GOD AND PUT INTO CHRIST

When the Thessalonians accepted the word preached by Paul, they accepted the Triune God. The word they received was the gospel preached to them. By accepting this word and thereby accepting the Triune God, they were born of God and put into Christ. On the negative side, this was a turning to God from idols. On the positive side, it was being born of God and also believing into the Son of God. In this way an organic union took place, and the Thessalonians came to be in God the Father and in the Lord Jesus Christ.

The new believers at Thessalonica were all in the Triune God. Because they were in the Father and the Son, they were no longer heathen or Jews. They were saints. They had become saints in God the Father and the Lord Jesus Christ. In 1:1 the phrase "in God the Father and the Lord Jesus Christ" not only qualifies the church, but also qualifies the Thessalonians. This means not only that the church was in God the Father and the Lord Jesus Christ, but also that the Thessalonians, being no longer Greeks or Jews, but believers, were also in the Father and in the Lord Jesus Christ.

Dean Alford makes three points concerning this part of 1:1. First he says that the phrase "in God the Father and the Lord Jesus Christ" indicates communion and participation. Alford did not use the expression organic union, but he speaks of communion, which means fellowship and a kind of co-union. He also speaks of the believers participating in God and Christ. Because of this participation, they have a common union with God. Second, Alford says that the words "in God the Father" mark out the believers as being no longer heathen, for as heathen they were not in God the Father. Third, he says that "in the Lord Jesus Christ" indicates that the believers are no longer Jewish, for the Jews were not willing to accept the Lord Jesus. Hence, the believers at Thessalonica, being in the Father and the Lord Jesus Christ, were no longer heathen or Jewish.

SERVING AND WAITING

In chapter one we have the Triune God and the preaching of the Triune God in the word, His embodiment. This word is the gospel that is accepted by the believers. When the Thessalonians accepted the word, they were born of God and united to Christ. Therefore, they became the church in God the Father and the Lord Jesus Christ. Then what did they do? They served the living God. The word serve used in verse 9 is all-inclusive. It includes everything we do in our daily living. God is living because He is true, not false. Thus, in 1:9 Paul speaks of serving a living and true God. The church of the Thessalonians was made up of believers serving a living God who is true. This is also what we are doing today. The fact that we are serving a living God proves that we are in God the Father.

Furthermore, in verse 10 Paul points out that we are waiting for the Son of God from the heavens. We are serving the living God, and we are waiting for His Son, the One whom He raised from among the dead. Jesus, the Son of God, delivers us from the wrath which is to come. Although the wrath will come in the future, He is now delivering us, and He will deliver us to the uttermost, until there is no longer any wrath.

To serve a living God indicates that we are in God the Father, and to wait for the Son indicates that we are in our Lord Jesus Christ. Thus, our serving and our waiting mark us out as those who are in God the Father and in the Lord Jesus Christ. If we were not in the Father, we would not be serving a living God, and if we were not in Jesus Christ our Lord, we would not be waiting for Him.

As we consider verses 1, 9, and 10, we see that the end of this chapter corresponds to the beginning. In the beginning Paul says that the church is in God the Father and the Lord Jesus Christ. At the end of this chapter he speaks of serving the living God and waiting for the Son. This is the holy life for the church life, a life constructed of faith, love, and hope. Faith is working, love is laboring, and hope is enduring.

THE WORD OF THE LORD AND FAITH TOWARD GOD

I would call your attention to verse 8: "For from you the word of the Lord has sounded out, not only in Macedonia and Achaia, but in every place your faith toward God has gone out, so that we have no need to speak anything." Notice here Paul says that from the Thessalonians the word of the Lord has sounded out and that in every place their faith toward God has gone out. This indicates that the word of the Lord and faith toward God are synonymous. The Thessalonians heard the word. When they accepted the word, it became their faith in both an objective and subjective way. As we have pointed out, objective faith denotes that in which we believe, and subjective faith denotes the action of believing. In verse 8 faith toward God includes both the subjective and objective aspects.

In your experience, is the word of the Lord simply the word, or is it also faith? If the word is faith to you, this means it has brought you a view, and you have seen this view. This seeing of the view results in your believing. In this way the word becomes your faith. Now when the word of the Lord is sounded out, it is not merely an objective word; it is also your subjective faith. Therefore, when such a word is sounded out, your faith goes out.

Faith is the foundation of the structure of a holy life for the church life. Upon this foundation a building is taking place. This is the labor of love. Then the topstone, the capstone, of this building will be the enduring hope. In this way we have the complete structure of a holy life for the church life: the work of faith, the labor of love, and the endurance of hope.

If we see the basic matters in chapter one of 1 Thessalonians—the Triune God, the word as the embodiment of the Triune God, the mark of being in the Father and the Lord Jesus Christ, and the work of faith, the labor of love, and the endurance of hope—then we shall know the burden in Paul's spirit when he composed this portion of the Word.

LIFE-STUDY OF FIRST THESSALONIANS

MESSAGE FIVE

THE TRIUNE GOD EMBODIED IN THE WORD TO PRODUCE A HOLY LIFE FOR THE CHURCH LIFE

(1)

Scripture Reading: 1 Thes. 1:1-10

It is accurate and correct to say that the books of 1 and 2 Thessalonians are on the church life. Although the expression "the church life" cannot be found in these Epistles, the church is mentioned emphatically at the beginning of each book. First Thessalonians opens with these words: "Paul and Silvanus and Timothy to the church of the Thessalonians in God the Father and the Lord Jesus Christ." Second Thessalonians opens in almost exactly the same way. The only difference is that 1 Thessalonians 1:1 says "the Father" and 2 Thessalonians 1:1 says "our Father." Both 1 and 2 Thessalonians were addressed to the church.

THE CHURCH OF THE THESSALONIANS

Each of the fourteen Epistles written by Paul opens in a particular way. The beginning of every Epistle matches the contents of that particular Epistle. For example, Romans 1:1 says, "Paul, a slave of Christ Jesus, a called apostle, separated to the gospel of God." First Corinthians begins in a somewhat different way: "Paul, a called apostle of Christ Jesus through the will of God" (1 Cor. 1:1). In contrast, the opening of both 1 and 2 Thessalonians is quite simple. Paul does not use any titles to refer to himself; he does not speak of himself as a slave of Christ or as an apostle. Instead, he simply says, "Paul and Silvanus and Timothy to the church of the Thessalonians in God the Father and the Lord Jesus Christ."

The expression, "the church of the Thessalonians in God the Father and the Lord Jesus Christ," is unique. On the one hand, the church is of certain persons; on the other hand, it is in God the Father and the Lord Jesus Christ. This way of referring to the church is very different from that found in 1 Corinthians 1:2. There Paul says, "To the church of God which is in Corinth," describing the church as being in a particular place. But in 1 and 2 Thessalonians Paul speaks of the church not as being in a certain place, but as being of certain persons, the Thessalonians, who are in God. In these Epistles the church is of the Thessalonians and in the Father and the Lord Jesus Christ.

According to history, Thessalonica was an immoral place. For the most part, the people of that city were not moral. Nevertheless, according to 1:1, the church in that city was "of the Thessalonians." It does not seem possible that a church could be composed of people who lived in a city like Thessalonica.

It is very positive to say that the church is in God the Father, but it is not positive to say that the church is of the Thessalonians. In 1:1 we have the church of the Thessalonians in God. The prepositions "of" and "in" here are very important. The church in Thessalonica was of people from an evil city, but it was in God the Father. This is similar to speaking of the church in San Francisco as being the church of the San Franciscans in God the Father. San Francisco has a world-wide reputation for being an evil, immoral city. Nevertheless, there is a church in San Francisco today, the church of the San Franciscans in God the Father and the Lord Jesus Christ.

HOLY PEOPLE LIVING A HOLY LIFE

We have pointed out that the books of 1 and 2 Thessalonians are concerned with the church life. From the content of these books we know that the church life depends on a holy life. Many San Franciscans may be evil, but those San

Franciscans who compose the church in San Francisco are holy. Praise the Lord that among today's San Franciscans there are a number of holy people living a holy life! The same is true of the church in Los Angeles. The Lord can boast to the demons and the evil angels that in such an immoral city as Los Angeles, the home of Hollywood, the Lord has a church composed of holy people living a holy life. In the local churches today, we are living a holy life for the church life.

We all need to see that 1 and 2 Thessalonians are on the church life. Not long ago, while I was working on these two Epistles, I was looking to the Lord that he would show me the main subject of these books. Eventually, I became impressed with the matter of the church life in these Epistles. I believe that impression came from the Lord. Apparently 1 and 2 Thessalonians are not related to the church. However, if you touch the depths of the truth in these books, you will see that they truly are concerned with the practice of the church life through the living of a holy life. Now we must go on to see how it was possible for people from an immoral city such as Thessalonica to become a holy people living a holy life for the church life. If we would understand this, we need to ask a very important question: What is the source of a holy life for the church life?

THE FATHER, THE SON, AND THE HOLY SPIRIT

The title of this message is "The Triune God Embodied in the Word to Produce a Holy Life for the Church Life." Those who are thoughtful may wonder why this title uses the term "The Triune God" when this expression is not found in 1 Thessalonians 1. Furthermore, such careful readers may wonder how we can speak, again from 1 Thessalonians 1, of the Triune God embodied in the Word. This chapter clearly mentions the word, but what about the Triune God and the embodiment of the Triune God in the Word? Let us consider this matter carefully.

First Thessalonians 1:1 speaks of God the Father. Moreover, in verse 3 we have the words "before our God and

Father." In verse 10 Paul speaks of the Son: "And to wait for His Son from the heavens, Whom He raised from among the dead—Jesus, Who delivers us from the wrath which is coming." Twice in this chapter Paul refers to the Holy Spirit. Verse 5 says, "Because our gospel did not come to you in word only, but also in power, and in the Holy Spirit, and in much assurance." In verse 6 Paul points out that the Thessalonians "accepted the word in much affliction with joy of the Holy Spirit." Therefore, in this chapter we have the Triune God, God the Father, God the Son, and God the Holy Spirit. Therefore, 1 Thessalonians 1 is a chapter on the Triune God.

Actually, the entire New Testament is related to the Triune God. The Triune God is the element for the construction of the New Testament. In preparing meals, sisters use various groceries as the elements of their cooking. Likewise, certain elements are the "ingredients" used in the composition of the New Testament. What are the elements found in 1 Thessalonians 1? The most basic element is the Triune God. Just as meat is an important element in the diet of many Americans, so the Triune God is the most important element in Paul's spiritual cooking. Hence, it is not surprising that in 1 Thessalonians 1 we can clearly see the Triune God. In this chapter Paul explicitly speaks of the Father, the Son, and the Spirit.

Both 1 Thessalonians 1:1 and 2 Thessalonians 1:1 speak of the church of the Thessalonians. This indicates that the church is composed of saved and regenerated sinners. From history we know that the cities of ancient Macedonia, where Thessalonica was located, and Achaia, where Corinth was situated, were evil and immoral. Those cities may have been worse than today's San Francisco. The Thessalonians in particular did not have a good name; instead, they had a reputation for sinfulness, uncleanness, and immorality. But some of these Thessalonians were saved and regenerated, born of God, through believing in Christ. As a result, in that evil city there came to be a church of the Thessalonians in God the Father and the Lord Jesus Christ.

In reading the New Testament, it is easy for us to take terms such as in Christ, in the Lord, and in God for granted and not pay much attention to them. We need to be deeply impressed by the expression "in God the Father and the Lord Jesus Christ." The utterance is marvelous. It is a tremendous matter for people to be in God! Suppose some very sinful people hear the gospel, receive the Lord Jesus, and are saved. They become Christians and are now in God the Father. We need to realize that this is a matter of great significance. Do you know where we are as believers? We are in God the Father and in the Lord Jesus Christ!

According to 1:1, the church is not only in God the Father, but also in the Lord Jesus Christ. The church has such a marvelous location in the Father and in our Lord. Actually, God the Father and Jesus Christ are one. They are the Father and our Lord. The Father is the first of the Trinity, and the Lord Jesus Christ, the Son, is the second. However, we should not regard the Father and the Son as separate persons. God is triune, that is, He is three-one. Yes, the Father, the Son, and the Holy Spirit are three; yet They are one. This is beyond the ability of the human mind to comprehend. Oh, our God, the Triune God, is wonderful! This Triune God is revealed in 1 Thessalonians 1. Furthermore, the church of the saved ones is in this wonderful God who is the Father and the Lord Jesus Christ.

THE CHURCH PEOPLE IN GOD THE FATHER AND THE LORD JESUS CHRIST

Recently, as I was studying 1:1, I realized that to speak of the church of the Thessalonians in God the Father and the Lord Jesus Christ is to utter something very weighty and deep. I consulted the writings of Dean Alford on this verse, and I was helped by what he had to say. First, Alford points out that the preposition "in" here denotes communion and participation in. What Alford means by participation is equal to the expression "organic union." Communion denotes a common union. The church is a group of people who have a common union with God and who are participating in Him.

Furthermore, Alford goes on to say that the expression "in God the Father" is a mark, an indication, that those in the church are no longer heathen, no longer of the Gentiles. Gentiles do not have God, but the church is composed of a group of people who are in God the Father. Those in the church, therefore, are no longer heathen.

Alford also says that "in the Lord Jesus Christ" indicates that those in the church are no longer Jewish. Jews do not believe in Jesus Christ, just as the heathen do not believe in the true God. Who are those who believe in God and in the Lord Jesus Christ? The church people are such believers. Today we are neither heathen, nor Jewish; we are the church people in God the Father and the Lord Jesus Christ. Those in the church life with a background in Judaism must realize that they are no longer Jewish. The church is composed of those who are no longer Gentiles or Jews, for we all now are in God the Father and in the Lord Jesus Christ.

Elsewhere in his Epistles, Paul speaks of the churches of Christ and of the church of God. Certain Christian groups have adopted these expressions as denominational titles. For example, today we have the Church of Christ, the Assembly of God, and the Church of God. But do you know of any Christian group with the title "The Church in God"? Surely there is no such group. Nevertheless, according to 1:1, it is a fact that the church is in God.

Which matter would you say is deeper, for the church to be of God, or for the church to be in God? For the church to be in God is deeper, more profound, than for the church to be merely of God. Hallelujah, the church is in God! The church is not only of God and of Christ; the church is also in God and in Christ. It is important for us to see that the church in our locality is of God and in God, of Christ and in Christ.

A RELATIONSHIP IN LIFE

I can testify that seeing the significance of the preposition "in" in 1:1 has caused the book of 1 Thessalonians to become very dear and lovable to me. In this book we have the revelation that the church is not only of God and of Christ, but also in God the Father and in the Lord Jesus Christ.

The church is not merely in God, but is in the Father. The word Father here indicates a relationship of life. God is no longer only our Creator; He is our Father. God is the Father of the church people, for we have all been born of Him. It is a wonderful fact that we have been born of God and that He is now our Father!

Suppose your father were the President of the United States. If such were the case, you could refer to him as "my father, the President." This would be very different from merely speaking of the President. To refer to our President may indicate that you are a citizen. But if you could say, "my father, the President," that would indicate that the President is your father and that you have a life relationship with him. In the same principle, we can speak of God as being our Father. No longer is God only our Creator. He has become our Father, for we have been born of Him. Furthermore, Jesus Christ is our Lord. Hallelujah, we have a Father and a Lord!

THE CHURCH IN THE TRIUNE GOD

To say that the church is in God the Father and in the Lord Jesus Christ is not the same as saying that the church is in two separate persons. No, the church is in the wonderful One who is the Father and the Son. Do you think that the church today on the one hand is in the Father and on the other hand in the Lord Jesus? In other words, do you think that the church, the unique church in a locality, is in two separate persons? We should not think of the church in this way. God is the Father and the Lord Jesus Christ, and the church is in this One. Do not ask me to explain how the church can be in the One who is both the Father and the Son. It is beyond my ability to explain such a mystery. All the centuries of Christian history prove that no one can explain the Triune God adequately. But in 1:1 we have the revelation of the tremendous fact that the church is in the unique God and that this God is our Father and our Lord Jesus Christ. Hallelujah, we have such a wonderful God, and we are in Him!

When Paul speaks of the church of the Thessalonians in God the Father and the Lord Jesus Christ, he actually means that the church of the Thessalonians is in the Triune God. Paul's word concerning the Father and the Lord Jesus Christ indicates or implies that God is triune. If God were not triune, how could He be the Father and the Son? It would be impossible. Furthermore, Paul's reference to the Father and Christ also implies the Holy Spirit. As we have pointed out, elsewhere in this chapter Paul explicitly speaks of the Holy Spirit. Therefore, 1 Thessalonians 1 clearly shows the Triune God—the Father, the Son, and the Holy Spirit. Both 1 Thessalonians 1:1 and 2 Thessalonians 1:1 reveal that the church is composed of a group of sinners who have been saved and regenerated and who are now in the Triune God. How wonderful!

LIFE-STUDY OF FIRST THESSALONIANS

MESSAGE SIX

THE TRIUNE GOD EMBODIED IN THE WORD TO PRODUCE A HOLY LIFE FOR THE CHURCH LIFE

(2)

Scripture Reading: 1 Thes. 1:1-10

In the foregoing message we saw that the Triune God is revealed in chapter one of 1 Thessalonians. In verses 1 and 3 Paul speaks of God the Father; in verse 10, of the Son; and in verses 5 and 6, of the Holy Spirit. According to 1:1, the church of the Thessalonians was in God the Father and the Lord Jesus Christ. This indicates that the church is in the Triune God. In this message we shall go on to consider, also from 1 Thessalonians 1, how this Triune God is ministered to us.

THE WORD OF THE LORD AND FAITH TOWARD GOD

In verses 5 and 6 Paul says, "Because our gospel did not come to you in word only, but also in power, and in the Holy Spirit, and in much assurance, even as you know what kind of men we were among you for your sake. And you became imitators of us and of the Lord, having accepted the word in much affliction with joy of the Holy Spirit." According to these verses, to preach the gospel is to preach the word. The gospel preached by the apostles was the word accepted by the Thessalonians. In verse 8 Paul goes on to say, "For from you the word of the Lord has sounded out, not only in Macedonia and Achaia, but in every place your faith toward God has gone out, so that we have no need to speak anything."

First the Thessalonians accepted the word, and then they sounded it out.

In verse 8 the word of the Lord and faith toward God are synonymous. This verse says that from the Thessalonians the word of the Lord sounded out and that their faith toward God went out. Thus, the word that is sounded out is the faith that goes out.

What is faith? Hardly anyone can give a satisfactory definition. It is very difficult to say what faith is. However, by considering these verses carefully, we can have a proper understanding of faith.

First, faith is a matter of having the word preached to us. Next, faith includes our accepting of the word and our sounding it out. This kind of word is faith. The word of the gospel is preached, accepted, and declared. In this way the word becomes faith within us. In the speaking of the preacher, the word is the gospel. But when we accept the word, and especially when we sound out the word, it becomes faith within us.

Suppose a preacher of the gospel speaks to an unbeliever concerning man's fall and God's salvation. The one who preaches the gospel tells the unbeliever that in Christ God was incarnate, that He was crucified for our sins, that He was resurrected from among the dead, and that He has become the life-giving Spirit in order to dwell in us. When this unbeliever receives the word of the gospel and declares it, it becomes faith.

THE CONTENT OF THE WORD PREACHED BY PAUL

Now we need to study the content of the word, the gospel, preached by Paul. No doubt, Paul preached the Triune God. In verse 4 he says, "Knowing, brothers beloved by God, your selection." Selection refers to the Father's work in eternity past. That was when God selected us. In verse 10 Paul speaks about the Son as the One who delivers us. The Son is the Savior, the Deliverer. In verse 5 Paul says that the gospel they preached came in power and in the Holy Spirit;

and in verse 6 we see that the Thessalonians accepted the word with joy of the Holy Spirit. The fact that the gospel was preached in the Holy Spirit indicates that the Spirit is the One who transmits the things of God into us. Thus, God the Father selected us, God the Son accomplished redemption to deliver us, and God the Spirit transmits all the divine things to us. This is the content of the word preached by Paul as the gospel. This is the reason I say that the Triune God is embodied in the word.

A brother may give a short gospel message in which he says that God created man, that man has become fallen, that Christ has come to die on the cross for our sins, and that now the Spirit is seeking to regenerate us. Even in such a short message, God the Father, God the Son, and God the Spirit are all included. This is the content of the proper gospel, a gospel that is the divine word embodying the Triune God and telling us what the Father has done, what the Son has done, and what the Spirit is doing. When someone believes this word and accepts it, it becomes faith within him.

Do you realize what happens when the Triune God is ministered to a person through the word, and that person receives the word so that it becomes faith within him? At that moment such a person experiences a new birth. He is born of God. We all were sinners, but through faith we have become sons of God. Through faith we experience a new birth.

Faith is not a matter of trying to believe something that we are not able to believe. Whenever you preach the gospel, do not force anyone to believe. Instead, present the Triune God as the One most dear, precious, and valuable. When others hear the presentation of such an attractive One, they will appreciate what you are saying and receive your word. The word they accept will then become their faith. This is what it means to believe.

TWO ASPECTS OF FAITH

Faith has two aspects: the objective aspect and the

subjective aspect. When we accept the word of God, it becomes both our objective faith and our subjective faith. Objective faith denotes the things we believe, and subjective faith refers to our action of believing. Through such a faith we are regenerated, born of God, and a relationship of life begins between us and God. Furthermore, through this kind of faith we are put into Christ. Formerly, we were outside of Christ. But now through faith we are in Christ. This means that there is an organic union between us and Christ. This is the beginning of the Christian life, and this life is a holy life that consummates in the church life. In this way the Triune God is transmitted into our being so that we may have a new life, the divine life. With this new life we have a relationship of life with God and an organic union with Christ. By means of this relationship and union we begin our Christian life, a life of holiness, a holy life for the church life.

THE WORK OF FAITH

Now that we have considered verse 1 in a rather full way, let us go on to verse 3. Here Paul says, "Remembering unceasingly your work of faith, and labor of love, and endurance of hope of our Lord Jesus Christ, before our God and Father." In this verse Paul speaks of three matters: the work of faith, the labor of love, and the endurance of hope. The work of faith comes first. Faith comes through our acceptance of the word that is the embodiment of the Triune God. When we accepted this word, faith was produced within us. We have seen that this faith is both objective and subjective.

In Greek there is a definite article in verse 3, the faith. This indicates that this verse speaks of the work of the faith. This faith is God's word accepted by us. The word preached to us and received by us becomes faith. Because this faith is living and active, it results in the work of the faith.

The Greek word for work in verse 3 is *ergon,* a word usually rendered as work. Paul uses this word in Romans 3:20: "Because by the works of law no flesh shall be justified before Him." In Romans 3:20 work mainly denotes our conduct, our behavior. Paul is saying that no fallen person can be justified before God by his conduct. Thus, in that verse work does not refer to an activity or a task that we do; it refers to particular deeds in our behavior. What, then, is the meaning of work in verse 3? Does it refer to deeds, or to some kind of task? Actually, in Greek this word denotes acts, actions, activities. It includes everything of our actions. Our actions involve deeds, conduct, and many other things as well. Therefore, the work of faith refers to all the acts, actions, of faith.

Suppose an evangelist preaches the gospel to an unbeliever. The unbeliever accepts the word, faith is produced in him, and through this faith he is born of God and put into Christ. Now that he has faith, certain actions are sure to follow. For example, he may spontaneously declare, "O Lord Jesus, You are so precious!" Then he may go home and speak to his wife and children about believing in the Lord Jesus. Both the declaration concerning the Lord and the preaching of the Lord are works of faith. Faith implies God, grace, power, light, and many other items. For this reason, when a new believer preaches Christ to his wife, the faith within him may enlighten him concerning his attitude toward her. Then he will confess his shortcomings to the Lord and apologize to his wife concerning certain matters. This also is a work of faith.

First Thessalonians 1:9 says, "For they themselves report concerning us what manner of entrance we had to you, and how you turned to God from idols to serve a living and true God." Here Paul speaks of turning to God from idols. This is the first action of faith. Anyone who has faith will turn to God from idols.

The work of faith includes all the actions that issue out of our living faith. This includes our relationship with others and all our behavior. Before a certain person was saved, he may have been unkind to others and harsh in many aspects of his behavior. But once he has faith in the Lord, this faith will not allow him to treat others in such an unkind way. Furthermore, it will be difficult for him to behave in a harsh way. I can testify of this from my experience. From my youth, I hated dogs and sometimes mistreated them. But after I was saved, the faith within me no longer allowed me to behave in that way. Such a change in behavior is an action that comes out of faith.

Those who have faith are very different from those who do not have faith. Before they had faith, some indulged in sinful things. Now that they have faith, they can no longer indulge in these things. Spontaneously, as an action, a work, of faith, they refrain from those things. Others before they were saved were not good neighbors. But after they were saved and came to have faith, they became very kind, gentle, loving, and considerate. No one taught them to be different. The change was produced by the faith within them. The faith caused them to be helpful to others, especially to other believers. This is another illustration of the work of the faith.

The work of faith denotes the proper actions of a genuine believer. It is not the performing of a certain task or the doing of certain good deeds to help others. No, it is our daily action as believers, the action that is a product of faith. This is Paul's understanding of the work of faith. As he was praying for the Thessalonians, he remembered their action of faith.

THE LABOR OF LOVE

According to verse 3, the labor of love comes after the work of faith. This labor of love is truly a labor; it is not merely an action or some kind of conduct. It involves endeavoring, striving, working.

We have pointed out that the work of faith begins with turning to God from idols. The work of faith surely implies this kind of turning. Thus, the turning to God from idols is related to the work of faith. Now we must see that serving the living God is related to the labor of love. We are laboring to serve our God, who is living. We serve this living One because we love Him. Galatians 5:6 says that faith operates through love. This love is related first to serving our living God.

The faith within us produces many different kinds of actions. Moreover, this faith operates in love. In love, we as believers should endeavor to serve our living God. Our God is living. As the living One, He speaks all the time, and we serve Him.

It is not easy to serve God; rather, it is a labor. Paul even says that it is a struggle. Therefore, if we would serve the living God, we must struggle. Whatever God speaks in us and whatever He indicates to us, we need to follow Him. This is to serve Him as the living God. This service requires love toward Him. We should first love God, and this love will cause us to labor in serving Him.

THE ENDURANCE OF HOPE

Finally, in verse 3 Paul speaks of the endurance of hope. No doubt, the endurance of hope in verse 3 corresponds to the waiting for the Son of God in verse 10. If we have the endurance of hope, we shall wait for God's Son from the heavens.

Now we can see what is the Christian life as a holy life for the church life. This life originates with the Triune God. Through the preaching of the word and our acceptance of the word, we enter into a life relationship with God the Father and have an organic union with Christ. This comes through faith. Then this faith works, acts, and issues in many things. In particular, it causes us to turn to God from everything else. Furthermore, in love we labor, struggle, and strive to serve the living God. At the same time, with the endurance of hope we wait for the coming back of the Son of God. This surely is a holy life, a life that is sanctified and separated. According to chapter four, verse 7, God has called us in such a life, and according to chapter five, verse 23, God is now sanctifying us wholly for this kind of life so that we may have the proper church life.

LIFE-STUDY OF FIRST THESSALONIANS

MESSAGE SEVEN

THE CHURCH IN THE TRIUNE GOD

(1)

Scripture Reading: 1 Thes. 1:1; 2 Thes. 1:1; Matt. 28:19; Acts 19:5; Rom. 6:3; Gal. 3:27; Rev. 1:11-12

Both 1 Thessalonians 1:1 and 2 Thessalonians 1:1 tell us that the church is in God the Father and the Lord Jesus Christ. I would ask you to carefully consider the expression "the church in God the Father and the Lord Jesus Christ." Suppose Paul had written in a brief way and had simply said "the church in God and Christ." It may seem to us that it is adequate to speak of the church in God and Christ instead of the church in God the Father and the Lord Jesus Christ. The longer description of the church contains three names not found in the shorter: the Father, the Lord, and Jesus.

THE FATHER, THE LORD, AND JESUS

By reading the New Testament we realize that the first basic matter concerning the divine titles is the revelation of the name of the Father. When the Lord Jesus came and lived on earth in the flesh, what He mainly did was reveal the name of the Father to His disciples. For example, in His prayer to the Father recorded in John 17, the Lord Jesus said, "I have manifested Your name to the men whom You gave Me out of the world" (v. 6). The Lord also said to the Father, "And I have made Your name known to them, and will make it known" (John 17:26). It is a matter of great significance to know the Father. It is a great thing to know God, but it is an even greater thing to know the Father.

It is also important that we pay adequate attention to the title Lord. In the Old Testament this was used as a divine title. It was not a simple matter for the man Jesus to become the Lord. According to Acts 2, after His resurrection and ascension, Christ was made Lord of all. This means that a man, even a Nazarene, has become Lord of all. As applied to the Lord Jesus, the title Lord implies incarnation, human living, crucifixion, resurrection, and ascension. It was through such a process that the man Jesus was made Lord of all.

Before the incarnation, Christ as God was already the Lord. However, He was the Lord, the Creator. But today, after a process going from incarnation to ascension, the man Jesus has been made Lord. As applied to Christ in the New Testament, this title is rich in meaning. Christ is not only the Creator, but the One who was incarnate, who lived on earth for thirty-three and a half years, who was crucified, who was resurrected, and who has ascended to the heavens. By His crucifixion Christ accomplished redemption, terminated the old creation, destroyed Satan and death, and abolished every separation between God and man and also all the separations between men. Hallelujah for what the crucifixion of Christ has accomplished! Like the crucifixion, Christ's resurrection is profound. In the words of the song entitled, "God Is Processed," crucifixion terminates, and resurrection germinates. After His crucifixion terminated the old creation, Christ's resurrection germinated the new creation. Now, as the incarnated, crucified, resurrected, and ascended One, Jesus Christ has been made the Lord of all. All this process and everything related to it is implied in the title Lord.

The name Jesus also is significant and meaningful. Jesus means Jehovah the Savior, or Jehovah our salvation. In order for Jehovah to become our Savior and our salvation, it was necessary for Him to pass through a long process.

Christ means the anointed One. As the Christ, the anointed One, the Lord Jesus is the One appointed by God to accomplish His eternal purpose. Christ has been anointed, commissioned, and appointed to fulfill God's purpose. Through the steps of His process, He, as the Christ, has fulfilled this commission and has accomplished God's purpose. Now in resurrection and ascension He is our Lord Jesus Christ.

God is not only our Creator; He is also our Father. For God to be our Father involves much more than His merely being our Creator. How was it possible for God the Creator to become our Father? In other words, how could we, creatures of God, become children of God the Father? God has no intention to become our Father by adoption, our step-father, or our father-in-law. On the contrary, He is our Father-in-life. This means that we have received God's life. This took place when we were born of God.

It should be more than mere doctrine for us to declare that we have been born of God. Hallelujah, we are sons of God in life! Having been born of God, we are now God's sons in life, and He is truly our Father. What a great matter this is!

We need to be very careful in reading the Bible. If we read carefully, we shall realize that 1 Thessalonians 1:1 and 2 Thessalonians 1:1 are very similar, but are not exactly the same. First Thessalonians 1:1 says, "Paul and Silvanus and Timothy to the church of the Thessalonians in God the Father and the Lord Jesus Christ: Grace to you and peace." Second Thessalonians 1:1 says, "Paul and Silvanus and Timothy to the church of the Thessalonians in God our Father and the Lord Jesus Christ." The former speaks of "the Father"; the latter, of "our Father." Furthermore, in 2 Thessalonians the blessing, "Grace to you and peace," is found in verse 2 instead of verse 1. This indicates that Paul's opening word in 2 Thessalonians is a little stronger than the one in 1 Thessalonians. Certainly Paul was not careless in writing his Epistles. Everything he wrote was with a definite purpose.

THE SPIRIT IMPLIED

Both Epistles tell us that the church is composed of human beings, in this case, of Thessalonians. Thessalonica was an evil city, and for the most part those in that city were immoral people. Nevertheless, some who were once immoral were saved and regenerated and composed the church in their locality in the Triune God. For this reason, Paul speaks of the church of the Thessalonians in God the Father and the Lord Jesus Christ. By this expression Paul denotes the Triune God.

When some read concerning the church of the Thessalonians in the Triune God, they may say, "You claim that 1:1 indicates that the church is in the Triune God. Yes, this verse mentions the Father and the Lord Jesus Christ, the Son, but nothing is said concerning the Spirit. If this verse speaks of the Triune God, where is the Spirit?" Here we have one of the many instances where what the Bible does not say is just as important as what it does say, if not more so. Often in our contact with the saints, we may refrain from saying something to them. This may be more important than what we do say to them. Why did Paul not say "the church of the Thessalonians in God the Father, the Lord Jesus Christ, and the Holy Spirit"? Eventually we shall see that there is a good reason for Paul to mention the Father and Christ the Son, but not the Spirit.

Be assured that the very God spoken of in 1:1 is the Triune God. We know this by the fact that Paul first mentions the Father, the first of the Trinity. Whenever we have the first, we also have the second, the Son, and also the third, the Spirit. The very fact that Paul speaks of the Father is a strong indication that he is thinking of the Triune God. Moreover, the expression "the Lord Jesus Christ" implies the Spirit. The expressions "God the Father" and "the Lord Jesus Christ" both imply the Spirit. Therefore, in 1:1 the Spirit is implied and understood.

We must believe that the God referred to in 1:1 is the Triune God. To be in God the Father and the Lord Jesus Christ implies that we are also in the Spirit. Hence, in 1:1 we have the Triune God implied. This verse indicates that the church is in the Triune God.

IN THE TRIUNE GOD ORGANICALLY AND IN LIFE

It is a rather simple matter to say that the church is of God or of Christ. But it is deeper and more profound to declare that the church is in God the Father and in the Lord Jesus Christ. For example, it is one thing to say that we are of a particular person. However, it is altogether another matter to claim to be in that person. Humanly speaking, it is possible to be of someone, but it is not possible to be literally in that one. Only in a way that is organic and of life can the church be in the Triune God. We do not adequately understand the way of life, but God does understand it in full. Furthermore, only God can do something in the way of life. In a way that is organic and of life, God has made it possible for the church to be in the Triune God.

For the church to be merely of God, it is sufficient that God be merely our Creator. But for the church to be in God, God must become our Father, and we need to have a life relationship with Him. Likewise, for the church to be in the Lord Jesus Christ, Christ must be the Lord and Jesus to us.

VEILED BY TRADITIONAL CONCEPTS

Perhaps you have read 1:1 many times without realizing that the church is in the Triune God. Nevertheless, this fact is revealed in the Bible. Why is it, then, that not many Christians have seen it? The reason they do not see that the church is in the Triune God is that they are veiled by traditional concepts concerning the church. Believers may be familiar with expressions such as the church of God, the church of Christ, and the assembly of God, especially in the way they are employed today as denominational titles. But not many have realized that the church is in the Triune God.

It is important to realize that the New Testament does not say that the church is in God. First Thessalonians 1:1 tells us that the church is in God the Father and the Lord Jesus Christ. This is different from speaking of the church as merely in God, for it reveals that the church is in the

Triune God. According to the Bible, there is no such thing as the church merely in God, but there is the church in the Triune God.

THE DIFFERENCE BETWEEN GOD AND THE TRIUNE GOD

Now we need to consider carefully the difference between God and the Triune God. To speak only of God is to regard Him as if He had not been processed. However, the Triune God denotes God in His process. Genesis 1:1 says, "In the beginning God created the heavens and the earth" (lit.). In this verse we cannot see the processed God; that is, we cannot see the Father, the Son, and the Spirit. But in the New Testament we have a full revelation of the Triune God.

In the New Testament the first main step regarding the revelation of the Triune God is the revelation of the name of the Father. In the four Gospels we have the revelation not mainly of God, but mainly of God the Father. The Lord Jesus spent much time with the disciples to reveal to them the name of the Father.

In the New Testament, of course, we also have the revelation that Jesus is the Son of God. One day, according to Matthew 16, the Lord Jesus led His disciples away from Jerusalem, with its religious atmosphere, to Caesarea Philippi, close to the northern border of the Holy Land, at the foot of Mount Hermon, on which He was soon to be transfigured (Matt. 17:1-2). Caesarea Philippi was far from the holy city with the holy temple, where the atmosphere of the old Jewish religion filled everyone's thought. The Lord purposely brought His disciples to a place with a clear atmosphere so that their thought could be released from the effects of the religious surroundings in the holy city and holy temple, and that He might reveal to them something new concerning Himself. It was there that the vision concerning Him as the Christ, the Son of the living God, was given to Peter.

Matthew 16:13 says, "Now when Jesus came into the district of Caesarea Philippi, He asked His disciples, saying,

Who do men say that the Son of Man is?" Because the disciples were not clear, they began to answer in a nonsensical way. According to verse 14, they said, "Some, John the Baptist; and others, Elijah; and still others, Jeremiah, or one of the prophets." Then the Lord Jesus said to them, "But you, who do you say that I am?" (v. 15). As we know, Peter, receiving the revelation from the Father, answered and said to the Lord Jesus, "You are the Christ, the Son of the living God" (v. 16). Thus, in the New Testament we first have the revelation of the name of the Father and then the revelation of the Son of God. The first title revealed in the New Testament, therefore, is the Father; the second is that of the Son.

Going on from Matthew 16 to John 14, we have the revelation of the Spirit. When Philip said to the Lord Jesus, "Lord, show us the Father and it suffices us" (John 14:8), the Lord replied, "Am I so long a time with you, and you have not known Me, Philip? He who has seen Me has seen the Father....Do you not believe that I am in the Father, and the Father is in Me?" (vv. 9-10). Here the Lord Jesus indicates that He is in the Father and that the Father is in Him. This means that He cannot be separated from the Father nor the Father from Him. After speaking in this way concerning Himself and the Father, the Lord went on to speak of the Spirit of reality, another Comforter, "And I will ask the Father, and He will give you another Comforter, that He may be with you forever; even the Spirit of reality" (vv. 16-17). Thus, the Spirit, another Comforter, is the third divine title revealed in the New Testament. Therefore, we have the revelation of the Father, the Son, and the Spirit. This is the Triune God.

The revelation of the Triune God requires the incarnation of Christ, the Lord's human living, and His crucifixion and resurrection. After the resurrection of Christ, we have the coming of the Spirit. Now we know that the Triune God is the Father, the Son, and the Spirit.

This Triune God is the processed God. He has passed through the process of incarnation, human living, crucifixion, and resurrection. In crucifixion, He accomplished redemption, the termination of the old creation, and the destruction of Satan and death. In resurrection, He germinated the new creation. Now He is the life-giving Spirit as the ultimate consummation of the Triune God. The church is in such a Triune God. The church is in the processed Triune God, the One who has become the life-giving Spirit with the Father and the Son.

LIFE-STUDY OF FIRST THESSALONIANS

MESSAGE EIGHT

THE CHURCH IN THE TRIUNE GOD

(2)

Scripture Reading: 1 Thes. 1:1; 2 Thes. 1:1; Matt. 28:19; Acts 19:5; Rom. 6:3; Gal. 3:27; Rev. 1:11-12

We have seen that 1:1 indicates that the church is in the Triune God. Paul speaks of the Triune God in 2 Corinthians 13:14: "The grace of the Lord Jesus Christ, and the love of God, and the fellowship of the Holy Spirit be with you all." Here we have the threefold blessing of the Triune God, the blessing of love, grace, and fellowship. The Triune God revealed in this verse is the processed God. The very God in whom the church is today is the processed Triune God, the Father, the Son, and the Holy Spirit.

THE FATHER'S DESIRE AND PLAN

What is it that God the Father desires? According to the New Testament, the Father wants many sons. The Father's concern is with sonship. In order to produce these sons, He has been begetting children. With Him, there need be no limit to the number of children. The more children He has, the better. The Father wants sons, and He is begetting them.

God the Father has a definite purpose in producing many sons. He is not a foolish father, one without a purpose. Rather, He has a purpose and a plan. God's selection and predestination are according to His purpose. First He selected us and then predestinated us. This indicates that God is the unique initiator and originator. Thus, for the church to be in God the Father implies that the church is in God's purpose, plan, selection, and predestination. No doubt, the church is also in God's calling. The church in God the Father is the church in the One who is the initiator and originator.

This understanding of the church in the Father is not merely a matter of doctrine; rather, it has much to do with us in our practical experience. A problem among Christians today is that they have many different purposes and plans. There are different initiators and originators. This is not right. We Christians all should have the unique purpose, the purpose of our Father. We should also have the unique plan of the Father. This means that only one—the Father—should be the initiator and originator. We should not originate anything or initiate anything. Imagine what would happen if all Christians gave up their own purposes and plans and had only one initiator and originator. What oneness there would be among us all! There would be no division whatever.

THE TERMINATION OF EVERYTHING NEGATIVE, NATURAL, AND OLD

We have seen a little of what it means for the church to be in the Father. Now let us go on to consider what it means for the church to be in the Lord Jesus Christ. It is a great matter to be in Christ. To be in Christ means that there is no sin, flesh, self, natural life, old creation, death, or Satan. If we are in Christ, everything negative has been terminated. Sin, death, the self, the flesh, Satan, and the old creation have all been terminated. For those who are in Christ everything other than God has been terminated.

If we realize what has been terminated in Christ, we shall know that it is shameful for so-called churches to designate themselves by certain names. For example, in China there was a group called the American Presbyterian Church. Recently in southern California I saw a sign which read "The Orange County Chinese Taiwanese Church." A brother recently told me about a group called the San Francisco Chinese Mennonite Church. There is no room for any such names or designations in the church. Those who take a name such as these indicate by doing so that they are not the church in the Lord Jesus Christ. The fact that they have a name indicates that many things among them have not been terminated.

The church is in the Lord Jesus Christ. This implies that with respect to the church everything natural, everything negative, everything of the old creation, has been terminated. This means that in the church there are no Chinese or Americans, no Japanese or Koreans, no French or Germans. In the church there is room only for Jesus Christ the Lord. This is the significance of the church being in the Lord Jesus Christ.

We in the Lord's recovery claim to be practicing the church life. Whenever we make such a claim, however, we need to check to see whether we are still holding to our culture or disposition. Regarding this matter, sometimes we expect others to sympathize with us. On occasion sisters have said to me, "Brother Lee, don't forget that we are sisters. According to the Bible, we sisters are weaker vessels." But in the Lord Jesus Christ there are no weak vessels. Therefore, we should not expect anyone to sympathize with our natural disposition. As long as you want others to sympathize with you, that is an indication that in your experience you are not buried with Christ. For the church to be in the Lord Jesus Christ in a practical way, we all need to be terminated and buried. We need to die and then be placed in the tomb. This is to be in the Lord Jesus Christ.

When I say this, does it seem that I am comparing the Lord Jesus Christ to a tomb? Listen to what Paul says in Romans 6:3: "Are you ignorant that as many as have been baptized into Christ Jesus have been baptized into His death?" This verse clearly says that to be baptized into Christ is to be baptized into Christ's death. How, then, can we be in Christ without also being in His death? To be in Christ is to be buried, terminated. Do you like to hear such a word? Whether we like to hear it or not, it is the truth that to be in Christ is to be terminated.

During special times of conference or training, saints

come together from different cities and regions. Outwardly, no one says anything in favor of his locality. But deep within we may be proud of coming from a certain place. In our heart we may say, "You have to realize that we are from such-and-such place. Our place is the best." To think in this way is to exalt ourselves. When we claim to be of a certain place, we are excluding ourselves from the Lord Jesus Christ. The church must be only in God the Father and the Lord Jesus Christ.

A NEW BEGINNING

There is an important reason why Paul opened the Epistle of 1 Thessalonians the way he did. In Paul's time, the Greeks for the most part were proud and evil. They had a complex mythology, and they proudly worshipped false gods. They were extremely superstitious. Thus, they were ruined and corrupted by their mythology, superstition, and philosophy. Like Egyptian, Babylonian, and Persian philosophy, Greek philosophy was not pure. On the contrary, it contained defiling elements. In a sense their philosophy promoted immorality and fornication.

When Paul speaks of the church of the Thessalonians in God the Father and in the Lord Jesus Christ, he was saying, "Dear saints in Thessalonica, you are still Thessalonians. But you must realize that now that you have believed in Jesus Christ, you are different. No longer are you in mythology or philosophy. Instead, you are in God the Father, for you have been regenerated, born of God, and have had a new beginning. You are also in the Lord Jesus Christ, since in Him you have been terminated on the cross. Therefore, you are no longer Greeks, and you are no longer immoral people. You should not be in philosophy or mythology any longer, but should be absolutely in God the Father. Do you know how it is possible for you to be in the Father? You can be in Him because you have been born of Him. Thus, now you are in the begetting God, the One who has become your Father. Furthermore, instead of being in your philosophy, you are in the Lord Jesus Christ. Being in the Father and the Lord

Jesus Christ, you are now a holy people, a separated people. From now on, you should live a life that is absolutely separated from Thessalonica, from Greece, from immorality, and from Greek mythology and philosophy. This holy life, this separated life, is for the church life, because the church is in God the Father and the Lord Jesus Christ."

It is important for us all to see that the church is in the Triune God. Because I have been naturalized to be an American citizen, in a good sense I have been somewhat Americanized. Actually, however, I do not regard myself as an American or a Chinese, but as someone in the Lord Jesus Christ. Whatever our status is in regard to earthly citizenship, we all need to realize that our real position is that we are in God the Father and the Lord Jesus Christ. Being in the Father and the Lord Jesus Christ implies that we have had a new birth, a new beginning. We have a new source—God the Father. All the old things, the negative things—sin, the flesh, the self, the old man, the natural life, Satan, death—have been terminated. Our being in the Lord Jesus Christ involves a termination of all these things. This means that in the Lord Jesus Christ there is no sin, death, or Satan. In Him there is no world, flesh, self, or old creation. In God the Father we have been born again, regenerated. In Him we have a new source and a new beginning. In the Lord Jesus Christ we have the termination of everything of the old creation. This is the implication of being in God the Father and the Lord Jesus Christ. Here in the Triune God is where the church is today.

A CONTROLLING VISION

It is basic to living a holy life for the church life to see that the church is in the Triune God. If we see this, we shall not care for teachings about improving our behavior or becoming more ethical. As long as we see that the church is an entity in God the Father and the Lord Jesus Christ, we shall realize that we have been absolutely separated by God Himself and are now encompassed by the Lord Jesus Christ. This makes us a holy people living a holy, separated life.

This life is for the church. When we see this, we can understand what is written in the book of 1 Thessalonians.

I have the full assurance that if you see what is covered in these messages on the church in the Triune God, you will be different both in your concept and in your activity. These messages convey a vision, a vision that will control our thinking, our activities, and our entire life. If we see the revelation that the church is in God the Father and the Lord Jesus Christ, we shall spontaneously realize that we should not hold to certain concepts or do certain things, for they are worldly, profane, unholy, not separated unto God. We shall realize that such things are not for the church which is in God the Father and the Lord Jesus Christ.

I can testify that I love Paul's expression in 1:1—"the church of the Thessalonians in God the Father and the Lord Jesus Christ." How marvelous that the church is of certain people in God the Father and the Lord Jesus Christ!

Both in 1 Thessalonians 1:1 and in 2 Thessalonians 1:1 and 2, Paul mentions grace and peace after speaking of the church in God the Father and the Lord Jesus Christ. Grace is the Triune God to be our enjoyment. When we are in the Father and the Lord Jesus Christ, we are in the place to enjoy all the things of God.

CONTACTING THE SPIRIT

We have pointed out that the Father is the One who plans and originates. He is the initiator and the originator. God the Son accomplishes everything that God the Father has purposed, planned, initiated, and originated. But what is the function of God the Spirit? The Spirit is neither the originator nor the accomplisher—He is the executor. The Spirit does not do anything for Himself or by Himself. Rather, He executes, carries out, what the Father has planned and originated and what the Son has accomplished. We all must see that everything the Father has planned and everything the Son has accomplished is now in the Spirit and with the Spirit. In our experience the One we contact is the Spirit. This Spirit is the Son, and in the Son we have the Father. For this reason we may say that the Father is in the Son and that the Son is now the life-giving Spirit dwelling in us. What we need to do is stay in the Spirit and walk according to the Spirit. When we walk according to the Spirit, we are actually walking according to the Triune God.

The Spirit is the ultimate consummation of the processed Triune God. The Spirit is the application, the reaching to us, of the Triune God. How does the processed Triune God reach us and contact us? He does this as the Spirit. How can the processed Triune God be applied to us in our experience? He is applied as the life-giving Spirit. The Spirit is not only the Spirit of God and the Spirit of Christ; He is the Spirit as God and as Christ. In our experience today, the Triune God is the very life-giving Spirit. Therefore, when we are in God the Father and the Lord Jesus Christ, we are in the Spirit. Because the Spirit is implied and understood in 1:1, we speak of the church being in the Triune God.

LIFE-STUDY OF FIRST THESSALONIANS

MESSAGE NINE

THE CHURCH BECOMING THE EMBODIMENT OF THE TRIUNE GOD

(1)

Scripture Reading: 1 Thes. 1:1; 2:12; 3:12; 4:7; 5:23-24; 2 Thes. 1:3, 5, 10; 2:13-14, 16; Col. 3:10-11; Rev. 1:11-12

We have emphasized the fact that in 1:1 Paul says that the church is in God the Father and the Lord Jesus Christ. We have considered what it means for the church to be in God the Father and also the significance of the church being in the Lord Jesus Christ. However, although we have emphasized the Father, the Lord, and Jesus, we have not explained fully what it means for the church to be in Christ.

When the name Jesus is used in the New Testament, it primarily refers to the Lord in His experiences on earth from His incarnation to His resurrection. Jesus is the name of the Lord with respect to His humanity. Hence, this name denotes His life experiences and the things He passed through before His resurrection. Christ is a divine title that mainly denotes the Lord's experience, position, life, and actions after His resurrection. This title refers to what the Lord is after His resurrection.

The life of the Lord Jesus Christ may be divided into two sections: the section before His resurrection, and the section after His resurrection. Resurrection, therefore, is a dividing line, a boundary line, of the Lord's life and experience.

The four Gospels may be regarded as biographies of the Lord Jesus. These biographies tell His life story between His incarnation and resurrection. This period of time is, for the most part, represented by the name Jesus. If we speak of Jesus according to the biblical use of this name, we mainly refer to His experience between incarnation and resurrection. After resurrection the life of the Lord Jesus is altogether in another sphere.

Today, however, many Christians are not clear in their understanding concerning Jesus and Christ. Some believers, especially those in Pentecostalism, say "Praise Jesus!" According to the Bible, it is better to say "Praise the Lord." It is much more common for Christians today to say "Praise the Lord" than it was twenty years ago, when the Lord's recovery came to this country. This may be due to the influence of the recovery. In any case, it is more fitting to say "Praise the Lord" than to say "Praise Jesus."

According to the New Testament, the title Lord applies to the entire life and ministry of Jesus Christ. This means that the title Lord is an all-inclusive title. But the name Jesus refers to the Lord in His humanity and to His human life prior to resurrection. Christ, as we have seen, refers to the resurrected Christ in ascension.

CHRIST ON THE THRONE AND IN US

The Christ in whom many of today's Christians believe is a Christ far away in the third heaven. But our Christ is not only the resurrected and ascended Christ in heaven; He is also the One who has descended and entered into our spirit. Hallelujah, Christ is now in our spirit!

In John 14 the Lord Jesus spoke to His disciples regarding His going and His coming. In John 14:1 He said, "Let not your heart be troubled; believe in God, believe also in Me." In the next verse the Lord spoke about the many abodes in the Father's house and about going to prepare a place for them. In verse 3 He said, "And if I go and prepare a place for you, I am coming again and will receive you to Myself, that where I am you also may be." Here the Lord Jesus seemed to be saying, "Do not be troubled by the fact that I am going. Apparently I am leaving you. But actually My going is for My coming. After I go, I shall come back again." The Lord Jesus was not saying that He was going to heaven. Rather, He was going to the cross and then to the tomb and to Hades. Then in resurrection He would come back to the disciples.

Nearly all Christians take the Lord's word in John 14 to refer to His second coming. This understanding is not accurate. In John 14:18 the Lord Jesus said to the disciples, "I will not leave you orphans; I am coming to you." If the Lord's coming in John 14 were His second coming, the disciples certainly would have been orphans. If the Lord Jesus were only in the heavens today, we all would be orphans. When the Lord said, "I am coming to you," He was speaking of His coming in another form. This coming was fulfilled on the day of His resurrection in John 20:19-22. After His resurrection, the Lord Jesus came back to His disciples to be with them forever, so that they were not left orphans.

The Lord's coming in John 14 refers to His coming in another form. The Lord first came in the form of the flesh. When He spoke to the disciples in John 14, He was still in that form. But in this chapter He seems to be saying, "I am now in the flesh. But I am going to the cross, where I shall be slain. Afterward, I shall be buried in a tomb. Then I shall rise up from among the dead and come again in another form. When I am in that form, I shall come back to you." And the Lord did come back in this form on the day of His resurrection.

Chapter twenty of John describes how the Lord came to His disciples on the day of His resurrection. John 20:19 says, "When therefore it was evening on that day, the first day of the week, and when the doors were shut where the disciples were for fear of the Jews, Jesus came and stood in the midst and said to them, Peace be to you." The Lord Jesus appeared in a splendid, excellent way, in a way beyond human ability to understand. The Jews were opposing the disciples and trying their best to destroy them. Therefore, the disciples were afraid and met behind closed doors. Perhaps they were groaning and wondering what to do. Suddenly the Lord Jesus appeared and said, "Peace be to you." This One who appeared to them was not Jesus in the flesh—He was Christ the Lord.

According to verse 21, the Lord said to them, "Peace be to you; as the Father has sent Me, I also send you." Then, as we see in verse 22, the Lord breathed into the disciples the holy *pneuma,* the Holy Spirit: "And when He had said this, He breathed into them and said to them, Receive the Holy Spirit." The Lord Jesus in His resurrection is now the *pneuma,* the Spirit. He appeared to the disciples in the form of *pneuma,* and He told them to receive the holy *pneuma,* the holy breath. In the Greek language the word *pneuma* means both Spirit and breath. Hallelujah, Christ in resurrection is the breath, the *pneuma,* the Spirit! After the disciples received Him as the holy *pneuma,* He began to live in them.

We also have received the Lord Jesus Christ as the holy breath, the holy *pneuma,* the life-giving Spirit, and now He is actually in us. I believe that if we have a proper realization of Christ in us, we shall be very excited, even beside ourselves with joy. The fact that we may not be at all excited about this may indicate that we do not realize that Christ is in us.

Where is Christ today? The answer is that Christ is on the throne in heaven and also living in us. Oh, we should be able to declare with a strong release of the spirit that Christ is in us. Our Christ today is the One who lives in us! In a very real sense, our Christ is different from the Christ in whom many Christians believe, for they have a Christ merely in heaven, but we have both the Christ in heaven and the Christ who dwells in our spirit.

I have been condemned and falsely accused of preaching another Christ. I do not preach a Christ different from the One revealed in the Bible. But, in a certain sense, I preach a Christ who is somewhat different from the One in whom many Christians believe, for the Christ I preach is both in the heavens and in me, whereas many Christians have a Christ only in heaven. Rather than enjoy the indwelling Christ today, they are waiting to die and to meet Christ in heaven. The Christ I preach is the Christ revealed in the Scriptures. He is the Lord Jesus Christ. He is the Lord in an all-inclusive sense. For Him to be the Lord means that He is both Jesus and Christ.

TERMINATION AND RESURRECTION

In the foregoing message we pointed out that to be in Christ is to be in His death, the death which terminates all negative things: sin, the world, the old creation, the old man, the flesh, the self, and Satan. When the Lord Jesus was crucified, He terminated all these negative things. This all-inclusive termination brings in resurrection. In the Bible there is a strong principle that death ushers us into resurrection. If there is no death, there can be no resurrection.

In resurrection Jesus is the Christ. Hallelujah, His crucifixion is still effective! Praise Him that He has been resurrected and that in resurrection He has become the Christ. Now as believers we are in Christ; we have entered into an organic union with Him.

Some Christian teachers speak of being in Jesus. This expression is not accurate. We can be in Christ, but we cannot be in Jesus. When the Lord was Jesus in the flesh, no one could be in Him. But after He was crucified and resurrected and had become the Spirit, we could be in Him. By the Spirit, with the Spirit, through the Spirit, and in the Spirit, we can be in Christ. Christ is the heavenly, spiritual air, and we are now in Him.

THE ANOINTED ONE AND THE ANOINTING ONE

The word Christ is an anglicized form of the Greek word *christos.* This Greek word is an equivalent to the Hebrew word for Messiah, meaning the anointed One. For the Lord Jesus to be the Messiah, the Christ, the anointed One, means that God's Spirit was poured upon Him. Today our Christ is not only the anointed One, but is also the anointing One. He Himself has become the life-giving Spirit. In resurrection Christ is both the anointed One and, as the anointing Spirit, the anointing One.

In experience we can know that Christ today is the anointing One. Suppose someone is suffering and is deeply sorrowful and depressed. According to his feeling, life is not worth living. Then he hears the gospel and learns of God's love for him. He hears how the Lord Jesus died for him, has been resurrected, and is waiting for him to receive Him by calling, "O Lord Jesus." Then he says, "Lord Jesus, I thank You." He finds that his sorrow has gone away. Within he has the sense of being watered. This watering is the Lord's anointing that results in peace, in rest, and in the sense of being loved by the Lord and being cared for by Him. This is the experience of Christ as the anointing One.

When we call on the Lord's name, the Person of the Lord comes to us. Just as a person responds when we call his name, so the Lord Jesus Himself responds when we call His name. The Lord's name is Jesus Christ, and His Person is the Spirit. For this reason, when we call on the name of the Lord Jesus, it is the Spirit who comes.

Our concept may be that the Lord is only in the third heaven. Therefore, when we call on Him, we may be surprised that He comes so quickly. Actually, as the Spirit He is already within us. Our intention may be to say, "Lord Jesus Christ, You are in heaven." But before we have finished saying the Lord's name, He has already responded. The Lord can respond so quickly to our calling on Him because in resurrection He is now the life-giving Spirit.

In Genesis 1 we have God, and in the four Gospels we have a record of the life of Jesus on earth. But today for our experience we have the Lord Jesus Christ as the Spirit. The moment we begin to call on His name, He comes to us from within us. This is Christ in resurrection.

THE RICHES OF RESURRECTION

The church is in God the Father and the Lord Jesus Christ. The title Christ in 1 Thessalonians 1:1 denotes all the riches of resurrection. If the Lord were only Jesus and not Christ, we could not be in Him. But because He is the Lord Jesus Christ, we can be in Him and we are in Him right now. Where are we? We are in the Lord Jesus Christ. The name Jesus implies that everything we are in the old creation and in the fall has been terminated, and the title Christ implies that we are no longer in ourselves, in the old creation, in sin and death, in the world, and in Satan. Instead, we are in resurrection, in the Spirit, and in righteousness, holiness, power, strength, and might. Because we are in Christ, we are even on the throne with Him. Oh, how marvelous it is to be in Christ.

To be in the Lord Jesus Christ means on the one hand that we are terminated and are no longer in the old creation. On the other hand, it means that by being in Christ we are in resurrection. To be in Christ is to be in resurrection, in the Spirit, in power, in strength, and in authority. However, because of the influence of traditional Christianity, we may not realize the significance of being in Christ. As a result, there may be a shortage of the experience of resurrection, strength, and authority.

Do you realize that because you are in Christ you are on the throne? Not only are you in power, might, strength, and authority, but you are also on the throne. After His resurrection Christ went to the heavens to be enthroned, and in Him we also are on the throne. Sometimes we need to say to Satan, "Satan, don't you see where I am? I am in Christ on the throne!"

Religion has deprived us, even robbed us, of the enjoyment of what we have in Christ. It has caused us in experience to be poor, pitiful. Therefore, we need to be impressed with the fact that to be in Christ is to be in resurrection, in the Spirit, in power, and on the throne. The church in Christ is the church in resurrection, in authority, and on the throne.

GROWING IN RESURRECTION LIFE

Before we go on to see that to be in Christ is also to be in the kingdom and glory, we need to emphasize the crucial matter of life. To be in Christ is to be in life, even in resurrection life. If we neglect life, we shall miss everything. Apart from life, there is no way to enter into the kingdom or the glory. The church today is in resurrection life, and this resurrection life is accomplishing many things for us.

I have learned much about life by observing how things grow in my garden at home. I am amazed how a tiny plant grows in life. This is a picture, an illustration, of how we are growing in resurrection life. Because we are in resurrection life, something within us is growing. The word growing implies a great deal. It includes transformation, blossoming, fruitfulness, and maturity. Some of the plants in my garden were rather uncomely before they had adequate growth. But by growing they have been transformed and have become beautiful. They have blossomed, they have borne fruit, and they have become mature. This matter of growth with all it implies is also included in the thought of the church being in God the Father and the Lord Jesus Christ.

It is indeed a tragedy that, under the influence of religion, so many Christians have been distracted from growing in resurrection life. Instead of paying attention to life and the growth of life, they pursue knowledge and try to improve themselves. There is no need for us to endeavor to improve ourselves, for we are in resurrection life. This resurrection life is the resurrected Christ, and this Christ in resurrection is the life-giving Spirit. The church today is in Christ, the One who in His resurrection has become the all-inclusive life-giving Spirit.

LIFE-STUDY OF FIRST THESSALONIANS

MESSAGE TEN

THE CHURCH BECOMING THE EMBODIMENT OF THE TRIUNE GOD

(2)

Scripture Reading: 1 Thes. 1:1; 2:12; 3:12; 4:7; 5:23-24; 2 Thes. 1:3, 5, 10; 2:13-14, 16; Col. 3:10-11; Rev. 1:11-12

According to both 1 Thessalonians 1:1 and 2 Thessalonians 1:1, the church is in God the Father and the Lord Jesus Christ. In the foregoing message we pointed out that for the church to be in Christ is to be in resurrection life. This resurrection life is Christ Himself in resurrection as the life-giving Spirit. What we need is not self-improvement but the growth of this resurrection life within us.

BROUGHT INTO THE FATHER

In John 14 we have a further indication that we the believers are in God the Father. According to the traditional religious understanding, this chapter speaks of heavenly mansions. However, what John 14 speaks about is not heavenly mansions; rather, it speaks of abodes, abiding places, in a divine Person, in God the Father. In verses 2 and 3 the Lord Jesus says, "In My Father's house are many abodes; if it were not so, I would have told you; for I go to prepare a place for you. And if I go and prepare a place for you, I am coming again and will receive you to Myself, that where I am you also may be." The Lord Jesus was telling His disciples that through His death and resurrection He would prepare the way to bring them into the Father.

The Lord Jesus is in the Father (John 14:10-11). He wanted His disciples also to be in the Father, as revealed in John 17:21. Through His death and resurrection, He brought His disciples into Himself. Since He is in the Father, they are also in the Father by being in Him. Hence, where the Lord Jesus is, there the disciples are also. Where is the Lord Jesus? He is in the Father. Therefore, for us to be where He is means that we also are in the Father.

It is actually superstitious to believe that John 14:2 and 3 mean that the Lord is building a heavenly mansion and that He will come back only after this work of building is complete. Some Christian teachers claim that the fact the Lord Jesus has not come back indicates that the building of the heavenly mansion is not yet finished. I was told this by a Christian teacher when I was very young. In their talk about the heavenly mansion, some have said, "How marvelous the heavenly mansion will be! The Lord Jesus has been there for more than nineteen hundred years, and still He hasn't finished the building of this mansion. The Lord said that after He prepares a place for us, He will come back and receive us to Himself. We know from the fact that He has not yet come back that He is still building the heavenly mansion."

While I was in England in 1958, I was enlightened to see from the Bible that John 14 has nothing to do with a heavenly mansion. The use of the word mansion in the King James translation of John 14:2 is not accurate. This verse speaks of abodes, not of mansions. The word used in Greek is a noun form of the verb abide. Here the Lord Jesus seems to be saying, "I am your abode, and you shall abide in Me. You are My abode, and I shall abide in you. I am going to prepare an abode in God the Father. The Father wants to receive you all. However, because you are sinful and unrighteous and He is holy and righteous, you cannot enter into Him unless I die on the cross to take away your sins. My death will open up the way for you to come into the Father. After I have prepared a place for you in the Father through My death and resurrection, I shall come again." Praise the Lord that in this sense the Lord Jesus has already returned! He has already come back, and He has brought us into the Father. Now as members of the church we can declare that we are in God the Father. The church, including all of us, is where the Lord Jesus is, that is, in God the Father. Hallelujah, where the Lord Jesus Christ is, there we are also! We are in the same abode as the Lord Jesus is. How wonderful!

When I began to teach that John 14 speaks not of heavenly mansions but of abodes in God the Father, I was criticized and condemned. Some accused me of taking away their heavenly mansion and complained that at a funeral they could no longer tell people that there is a heavenly mansion for the dead believers.

THE RESURRECTED CHRIST IDENTICAL TO THE SPIRIT

I have also been accused of teaching heresy for saying, according to the Bible, that Christ today is the life-giving Spirit. We should not regard the life-giving Spirit as a Person separate from the Lord Jesus Christ. When the Lord was in the flesh, He was Jesus. But in resurrection He has become the life-giving Spirit. We are not the only ones who have seen this fact and teach it. A number of other Christian writers have said that, in Christian experience, Christ is identical to the Spirit. In doctrine or in theology it is very difficult to explain how the second of the Trinity, the Son, can be identical to the third, the Spirit. Nevertheless, in Christian experience the resurrected Christ is identical to the Spirit. Second Corinthians 3:17 says explicitly, "The Lord is the Spirit." First Corinthians 15:45, a confirming verse, says, "The last Adam became a life-giving Spirit." Although it is according to the Bible to say that Christ is the Spirit, I have been condemned as heretical for teaching this.

The Bible reveals that the resurrected Christ, the very Christ in resurrection, is the life-giving Spirit. This can be confirmed by our experience. We have Christ within us, and we also have the Spirit within us. But in your experience do you have two in you, Christ and the Spirit, or do you have one? Although both Christ and the Spirit are in us, in experience we have one in us, not two, for Christ today in resurrection is identical to the Spirit.

In resurrection the Christ who dwells within us is a wonderful Spirit. This Spirit is life, power, holiness, love, righteousness, might, strength, wisdom, grace, kindness, mercy. Oh, this Spirit is everything! This is why we say that this Spirit, who is God and Christ, is all-inclusive.

In particular I wish to point out that this Spirit contains the effectiveness of Christ's death. The Spirit certainly does not contain death, but it does include the effectiveness of the crucifixion of the Lord Jesus.

WALKING ACCORDING TO THE SPIRIT

In the New Testament we are commanded to walk according to the Spirit. For example, Galatians 5:16 says, "Walk by the Spirit and you shall by no means fulfill the lust of the flesh." In Galatians 5:25 Paul says, "If we live by the Spirit, let us also walk by the Spirit." Referring to the mingled spirit, the Spirit mingled with our regenerated human spirit, Romans 8:4 says, "That the righteous requirement of the law might be fulfilled in us, who do not walk according to flesh, but according to spirit." Therefore, we should simply walk according to the Spirit. There is no need for us to do anything else.

Married brothers and sisters may be concerned about how to have a good marriage or how to be a proper husband or wife. If a brother were to ask me how to be a proper husband or how to have a good married life, I would give just one answer: Walk according to the Spirit. This word applies to brothers and sisters, to husbands and wives. Today many books have been written by Christians on how to have a good family life or how to avoid divorce. There is no need for us to read those books. Do you want to be a good husband or wife? Walk according to Spirit. Do you want to have a good marriage? The answer is the same—walk according to Spirit. Because the Spirit is all-inclusive, it is sufficient for us to walk according to Spirit.

Our problem is that we are not faithful always to walk according to Spirit. Of the approximately sixteen waking hours of each day, how much do you walk according to Spirit?

If daily we walk according to Spirit for even one hour and a half, we would be an outstanding saint. Even in the church meetings we may fail to be in the Spirit. For example, you may not sing according to Spirit. Instead, you may sing according to your emotion. If you are excited, you sing in a certain way according to your emotion. But perhaps at the next meeting, you may be very cold in your emotion. Nothing can stir you up because you care for your emotion, not for the Spirit. Your coldness in the meeting may be due to the fact that someone has offended you. Because you have been offended, you will not allow anything to stir you in the meeting. You may be low for several days, until something happens to stir you up again or to cause you to be excited. Then in the meeting you may praise the Lord in a loud way. However, in that kind of situation your praise is according to emotion, not according to Spirit.

We all must see that the church is in God the Father and the Lord Jesus Christ. We have pointed out that to be in Jesus Christ means that everything negative and everything of the old creation has been terminated. This means that our natural emotion and our self should be terminated. If this is your situation, you will not be offended by others. How can a dead person be offended by anything or anyone? It is impossible. No matter what you may say or do to a dead person, he will not be offended. To be in Jesus Christ is to be terminated and buried, for to be in Christ is to be in His death. If we truly are the church in God the Father and the Lord Jesus Christ, we shall not function in the meeting according to our emotion, but we shall function according to the Spirit.

We have seen that to be in Christ is to be in the spiritual air, in the life-giving Spirit. If in our experience we are in this spiritual air, we shall not be offended by others. The more others give us a difficult time, the more we shall be able to praise the Lord. This is the church in Christ as the life-giving Spirit.

The reality of the resurrected Christ as the life-giving Spirit is far beyond our ability to describe. Power, strength, might, authority, the throne, holiness, righteousness—all the divine virtues are involved with this resurrected Christ. Thus, when we are in Him, we have all these virtues. We have patience, endurance, and all that Christ is. Christ is the reality of the divine attributes and the human virtues. If in our practical living we are in Him, we shall be humble, kind, and enduring. We shall be those in resurrection, in the resurrected Christ.

WALKING WORTHILY OF GOD

We have placed a strong emphasis on the fact that, according to 1:1, the church is an entity in God the Father and the Lord Jesus Christ. Now let us go on to consider 2:12: "That you should walk worthily of God, Who calls you into His own kingdom and glory." What does it mean to walk worthily of God? To walk worthily of God is to have a life in the Lord Jesus Christ. First Thessalonians 2:12 is an explanation of 1:1. What does it mean for the church to be in God the Father and the Lord Jesus Christ? For the church to be in God the Father and the Lord Jesus Christ in a practical way is for there to be a company of human beings who walk worthily of God.

What can compare with God? What can match Him? The answer to these questions is that only God Himself can compare with God or match Him. This indicates that to walk worthily of God actually means to live God. Our daily life must actually be God Himself, since only God can be worthy of God, match God, or compare with God. Therefore, in our living we must express God.

Because we have God's life, we can live God. A dog obviously has a dog's life and therefore lives a dog. In the same principle, we have God's life and therefore we can live God. Hallelujah, God is our Father, and we are His children! As God's children with His life, it is possible for us to live Him.

Whereas 1:1 speaks of the church in God the Father, many Christians instead speak of the church in God the Almighty. In Christian services often that hymn is sung which begins, "Holy, holy, holy, Lord God Almighty." To you, is God only the Almighty, or is He also your Father? Because we have been born of Him, God is now our Father. As the Almighty, God does not have any life relationship with you, and you may not have anything to do with Him. You may be apart from Him and outside of Him. But if God has become your Father, you now have a life relationship with Him, and you are in Him.

Whom do you love more, the President of the United States, or your own father? The President may be wealthy, and your father may be poor, but certainly you love your father more than you love the President. In a far deeper way, we love God more as our Father than as merely the Almighty. Hallelujah, because we are children of God we can live God! We all should declare boldly, "Because I have God's life, I can live Him."

Now we see what it means to walk worthily of God. Only God can be worthy of Himself, and only God can match Himself or be compared with Himself. Therefore, to walk worthily of God is to live God. Praise the Lord that we have God's life and that we can walk worthily of Him by living Him!

LIFE-STUDY OF FIRST THESSALONIANS

MESSAGE ELEVEN

THE CHURCH BECOMING THE EMBODIMENT OF THE TRIUNE GOD

(3)

Scripture Reading: 1 Thes. 1:1; 2:12; 3:12; 4:7; 5:23-24; 2 Thes. 1:3, 5, 10; 2:13-14, 16; Col. 3:10-11; Rev. 1:11-12

CALLED INTO GOD'S KINGDOM AND GLORY

First Thessalonians 2:12 says, "That you should walk worthily of God, Who calls you into His own kingdom and glory." In the foregoing message we considered what it means to walk worthily of God. Let us go on to see what it means in a practical way to be called by God into His kingdom and glory.

Many Christians, including us, take things in the Bible for granted. For example, we may read 2:12 and take for granted that we understand it. However, we may not have a proper understanding of God's kingdom and glory. Of course, I do not claim to understand 2:12 in full. However, I do have some understanding from study and experience. What I wish to say concerning the kingdom and glory in 2:12 is mainly according to my spiritual experience.

In this verse Paul says that God has called us into His own kingdom and glory. No doubt, God's kingdom and glory are the goal of His calling. It is unfortunate that Christians think that God has called us into a heavenly mansion. God's calling is not to a heavenly mansion; it is to His kingdom and glory.

According to the understanding of many Christians, at present the earth is not God's kingdom, but one day the Lord Jesus will come back, take over the earth, and establish His rule upon it. That rule will be God's kingdom. Many of us have probably held such a concept concerning the kingdom of God. I do not say that this understanding is not accurate at all. However, I must say that it is not entirely accurate, and it is certainly much too superficial.

What is God's kingdom? The kingdom of God is God being manifested through us. Whenever we express God in our daily walk, that is the kingdom. The expression of God Himself from within us is the kingdom. Suppose a brother works in an office. Certain of his colleagues may oppose him because he is a believer. They may not be happy to have him there. But if he expresses God daily in the office, his fellow workers will realize that there is something unusual about him. They will know that with this brother there is something special. This is God's kingdom, God expressed from within that brother. On the one hand, others may oppose us, criticize us, and be unhappy with us. On the other hand, they sense something indescribable about us. This is God's kingdom as His manifestation through us. How marvelous it would be if all Christians expressed God! This expression truly would be the kingdom of God on earth.

When I was a young Christian, I understood 2:12 in the traditional way. I thought that God had called me merely to enter into His kingdom and glory in the future. My concept of the kingdom of God and the glory of God was very shallow and altogether too objective. Paul did not have such a view of God's kingdom and glory. From the context of 2:12 we can see that being called into God's kingdom and glory is related to walking worthily of God. When we walk worthily of God, there is with us a particular kind of atmosphere, and this atmosphere is God's kingdom. Furthermore, where the kingdom of God is, there the glory of God is also.

It is possible for the kingdom of God and the glory of God to be manifested in our married life. If a brother and his wife live God, they will walk worthily of God. Then in their married life there will be a certain kind of atmosphere. When others come into this atmosphere, they will spontaneously have a sense of respect. This is the kingdom of God with God's glory. If today's Christians would walk worthily of God, would walk in a way that expresses Him, the kingdom would come. God's kingdom would then be seen on earth.

As we have pointed out a number of times, glory is God Himself expressed. Whenever the Lord is expressed from within us, we are in a situation that can be described as glorious. If someone would walk into a brother's home when he is arguing with his wife, there would not be any glory. However, if you visit a brother's house and find him and his wife glowing, shining, and flowing, you would see the expression of God, God's glory.

Many of us can testify that when we live God and walk worthily of God, matching Him, there is an atmosphere around us that is nothing less than God's kingdom. Spontaneously the Lord is expressed. This expression is God's glory. Concerning the kingdom and the glory in 2:12, we have a further explanation of 1:1, where we are told that the church is in God the Father and the Lord Jesus Christ.

INCREASING AND ABOUNDING IN LOVE

In 3:12 Paul says, "And the Lord cause you to increase and abound in love to one another and to all, even as we also to you." The church in God the Father and the Lord Jesus Christ should be composed of those who are increasing and abounding in love to one another and to all men. No matter how many believers there may be in the church—fifty, five hundred, or five thousand—all the saints should love one another. Furthermore, they should increase in this love and abound in it. This kind of love is surely not of our human nature. As fallen human beings, we are not capable of such love. But the church in God the Father and the Lord Jesus Christ is characterized by this increasing and abounding love. If we truly are a church in God the Father and the Lord Jesus Christ, the love we have for one another will increase and abound.

BOXED IN TO GOD

In 4:7 Paul goes on to say, "God has not called us for uncleanness but in sanctification." To be in God the Father and the Lord Jesus Christ is to be in sanctification. The Greek word sanctification means separation. Only when we are in God the Father and in the Lord Jesus Christ are we truly separated unto God from everything other than God. If we are not in the Triune God, we are still common. Instead of being separated from the world, we are still involved, mixed up, with worldly people and worldly matters.

I wish to say a word especially to the young ones. Even though you are still young, you need to realize that as those who belong to the Lord Jesus, you are part of the church, and the church is in the Triune God. If we compare God to a box, we may say that God is boxing you in to Himself. You all need to be boxed in to Him more and more. God has placed you into Himself as a spiritual, divine, and heavenly box. Being in this box separates you to God. In other words, this being boxed in to God, this separation, is sanctification.

God has called you in sanctification. In 4:7 the phrase "in sanctification" modifies God's calling. God has called us in the "box" of sanctification. Now we all need to see that we are those separated unto God, boxed in to Him. We have no right to leap out of this box.

In 5:23 and 24 Paul says, "And the God of peace Himself sanctify you wholly, and may your spirit and soul and body be preserved complete, without blame, at the coming of our Lord Jesus Christ. Faithful is He Who calls you, Who also will do it." For the God of peace to sanctify us wholly means that He will completely box us in. No part of our being will be left out of God as the spiritual box. God as the divine box is not small. On the contrary, He is infinitely large and deep.

If a young person is tempted to indulge in a certain kind of worldly entertainment, this means that he is planning to come out of this heavenly box. However, many have testified that when they tried to get out of this box, they found that they were not able to do so. It seems that their arms were powerless to climb out.

According to these verses, God intends to box us in to Himself wholly, that is, entirely. Have you been completely boxed in by God? Verse 23 says that God will preserve our spirit and soul and body without blame at the coming of our Lord Jesus Christ. Verse 24 says that God, the One who calls us and who does the sanctifying, separating, work, is faithful. He will do the boxing-in work until we are completely separated from the world. Wherever we may be—at school, at work, at home, or with our neighbors—we shall eventually be fully boxed in to God. Young people, if you are invited to do something worldly, you may need to say, "I cannot participate in that, for I have been boxed in to God. Because I am in a heavenly box, I am not free to go to that place."

In 1 Thessalonians we have seen certain qualifications of the church in God the Father and the Lord Jesus Christ. If we would be such a church in reality and in a practical way, we need to walk worthily of God and fulfill His calling into His own kingdom and glory. As we have pointed out, we should not regard the kingdom and the glory as only something for the future and not for our experience today. We need to be in the kingdom of God and the glory of God today. Furthermore, we need to increase and abound in love, and we need to be fully sanctified, entirely boxed in, by the Triune God.

FURTHER CHARACTERISTICS OF THE CHURCH IN THE TRIUNE GOD

In 2 Thessalonians 1:3 Paul says, "We ought to thank God always concerning you, brothers, even as it is fitting, because your faith grows exceedingly, and the love of each one of you all to one another is increasing." In this verse Paul speaks of two matters: faith growing and love increasing. The growth of faith and the increase of love are also conditions, requirements, of being the church in God the Father and the Lord Jesus Christ.

In 2 Thessalonians 2:13 Paul continues, "But we ought to thank God always concerning you, brothers beloved by the Lord, because God chose you from the beginning unto salvation in sanctification of the Spirit and belief of the truth." The matter of salvation in sanctification of the Spirit is profound. God has chosen us from the beginning unto this salvation in sanctification. This is related to a life in God the Father and in the Lord Jesus Christ. This is also a qualification of being a church in God the Father and the Lord Jesus Christ.

Verse 14 says, "To which also He called you through our gospel unto the obtaining of the glory of our Lord Jesus Christ." Here we see that God has called us unto the obtaining of His glory. Once again, this is an aspect of the life of the church in God the Father and the Lord Jesus Christ.

Second Thessalonians 2:16 says, "Now our Lord Jesus Christ Himself, and God our Father, Who has loved us and given us eternal encouragement and good hope in grace." How profound! God has given us eternal encouragement and good hope in grace. Although we may not understand these matters adequately, we have nonetheless received them. We have an encouragement that is eternal and a hope that is good. God has given us both this encouragement and this hope in grace. This is marvelous! It is an incentive to have the church life in God the Father and in the Lord Jesus Christ.

We are not without incentive, and we are not lacking in hope. Never say that you are hopeless. Instead, you should declare, "I am full of hope. I have a good hope, the hope God has given me in grace. Furthermore, with this good hope there is eternal encouragement."

THE NEW MAN

In Colossians 3:10 and 11 Paul speaks of the church as the new man: "And having put on the new man, which is being renewed unto full knowledge according to the image of Him Who created him; where there cannot be Greek and Jew, circumcision and uncircumcision, barbarian, Scythian, slave, freeman, but Christ is all and in all." The word image in verse 10 refers to Christ, God's Beloved, as the very expression of God (Col. 1:15; Heb. 1:3). The relative pronoun "who" in this verse refers to God the Creator, the One who created the new man in Christ (Eph. 2:15). As the embodiment of the Triune God, the church eventually will bear the image of God.

THE GOLDEN LAMPSTAND

In the Bible there are many different symbols of the church: the house of God, the kingdom of God, the habitation of God, the fullness of God, the warrior, the bride. In the book of Revelation the church is symbolized by a golden lampstand. In Revelation 1:12 the Apostle John says, "And I turned to see the voice that spoke with me; and having turned I saw seven golden lampstands." Verse 20 of Revelation 1 says clearly, "The seven lampstands are seven churches."

In Exodus 25 there is a description of a golden lampstand. That lampstand is a type of Christ. Christ is the embodiment of God, and the lampstand is a type of Christ as this embodiment. Elsewhere we have pointed out that the lampstand signifies the Triune God. The lampstand is gold in substance, in element. In typology gold signifies the divine nature, the nature of God the Father. Second, the gold of the lampstand is in a definite form. This form signifies God the Son. God the Father is the element, and God the Son is the form. Finally, the seven lamps of the lampstand signify the seven Spirits of God as God's expression. As we consider the lampstand, therefore, we see the element signifying God the Father, we see the form signifying God the Son, and we see the seven lamps signifying the Spirit of God as the expression. Hence, the lampstand portrays the Triune God embodied in a single entity.

In Exodus 25 the lampstand is a type of Christ, but in Revelation 1 the lampstand signifies the church. Every church is a golden lampstand. This means that the church is the embodiment of the Triune God, for the church is an entity in the Triune God. Do you realize what the Lord is doing today? He is seeking to mold us, transform us, and conform us, the entire church, into the image of the Triune God. In this way all the churches become golden lampstands as the embodiment of the Triune God.

How blessed we are to see that the church is the embodiment of the Triune God! Our ears are blessed to hear this word. Many believers in the past never heard or saw anything concerning this. Hallelujah, we are in the church which is in God the Father and the Lord Jesus Christ! Now we are being transformed into the image of the Triune God and conformed to this image to be in reality and practicality the embodiment of the Triune God, having the Father as our element, the Son as our form, and the Spirit as our expression, shining the glory of the Triune God to the universe. This is the church filled with the Triune God.

LIFE-STUDY OF FIRST THESSALONIANS

MESSAGE TWELVE

THE CARE OF A NURSING MOTHER AND AN EXHORTING FATHER

Scripture Reading: 1 Thes. 2:1-12

In the book of 1 Thessalonians Paul does not speak of miracles. He does not say that the gospel came to the Thessalonians in miracles, wonders, and healings. If we study this book carefully, we shall see that Paul's emphasis is on daily living. In 1:5 he says, "You know what kind of men we were among you for your sake." Instead of emphasizing the supernatural and the miraculous, Paul takes his living as a factor for the preaching of the gospel. Furthermore, with respect to Christian living, he stresses three matters: turning to God from idols, serving the living God, and waiting for the coming back of the Lord Jesus.

A NORMAL LIFE

Throughout the centuries the human mind has been interested in things that are fantastic, miraculous, and supernatural. However, miraculous things do not last. But a work that is carried out by a proper living will last.

God's salvation enables us to live a normal life. This is a strong testimony of the gospel. Christians should live a normal life, not a miraculous, supernatural life. Therefore, a proper life for the church life must be common, regular, and normal. Such a life is characterized by turning to God from idols, serving the living God, and waiting for the coming back of the Lord Jesus. To have this kind of life means that nothing on earth occupies us. We are free from all idols, from all things other than God, and we are occupied by the living God Himself. This living God is testified in our daily life. We have a life which testifies that the God whom we serve is living. Furthermore, our goal, hope, and expectation are not related to things on earth, but are focused on the coming back of the Lord Jesus. A life with these three characteristics is a proper Christian life as a testimony to our God. These aspects of a proper Christian life are all covered in chapter one.

THE FOSTERING OF A HOLY LIFE FOR THE CHURCH LIFE

The first chapter of 1 Thessalonians covers two main points: the structure of a holy life for the church life and the origin of a holy life for the church life. The structure is composed of the work of faith, the labor of love, and the endurance of hope. The origin of such a life is the preaching of the gospel and the acceptance of the word preached, an acceptance resulting in turning to God from idols, serving a living and true God, and waiting for the Son. Now in chapter two we come to the third aspect of a holy life for the church life, the aspect of fostering.

Although the word fostering cannot be found in 1 Thessalonians 2, the fact of fostering can be seen in this chapter. Here Paul likens the apostles both to a nursing mother and to an exhorting father. This means that the apostles were mothers and fathers to the new believers. They regarded the believers as children under their fostering care. Just as parents care for their children, fostering their growth, so the apostles cared for the new believers. Thus, in 1 Thessalonians 2 we see the fostering of a holy life for the church life. In verses 1 through 12 we have the care of a nursing mother and an exhorting father, and in verses 13 through 20 we see the reward given to those who foster believers in this way. Because the apostles rendered such a care to the new believers, the apostles will eventually receive a reward from the Lord.

First Thessalonians 2:1-12 surely is a word to new believers. In these verses we do not have much that is weighty or deep. Here we do not have profound doctrines. Instead, we have a word that can be compared to the way parents speak to young children. Let us consider this portion verse by verse so that we may be impressed how to help new believers.

THE APOSTLES' ENTRANCE

Verse 1 says, "For you yourselves know, brothers, our entrance to you, that it has not been in vain." The apostle stresses repeatedly their entrance to the believers (1:5, 9). This shows that their manner of life played a great role in infusing the gospel into the new converts. It was not only what the apostles said, but also what they were.

The apostles came to the Thessalonians with the gospel in such a way that the Thessalonians were convinced. The apostles' entrance was not in vain. They were a pattern of how to believe in the Lord and follow Him. Because many came to believe in the Lord Jesus through the apostles, a church was raised up in less than a month. This happened not mainly as a result of preaching and teaching, but through the kind of entrance the apostles had among the Thessalonians.

SPEAKING THE GOSPEL IN MUCH STRUGGLE

Verse 2 continues, "But having suffered before and having been outrageously treated, even as you know, in Philippi, we were bold in our God to speak to you the gospel of God in much struggle." In the preaching of the gospel, the apostles experienced God. They enjoyed Him as their boldness in the struggle for the gospel. They were bold not in themselves, but in God, even after they had been outrageously treated by the Philippians. Suffering and persecution could not defeat them because they were in the organic union with the Triune God. According to verse 2, they spoke the gospel of God in much struggle. This indicates that while they were preaching, they were fighting, because persecution was still going on. Hence, they were struggling and speaking the gospel to the Thessalonians in the boldness of God.

HONEST AND FAITHFUL

In verse 3 Paul says, "For our entreaty was not of deception, nor of uncleanness, nor in guile." Deception refers to the goal, uncleanness to the motive, and guile to the means. All three are of and by the subtle and deceiving Devil. The word entreaty includes speaking, preaching, teaching, instructing, and exhorting. Paul's exhorting was free from deception, uncleanness, and guile. The apostles were not greedy, and they had no intention of making a gain of anyone. Their coming to the Thessalonians with the gospel was altogether honest and faithful.

APPROVED BY GOD

Verse 4 says, "But even as we have been approved by God to be entrusted with the gospel, so we speak, not as pleasing men, but God, Who proves our hearts." God's entrusting depends on His approval by His testing. The apostles were first tested and approved by God and then were entrusted by Him with the gospel. Hence, their speaking, the preaching of the gospel, was not of themselves to please men, but was of God to please Him. He proves, examines, and tests their hearts all the time (Psa. 26:2; 139:23-24).

The word "approved" in verse 4 implies being tested. God tested the apostles before He approved them. Based upon this approvedness, God entrusted them with the gospel. God did this in a careful way, for He knows our hearts.

According to our opinion, since God already knows everything, it is not necessary for Him to test us. Yes, before we were born, He already knew what kind of person we would be. Why, then, does God test us? God's testing is not mainly for Himself; it is primarily for us. God knows us, but we do not know ourselves. Because we do not know ourselves adequately, we may think that we are upright, honest, and faithful. However, when we are put to the test, we shall see what we really are and discover that in ourselves we are not honest, faithful, or trustworthy. God's testing, therefore, proves us to ourselves. Only after God proves us in this way shall we have approvedness.

I would encourage the young people not to have confidence in themselves, for they have not yet been tested. I have the assurance that God will use the young people. But God's using of them will come after His testing of them. God cannot entrust anything to us until we have the approvedness that comes from His testing. God's entrusting is based on our approvedness. But we cannot approve ourselves. Only after God has tested us will He grant us approvedness. Then He will entrust something to us and begin to use us.

It was in this way that God entrusted the apostles with the gospel. Because the apostles had been entrusted with the gospel, they spoke not as pleasing men, but as pleasing God, who proves our hearts. Their speaking was based on God's entrusting. Because He had entrusted them with the gospel, they spoke as pleasing God.

In verse 4 we see that we must be approved and then have something entrusted to us. Then we need to speak as pleasing God, the One who proves us. This indicates that we need to pass through testing, approving, and entrusting. Then we shall have something to preach and teach.

NO FLATTERY OR PRETEXT

Verse 5 says, "For neither at any time were we found with a word of flattery, even as you know, nor with a pretext for covetousness—God is witness." The Greek word rendered pretext also means pretense, cloak. To have any pretext for covetousness is to peddle or adulterate the word of God (2 Cor. 2:17; 4:2). It is also to pretend to be godly for gain (1 Tim. 6:5; Titus 1:11; 2 Pet. 2:3).

According to verse 5, the apostles were never found with a word of flattery. We all must avoid flattery, never speaking in a way to flatter others. In this verse Paul also says that the apostles did not have a pretext, a cloak, for covetousness. They did not have an evil motive that was covered in some way. Because they did not have any pretext or pretense, they did not peddle the word of God or adulterate it. To adulterate something is to mix it with an inferior material, for example, to mix gold with copper or wine with water, and then to sell it as if it were pure. Throughout the centuries, many preachers and teachers have adulterated the word of God in this way. They preached under a pretext in order to make gain for themselves.

From verse 5 we learn to avoid flattery and a pretext for covetousness. In our Christian work we must give no place to such unclean things. No servant of the Lord should use flattery or have some kind of pretext for covetousness. May the Lord have mercy on us and purify us from all these things. May we be able to say that God is our witness that we do not speak words of flattery or have any pretext for covetousness.

NOT SEEKING GLORY FROM MEN

In verse 6 Paul goes on to say, "Nor seeking glory of men, neither from you, nor from others, when we might have stood on our dignity as apostles of Christ." To seek glory of men is a real temptation to every Christian worker. Many have been devoured and spoiled by this matter.

The Greek words rendered "stood on our dignity" also mean "asserted authority." A literal translation would be "been able to be in weight," that is, been burdensome (see v. 9; 1 Cor. 9:4-12). To assert authority, dignity, or right in Christian work also damages it. The Lord Jesus, while on earth, gave up His dignity (John 13:4-5), and the apostle would rather not use his right (1 Cor. 9:12).

Apparently seeking glory from men is not as evil as covetousness. However, it is more subtle. The fall of the archangel was due to the seeking of glory. He became God's adversary because of his glory-seeking. Even though he was a leading angel with a very high position, he was still seeking glory. That was the cause of his fall. According to the New Testament, anyone who seeks glory of men is a follower of Satan. The seeking of glory is a trap spread by Satan to snare Christian workers. Therefore, it is very important that all Christian workers learn to avoid the snare of glory-seeking. However, not many have escaped this trap.

How much we shall be used by the Lord and how long our usefulness will last depends on whether we seek glory of men. If we seek glory, our usefulness in the hand of the Lord is finished. The seeking of glory for the self always kills one's usefulness. Therefore, may we all, especially the young, be warned never to seek glory in the Lord's work.

NOT STANDING ON THEIR DIGNITY

Verse 6 indicates clearly that the apostles did not stand on their dignity as apostles of Christ. They did not assume any standing or dignity. They had to forget that they were apostles and serve God's people as slaves. They were not to remind others of the fact that they were apostles of Christ. Instead, they were to keep in mind that they were brothers serving believers. They were not to assume any standing or dignity.

Those who are believers and also those who are not believers may consider the leading ones, the elders, or the apostles as dignitaries. However, in the local churches there are no dignitaries. Instead of being dignitaries, we are slaves serving one another. Nevertheless, I know of certain ones who did not assume anything when they did not have a position or title. But as soon as they were given a position, perhaps in a service group, they began to assume dignity. This is shameful. We should learn of Paul never to stand on our dignity or assert authority.

A sister whose husband is an elder should not assume dignity because she is the wife of an elder. An elder's wife is not the "First Lady." She is simply a little sister serving the church. Furthermore, her husband is not a dignitary; he is a slave. As an elder, he has been appointed to serve the church as a slave. We all should have this attitude.

Paul's statement, "We might have stood on our dignity as apostles of Christ," indicates that even in the early days there was the temptation of assuming dignity. People were the same in Paul's time as they are today. Then as well as now, there was the temptation to assume some kind of dignity or standing. Paul, however, did not stand on his dignity as an apostle in order to claim something for himself. By refusing to stand on his dignity or assert authority Paul is a good pattern for us all. If we follow this pattern, we shall kill a deadly disease germ in the Body of Christ, the germ of assuming a position.

CHERISHING THE BELIEVERS

In verse 7 Paul says, "But we were gentle in your midst, as a nurse would cherish her own children." The Greek word rendered nurse, *trophos,* sometimes means a mother; hence, it may denote a nursing mother (see Gal. 4:19). Cherishing includes nourishing. Therefore, this word not only includes nourishing but also includes tender care.

Even though Paul was a brother, he considered himself a nursing mother. Surely, he had no thought of position, dignity, or authority. The thought of being a nursing mother is very different from the thought of dignity or position. What position does a nursing mother have? What rank, dignity, or authority belongs to her? Her dignity consists in nourishing and cherishing her children, in taking care of them in a tender way.

The word cherish is lovely, a word of utmost tenderness. Paul regarded himself as a cherishing one, not merely as one who serves. He certainly did not control the believers. Neither did he merely serve them. Rather, he cherished them. His care for them was full of tenderness.

IMPARTING THEIR OWN SOULS

In verse 8 Paul continues, "Thus, yearning over you, we were well pleased to impart to you not only the gospel of God, but also our own souls, because you became beloved to us." The word yearning indicates being affectionately fond of, affectionately desirous of, like a nursing mother affectionately interested in her child whom she nourishes and cherishes. This was what the apostles did with the new believers.

The apostles not only imparted the gospel of God to the Thessalonians; they also imparted their own souls.

To live a clean and upright life as portrayed in verses 3 through 6 and 10, and to love the new converts, even by giving our own souls to them, as described in verses 7 through 9 and 11, are the prerequisites for infusing others with the salvation conveyed in the gospel we preach.

Paul's word in verse 8 about imparting their own souls to the Thessalonians can be compared to his word in 2 Corinthians 12 about being spent for the sake of the believers. Paul was willing to spend not only what he had, but was willing to spend himself, his very being. The apostles were willing to impart what they were into the believers. This can be compared to a nursing mother giving herself to her child.

THE APOSTLES' CONDUCT

Verse 9 says, "For you remember, brothers, our labor and hardship: working night and day so as not to be burdensome to any of you, we proclaimed to you the gospel of God." The apostles did not want to be a burden on the Thessalonians. Therefore, they labored night and day in order to proclaim to them the gospel of God.

In verse 10 Paul continues, "You are witnesses, and God, how holily and righteously and blamelessly we conducted ourselves with you who believe." Holily refers to conduct toward God, righteously to conduct toward men, and blamelessly to all—God, men, and Satan. In order to conduct himself in this way, Paul had to exercise strict control over himself. Verse 10 reveals that the apostles were those who practiced self-control.

A FATHER EXHORTING HIS CHILDREN

Verse 11 says, "Even as you know how we were to each one of you, as a father his own children, entreating you and consoling and testifying." The apostle was strong in stressing what or how they were (1:5), for what they were opened the way to bring the new converts into God's full salvation.

In verse 11 Paul likens himself to a father exhorting his children. In cherishing the believers as their own children, the apostles considered themselves as nourishing mothers. In exhorting them, they considered themselves fathers.

WALKING WORTHILY OF GOD

Verse 12 says, "That you should walk worthily of God, Who calls you into His own kingdom and glory." God's calling is according to His selection, and it follows His selection (1:4). As worshippers of idols (1:9), the believers were in the kingdom of Satan (Matt. 12:26). Now, through the salvation in Christ, they are called and have believed into the kingdom of God, which is the sphere for them to worship and enjoy God under the divine ruling with a view of entering into God's glory. God's glory goes with His kingdom.

In verse 12 Paul exhorts the believers to walk worthily of God. If he himself had not walked worthily of God, how could he have exhorted others to do so? In this matter also, he set an example for the believers to follow.

Verse 12 indicates that walking worthily of God is related to entering into His kingdom and being ushered into His glory. The thought here, in contrast to that in verses 1 through 11, is quite deep. Here we have a matter often neglected by Christians. Not many believers are taught to have a Christian walk that will enable them to enter into the kingdom of God, a walk that will usher them into God's glory. Many Christians have never heard such a word. Nevertheless, this is included as part of Paul's teaching to young believers.

A GOOD PATTERN

First Thessalonians 2:1-12 shows us how we should conduct ourselves as a pattern for new believers. In order to be a proper pattern, we need to be pure in our motives, especially concerning money. Much of what is written in these verses is related to money, greed, and covetousness. If we are not pure concerning money, if we are not sincere, honest, and faithful regarding it, we may be among those who adulterate the word of God and peddle it. Furthermore, this motive may cause us to use flattery and to have a pretext for covetousness. All these are serious matters. Therefore, if we would be a proper pattern for young saints, our greed must be dealt with, and money matters must be under our feet. We should never speak words of flattery, we should never have any pretext, and we should never seek glory for ourselves. Moreover, instead of trying to please man, we should do our best to please God. Then other believers will have a good pattern to follow.

If you consider the situation among believers today, you will realize that many Christians have no sense of direction. The reason for this lack of direction is that they do not have a proper pattern. We need to be a pattern to others and foster them, cherishing them as mothers and exhorting them as fathers to walk worthily of God. As we have pointed out in a foregoing message, to walk worthily of God is actually to live God. Only a life that lives God is worthy of God. When we live God, we walk worthily of Him. Such a walk will lead us into the kingdom and usher us into the glory of God. This is the goal of God's calling. God has called us to enter His kingdom and glory.

LIFE-STUDY OF FIRST THESSALONIANS

MESSAGE THIRTEEN

THE REWARD OF FOSTERING

Scripture Reading: 1 Thes. 2:13-20

In chapter one we have the structure and origin of a holy life for the church life. In chapter two we have the fostering of this life. When reading chapter two, we may have the feeling that Paul places too much emphasis on the apostles' entrance among the Thessalonians and the way they lived among them. We may think that Paul should have given the new believers more doctrine, teaching, and instructions. Instead, Paul emphasizes the apostles' coming, their preaching and teaching of the Word, and how the new believers accepted this word. Paul's emphasis is on the apostles' conduct, on their living and manner of life. The reason for this emphasis is that Paul wanted to nourish the believers, to cherish and foster them. It was not Paul's intention to give them a lot of knowledge. He did not have the burden to teach them so many things. In the twenty verses of chapter two there is actually very little teaching. In verse 12 he does say that God has called the believers into His kingdom and glory; however, he does not develop these matters or explain them. Rather, in verse after verse, Paul mentions his manner of life, his way of preaching, and his being a pattern to the believers.

THE WORK OF FOSTERING

What we have in chapter two of 1 Thessalonians is the fostering of the young Christian life. In this chapter Paul is nourishing and cherishing the believers. According to his writing, he behaves himself as a nursing mother and an exhorting father. On the one hand, he is a mother cherishing; on the other hand, he is a father exhorting. His main concern is not teaching, but the carrying out of a fostering work to help the young saints to grow.

Most Christian workers lack the concept that their work should not mainly be a work of teaching, but should be a work of fostering. Paul's concept concerning his work was one of helping believers to grow. For this reason, in 1 Corinthians 3 he says that he planted and Apollos watered, and then God gave the growth. This indicates that Paul's concept of Christian work is that it is a work of life. It is not work in a school: on the contrary, it is work on a farm, in an orchard, in a garden. Hence, it is not mainly a work of teaching others or educating them. But today the work of most Christians is mainly for education and somewhat for edification. This edification, however, is not directly related to life. Instead, it is related to ethics, morality, or the improvement of character. But with Paul the concept of Christian work was altogether different.

According to what he says in chapter two, Paul regards the believers as members of a large family. Of course, in a family there is the need for some amount of teaching. Both a mother and a father teach their children. However, in a family the focus is not on teaching the children, but is on raising them by cherishing, nourishing, and fostering them so that they may grow. Their growth is not mainly in knowledge: it is primarily a growth in life. As children grow in life, they spontaneously receive more education. The knowledge they acquire always goes along with their growth in life. They should not be given knowledge prematurely. This means that their knowledge should not exceed their growth of life. This is the proper concept of Christian work.

Concerning this matter, we in the Lord's recovery must have a change in our concept. Do not think that in the recovery we regard work higher than life. No, we need to concentrate on life. The church is a family. The church may also be compared to a farm or a garden. A family is a place where children grow up, and an orchard is a place where trees grow and produce fruit. Paul's concern in chapter two is with the growth of his children. He is fostering the young believers so that they may grow. We may also say that he is watering, nourishing, and cherishing the tender young plants so that they may grow in life. This is the reason that instead of giving the believers a great deal of teaching, he presents them a pattern of life. This pattern of a proper living is actually Paul himself.

GROWING BY IMITATING

Some Christian teachers say that a believer should not give a testimony concerning himself. According to these teachers, to testify of our experience is to preach ourselves. Therefore, they advise others not to speak of how they have repented, believed in the Lord, received grace, and have been saved. These teachers insist strongly that we should preach only the Lord Jesus and teach the Bible, but should never say anything about ourselves. In 1 Thessalonians 2, however, Paul certainly speaks about himself. He gives a strong testimony of his living among the Thessalonians. He reminds them of the apostles coming and of their manner of life among them. Why did Paul emphasize this? He emphasized it because he was presenting a pattern of a proper living to the young saints. I hope that all the elders and leading ones will see from Paul's example that we must be a pattern to the saints. In every local church there must be some patterns, some models, for others to follow.

In 1:6 Paul says to the Thessalonians, "You became imitators of us and of the Lord." Imitating is related to growing. In fact, in many ways to imitate is to grow. In a family children imitate their parents and older brothers and sisters. The little ones do not invent anything; instead, they imitate others. A very good illustration of this is in the use of language. A child learns the language spoken by his parents. He speaks the same language with the same accent. A child learns the language and the accent by imitation. This illustrates the fact that children grow by imitating their parents. Therefore, in a family to imitate actually means to grow. The children imitate their parents in many things—in gestures, in speech, and even in character. Parents are patterns, models, for their children. Whatever the parents are, the children will be also.

PRESENTING A PATTERN

To give the new believers and young ones a lot of teaching is not the proper way to take care of them. The proper way to foster them is to show them a pattern. By showing them a pattern you water them, supply them, nourish them, and cherish them. This is fostering. If you find that your experience is somewhat lacking, point the new believers to different people in the Bible, for example, to ones such as Enoch, Noah, Abraham, and David in the Old Testament and Peter, John, Paul, and Timothy in the New Testament. We can present the lives of Bible characters in such a way as to foster the growth of the young ones.

If we give too much teaching to new ones and young ones, we shall damage them. Every mother knows that one of the most important matters in the raising of children is proper feeding. Caring for children is ninety percent a matter of feeding and ten percent a matter of teaching. This also should be our practice in caring for new believers in the church. We must learn to have ninety percent feeding and ten percent teaching. Feeding involves the presenting of patterns either from the Bible or from church history. By reading the biographies of saints throughout the ages, we nourish ourselves and experience a kind of fostering. The point here is that the best way to feed others and foster them is to give them a proper pattern. If there is no pattern, there can be no fostering. Only by having a pattern can we feed others.

In the book of 1 Thessalonians Paul was not preaching himself. Rather, he was feeding his spiritual children with his own living of Christ. This means that Paul's way of living was used to feed his spiritual children. This was the reason he emphasized his coming to the Thessalonians, his preaching, his way of handling the word of God, and his manner of living.

THE OPERATING WORD OF GOD

In 2:13 Paul says, "And therefore we also give thanks to God unceasingly that, having received the word of the report from us of God, you accepted it not as the word of men, but even as it truly is, the word of God, which also operates in you who believe." This verse indicates that the source, the origin, of the apostles' preaching was God and not themselves. The Thessalonians received their word not as the word of men, but as the word of God. Here we see a governing principle: whenever we preach or teach, we must impress others with the fact that what we are saying is not the word of man, but is truly the word of God.

In verse 13 Paul says that the word of God operates in those who believe. Because the word of God is living and operative (Heb. 4:12), it operates in the believing ones. Once we receive and accept the word, it operates within us.

IMITATORS OF THE CHURCHES

In verse 14 Paul continues, "For you, brothers, became imitators of the churches of God which are in Judea in Christ Jesus; for you also suffered the same things of your own countrymen, even as they also of the Jews." The apostle taught the same thing in all the churches (1 Cor. 4:17; 7:17; 11:16). This indicates that all the churches should bear the same testimony of Jesus. Hence, they all are lampstands of the same kind (Rev. 1:9, 20).

The church in Thessalonica imitated the churches in Judea. Certainly reports concerning the churches in Judea reached the believers in Thessalonica. How could the Thessalonians have imitated the churches in Judea if they had not heard anything concerning them? They must have heard about the churches and the saints. These reports fostered the growth of the Thessalonian believers. Once again we see that nothing can foster a church or a saint as much as a true story about other saints or churches.

In verse 14 Paul points out that the Thessalonians suffered the same things of their own countrymen as the churches in Judea suffered of the Jews. This is a comforting, strengthening, and fostering word. When Paul wrote, the church in Thessalonica was suffering and was being persecuted. In the midst of their persecution, they heard about the sufferings of those in Judea. This report strengthened, comforted, and established them. It helped to foster them in their growth.

INOCULATION

Verse 15 continues, "Who have both killed the Lord Jesus and the prophets, and drove us out, and are not pleasing to God, and are contrary to all men." Paul was wise in writing this verse. Here he is inoculating the believers against the eventual coming of the Judaizers. Paul injected a healthy warning concerning the Judaizers into the Thessalonian saints. Here Paul seems to be saying, "Brothers, don't regard Jewish things as marvelous. The Jews are not for God, and they are not one with God. They killed the Lord Jesus, and they also drove us out. Be prepared, Thessalonians, for one day the Judaizers will come to you to undermine what we have done. Don't take their word, for they are against us. They are contrary to all men, and they are not pleasing to God." This surely was an excellent inoculation.

This inoculating word was also part of Paul's fostering of the saints. Even inoculation is included in fostering. In caring for their children, parents seek to protect them from disease. Even in caring for a garden we try to protect the plants from disease or insects. Otherwise, disease may ruin the plants, and the insects may devour them, especially the tender parts. Therefore, in order to protect a garden, we may spray the plants with insecticide. We may say that in this verse Paul was giving the believers at Thessalonica a divine germ-repellent. He warned them not to have any confidence in the Jews or to give them any credit. On the contrary, the Thessalonians were to reject them.

Paul continues this warning in verse 16, where he says of the Jews, "Forbidding us to speak to the nations that they may be saved, that they may fill up their sins always. But wrath has come upon them to the end." Paul points out that the Jews did not want the Thessalonians to hear the word of the apostles in order to be saved. This word is part of Paul's inoculation.

BEREAVED OF THE SAINTS

In verse 17 Paul goes on to say, "But we, brothers, being bereaved of you for a little while in presence, not in heart, were more abundantly eager with much desire to see your face." This word implies that the apostles considered the new converts precious and dear to them. Paul likened their departure from them to a bereavement, a loss they suffered from being separated from them and that caused them to miss them. In this verse we also see the apostles' yearning over the new converts.

In verse 17 Paul seems to be saying, "Brothers, we have been bereaved of you. We wanted to stay with you, and we miss you very much. But although we are bereaved of you in presence, we are not bereaved of you in heart. In our heart we are still with you. We are very eager with much desire to see your face."

Paul's word in verses 15 through 17 is emotional. Because he was emotional, he could touch the emotion of others. When Paul spoke about the Jews negatively, he was emotional. Likewise, when he spoke about the apostles positively, he was also very emotional. Paul's expression of deep emotion caused the believers to love the apostles and to shut out the Judaizers. This too is related to fostering children, to protecting them, to raising them without their being damaged by negative things.

Paul certainly knew how to foster the saints. He spoke about himself in such a way as to foster them and also to inoculate them. In fostering the Thessalonians, Paul pointed out to them that the Jews who opposed and persecuted needed to be shut out, but the Jews who came to them as apostles were lovable.

HINDERED BY SATAN

In verse 18 Paul says, "Wherefore we wanted to come to

you, indeed, I Paul, both once and again, and Satan hindered us." Because the apostles were carrying out the will of God, Satan frustrated them. Paul put the blame on Satan. In so doing he was telling the Thessalonians to shut out the Judaizers and to hate Satan. The apostles were eager to see the believers at Thessalonica, but they were hindered by Satan.

HOPE, JOY, AND CROWN

In verses 19 and 20 Paul concludes, "For what is our hope or joy or crown of boasting? Are not even you, before our Lord Jesus at His coming? For you are our glory and joy." The Greek word rendered coming in verse 19 is *parousia,* a word that means presence. The Lord's coming is His presence with us. In this light these two earlier Epistles were written. Every chapter of the first Epistle ends with the Lord's coming back.

Verse 20 indicates that since the apostles were the believers' nursing mother and exhorting father (vv. 7, 11), the believers, as their children, were their glory and joy. Apart from them, the apostles had no hope, glory, or crown of boasting.

Here Paul seems to be saying, "You are our hope, our joy, and our crown of boasting. Brothers, we are here only for you; we are not here for anything else. If we do not have you, we do not have anything. You are our hope, even as your hope is the Lord's coming back. Without you, at the Lord's coming back we shall be short of joy and glory. We need you! You are our hope, our joy, our crown, and our glory before the Lord Jesus at His coming." Once again Paul expressed deep emotion in caring for his children. He certainly was a father exhorting his children. As such an exhorting father, it seems as if Paul was saying, "Children, we are here only for you. Without you, life is meaningless. If it were not for you, we would not want even to live." Such a word from parents is deeply touching; it touches the heart of the children.

Would you not be touched deeply if your parents wrote such a word to you? Would you not be touched if they said that without you life is meaningless, that they are living on earth only for you? No doubt, when you heard or read such a word, your tears would flow. This kind of speaking fosters children and helps them to grow.

As a good father, Paul knew how to touch the heart of his children. If you are able to touch the heart of others, you will be successful in fostering their growth. The best way to foster others is to touch their heart deeply.

THE GOAL OF THE CHRISTIAN LIFE

Let us look once again at verse 12. Here Paul says, "That you should walk worthily of God, Who calls you into His own kingdom and glory." This verse indicates that our Christian life is a life with the kingdom as its goal. We need to walk worthily of God, the One who calls us into His kingdom and glory. This verse tells us clearly that the Christian life has a goal and that this goal is the kingdom of God. We are moving toward this goal, this destination. Our destination, and also our destiny, is to enter God's kingdom. The kingdom, a major subject in the New Testament, is the unique goal of our Christian walk.

Our goal is not heaven. According to the New Testament, the kingdom is our goal. First Thessalonians 2:12 does not say that God has called us to heaven, but says that He has called us with the goal of entering into His kingdom. This kingdom involves God's glory. When we enter into the kingdom, we shall certainly be in glory. The kingdom of God with the glory of God is far more excellent than a so-called heavenly mansion.

Paul's work with the new believers nourished them, cherished them, and fostered them to walk worthily of God so that they might enter into His kingdom and participate in His glory. This is the goal of the Christian life.

RECEIVING A REWARD

In verses 19 and 20 Paul indicates that those who work with the Lord in fostering the believers to walk worthily of God will receive a reward. This reward will be the believers we have fostered becoming our crown, glory, and joy. What a glory it would be to any Christian worker for the ones he has fostered to be matured at the Lord's coming back! What a crown and joy this would be to him! But on the contrary what a shame it would be if none of the believers had grown and matured.

Many of us are working with young saints. The result of our work should be the maturing of these believers. If they mature properly, they will be in the kingdom participating in God's glory. This maturity will then become our crown, joy, and boast before the Lord Jesus at His coming. Suppose, however, that we work continually with new believers, but to no avail. If this is the situation, at the Lord's coming back there will be no result of our work. What a shame that would be! When the Lord Jesus comes, the result of our work will be manifested. That result will also be our reward, our crown, our joy.

We see the same principle in 1 Peter 5:4. Here Peter says that the elders will be rewarded with a crown of glory. However, this reward will depend on the result of their eldership. If as a result of their eldership the saints mature, that maturity will become a crown of glory to the elders. That will then be their reward.

Chapter two of 1 Thessalonians is a healthy word for us all. From this chapter we learn how to work with the young ones and the new ones so that they may be fostered to grow into maturity and that there may be a positive result of our work before the Lord at His coming. This result will then be our crown and glory as the reward of our work today.

LIFE-STUDY OF FIRST THESSALONIANS

MESSAGE FOURTEEN

ENCOURAGEMENT FOR FAITH, LOVE, AND HOPE

Scripture Reading: 1 Thes. 3:1-13

ESTABLISHING AND ENCOURAGING

In chapter one of 1 Thessalonians we have the structure and origin of a holy life for the church life, and in chapter two we have the fostering of this life. Now in chapter three we have the establishing of a holy life for the church life. We have seen that this holy life is constructed of faith, love, and hope. Along with fostering, this life needs to be established. Its establishment involves the three main aspects of its structure; that is, it involves faith, love, and hope. In chapter three Paul is establishing the believers' faith, love, and hope.

We should keep in mind that 1 Thessalonians is a book written to new believers. Therefore, everything in this Epistle is presented in a brief way, not in a profound way. This principle applies in particular to chapter three. In writing this chapter, Paul sought to avoid profound terms. His word here can be compared to that of a father given to young children. But although Paul speaks in a brief way, he covers a number of crucial points.

In 3:1 Paul says, "Wherefore, when we could bear it no longer, it seemed good for us to be left in Athens alone." Athens was the chief city of the province of Achaia of the Roman Empire. In this city the Apostle Paul preached the gospel to philosophical Greeks (Acts 17:15-34).

The word "wherefore" at the beginning of this verse refers us to the previous chapter, especially to verses 17 and 18. These verses say, "But we, brothers, being bereaved of you for a little while in presence, not in heart, were more abundantly eager with much desire to see your face. Wherefore we wanted to come to you, indeed, I Paul, both once and again, and Satan hindered us." The apostles had been bereaved of the Thessalonian believers in presence and were intensely eager to see them again. This was the reason Paul says in 3:1 that he could bear the situation no longer. The word "wherefore" in verse 1 indicates that chapter three is a continuation of 2:17 and 18. Paul was willing to remain in Athens alone and, as he says in verse 2, to send Timothy to Thessalonica.

Verse 2 continues, "And we sent Timothy, our brother and God's fellow-worker in the gospel of Christ, to establish and encourage you for the sake of your faith." Instead of fellow-worker, some manuscripts read "minister of God." The minister of God is God's fellow-worker (1 Cor. 3:9; 2 Cor. 6:1). What a privilege! What a blessing!

Timothy was sent to the Thessalonians to encourage them for the sake of their faith. This indicates that what is covered in chapter three is related to establishing and encouraging. In speaking of the Thessalonians' faith, Paul returns to the matter of the structure of a holy life for the church life covered in chapter one. His concern in chapter three is with the establishing of such a life.

If we are established in our faith, we shall not be shaken by affliction. Concerning this, Paul says in verse 3, "That no one be shaken by these afflictions; for you yourselves know that we are appointed for this." If we are established in the faith, afflictions will do good to us (Rom. 8:28) according to God's purpose in His appointment. Otherwise, we may be shaken by the tempter (1 Thes. 3:5) through the afflictions. The Greek word rendered "appointed" also means destined, set, located. God has destined, appointed, us to pass through afflictions. Hence, afflictions are God's allotted portion to us, and He has set us, located us, in the situation of afflictions.

TWO ASPECTS OF FAITH

We need to consider carefully the meaning of faith in 1 Thessalonians 3. In verse 2 faith is not only subjective, referring to the saints' believing, as in verses 5, 6, and 10, but also objective, referring to what they believe in, as in 1 Timothy 3:9; 4:1; and 2 Timothy 4:7. These two aspects of faith involve each other. Our believing (subjective faith) is out of the things we believe and in the things we believe (objective faith).

The word faith in 1 Thessalonians is somewhat difficult to understand. The reason for this difficulty is that in the New Testament there are two aspects of faith, the objective aspect and the subjective aspect. Doctrinally speaking, the objective aspect comes first and produces the subjective aspect. The objective faith denotes those things in which we believe for our salvation. It includes the content of the new covenant. Thus, the content of the new covenant is equal to the objective faith. This aspect of faith is emphasized strongly in a book like 1 Timothy. For example, 1 Timothy 1:19 speaks of the faith. The faith in that verse is objective and refers to the things we believe in. However, the same verse also mentions subjective faith when it speaks of "holding faith and a good conscience." This subjective faith refers to our act of believing.

Christians often speak of the faith in an objective sense. Someone may ask what your faith is, meaning what you believe. This aspect of faith, the objective aspect, is not a matter of our action of believing, but a matter of what we believe. This objective faith includes the contents of God's New Testament economy.

When we receive a word concerning the objective faith, the contents of God's New Testament economy, spontaneously subjective faith is produced in us. We respond to the objective faith by believing. This means that we hear of the objective faith, and then subjective faith rises up in us. This subjective faith is our act of believing.

Subjective faith does not happen once for all. On the contrary, from the time we began to believe, the action of believing has been going within us, for the Christian life is a life of faith, a life of believing. Day by day we are living a believing life. We do not live according to what we see; we live according to what we believe. As Paul says, "We walk by faith, not by appearance" (2 Cor. 5:7). Our walk is by faith, not by sight.

All the matters we are talking about in these messages are matters of faith. For example, Colossians 1:27 says that Christ is in us to be our hope of glory. We receive this word in faith. By faith we believe in His coming back, and by faith we await a crown. Our speaking concerning these things is altogether by faith. Therefore, those who do not have faith do not have any idea of what we are saying. To them, our word is either superstitious or nonsensical. They can neither believe it nor accept it. Worldly people, unbelievers, do not have faith. As a result, they cannot understand what we are saying or the way we are living. Our living is absolutely a life of believing.

The objective aspect of faith is profound. We cannot say that we are perfect or altogether complete with respect to the objective faith. God's economy is profound. The content of His economy is Christ as the all-inclusive and all-extensive One. It is because God's economy is so profound and rich in its content that we dare not say that the objective faith has been perfected among us. We need to see that our objective faith includes the all-inclusive and all-extensive Christ as the content of God's economy. We do not yet know this content adequately or realize it fully. Thus, we still need to lay hold of more of the all-inclusive Christ, more of Christ as the content of our objective faith.

Praise the Lord that this objective faith produces subjective believing! When we receive a revelation concerning Christ, we cannot keep ourselves from believing in Him. Faith is spontaneously infused into our being, and we automatically believe in Christ. Unbelievers find it impossible to believe that Christ is in us. We, however, cannot help but believe that Christ lives in us. He is in us to be our life, our life supply, and our everything. We have seen a vision of the indwelling Christ, and we have no choice except to believe that He is actually in us. Because we have seen a revelation regarding the content of God's economy, we cannot help believing in what we have seen. We have been infused with the ability to believe, and now we have subjective faith, the inward action of believing.

PAUL'S CONCERN

When Paul says that Timothy was sent to establish and encourage the believers for the sake of their faith, did he mean objective faith or subjective faith? It is not easy to determine whether the faith in verse 2 is objective or subjective. Actually, faith in this verse denotes both the objective and subjective aspects of faith. It includes both what we believe and our action of believing. The brothers sent Timothy to see how the believers in Thessalonica were doing in these two aspects of faith. Were they still holding the objective faith, and how strongly did they believe in it? How well were they keeping the objective faith, and to what extent were they believing in it? Paul's concern was to know this. In verses 2 and 3 he seems to be saying, "Brothers, I am concerned that you may have been shaken through the afflictions. To be shaken is to lose faith. It is to lose the view of the objective faith and also to lose the subjective ability to believe! I am concerned about both aspects of your faith."

Those who are burdened to work with new believers must learn to watch over their faith and to care for how they are doing in both the subjective and objective aspects of faith. Is their faith increasing or decreasing? Are they growing in their ability to believe? We must ask questions such as these in caring for young believers. This is to have the concern Paul had for the faith of the Thessalonians in sending Timothy to establish and encourage them.

In verse 4 Paul says, "For even when we were with you, we told you beforehand that we are about to be afflicted, even as it also came to pass, and you know." The Greek word rendered "told" is in the imperfect tense, a tense indicating repeated action. Paul was continually telling the believers beforehand that the apostles would be afflicted. This affliction came according to Paul's prediction.

In verse 5 Paul goes on to say, "Because of this, when I

also could bear it no longer, I sent to know your faith, lest somehow the tempter had tempted you, and our labor would be in vain." The tempter here is the subtle Devil, the old serpent, who tempted Eve (Gen. 3:1-6; 1 Tim. 2:14). The aim of this subtle tempter is to destroy the gospel work accomplished through God's fellow-workers. Paul was concerned that the afflictions, sufferings, and persecutions would be used by the tempter to shake the Thessalonians from their faith and to cause a loss of faith among them. Because he could no longer bear not knowing about their faith, Paul sent Timothy to them to know what was the situation with them regarding their faith.

Once again, the faith in verse 5 includes both objective faith and the subjective faith. Paul was eager to know both aspects of the Thessalonians' faith.

Faith is the first item in the basic structure of the Christian life, a holy life for the church life. Those who backslide, including many who leave the church life, experience some loss of faith. They may not lose their faith absolutely, but they may lose it at least in part. They may no longer have a view of the objective faith, of the contents of God's New Testament economy. While such ones were in the church life, they did have a view. They saw Christ, they saw the church, and they saw God's economy. They saw God's recovery and how the Triune God is dispensing Himself into us. However, they have gradually come to lose sight of these matters. Whenever someone loses sight of the contents of God's economy, the subjective faith, the believing action within him, also diminishes. The ability within us to believe is always a product, a result, an issue, of having a proper view of God's economy. Therefore, it is a dreadful matter to lose sight of God's economy.

In the meetings of the church and of the ministry, it is as if we are all watching a heavenly television to see more of God's economy. The more we see this heavenly television, the more we believe. We spontaneously believe in what we see. Therefore, we come away from meetings full of the ability to believe. The meetings of the church and the ministry enlarge our capacity to believe.

A good Christian worker is a person who continually infuses others with the divine view, helping them to see the marvelous scenes on the heavenly television and to be impressed by them. When the heavenly view is conveyed into us, transmitted into us, we have the ability to believe. By believing we are connected to a divine transmission. This transmission is the flowing of heavenly electricity. By believing we "switch on" to this flow.

We know from verse 5 that Paul was concerned that the tempter had tempted the Thessalonians and that the apostles' labor among them had been in vain. Paul knew that once we lose sight of the contents of God's economy, we shall be shaken and removed from the line of faith. Then whatever we have heard concerning God's economy will be in vain. This fact is illustrated in the lives of many who have left the church life. Their situation confirms that when we lose sight of God's economy, all that we heard becomes vain.

ENCOURAGED THROUGH THE BELIEVERS' FAITH

Timothy returned to Paul with good news, telling him that their labor among the Thessalonians was not in vain. Paul refers to this report in verse 6: "But Timothy, having just come to us from you, and bringing good news to us of your faith and love, and that you have good remembrance of us always, longing to see us, even as we also you." This good news concerning the Thessalonians' faith assured Paul that their labor among them had not been in vain.

The apostle was in Corinth after leaving Athens (Acts 17:15-16; 18:1, 5). It was here that he wrote this loving letter to the dear saints in Thessalonica for their encouragement.

In verse 6 Paul speaks of both faith and love. Love is the outflow, the issue, of faith. We have seen that faith is the foundation, love is the building, and hope is the topstone. In writing an establishing word to the Thessalonians, Paul first covers faith and gradually brings in love. Therefore, in verse 6 he speaks of the believers' faith and love.

Verse 7 says, "Because of this we were encouraged over you, brothers, in all our necessity and affliction, through your faith." The sound condition of the believers is always an encouragement to God's fellow-workers, who work with them and bear them as a burden. The Greek word rendered "necessity" can also be translated distress. It denotes an urgent need resulting from calamity. A calamity puts people into a position of having an urgent need for necessary supplies such as food, water, clothing, and housing. Even though the apostles were in necessity, in distress, they were encouraged over the Thessalonians through their faith. Once again Paul speaks concerning faith.

In verse 8 Paul goes on to say, "Because now we live if you stand firm in the Lord." The believers' firm standing in the Lord ministers life to the apostles. To stand firm in the Lord is in contrast to being shaken from the faith (v. 3). If the young believers you are working with stand firm in the Lord, that standing will certainly minister the life supply to you.

PERFECTING WHAT IS LACKING

Verses 9 and 10 say, "For what thanks can we return to God concerning you, for all the joy with which we rejoice because of you before our God, night and day beseeching exceedingly that we may see your face and perfect what is lacking in your faith?" The Greek word translated "perfect" in verse 10 also means complete. The same Greek word is used in 2 Corinthians 13:9. The believers at Thessalonica, being young in the Lord, were still lacking in their new faith. The apostle realized this with much loving concern for them. This is the reason he wrote this Epistle.

When Paul wrote the book of 1 Thessalonians, the believers at Thessalonica probably had been Christians for less than a year. To be sure, they needed to see much more concerning the contents of God's economy. Likewise, even many of us who have been in the recovery for years may still be lacking in our view of the all-inclusive and all-extensive Christ as the content of God's economy. This means that we still have a lack in the objective faith. Having such a lack in the objective faith, we also have a shortage in subjective faith. Because our seeing is limited, our believing ability is also limited. Our ability to believe depends on our seeing, on our view. During the time we have been in the recovery, our view concerning Christ and God's economy has been broadened. Since our view has been broadened, our objective faith has increased. This results in an increased ability to believe.

Night and day, exceedingly, Paul prayed that the apostles might see the Thessalonians face to face in order to perfect what was lacking in their faith. In these verses Paul seems to be saying, "You Thessalonians have been in the Lord only a short time. Surely there is a lack both in your objective faith and subjective believing. Many things have not yet been opened to you or shown to you. We would like to visit you again in order to show you more of Christ. Then, having a greater view of Christ, your objective faith will be broadened and, spontaneously, your subjective faith will be increased. This is your need, and this is our burden in praying to see you again."

AN EMPHASIS ON LOVE

In 3:1-10 Paul has mainly dealt with faith as the first item of the structure of a holy life for the church life. Beginning in verse 11 he emphasizes love: "Now our God and Father Himself, and our Lord Jesus, direct our way to you; and the Lord cause you to increase and abound in love to one another and to all, even as we also to you." Verses 11 and 12 are mainly on love. The apostle's concern for the young believers is first their faith. Following faith is love, which issues from faith and works together with faith (Gal. 5:6; 1 Tim. 1:14) as an indication of growth in life (1 Thes. 1:3). It was necessary for the Thessalonians' love to increase, to grow. Therefore, Paul first wanted to perfect their faith and then encourage them to increase and abound in love. He knew that love would flow out of their faith.

Then they would have a living in love, a love to the saints in their locality and to all believers everywhere.

In verse 11 the word "direct" in Greek is in the singular. This indicates that the apostle considers God the Father and the Lord Jesus as one. How good it is to have our way in the ministry directed by such a One! And how beautiful are the footsteps of the apostles in their carrying out of this One's ministry for the fulfilling of His purpose!

HEARTS ESTABLISHED BLAMELESS IN HOLINESS

In verse 13 Paul concludes, "That He may establish your hearts blameless in holiness before our God and Father at the coming of our Lord Jesus with all His saints." The establishing of the believers' hearts blameless issues from faith and love, as mentioned in the preceding verses. This spontaneously produces the hope of the coming back of our dear Lord, in whom we believe and whom we love. Hence, faith, love, and hope are again the implied factors in the construction of this Epistle.

If our faith is perfected and our love grows, increases, and abounds, the result will be a hope of having our hearts established blameless in holiness before our God and Father at the coming of the Lord Jesus with all His saints. These saints are the believers in Christ, including the Old Testament saints (Dan. 7:18, 21-22, 25, 27; Zech. 14:5). Although verse 13 does not use the word hope, hope is nonetheless implied or indicated. The establishing of a holy life for the church life is thus related to its structure composed of faith, love, and hope.

WORKING WITH NEW BELIEVERS

Paul's way to take care of new believers is very different from that followed by many Christians today. His way is to show the new believers that they have been regenerated of God the Father and brought into an organic union with the Lord Jesus Christ and thereby have the structure of a holy life. All genuine Christians, whether old or young, have such a structure of a holy life for the church life. This life is the proper Christian life.

Many Christians do not have a proper Christian life. Furthermore, they do not have any idea concerning the church life. Many do not even know what it means to live a holy life. A holy life is a life entirely separated unto God, sanctified. To live a holy life is to have a life absolutely for God, by God, with God, and in God. This holy life is for the church life. The holy life for the church life is what Paul is covering in this Epistle addressed to new believers.

As real Christians, we all have this kind of life within us. Now we need to live it. This life has a structure composed of faith, love, and hope. Our work with new believers should foster this life; it should nourish and cherish it so that it may grow. Moreover, we must learn how to establish, strengthen, and encourage this life in its structure of faith, love, and hope.

Faith is a matter of seeing a view of the contents of God's New Testament economy. Once we have the view, we shall believe in what we see. This faith is the foundation of our Christian life. Out of our faith love will flow forth. In the church life we are living a life of love. We should love everyone: those believers who meet with us and those who do not and also the unbelievers. This love is the issue of our faith. Furthermore, we shall then have a life that is full of hope. We are living for Christ, we are expressing Him, and we are even His Body. As we wait for His coming back, we are filled with hope. Our hope, destiny, and destination are not on this earth. They are altogether focused on the coming back of the Lord Jesus.

If we see the structure, origin, fostering, and establishment of a holy life for the church life, we shall have a direction in our work with new believers. We shall help them to realize that, as genuine Christians, they already have the structure of a holy life for the church life. Then we shall foster this life and establish its faith, love, and hope.

LIFE-STUDY OF FIRST THESSALONIANS

MESSAGE FIFTEEN

AN EXHORTATION CONCERNING A HOLY LIFE FOR THE CHURCH LIFE

Scripture Reading: 1 Thes. 4:1-12

The Epistle of 1 Thessalonians was written to new believers, to those who had been in the Lord less than a year. For this reason, in the first three chapters of this book, we cannot find anything to compare with what is revealed in Romans, Ephesians, or Galatians. Paul stayed with the Thessalonians for approximately a month. In that short period of time he did not have the opportunity to cover many deeper truths. For this reason, in 3:10 he expressed his desire to come to the Thessalonians and perfect what was lacking in their faith. To be sure, these new believers were lacking in many aspects of the faith revealed in Romans, Ephesians, and Galatians. Therefore, Paul wanted to visit them again so that he could minister to them the contents of the faith so that their faith would increase and be perfected.

We all need to have a broad view of God's economy. Once we see such a view, we shall spontaneously believe in what we see. We cannot help but believe after seeing a view. Believing comes from this kind of spiritual seeing. Paul's writings take us on a tour to show us heavenly, spiritual things concerning Christ, His achievements and attainments, and what He has obtained. The more we see concerning this, the more we shall be impressed, and the more faith we shall have. We shall find that it is simply impossible not to believe.

We have emphasized the fact that in 1 Thessalonians we have a word to beginners, to new believers. Those who are working with young people or with new believers can receive from this book both a direction and an outline to follow. If they follow this outline and direction, they will lay a good foundation in their work with new believers.

A WORD OF WARNING

In this message we come to chapter four of 1 Thessalonians. In chapter one we have the structure and origin of a holy life for the church life; in chapter two, the fostering of such a life; and in chapter three the establishing of the three items of the basic structure of this life. After covering these matters, in chapter four Paul injects an inoculation into the believers concerning the most serious germ that damages the church life, the germ of fornication.

Fornication has its source in lust. People would never have a chance to indulge themselves in this lust if they did not have some form of social life. Social life is a hotbed of fornication. A person who does not have a social life is not in danger of falling into fornication. If you live alone and have little contact with others, it is very unlikely that you will commit fornication. But the church life is a meeting life, a communal life. In other words, the church life is a social life. In order to have the church life, we cannot avoid having a communal life, a social life, in which we have considerable contact with one another.

According to history, the problem of fornication has come up over and over again in one church after another. The facts prove that Christian workers in particular are often snared by fornication because they have so much contact with others. Furthermore, fornication has been the factor in damage caused to those in the Pentecostal movement. In certain places this movement has been limited because of the sin of fornication.

In 4:3 Paul says, "For this is the will of God, your sanctification; that you abstain from fornication." God's will is that His redeemed people, the believers in Christ, should live a life of holiness according to His holy nature, a life wholly separated unto Him from anything other than Him. For this He is sanctifying us thoroughly (5:23).

At Paul's time, both in Corinth and Thessalonica sensuality and immorality were rife in the pagan religions and even fostered by their pagan worship. Man was made for expressing God (Gen. 1:26). Nothing ruins man for this purpose more than fornication. This prevents man from being holy, separated unto God, and contaminates man to the uttermost in the fulfilling of God's holy purpose. Hence, the apostle strongly charges the newly converted Gentile believers, by sanctification unto God, to abstain from the damage and contamination of fornication, the most gross sin in the eyes of God.

Here in 1 Thessalonians 4 Paul gives us a warning concerning fornication. He also spoke strongly about fornication in 1 Corinthians. Because there was so much immorality in Corinth and Thessalonica, Paul realized that along with fostering and establishing the saints in Thessalonica, it was necessary for him to warn them about the sin of fornication. Now we can understand why in a book to new believers Paul thought it necessary to speak about fornication. He wanted the saints in that evil city to be aware of the danger. As the church in such a place, they needed a warning about fornication.

In 1 Corinthians 16:20 Paul says, "Greet one another with a holy kiss." Paul did not forbid the Corinthians to have contact with one another, for that would have been inhuman. However, Paul charged them to greet one another with a holy kiss. Such a word was written against the background of the situation in Corinth. In the same principle, fornication is dealt with in 1 Thessalonians 4 because of the environment of Thessalonica. A young church had been raised up in the midst of an evil, immoral environment. Knowing that it would be difficult for the church in that city to avoid problems with fornication, Paul issued a warning regarding it.

We also need this warning today. In the United States and Europe males and females have social contact with hardly any limitation. Because of this situation, it is easy for people to fall into fornication. In order for churches to exist in these regions, there is a need of a warning concerning fornication.

As we read 4:1-12, we see that Paul's tone here is one of warning. The tone is different from that found in the first three chapters. After Paul has completed his task of fostering and establishing a holy life for the church life, he changes his tone. The first warning he gives us concerns fornication. As we shall see, in his warning about fornication, Paul brings in the wonderful matter of sanctification.

SANCTIFICATION VERSUS FORNICATION

In 4:1 Paul says, "For the rest therefore, brothers, we ask and entreat you in the Lord Jesus, that even as you received from us how you ought to walk and to please God, even as indeed you do walk, that you abound more." In verse 3 Paul says that the will of God is our sanctification. This sanctification is versus fornication. In order to have a walk that pleases God, we need to be sanctified.

Nothing damages a believer as much as fornication. According to Paul's word in 1 Corinthians 6, fornication ruins a person's body. Other sins may not damage us subjectively, but fornication damages our body, contaminates our entire being, and makes us utterly unholy. Moreover, fornication is used by God's enemy to spoil the man God created for the fulfillment of His purpose. Therefore, fornication must be altogether abandoned. This is the reason Paul says in 4:3, "Abstain from fornication." The word "abstain" is strong, and it indicates that we should run away from fornication. God's will is to have us fully separated unto Himself, wholly sanctified for the fulfillment of His purpose. This requires that we abstain from fornication.

In verses 4 and 5 Paul continues, "That each one of you know how to possess his own vessel in sanctification and honor, not in the passion of lust, even as also the nations who do not know God." To possess one's vessel is to keep it, to preserve it. There are two schools of interpretation of the word vessel here; one refers the vessel to man's body, as in 2 Corinthians 4:7; the other to his wife, as in 1 Peter 3:7. The context in this verse and the following one, with phrases "each one of you," "in sanctification and honor," and especially "not in the passion of lust," does not justify the interpretation of the second school, but that of the first. The apostle considers man's body here as his vessel, just as David did in 1 Samuel 21:5. In the same matter concerning the use of the body, both Paul and David consider man's body as his vessel. To keep or preserve man's vessel in sanctification and honor, not in passion of lust, is the safeguard against committing fornication.

Sanctification refers more to a holy condition before God; honor, more to a respectable standing before man. Man was created for God's purpose with a high standing, and marriage was ordained by God for the propagation of man to fulfill God's purpose. Hence, marriage should be held in honor (Heb. 13:4). To abstain from fornication is not only to remain in a sanctified condition before God, but also to hold and keep a standing of honor before man. Whenever someone becomes involved in fornication, he is contaminated, and his sanctification is annulled. Moreover, he loses honor before man. Not even unbelievers honor those who commit fornication. Therefore, we must know how to possess, keep, preserve, our own body in sanctification toward God and in honor before man. We must be those who are sanctified unto God and those who have honor before man. In order to be such persons, we must absolutely abstain from fornication and not give ground for suspicion in this matter.

According to verse 5, we should not possess our body in the passion of lust as the nations who do not know God. Not knowing God is the basic reason for indulgence in the passion of lust.

In verse 6 Paul goes on to say, "That no one overstep and take advantage of his brother in the matter, because the Lord is the avenger concerning all these things, even as we also said before to you and solemnly charged." Literally, the Greek word rendered "overstep" means to overpass limits, that is, overreach, transgress, go beyond. "Overstep...his brother" refers to adultery with the brother's wife. In Greek "take advantage of" also means make a gain of; hence, defraud. By "the matter" Paul means the matter of fornication, mentioned in verse 3. In verse 6 Paul also says that the Lord is the avenger concerning these things, things such as overstepping and taking advantage of others. The Lord judges the fornicators and adulterers as an avenger, as a punisher, meting out justice.

Fornication always involves overstepping the regulation of the marriage relationship. The relationship between male and female was ordained by God. Marriage is a holy matter that was ordained by God and is under His strict regulation. Therefore, the contact between male and female must be according to God's ordination and regulation. Otherwise there may be some kind of transgression, overstepping, breaking of God's regulation.

In verse 7 Paul says, "For God has not called us for uncleanness but in sanctification." The Greek preposition translated "for" in this verse, *epi,* means upon, on condition of. Uncleanness in this verse denotes uncleanness in things like fornication and adultery. Some teachers say that verse 6 speaks of taking advantage of a brother in doing business. To refer uncleanness here to unfair gain in business is not acceptable according to the context of this section, which begins in verse 3 with the charge to abstain from fornication. Actually, verse 7 is the concluding word of this charge.

The apostle's charge to abstain from fornication is based upon sanctification (v. 3), strengthened by sanctification (v. 4), and concluded here with sanctification, because fornication, as the most unclean thing, destroys the holy standing and character of God's called saints.

God has not called us on condition of uncleanness, but He has called us in sanctification. This indicates that we must always remain in sanctification. God's calling has nothing to do with uncleanness. His calling is in sanctification, and this sanctification is versus fornication.

Verse 8 says, "Consequently, he who rejects, rejects not man but God, Who also gives His Holy Spirit to you." This verse is the conclusion of the section which begins in verse 3. The word "rejects" here refers to the charge given in the preceding verses. Here Paul seems to be saying, "I have given you a warning. If you reject it, you are not rejecting me, but you are rejecting God, the One who gave His Holy Spirit to you." Here the Holy Spirit is referred to as the Holy One who sanctifies us, making us holy before God (Rom. 15:16; 1 Pet. 1:2; 1 Cor. 6:11).

The will (v. 3), the call (v. 7), and the Spirit of God are all for our sanctification. God had His will first, then His call, and then the giving of His Holy Spirit. By His Spirit we may be sanctified to answer His call and fulfill His will.

God has given His Holy Spirit to us to sanctify us, to make us holy, to separate us unto God for His purpose. Thus, this Holy Spirit is moving, working, and acting within us constantly for a purpose. If we fall into fornication, we reject this indwelling Spirit who is working within us to sanctify us unto God. This is Paul's meaning here, in the verse that concludes a section on sanctification versus fornication.

May we all, especially the young people, be impressed with Paul's word of warning. The age in which we live certainly is no better than the age in which Paul lived. Furthermore, the cities where we live today are not better than Corinth or Thessalonica. On the contrary, both the age and the cities may be worse. Therefore, we need this warning concerning sanctification versus fornication.

BROTHERLY LOVE

In verses 9 and 10 Paul goes on to exhort the believers regarding brotherly love: "Now concerning brotherly love, you have no need for me to write to you, for you yourselves are taught of God to love one another; For indeed you do it unto all the brothers in the whole of Macedonia. But we entreat you, brothers, to abound more." The words "brotherly love" are a translation of the Greek word *philadelphia,* composed of *phileo,* to love, and *adelphos,* brother. Here Paul reiterates his word in 3:12 concerning love: "And the Lord cause you to increase and abound in love to one another and to all, even as we also to you." This emphasis on love indicates that love is a vital factor in the Christian life. According to Galatians 5:14 and Romans 13:10, love is the fulfillment of the law. If we love others, certainly we shall not commit fornication, steal, or lie.

A BECOMING WALK

In 4:11 and 12 Paul speaks concerning a becoming walk: "And to be ambitious to be quiet, and to attend to your own affairs, and to work with your hands, even as we charged you; that you may walk becomingly toward those outside, and you may have need of nothing." In verse 11 Paul gives us a good word: "Be ambitious to be quiet." It is extremely difficult for a talkative person to be quiet. If such a person can be quiet for half an hour, that would be a victory.

The church life is damaged the most by fornication, then by jealousy, and after that by busybodies. A busybody wants to be everybody when actually he is nobody. Therefore, Paul charges the busybodies to be ambitious to be quiet. This means that they should have the ambition of calming themselves down. Certainly I would encourage the saints to have more fellowship. But those who are busybodies should be encouraged to be somewhat less active and to be more quiet. They should not seek to be the church information desk or be interested in knowing about others' affairs. Instead, as Paul says, they should attend to their own affairs. Perhaps they should spend more time cleaning house or arranging their things. They should avoid the kind of busyness that damages the church life.

Those who are too interested in others' affairs should be ambitious to be quiet and attend to their own affairs. But those who do not care for others and who spend too much time on their own affairs should be encouraged to spend more time caring for others in a proper way. In this matter, because we were born with different dispositions, we all need to be balanced.

In verse 12 Paul charges us to walk becomingly. We should not walk in a way that is strange or peculiar. In the eyes of others, our walk should be very becoming.

Today young people like to be peculiar. Some think that the more peculiar they are, the better it is. By being peculiar they attract the attention of others. We, however, should conduct ourselves in a way that is normal, becoming, and ordinary. However, in so doing we are not following any code or regulations. I believe that if we desire to love the Lord, to live Him, to walk according to His heart, deep within we shall sense something requiring us to be normal and becoming in all we do. In the way we drive, in the way we wear our hair, in the clothes we wear, and in all other things, we shall want to be becoming.

Anything that attracts the attention of others in a peculiar way is not becoming. We need to behave and walk becomingly. In particular, we must walk becomingly toward those outside, toward the outsiders.

CARING FOR NEW BELIEVERS

The more we read 1 Thessalonians and consider its contents, the more we realize that this Epistle was written to new believers. First Thessalonians is absolutely different from Ephesians. The book of Ephesians contains many profound terms: the mystery of Christ, the Body of Christ, the fullness of Him who fills all in all. By contrast, 1 Thessalonians does not use profound terms. Instead, there are a number of simple warnings. For example, we are told that it is God's will for us to be sanctified. This is an elementary way of speaking. Another example concerns Paul's exhortation to brotherly love. He tells us that we have been taught of God to love one another, and then he encourages us to abound in this love. Furthermore, Paul exhorts us to be ambitious to be quiet, not to be busybodies, to work with our hands, and to attend to our own affairs. Such words are elementary; however, they are very practical, and we need them.

Why in his exhortation in chapter four does Paul mention

only three things? Why does he speak only of sanctification versus fornication, of brotherly love, and of a becoming walk? The answer to these questions is that if we take care of sanctification, brotherly love, and walking becomingly, we shall be perfect. Therefore, we all need to take care of our sanctification, of our love for others, and of having a proper and becoming walk.

First Thessalonians certainly is a book for new believers. In this Epistle Paul takes care of the beginners in a very practical way. This does not mean, however, that new believers do not need books such as Romans, 1 and 2 Corinthians, Galatians, Ephesians, Philippians, Colossians, and Hebrews. They certainly have a need for these books. But because they are young, they first need something simple and practical. This is the reason Paul wrote 1 Thessalonians in the way he did. He knew that the believers had been in the Lord less than a year, and therefore he wrote them in a very practical way. May we all follow Paul's example and adopt his way to work with young saints and new believers.

LIFE-STUDY OF FIRST THESSALONIANS

MESSAGE SIXTEEN

THE HOPE OF THE CHRISTIAN LIFE

Scripture Reading: 1 Thes. 4:13-18

In 4:13-18 Paul gives an elementary word concerning the Lord's coming and the rapture of the believers. Here, as a word of comfort, the rapture of believers at the Lord's coming is mentioned in a general way. Concerning this matter, details are revealed in other books of the New Testament, such as Matthew and Revelation.

What Paul describes in 4:13-18 is the general hope of all believers. This is the hope of a holy life for the church life. This kind of life is neither sinful nor worldly. On the contrary, it is pure and holy. Furthermore, this holy life for the church life has a hope.

Because of man's fall there is no hope for the fallen human race. The only expectation unbelievers have is death. Death is their destination. Day by day, they are living with a view toward their death, and they are on the way to death. Thus, death is their future.

In Ephesians 2:12 Paul describes the hopeless situation of unbelievers: "You were at that time apart from Christ, alienated from the commonwealth of Israel, and strangers from the covenants of the promise, having no hope and without God in the world." Unbelievers have no hope because they do not have God. Because they are apart from Christ and their living is without God, they do not have any hope. The only thing that awaits them is death. Everyone realizes this and takes it for granted. For this reason, unbelievers do not like to think about their future. Actually, they do not have a positive future. In their future looms the darkness of death.

As those who believe in Christ, we have a life full of hope. Our hope is the Lord's coming back. Furthermore, our hope includes resurrection and rapture. Resurrection is not only a matter of life, but a matter of life overcoming death. When life overcomes death, that is resurrection. Rapture is something that goes even beyond resurrection. A person may be resurrected and yet not be raptured.

RESURRECTION AND RAPTURE

The holy life for the church life is a life with a future, a life with hope. This hope is not merely the Lord's coming; it is the Lord's coming with resurrection and rapture. The coming back of the Lord Jesus will cause the resurrection and the rapture to occur. As we have just pointed out, resurrection and rapture are both in addition to life. Today life is our possession. We have life, we are in life, and we are enjoying life. However, we are awaiting the Lord's coming, and His coming will bring resurrection and rapture.

Resurrection, of course, is for those who have died. Today we are living a holy life for the church. If the Lord delays His coming back, we all shall eventually "sleep," that is, die physically. All the believers who have died are waiting for resurrection. If we live until the coming back of the Lord Jesus, we shall not need resurrection. However, we shall still need rapture. Furthermore, those who have died will need to be resurrected and raptured as well. All believers, the dead as well as the living, need rapture. Rapture, therefore, is actually the end of our life on earth. This means that the conclusion of our life is neither death nor resurrection—it is rapture.

In the Scriptures there is not such a word as rapture, but the thought of rapture is there. As used by Christian teachers, the word rapture means to be taken away, as what happened to Enoch and Elijah (Gen. 5:24; 2 Kings 2:1, 11). Matthew 24:40-41; Luke 17:34-36; 21:36; 1 Thessalonians 4:17; Revelation 3:10; 7:9; 11:12; 12:5; 14:1, 16; 15:2 all refer to rapture, to the taking up of the believers to the heavens.

In the New Testament the rapture is an important subject. In 4:13-18 Paul speaks of it only in a general, elementary way. He tells us that the living, together with those believers who have died and have been resurrected, will be caught up to a meeting of the Lord in the air. In these verses Paul does not go further to explain the details. What he says here can be compared to an elementary school teacher giving his students some basic principles of mathematics. Actually, the rapture is not a simple matter. For this reason, there has been much debate among Bible teachers concerning it.

Paul's intention is to give the new believers a basic concept of the hope of our Christian life. He wants to impress them with the fact that the Christian life, which is a holy life for the church life, has a hope. Therefore, this life is absolutely different from the hopeless life of fallen mankind. The hope of the Christian life is the Lord's coming back, and this hope includes resurrection and rapture.

In verse 13 Paul says, "But we do not want you to be ignorant, brothers, concerning those who are sleeping, that you may not sorrow even as also the rest who have no hope." The words "those who are sleeping" refer to the dead (v. 16; John 11:11-14; 1 Cor. 11:30). The death of believers is considered by both the Lord and the apostle as sleep. Perhaps by the time Paul wrote this Epistle some of the believers in Thessalonica had died. Otherwise, there would have been no reason for Paul to write about this matter.

In verse 14 Paul continues, "For if we believe that Jesus died and rose, so also those who are asleep will God, through Jesus, bring together with Him." To believe in the hope described here includes believing in the Lord's resurrection. Anyone who does not believe in Christ's resurrection will not believe in this hope. But if we believe in this hope, this indicates that we have already believed in Christ's resurrection.

Some may refer to verse 14 and say, "When the saints die, they go to heaven, and when the Lord Jesus comes back, He will bring them from heaven with Him." To interpret the verse in this way is to neglect the first half of the verse, where we are told that Jesus died and rose. This, of course, refers to His resurrection. If the dead saints are already in heaven, and if the Lord will bring them with Him from heaven when He comes, then the dead saints do not need resurrection.

Verses 15 and 16 will help you to understand what I mean: "For this we say to you by the word of the Lord, that we who are living, who remain unto the coming of the Lord, shall by no means precede those who have slept; because the Lord Himself, with a cry of command, with the voice of an archangel, and with a trumpet of God, will descend from heaven, and the dead in Christ shall rise first." Please pay careful attention to the word "rise" in verse 16. If the dead are already in heaven, what need is there for them to rise? If they are truly in heaven, they do not need to rise. Furthermore, they do not need to be raptured or to be caught up to the Lord. Their only need would be to descend from heaven with the Lord Jesus. The fact that verse 16 says that the dead in Christ shall rise indicates that they must be in some place other than heaven.

In verse 15 the Greek word translated "coming" is *parousia,* presence. In verse 16 the Greek words rendered "cry of command" may also be translated shout of command, as a signal for assembling. The trumpet of God is the last trumpet (1 Cor. 15:52), a trumpet for assembling God's redeemed people (see Num. 10:2).

In verse 17 Paul goes on to say, "Then we who are living, who remain, shall be caught up at the same time together with them in clouds into a meeting of the Lord in the air; and so we shall be always together with the Lord." According to this verse, both the dead and the living believers will be caught up to the Lord. First the dead will be raised, and then together we shall be caught up to a meeting of the Lord in the air.

The manchild in Revelation 12, the overcomers, will be caught up, raptured, to the throne of God in the third heaven before the last three and a half years of the great tribulation (Rev. 12:5-6, 14). Here, the majority of believers will be raptured to the air at the time of the Lord's coming.

THE DEAD SAINTS IN PARADISE

Some among us may still hold the concept that saints who have died have gone to heaven and are now there with the Lord Jesus. If Paul had not gone beyond what he says in verse 14, there might be ground for this concept. But in verse 16 Paul says that when the Lord Jesus comes, the dead saints will rise up. Where will they rise up from? From heaven? If they are already in heaven, what need will they have to rise up? And to what place would they rise if they are already in the third heaven with the Lord?

Many Christians have been cheated by sugar-coated religious teachings. One of these teachings says, "Oh, you don't need to weep about your mother who has died. Because she believed in the Lord Jesus, she is now in heaven with Him. She is in a heavenly mansion, a home that is much better than yours. Why, then, should you weep? One day you will join her in heaven." This kind of teaching is full of leaven and is very deceitful. I have studied the Bible for more than fifty years, and I have not found even one verse that teaches such a thing. This is a superstition that has its source in paganism, or in Buddhism, and was adopted by Catholicism.

According to the Bible, the dead believers are in Paradise (Luke 23:43), the comfortable section of Hades (Luke 16:22, 25-26). In Hades, there are two sections: a section of comfort and a section of torment. The section of suffering is different from the lake of fire. The unpleasant part of Hades may be compared to a jail in contrast to a prison. A jail is a place where criminals are held temporarily. But after a criminal has been tried and judged, he is taken from jail and put into prison. The sinners now in the section of torment in Hades are awaiting the final judgment, which will take place at the white throne of God. After that, the sinners will be cast into the lake of fire, the eternal prison.

The dead saints are in Paradise, and when the Lord Jesus comes, they will rise up. They will not rise up to heaven; rather, they will rise up and then be caught up together with the living saints. This is the reason verse 16 says that the dead in Christ will rise first. Then, according to verse 17, those who are living will be caught up at the same time with them to a meeting of the Lord. This means that all believers, the dead as well as the living, will be raptured to the air. This teaching is not sugar-coated, and it does not contain any leaven. On the contrary, it is according to the pure Word of God.

According to the Word of God, when the Lord Jesus descends from heaven, the dead saints will rise up. Their spirit and soul will rise out of Paradise, their body will rise up from the tomb, and their spirit and soul with the body will make them perfect. They will then join the believers who are living, and together we shall all be caught up to the Lord.

THE RAPTURE OF THE LIVING

In verse 15 Paul says, "We who are living, who remain unto the coming of the Lord." In verse 17 he also says, "We who are living, who remain." Why does Paul add the clause "who remain unto the coming of the Lord" in verse 15 and the clause "who remain" in verse 17? If you consider this matter thoughtfully, you will realize that this indicates, or at least implies, that there are some living ones who do not remain. Some living ones are gone. These living ones who do not remain are overcomers.

There is a difference between the rapture of the overcomers and the rapture of those believers who are alive and remain until the Lord's coming. The rapture of the overcomers will take place before the last three and a half years, a period known as the great tribulation. In other words, the overcomers will be raptured before the tribulation (Rev. 3:10). But those who are alive and remain will be raptured at the end of the tribulation, that is, at the last trumpet (1 Cor. 15:52). This is the rapture mentioned in 1 Thessalonians 4.

Regarding time, these two raptures are different: one takes place before the great tribulation, and the other, at the end of the tribulation. Furthermore, there is a difference regarding location. According to Revelation 12, the overcomers are raptured to the throne of God in the third heaven. But according to 1 Thessalonians 4, the rapture of those who are alive and remain will be to the clouds in the air.

THE PAROUSIA

We have pointed out that the Greek word for "coming" in verse 15 is parousia, the same word as used in Matthew 24:3. Christ's coming will be His presence with His believers. This parousia will begin from the time the overcomers are raptured to the throne, continue with His coming to the air (Rev. 10:1), and end with His coming to the earth. Within His parousia, there will be the rapture of the majority of the believers to the air (1 Thes. 4:15-17), the judgment seat of Christ (2 Cor. 5:10), and the marriage of the Lamb (Rev. 19:7-9).

Parousia denotes the Lord's presence; it does not directly denote His coming. Of course, His presence involves His coming. If I am away from my family and then am present with them again, my presence includes my coming. Actually, my presence equals my coming. For this reason, the word parousia may be translated coming. It would be rather awkward to literally render it as presence. But even though this translation may be awkward, it would be correct to say "unto the presence of the Lord."

According to the New Testament, the Lord's parousia, His presence, will last a period of time. It may begin immediately before the start of the great tribulation. The Lord's coming (the parousia) will begin probably near the start of the tribulation. At present, the Lord is in the third heaven. When the great tribulation begins on earth, the Lord will leave the throne in heaven and descend from the throne, concealed in a cloud, to the sky. Revelation 10:1 speaks of a "strong Angel coming down out of heaven, clothed with a cloud." This strong Angel is Christ, who descends secretly from the third heaven to the air. Probably the Lord will stay in the air concealed by the cloud for a period of time, possibly more than three years. This is the reason we say that the Lord's parousia will last a certain length of time.

When the Lord is in the air, He will do a number of things. He will rapture both the resurrected and the living believers. He will judge all the saved ones at His judgment seat. At that time the decision will be made by Him concerning who will join Him in the millennial kingdom and who will not. This judgment will, of course, take place after the rapture mentioned in 1 Thessalonians 4. This sketch should give us a general idea of the Lord's coming according to the pure Word. This sketch is not according to strange or traditional teachings.

As Christians, we should live a holy life for the church life. This life has a hope, the hope that the Lord whom we are serving today will come back. At His coming back, the saints who have died will rise up from Paradise and the tomb to be caught up with those who are alive and remain.

AN ELEMENTARY WORD

This word concerning our hope was written to the believers as a comfort and encouragement in the death of their relatives. It is an elementary word concerning the Lord's coming back and our being caught up to Him. If we would know the details, we need to study Matthew 24 and 25, the whole book of Revelation, 1 Corinthians 15, and other portions of the Word, including 2 Thessalonians. Once we study all these portions of the Scriptures, we shall see that the matters of the Lord's coming and our rapture are not as simple as what is presented by many today. The details include the rapture of the overcoming saints, the judgment at the judgment seat of Christ, the reward in the kingdom, and the discipline by the kingdom. All these things are involved in the Lord's coming and our rapture.

LIFE-STUDY OF FIRST THESSALONIANS

MESSAGE SEVENTEEN

WATCHFULNESS AND SOBERNESS

Scripture Reading: 1 Thes. 5:1-11

Immediately after Paul presents the hope of a holy life for the church life, he covers the matter of the watchfulness and soberness of this life. We have a wonderful hope, a hope that the Lord Jesus will come back and that we shall be raptured to Him. Along with this hope, we need watchfulness and soberness. As we are hoping, we need to watch and be sober. For this reason, 1 Thessalonians does not end with chapter four. In this wonderful book for new believers, Paul adds yet a further word concerning watchfulness and soberness. Once again, we should follow Paul's pattern. We should not simply encourage new believers in their hope. We should also go on to tell them that along with this hope, they need to be watchful and sober. They should not be asleep, and they should not be drunk or in some kind of stupor.

As Paul was writing the last part of chapter four, I believe that he was burdened to speak a word on the watchfulness and soberness of a holy life for the church life. If this book concluded at the end of chapter four, and if we did not have 5:1-11, some believers may be misled. In fact, because they isolate 4:13-18 from the rest of this Epistle, Christians have been misled or even drugged in their mentality. Therefore, as we apply chapter four to our situation, we should not neglect 5:1-11. This means that as we wait for the Lord's coming back, we need to be watchful and also sober.

TIMES AND SEASONS

In 5:1-3 Paul indicates that the day of the Lord comes as a thief in the night. Verse 1 says, "But concerning the times and the seasons, brothers, you have no need for anything to be written to you." Times and seasons here refer to the Lord's coming. This is confirmed by the expression "the day of the Lord" in verse 2.

THE DAY OF THE LORD

In verse 2 Paul goes on to say, "For you yourselves know accurately that the day of the Lord so comes as a thief in the night." The coming of the Lord in the preceding chapter is mainly for comfort and encouragement. The day of the Lord in this chapter is mainly for warning (vv. 3-6), since it is mentioned in the Word mostly in relation to the Lord's judgment (1 Cor. 1:8; 3:13; 5:5; 2 Cor. 1:14; 2 Tim. 4:8).

The fact that the day of the Lord comes as a thief in the night indicates that its coming is kept secret and that it will come suddenly. It is not known beforehand by anyone (Matt. 24:42-43; Rev. 3:3; 16:15). This thought is strengthened by what Paul says in verse 3: "Whenever they say, Peace and security, then sudden destruction comes upon them, as birth pangs to a woman with child, and they shall by no means escape."

THE SAFEGUARD OF FAITH, LOVE, AND HOPE

In verses 4 through 11 we see the safeguard of faith, love, and hope. In verse 4 Paul reminds us that we are not in darkness that the day should overtake us as a thief, and in verse 5 he points out that we are sons of light and of the day, and thus are not of the night nor of darkness. Then in verse 6 he exhorts us to watch and be sober: "So then, let us not sleep as the rest, but let us watch and be sober." To sleep here is to be unwatchful. Watch is versus sleep (see v. 7), and sober is versus drunk. In verse 7 Paul says, "For those who sleep, sleep in the night, and those who are drunk, are drunk in the night." Here to be drunk is to be in a stupor.

Christians are familiar with the word watchful. However, we probably do not know the real meaning of this word. What does it mean to be watchful? Our answer will be too vague if we merely say that to be watchful is not to sleep. In this case, as with many other things, we may take for granted that we understand what the Bible says, when actually we do not understand the matter at all. The same is true about what it means to be sober.

To be watchful and to be sober are related to safeguarding the three basic structures of the holy life for the church life: faith, love, and hope. Verse 8 indicates this: "But we who are of the day, let us be sober, putting on the breastplate of faith and love, and a helmet, the hope of salvation." The words breastplate and helmet both indicate spiritual warfare. The breastplate is of faith and love, covering and protecting our heart and spirit according to God's righteousness (Eph. 6:14). The helmet is the hope of salvation (Eph. 6:17), covering and protecting our mentality, the mind. Faith, love, and hope are the three basic structures of the genuine Christian life as depicted in 1 Thessalonians 1:3. Faith is related to our will—a part of our heart (Rom. 10:9)—and to our conscience—a part of our spirit (1 Tim. 1:19). Love is related to our emotion, another part of our heart (Matt. 22:37); and hope is related to our understanding—a function of our mind. All of these need to be protected that a genuine Christian life may be maintained. Such a life is watchful and sober. At the beginning of this Epistle, the apostle praised the believers' work of faith, labor of love, and endurance of hope (1:3). Here, at the conclusion of the Epistle, he exhorts them to keep these spiritual virtues covered and protected by fighting for them.

HOPE IN THE LORD'S COMING BACK

The hope spoken of in verse 8 is the hope of our Lord's coming back, which will be our salvation from both the coming destruction and from the slavery of corruption of the old creation (Rom. 8:21-25). Salvation in verses 8 and 9 is not salvation from eternal perdition through the Lord's death, but salvation from the coming destruction through the Lord's coming back.

According to verse 8, we need armor to safeguard our faith, love, and hope. If we would protect these aspects of the basic structure of a holy life for the church life, we need to be watchful and sober. Therefore, being watchful and sober is part of the living we should have as we hope in the Lord's coming back.

We have pointed out that in chapter four Paul comforts us with this hope, telling us that at the Lord's coming we shall be raptured. We shall be transported into a state of ecstasy to meet with the Lord in the air. However, this hope requires a living of watchfulness and soberness. We need a life of watchfulness and soberness in order to wait for the Lord's coming. In other words, as we exercise our hope in the Lord's coming back, we need a watching life and a sober life. If we are watchful and sober, we shall protect, safeguard, the basic structure of our Christian life.

THE MEANING OF WATCHFULNESS

Now we come to the crucial matter of understanding what it means to be watchful and sober. Watchfulness here is related to a battle, a fighting. Some versions use the word vigilant, a word related to warfare. Soldiers in a battle need to be watchful, vigilant. The fact that watchfulness is related to fighting is confirmed by Paul's mention of the breastplate and helmet in verse 8. A breastplate and helmet are not ordinary items of dress. They are, of course, part of the armor used by soldiers in fighting. Paul's concept of being watchful and sober, therefore, is related to fighting, to warfare. In these verses Paul is talking about some kind of battle.

There are sugar-coated teachings about the Lord's coming and the rapture revealed in chapter four, but these teachings do not prepare believers for fighting. Instead, they cause them to be drugged and in a stupor. It is important for us to see that watchfulness refers to a proper spirit in fighting a battle. If we grasp this thought, we shall have in large measure the proper understanding of what it means to be watchful.

To be watchful is to continue fighting. Soldiers in a battle do not merely look around. That is not to be watchful. They are watchful because they are fighting. When they stop fighting, they are no longer watchful. According to our understanding, to be watchful is simply to look out for something, for example, to watch our step as we are walking. But this is not the meaning here. In these verses to be watchful is to remember that we are in a battle, that we are fighting and are surrounded by enemies. This is the reason we need a helmet and also a breastplate.

Again and again we have emphasized the fact that 1 Thessalonians is an epistle written to new believers. This book contains many basic concepts regarding the Christian life. In each of the five chapters certain basic principles, certain elementary teachings, are covered. But even in a book concerned with elementary teachings, Paul includes the matter of spiritual warfare. Paul does not explicitly tell the believers that they are on a battlefield and need to fight. But what he says in 5:1-11 implies spiritual fighting.

SALVATION FROM THE COMING DESTRUCTION

In verse 3 the word destruction is used: "Whenever they say, Peace and security, then sudden destruction comes upon them, as birth pangs to a woman with child, and they shall by no means escape." What is this destruction? It is related to the salvation mentioned in verses 8 and 9. Salvation in these verses is salvation from the coming destruction through the Lord's coming back, not salvation from eternal perdition through the Lord's death. Fallen man will perish for eternity. That is eternal perdition. We who have believed in the Lord Jesus will be saved from eternal perdition. We have already obtained salvation in this respect. We have been saved from eternal perdition, and we shall never perish.

Biblical salvation from eternal perdition is eternal salvation. Once we are saved, we are saved for eternity. Contrary to the teaching of the Arminian school of theology, we cannot lose our salvation. Salvation is once for all. But here Paul is speaking about salvation in another respect, that is, salvation from the coming destruction.

Furthermore, in the light of Romans 8:21-25, we shall also be saved from the slavery of corruption of the old creation. All created things are today subject to the slavery of corruption. The entire old creation is enslaved to corruption. Everything, including our physical body, is decaying. Do you know what it means to get old? To get old is to decay. We all are in the process of decaying. The slavery of corruption in the old creation is controlling us, and we are subject to it. But when the Lord Jesus comes and we are raptured, we shall be saved from the slavery of corruption of the old creation. Therefore, the Lord's coming and our rapture will save us from two things: destruction and the slavery of corruption. This is the salvation mentioned in verses 8 and 9. However, the primary meaning is the salvation from the coming destruction.

Now we must go on to find out what this coming destruction is. This destruction is related to the battle that is raging between God and Satan. Near to the time of the Lord's coming, destruction will take place suddenly. That destruction will come primarily from God, but a portion of it will be caused by Satan. God will judge this rebellious world, and Satan will fight back. The result of the intense battle raging between God and Satan will be sudden destruction. It will be when people say, "Peace and security," that this destruction will come suddenly.

We need to be saved from this sudden destruction. The way to be saved from it is to be watchful and sober. As God is fighting, we must take sides with Him and fight for His interests. Since He is fighting, we should be fighting also.

Actually, to fight is to be watchful. Only those who are fighting are truly watchful. The more we are fighting, the more watchful we shall be. As long as you are fighting, you need not try to be watchful, for you will be watchful automatically. Sometimes soldiers in an army go for days without sleep. The battle does not allow them time to sleep. This illustrates the fact that to fight is to be watchful. The Christian life, a holy life for the church life, is a life of fighting. We are on the battlefield, and we need to be alert, watchful, vigilant.

THE MEANING OF SOBERNESS

Soberness is related to watchfulness. To be sober is to be clear about the situation in which we are fighting. It is to have a proper understanding concerning where we are and where the enemy is. It is to see how the enemy is attacking and how we should fight back. If we are sober, we shall be clear about our direction.

To be sober is to be clear about everything related to the battle. It is to be clear about where the enemy is, what the enemy is doing, and how the enemy is attacking. It is also to be clear about how to protect ourselves and how to fight back. Those who are sober are fully clear about their situation.

THE LACK OF WATCHFULNESS AND SOBERNESS

Most of today's Christians do not have such a soberness. As a result, they are drugged, they are in a stupor, and they do not have the proper sense of direction. This is the reason it is often difficult to have fellowship with them. If you fellowship with certain ones about a particular matter, they will argue with you. Should you try to fellowship about something else, they may condemn you or even slander you.

In verse 6 Paul says, "So then, let us not sleep as the rest, but let us watch and be sober." The word watch here is versus sleep in the following verse, and sober is versus drunk. As we talk about the hope of the Lord's coming, we need to consider ourselves and ask whether we are watchful or sleeping, whether we are sober or drunk. Certain slogans on bumper stickers concerning the Lord's coming indicate that many Christians are drugged and in a stupor. With respect to the coming of the Lord, there is no watchfulness or soberness. We, therefore, need to be on the alert. Are we fighting for the Lord's interests? Are we watchful? Are we sober and clear about our situation? We need to ask ourselves questions such as these.

We have emphasized the fact that Paul wrote the Epistle of 1 Thessalonians in an elementary way, talking about basic matters. He speaks concerning the Lord's coming and our being caught up to Him. But instead of stopping there, he goes on in chapter five to speak of watchfulness and soberness.

PUTTING ON THE ARMOR

If we are watchful and sober, we shall put on the armor. According to verse 8, we should put on the breastplate of faith and love and also a helmet, the hope of salvation. This breastplate protects our faith and love; the helmet guards our hope. Hence, by the armor, the basic structures of the Christian life—faith, love, and hope—are protected.

If we read 1 Thessalonians 5 carefully and compare it with Ephesians 6, we shall see that in 1 Thessalonians we have an elementary teaching concerning spiritual warfare. In Ephesians 6, however, the teaching about spiritual warfare is much more advanced. Therefore, we need to go on from 1 Thessalonians 5 to Ephesians 6.

We have pointed out strongly that to fight properly is to be watchful and also sober. This fighting safeguards our Christian life; it preserves and protects the basic structure of the Christian life.

Some who formerly were with us in the Lord's recovery put off the armor and thereby were exposed to the enemy's attack. Because they had no covering, no protection, and no safeguard, they were defeated by the enemy. Instead of being watchful and sober, they were sleeping and in a stupor.

We need to be watchful and sober. This means that we need to keep on fighting. We also need to safeguard the structure of our Christian life by wearing the armor. Then when the Lord Jesus comes, we shall be saved from the sudden destruction.

SUDDEN DESTRUCTION

God will one day judge the world, and Satan will seek to destroy it. If we read the book of Revelation carefully, we shall see that during the last three and a half years, God will be angry with this evil, sinful, and rebellious world and judge it. Moreover, Satan will not want the world to exist any longer and will seek to destroy it. The result will be sudden destruction.

In verses 9 and 10 Paul says, "Because God did not appoint us to wrath, but to the gaining of salvation through our Lord Jesus Christ, Who died for us that, whether we watch or sleep, we may live together with Him." Since God did not appoint us to wrath, we should watch, be sober, and fight to cooperate with God that we may gain His salvation through the Lord Jesus. As we have pointed out, salvation in this verse is not eternal salvation; it is salvation from the coming destruction and also from the slavery of the corruption of the old creation. We are waiting for salvation from destruction and from the slavery of corruption. Then we shall enjoy the freedom of the glory of the sons of God.

LIVING TOGETHER WITH THE LORD

In verse 10 Paul speaks of living together with the Lord. The Lord died for us not only that we may be saved from eternal perdition, but also that we may live together with Him, through His resurrection, a life that can save us from the coming destruction. We may live together with Him whether we watch or sleep, that is, whether we live or die. On the one hand, the Lord is away from us and we are awaiting His coming back; on the other hand, He is with us (Matt. 28:20), and we can live together with Him (Rom. 6:8).

LIFE-STUDY OF FIRST THESSALONIANS

MESSAGE EIGHTEEN

COOPERATION WITH THE DIVINE OPERATION

(1)

Scripture Reading: 1 Thes. 5:12-28

Chapter five begins with the word "but." This indicates that the last part of chapter four, which is concerned with the rapture, needs a further word about another matter. According to 5:1, this further word is related to the times and the seasons.

As a young believer, when I heard messages about the Lord's coming, I was very excited. It is common for new believers to be excited when they hear about the Lord's coming back. They may expect the Lord to come at any moment. For this reason, they need Paul's further word in chapter five.

The "times and the seasons" in verse 1 refer to the Lord's coming. This is confirmed by the expression "the day of the Lord" in the following verse. The coming of the day of the Lord is different from what we imagine. Actually, it is a mystery. The Lord Jesus even said that, as a man, He did not know the time of His coming. The date of the Lord's coming is absolutely hidden as a mystery in the Father's heart, and this mystery has not been revealed. Therefore, in 5:2 Paul says that the day of the Lord "so comes as a thief in the night." To be sure, no thief would give an advance warning that he is coming to steal something. In the same principle, the day of the Lord will come suddenly and unexpectedly. Thus, we need to be watchful and sober. Because we have no way to figure out the time of the Lord's coming, we need to be watchful and sober.

After covering the matter of watchfulness and soberness

in 5:1-11, Paul turns in 5:12-24 to our cooperation with the divine operation. In these verses Paul covers a number of items in an elementary way.

In the New Testament there is no book that ends in such a marvelous and all-inclusive way as 1 Thessalonians. Paul's concluding word includes a number of crucial things, which Paul did not have the time to cover in detail. Therefore, he listed them together in one section toward the end of this Epistle.

RESPECTING THE LEADING ONES

Verse 12 says, "Now we ask you, brothers, to know those who labor among you and take the lead among you in the Lord, and admonish you; and to regard them most highly in love because of their work. Be at peace among yourselves." The word "know" here means first to recognize and then render respect and regard. According to Matthew 7:23, when the Lord Jesus comes back, He will say to certain ones, "I never knew you." The expression, "I never knew you" means not to appreciate or respect what was done. In the same principle, in verse 12 the word "know" means to appreciate and respect those who labor among us and who take the lead among us. Here Paul probably refers to the elders who labor in teaching and take the lead among the believers (1 Tim. 5:17).

To take the lead is not mainly to rule, but to set an example in doing things first that others may follow. The elders should not only labor in teaching, but also do things as an example. The example may become a ground for their admonition.

It is indeed marvelous that, although the church in Thessalonica had been in existence less than a year and Paul had spent only three Sabbaths working there, some leading ones had been raised up. In a short period of time a church was established, and some leading ones were produced. Paul surely was a qualified and skillful Christian worker.

In verse 13 Paul charges us to regard the leading ones most highly in love because of their work. The word "regard" here means to lead the mind through a reasoning process to a conclusion; hence, it is to think, consider, estimate, esteem, regard. The leading ones should regard themselves as slaves serving the saints. But the believers should regard them highly in love because of their work.

As Paul was writing this Epistle, one thought followed upon another. As we have pointed out, the subject of the preceding section (5:1-11) is watchfulness and soberness. The Christian life is a life of fighting for God's interests, and we need to be watchful and alert. Then Paul goes on to say that we must learn to respect, honor, the leading ones in the church. It seems that the matters of watchfulness and soberness and respecting the leading ones have no logical connection. However, they are related in a very practical way. If we are on the alert, full of watchfulness in spiritual warfare, we shall surely honor the leading ones. Those who have had experience in military service know that soldiers must respect their commanding officers. If they have no respect for the officers, the leaders, the army will not be able to fight properly. The first thing a soldier must learn in order to fight is to respect the one leading him. I believe that this was Paul's concept in turning to the matter of respecting the leading ones at this point.

TO BE AT PEACE

In verse 13 Paul gives this exhortation: "Be at peace among yourselves." To regard the leading ones and to be at peace with one another is a proper condition of a local church. But if the saints in a local church do not respect the leading ones, there will be no peace. The same principle applies to the family life. If the children do not respect their parents, how can there be peace? In such a situation it will be impossible for a family to have peace. In like manner, there will not be peace in an army if the soldiers have no respect for the officers.

The sequence of Paul's thoughts in these verses is significant. First, we need to be watchful and sober in fighting the spiritual warfare. Second, we must highly regard the leading ones. Then we shall be at peace among ourselves.

ADMONISHING, ENCOURAGING, UPHOLDING, AND BEING LONGSUFFERING

In verse 14 Paul continues, "And we entreat you, brothers, admonish the disorderly, console the fainthearted, uphold the weak, be longsuffering toward all." Those who are disorderly are idle or busybodies; they are not disciplined, but are unruled and rebellious. Acting on their own, they are disorderly and do not care for the proper order in the church life. According to verse 14, all the brothers, not only the leading ones, should admonish the disorderly. This means that all the saints must function to shepherd others and edify them.

In verse 14 Paul also encourages us to console the fainthearted. Literally, the Greek word for fainthearted is "of little soul." It refers to being narrow and weak in the capacity of mind, will, and emotion. Those who are little-souled have a very limited capacity to bear sufferings or difficulties. Among the saints there are some who are born with such a small soul. They need to be comforted, consoled.

In verse 14 Paul also encourages us to uphold the weak. The weak here probably refers to the weak ones in general, who are weak either in their spirit, soul, or body, or weak in faith (Rom. 14:1; 15:1). Some saints among us are weak. They may be weak in body or in spirit, weak in heart or in will. Some are weak in their faith or weak in praying. What shall we do with these weak ones? According to Paul's word, we need to uphold them.

In verse 14 Paul exhorts us to be longsuffering toward all. This implies that in a local church, besides some being disorderly who need admonishing, some being of little soul who need consolation, and some being weak who need upholding, all the members may be a problem in some way and need our longsuffering toward them.

Today we are still in the old creation, not in the New Jerusalem. This is the reason there are many problems among the saints. According to my experience, every one of us can be a problem to others. I may be a problem to you, and you may be a problem to me. On the one hand, we may love all the saints; on the other hand, they may cause us problems. Therefore, we need to be longsuffering toward all.

We should not dream that the church will be a utopia. On the contrary, the church life is full of problems. If a believer does not have any problems, it is not likely that he will come into the church life. Those who have no problems have no need for the church life. In a sense, the church is a hospital filled with those who are sick. For this reason, we need to be longsuffering toward all the saints.

Do not be bothered when others come to you with problems, even with problems that seem to be small and insignificant. In particular, those who are little-souled may come to you with minor problems. To such ones, even a hair is like a heavy weight. Instead of being angry at them for bringing such a small thing to you, help them to deal with their problems. However, an elder may be irritated by one who brings a little problem to him. Elders, learn to be longsuffering, especially toward the weak and those with a little soul. Any brother who expects to be an elder must be longsuffering. Paul's word in verse 14, however, is not limited to elders; it is a word for all the saints.

A number of times saints have come to me saying that they cannot tolerate the church life in their locality and want to move elsewhere. I told them that if they move to a different place, they will find the situation in the new place to be even worse. If they travel from place to place, eventually they will probably prefer the locality where they began. This is a common experience among church travelers. Instead of seeking to move to a different locality where you think the situation in the church will be better, remain where you are and be longsuffering toward all. Because no church is heavenly, free of problems, all the saints, and not only the elders, need longsuffering.

In verse 15 Paul goes on to say, "See that no one renders to anyone evil for evil, but always pursue what is good for one another and for all." This means that regardless of how others treat us, even if their treatment is evil, we should pursue good for them. If we do not have longsuffering, however, we shall render evil for evil.

REJOICING, PRAYING, AND GIVING THANKS

Verse 16 says, "Always rejoice." This exhortation is based upon the conditions mentioned in verses 14 and 15. Rejoicing includes calling on the name of the Lord. Can you rejoice in the Lord without calling on Him? I do not believe this to be possible. We simply cannot rejoice in the Lord without uttering His name. Hence, the name of the Lord is implied in Paul's charge to always rejoice. When we rejoice, therefore, we rejoice with the Lord's name.

In verse 17 Paul says, "Unceasingly pray." This is to have uninterrupted fellowship with God in our spirit. It requires perseverance (Rom. 12:12; Col. 4:2) with a strong spirit (Eph. 6:18).

In verse 18 Paul continues, "In everything give thanks; for this is the will of God in Christ Jesus for you." We should give thanks in everything because all things work together for our good that we may be transformed and conformed to the image of Christ (Rom. 8:28-29). The clause "for this is the will of God in Christ Jesus for you" modifies all the three preceding items. God wants us to live a rejoicing, praying, and thanking life. Such a life is a glory to God and a shame to His enemy.

The sequence in verses 16 through 18 is according to Paul's experience. Paul knew that first we rejoice, then pray, and then give thanks. If you try to practice these in the opposite order, you will find that Paul put them in the correct sequence according to experience. The will of God in Christ Jesus for us is that we rejoice, pray, and give thanks.

NOT QUENCHING THE SPIRIT

In verse 19 Paul goes on to say, "Do not quench the Spirit." The Spirit makes our spirit burning (Rom. 12:11) and our gifts flaming (2 Tim. 1:6). So we should not quench Him.

The Christian life is a life inspired and stirred up by the Spirit. Throughout the day we must have the Spirit inspiring us, stirring us, and moving and acting within us. Thus, instead of quenching the Spirit, we need to fan the flame that is within us. The word "quench" implies fire. The Spirit is burning within us. We should not quench this fire, but instead we should fan it into flame.

NOT DESPISING PROPHECIES

In verses 20 and 21 Paul says, "Do not despise prophecies; but prove all things; hold fast what is good." To despise here is to count as nothing, lightly esteem. The prophecies in verse 20 refer mainly to prophesying, to prophetic speech from a revelation. This does not need to be a prediction (see 1 Cor. 14:1, 3-4). To prophesy is to speak for the Lord and to speak forth the Lord. Only a small percentage of prophecy is related to prediction. We should not despise this kind of speaking. To prove all things includes to discern the prophecies (1 Cor. 14:29), to discern the spirits (1 Cor. 12:10), to test the spirits (1 John 4:1), to prove what is the will of God (Rom. 12:2), and to prove what is well-pleasing to the Lord (Eph. 5:10). On the one hand, we should not despise prophecies; on the other hand, we should not follow blindly. We need to prove things, to test them, and then hold fast what is good.

ABSTAINING FROM EVERY FORM OF EVIL

Verse 22 says, "Abstain from every form of evil." The King James Version of verse 22 says, "Abstain from all appearance of evil." Using this translation, a number of Bible teachers have misunderstood this verse, thinking that it tells us to avoid not only evil but even the appearance of evil, anything that may be suspected of being evil. In the past, we also were influenced by this understanding. But if we consider the meaning of the Greek word rendered "form," we shall have the proper understanding of this verse. Literally, the word is species, as subordinated to the genus; hence, kind. It denotes anything in view, anything in perception; hence, a sight. It does not refer to the appearance of evil, but the kind, the form, the shape, the sight, of evil. The believers who live a holy life in faith, love, and hope should abstain from evil in any form and of any kind.

LIFE-STUDY OF FIRST THESSALONIANS

MESSAGE NINETEEN

COOPERATION WITH THE DIVINE OPERATION

(2)

Scripture Reading: 1 Thes. 5:12-28

When Paul wrote verses 12 through 22 of chapter five, he had much on his heart that he still wanted to say to the new believers in Thessalonica. He had many things that he yet wanted to teach them. However, because he did not have the time to write further, he listed many different items together in these verses: honoring the leading ones, being at peace, admonishing the disorderly, consoling the fainthearted, upholding the weak, being longsuffering toward all, not rendering evil for evil, always rejoicing, praying unceasingly, giving thanks in everything, not quenching the Spirit, not despising prophecies, proving all things, holding fast what is good, abstaining from every form of evil. Actually, nearly every item requires a full chapter to be developed adequately.

COOPERATING WITH GOD

In verse 23 Paul goes on to say, "And the God of peace Himself sanctify you wholly, and may your spirit and soul and body be preserved complete, without blame, at the coming of our Lord Jesus Christ." "And" conjoins the blessing of God's sanctifying of our entire being, given in this verse, with the charge of our abstaining from every kind of evil, given in the preceding verse. On the one hand, we abstain from every form of evil; on the other hand, God sanctifies us wholly. We cooperate with God for a holy living.

According to verses 16 through 22, we should rejoice,

pray, give thanks, not quench the Spirit, not despise prophecies, prove all things, hold fast what is good, and abstain from every form of evil. If we take care of these things, the God of peace will sanctify us wholly. Here we see the matter of the believers' cooperation with the divine operation. In verses 12 through 22 we have the believers' cooperation in living a spiritual and separated life. In verses 23 and 24 we have God's operation in sanctifying and preserving the believers.

If we would live a holy life for the church life, we must cooperate with God's operation. God is now dwelling in us. The indwelling Triune God is operating within us all the time. This is the reason we should not quench the Spirit. Actually, the Spirit is the processed Triune God. The inward burning of the Spirit is the operation of the Triune God within us, an operation with which we need to cooperate. We cooperate by taking care of all the matters covered in verses 12 through 22. On our side, we need to cooperate. On God's side, God is operating within us. The God of peace Himself will sanctify us wholly. The Triune God indwells, and we are the ones indwelt by Him. Hence, there must be two sides: God's side and our side. He operates, and we cooperate with His operation.

In verse 23 Paul expresses his wish, his desire, that the God of peace would sanctify us wholly. Actually, this is the apostle's prayer. Paul prays that the God of peace Himself sanctify us wholly. We may also say that the first part of verse 23 is Paul's blessing, that he blesses the believers with a word concerning the God of peace sanctifying them.

In the second part of this verse Paul says, "May your spirit and soul and body be preserved complete." In the first part of the verse, concerning God's sanctifying us, it is God who takes the initiative. But in the second part of the verse, concerning our spirit, soul, and body being preserved, we are the ones who should somehow take the initiative.

BE PRESERVED

The command "be preserved" may be regarded as an

active-passive verb. This means that we take the initiative to be preserved. However, God is the One who preserves our spirit, soul, and body. Therefore, we take the initiative, but God does the work of preserving our entire being. Therefore, we should pray, "Lord, I long to have my spirit, soul, and body preserved. However, I cannot do this work. I take the initiative, Lord, to ask You to do this."

Do you have the desire, the aspiration, that your entire being would be preserved complete? If we do not have this desire, we should ask the Lord to have mercy on us and grant us such an aspiration. But if we already have this longing, we then need to take the initiative to pray that the Lord would preserve us.

Paul wrote verse 23 not according to doctrine, but according to his experience. It is difficult for us to say whether in this verse we have Paul's prayer or his blessing. It is certain that here we see Paul's desire, his wish. Paul desired that the God of peace would wholly sanctify the believers and that the believers would have an aspiration for their spirit, soul, and body to be preserved complete and without blame. Can you see in this verse God's operation and our cooperation? No doubt, the apostle represents God. Thus, Paul's wish is God's wish. His desire is God's desire. This means that God wishes, desires, to sanctify us wholly. But do we have the aspiration for our spirit, soul, and body to be preserved? The sanctifying work is God's operation, but the aspiration to be preserved is our cooperation. When we have both God's desire and our aspiration, we then have our cooperation with God's operation to sanctify us wholly and to preserve our entire being.

THE COMING OF THE LORD

In verse 23 Paul refers to "the coming of our Lord Jesus Christ." This is a further reminder of what Paul has written in chapter four. In verse 23 Paul seems to be saying, "Are you believers excited that the Lord Jesus will come back? Are you waiting for His coming? If you are excited and are waiting, you need to practice what I have just written concerning being sanctified and having your spirit, soul, and body preserved. If you do not practice this matter, you will not be ready for the Lord's coming back. You must be sanctified and preserved. Then you will be ready, prepared, qualified, for the coming back of the Lord Jesus. You must admit that at present you are not ready for the Lord's coming. This means that He must delay His coming until the believers are ready. Dear ones, I urge you to get ready for the Lord's coming by being sanctified wholly and by being preserved in your spirit, soul, and body complete and without blame."

SANCTIFIED WHOLLY

According to verse 23, the Sanctifier is the God of peace. His sanctification brings in peace. When we are wholly sanctified by Him from within, we have peace with Him in every way.

The word "sanctified" here means to be set apart; it is to be separated unto God from things common or profane.

The word "wholly" means entirely, thoroughly, to the consummation. God sanctifies us wholly, so that no part of our being, either of our spirit or soul or body, will be left common or profane.

Paul's word concerning our spirit and soul and body strongly indicates that man is of three parts: spirit, soul, and body. The spirit is our inmost part, the inner organ, possessing God-consciousness, that we may contact God (John 4:24; Rom. 1:9). The soul is our very self (Matt. 16:25; Luke 9:25), a medium between our spirit and our body, possessing self-consciousness, that we may have our personality. The body is our external part, the outer organ, possessing world-consciousness, that we may contact the material world. The body contains the soul, and the soul is the vessel of the spirit. In the spirit of the regenerated ones, God as the Spirit dwells; in the soul, our self; and in the body, the physical senses. God sanctifies us first by taking possession of our spirit through regeneration (John 3:5-6); second, by spreading Himself as the life-giving Spirit from our spirit into our soul to saturate and transform it (Rom. 12:2; 2 Cor. 3:18); and last, by enlivening our mortal body through our soul (Rom. 8:11, 13) and transfiguring it by His life power (Phil. 3:21).

God not only sanctifies us wholly, but also preserves our spirit, soul, and body complete. "Wholly" is quantitative: "complete" is qualitative. In quantity God sanctifies us wholly; in quality God preserves us complete, that is. He keeps our spirit, soul, and body perfect. Through the fall our body has been ruined, our soul has been contaminated, and our spirit has been deadened. In God's full salvation our entire being is saved and made complete and perfect. For this, God is preserving our spirit from any deadening element (Heb. 9:14), our soul from remaining natural and old (Matt. 16:24-26), and our body from the ruin of sin (1 Thes. 4:4; Rom. 6:6). Such a preservation by God and His thorough sanctification sustain us to live a holy life unto maturity that we may meet the Lord in His *parousia,* His presence.

In verse 24 Paul says, "Faithful is He who calls you, who also will do it." The faithful God who has called us will also sanctify us wholly and preserve our entire being complete. This is Paul's word of assurance to the believers.

THE CONCLUSION OF THE EPISTLE

In verses 25 through 28 we have the conclusion of this Epistle. Verse 25 says, "Brothers, pray concerning us." Is it not surprising that Paul would ask those who have been in the Lord less than a year to pray for him? Would you have asked such young believers to pray for you? Paul's request in this verse for prayer can be compared to a grandfather asking his young grandchild to pray for him. Nevertheless, Paul asked new believers, those who had been in the Lord for only a short time, to pray for the apostles. Paul knew that, no matter how little was their experience in prayer, it still would be helpful for them to pray. By this we see that we should not despise the new ones or the young ones. On the contrary, we should ask them to pray for us.

In verses 26 and 27 Paul says, "Greet all the brothers

with a holy kiss. I adjure you by the Lord that this letter be read to all the brothers." Some manuscripts insert the word "holy" before brothers. This would mean that since this Epistle is concerned with the holy life of the believers, the apostle in his concluding charge calls the believers holy brothers.

Paul's concluding word is this: "The grace of our Lord Jesus Christ be with you." Grace is God in the Son as our enjoyment. According to John 1:17, "The law was given through Moses; grace and reality came through Jesus Christ." The law makes demands on man according to what God is, but grace supplies man with what God is to meet what God demands. No man can partake of God through the law, but grace is the enjoyment of God for man. Thus, grace is God enjoyed by man.

In 1 Corinthians 15:10 we have a further word concerning grace. Here Paul says, "But by the grace of God I am what I am; and His grace unto me was not in vain, but I labored more abundantly than all of them, yet not I, but the grace of God with me." Grace in this verse is the resurrected Christ becoming the life-giving Spirit to bring the processed God in resurrection into us to be our life and life supply that we may live in resurrection. Therefore, grace is the Triune God becoming life and everything to us.

The grace that motivated Paul and operated in him was not a matter or a thing, but a living Person, the resurrected Christ, the embodiment of God the Father becoming the all-inclusive life-giving Spirit, who dwelt in Paul as his everything. It is only when we enjoy the Lord as grace that we can live a holy life for the church life, a life that is genuine and proper for the church by the Lord as the life supply.

LIFE-STUDY OF FIRST THESSALONIANS

MESSAGE TWENTY

OUR HEART TO BE ESTABLISHED BLAMELESS IN HOLINESS

(1)

Scripture Reading: 1 Thes. 3:6a, 10, 12-13; Prov. 4:23; Jer. 17:9; Psa. 73:1; 78:8; Ezek. 36:26; Matt. 5:8; 15:8, 18-19; 12:34-35; 22:37; Acts 28:27; 2 Cor. 3:15-16; Rom. 10:10; Heb. 4:12; 1 Tim. 1:5; 2 Tim. 2:22

In this message we shall consider what it means to have our heart established blameless in holiness. First Thessalonians 3:13 says, "That He may establish your hearts blameless in holiness before our God and Father at the coming of our Lord Jesus Christ with all His saints." Three important words here are heart, blameless, and holiness. What does it mean to have our heart established blameless? This certainly is an unusual expression. Of course, this establishing is not our work; it is the Lord's doing.

HOLINESS AND SANCTIFICATION

What is your understanding of the phrase "blameless in holiness"? The words "in holiness" do not qualify the verb "establish." Rather, they qualify the word "blameless." In this verse Paul is not saying that the Lord establishes our heart in holiness. Instead, he is saying that the Lord is making our heart blameless, and making it blameless in holiness. Thus, we need to find out what it means for our heart to be blameless in holiness.

Second Thessalonians 2:13 says, "But we ought to thank God always concerning you, brothers beloved by the Lord, because God chose you from the beginning unto salvation in sanctification of the Spirit and belief of the truth." This verse speaks of salvation in sanctification, and 1 Thessalonians 3:13, of being blameless in holiness. To be in holiness is different from being in sanctification. Of course, holiness and sanctification both refer to an element that is holy. However, holiness refers to the element itself, and sanctification refers to the process of being made holy, the process of being sanctified. A process is going on to make us holy; this process is sanctification. Therefore, to be in holiness is to be in the element, and to be in sanctification is to be in the process of being made holy.

God's salvation is in sanctification. This means that God's salvation involves a continuing process through which we are being made holy. As this process is taking place, we enjoy God's saving power. Holiness is the element of God's holy nature. It is in this element that we are to be blameless.

Once again I would like to take as an illustration the simple matter of making tea. Tea is an element, and "teaification" is the process of making tea. Suppose you have a cup of plain water. In order to tea-ify the water, you need to place a tea bag into it. When a tea bag is first put into water, the water may seem to remain the same. It seems to be little more than plain water. But after a period of time and some action of stirring, the water will become tea-ified; that is, tea is added to the water and mingled with it. Hence, we may say that the water is under the process of tea-ification. Eventually, the tea is in the water, and the water is in the tea. This means that the element of tea is mingled with the water. As a result of this tea-ification, the tea and water are blended together to make one beverage. Actually, this kind of drink is tea-water.

For the tea to be in the water is one thing, but for the water to pass through the process of tea-ification is another. In like manner, we need to be blameless in the element of holiness, and we also need to undergo the process of sanctification so that we may enjoy God's salvation daily and even hourly.

FAITH AND LOVE

If we have a bird's-eye view of 1 Thessalonians, we shall see that the first three chapters make up one section, and the last two chapters make up another. We have seen that this Epistle has a basic structure containing three elements: the work of faith, the labor of love, and the endurance of hope. Paul speaks of this in 1:3: "Remembering unceasingly your work of faith, and labor of love, and endurance of hope of our Lord Jesus Christ, before our God and Father." With this structure as a basis, Paul says in 1:9 and 10 that the believers turned from idols to serve a living and true God and to wait for His Son from the heavens. In chapter two we have the fostering of a holy life for the church life. This fostering is the work of a cherishing mother and exhorting father. The result of the proper fostering is that we walk worthily of God, who calls us into His own kingdom and glory (2:12). In order to have such a walk, we need to be perfected in our faith, and we need to increase and abound in our love. In chapter three Paul is deeply concerned about the Thessalonians' faith and love. According to 3:10, his desire was to perfect anything that was lacking in their faith. Yes, the Thessalonians had faith, yet it needed perfecting. Paul longed to see them in order to perfect what was lacking in their faith. In 3:12 he goes on to say, "And the Lord cause you to increase and abound in love to one another and to all, even as we also to you." As believers, we all need to be perfected in faith and to increase and abound in love.

In verse 13 of chapter three we see the specific reason we need to be perfected in faith and to increase and abound in love: it is that the Lord may establish our hearts blameless in holiness. The establishing of our heart is the issue, the result, of the perfecting of our faith and of the increase and abounding of our love. The Lord is doing a work of building. This building work is to establish our heart. Our heart needs to be built up, to be established blameless. Later we shall seek to explain what the word blameless in verse 13 means.

In 3:13 Paul says that the Lord will establish our hearts blameless in holiness. He does not say that our heart will be established blameless in purity or in cleanness. The New Testament emphasizes the matter of a pure heart. The Lord Jesus said, "Blessed are the pure in heart, for they shall see God" (Matt. 5:8). Paul exhorted Timothy to be with those who call on the Lord out of a pure heart (2 Tim. 2:22). Furthermore, in Psalm 51:10 David prayed that the Lord would create in him a clean heart. Why, then, does Paul not say blameless in purity or in cleanness, but instead says blameless in holiness? The reason is that the book of 1 Thessalonians is on a holy life for the church life. The conclusion of the first section of this Epistle, composed of chapters one, two, and three, is that the Lord will establish our heart blameless in holiness.

I believe that we all have faith, love, and hope. We have turned to God from idols, we are serving the living God, and we are waiting for the coming back of the Lord Jesus. Therefore, we have faith, love, and hope, and we have the turning, the serving, and the waiting. But we still need to be perfected in our faith. In 1 Thessalonians faith refers to our believing ability and also to what we believe. Faith, therefore, is a great matter. The aspect of objective faith, the things we believe in, is a vast field including many things. The messages we have put out over the years have covered different matters in this field of faith. These messages show us how much the Christian faith, Christian belief, comprises. It even includes the matter of the mingling of the Triune God with saved and regenerated human beings.

Through the preaching of Paul, the Thessalonians heard the gospel. This means that they heard the faith. Not only did the Thessalonians hear the faith—they received it. However, because Paul was with them such a short time, approximately three weeks, he could not have presented all the contents of the New Testament faith. No wonder he was eager to visit them and see them face to face in order to speak further to them concerning the faith and to perfect them in the faith. Like the Thessalonians, we also need to have our faith perfected.

The Thessalonians had faith and also had love. As believers in Christ, we also love one another. The divine love is without measure; it is immeasurable. Hence, we need to increase and abound in our love.

If we are perfected in our faith and if we increase and abound in our love, we shall have a living, a daily walk, that is worthy of God's calling. If we would have this kind of living, the Lord must set our heart on a fixed foundation. This is to establish, to build up, our heart.

A CHANGEABLE HEART

Instead of having an established heart, most Christians have a changeable, movable heart. We need a heart that is solidly established, not a heart that is changeable. According to our natural birth, however, our heart is changeable. The most changeable thing about us is our heart. For example, in the morning a brother may be very kind to his wife. But during breakfast he may become bothered by something and treat her in an unkind way. This is an illustration of the changeableness of our heart.

Our heart is changeable not only in relation to other people, but even in our relationship with the Lord. God is the unchanging One; He never changes. We are the ones who are changeable, and we are changeable in our heart. For this reason, Paul was concerned that the hearts of the new believers at Thessalonica would be set, built up, and established.

Verse 13 opens with the word "that." The Greek word here actually means "in order that"; that is, it indicates an issue, a result, of the foregoing verses, especially verses 6 through 12. We need to read verses 6 through 13 as a complete section. Then we shall see that verse 13 is a conclusion of what Paul covers in this section. In these verses Paul's concern is for the Thessalonians' faith and love. His desire is that their faith would be perfected and that their love would increase and abound in order that the Lord may establish their hearts.

Our heart still needs to be established. This is true both of the young and of the old. I know the experiences of young people. I also know that young people are changeable. I can recall my experience as a young person many years ago. Young people are not steadfast. Now as an elderly man I can speak concerning those who are old. Old people are not more steadfast than young people. Actually, there is no one who, according to his natural, human life, is steadfast in his heart. As human beings, we all are changeable. Simply because we grow older does not mean that there is a basic change in our nature. For example, a piece of glass may be very fragile. After fifty years, the glass will still be fragile. Age will not make it any stronger. The same is true in human life. Both the old and the young are changeable in heart. Therefore, I urge you, especially those who are not so young, not to have any confidence in your heart. Because our heart changes so easily, it is not at all trustworthy.

In my ministry I have met thousands of people. Throughout the years I have seen the changeableness of the human heart. Time after time I have seen someone have a change of heart. Because our heart is changeable, a crucial need in our Christian life is the establishing of our heart.

Although we need our heart to be established, we are not able to do this ourselves. Only the Lord can establish our heart. Therefore, we need Him to cause our heart to be solidly established and built up.

A BLAMELESS HEART

We have seen that according to verse 13 the Lord seeks to establish our hearts blameless. Do you know why our heart is blamable, worthy of blame? Our heart is blamable because it is changeable. If your heart is set, built up, and established upon a solid foundation, it will then become blameless. An unchanging heart is a blameless heart.

Sometimes we criticize others for being changeable when we ourselves are also changeable. For example, a brother may tell his daughter not to trust in a particular young man because he is fickle and changeable. As parents we may speak this way in order to protect our children. Also, in order to care for new believers, we may warn them not to trust certain people who are changeable. But how about ourselves? Are we not changeable? I must confess that in the natural life I am changeable. Further, most of the changes I am referring to are negative. Years ago I recorded certain things in my diary, for instance, a record of how I had dealt with a particular matter thoroughly before the Lord. But years later I dare not read what I have written, for even after writing such a record I experienced some change.

We need to realize and admit that our heart is changeable. Therefore, we need to receive the mercy and grace from the Lord that we may give Him the permission to establish our heart. He is waiting for our permission before He works within us to do the establishing. When our heart has been established, it will become blameless.

LIFE-STUDY OF FIRST THESSALONIANS

MESSAGE TWENTY-ONE

OUR HEART TO BE ESTABLISHED BLAMELESS IN HOLINESS

(2)

Scripture Reading: 1 Thes. 3:6a, 10, 12-13; Prov. 4:23; Jer. 17:9; Psa. 73:1; 78:8; Ezek. 36:26; Matt. 5:8; 15:8, 18-19; 12:34-35; 22:37; Acts 28:27; 2 Cor. 3:15-16; Rom. 10:10; Heb. 4:12; 1 Tim. 1:5; 2 Tim. 2:22

The Bible tells us that, as human beings, we have inward parts in addition to the outward members of our physical body. The inward parts are the parts of our inner being. According to the Bible, man is composed of spirit, soul, and body. The body, our physical being, is visible. This is our outer being. But the spirit and the soul, our inner being, are invisible. The soul includes the mind, the emotion, and the will. Along with all these inward parts of our being, the Bible also speaks of the heart and the conscience. We may say that the Bible is a book that deals with the genuine psychology, for it treats in a full way man's seven inward parts: the spirit, the soul, the heart, the mind, the will, the emotion, and the conscience. These inward parts are the components of our inward being.

THE POSITION OF THE HEART

At this point I would like to raise two questions. First, what is the position of the heart in our inner being? Second, what is the function of the heart? In our study of 1 Thessalonians it is important that we find the answer to these questions. In this basic book to new believers Paul tells them in chapter three that they need to be perfected in their faith, and they need their love to increase and abound so that the Lord may establish their hearts. Surely Paul's word concerning the heart in 3:13 indicates something crucial. Why does Paul not say that the Lord would establish their conscience, or that He would establish their mind, will, or emotion? It is very important that here Paul speaks of the Lord establishing the heart.

Throughout the years we have emphasized the spirit, and we have stressed the importance of turning to our spirit. Although we have given a number of messages on the heart, we have not emphasized the matter of the heart as much as we have emphasized the spirit. Now we would ask why in 3:13 Paul does not say that the Lord would establish our spirit or our soul, but our heart.

We know that our being is composed of three main parts—the spirit, the soul, and the body. But in 3:13, the end of the first section of 1 Thessalonians, Paul says, "That He may establish your hearts blameless in holiness before our God and Father at the coming of our Lord Jesus with all His saints." However, at the end of the second section, composed of chapters four and five, Paul says, "And the God of peace Himself sanctify you wholly, and may your spirit and soul and body be preserved complete, without blame, at the coming of our Lord Jesus Christ" (5:23). Why at the end of this Epistle does Paul mention nothing concerning the heart? What has become of it? What, then, is the relationship of the heart to the three main parts of our being? In order to answer this question, let us consider some verses that indicate the close relationship of the heart to the spirit and the soul.

Hebrews 4:12 says, "For the word of God is living and operative and sharper than any two-edged sword, and piercing even to the dividing of soul and spirit, both of joints and marrow, and able to discern the thoughts and intents of the heart." This verse speaks of the spirit, the soul, and the heart. Once the soul is divided from the spirit, we are able to discern the thoughts and intents of the heart. The thoughts, of course, are of the mind, and the intents are of the will. According to this verse, the mind and the will are related to the heart, since the thoughts and intents are of the heart. The heart, therefore, includes the mind for thinking and the will for making decisions. This verse indicates that the heart is very close to the soul and the spirit.

Psalm 78:8 says, "And might not be as their fathers, a stubborn and rebellious generation; a generation that set not their heart aright, and whose spirit was not steadfast with God." In this verse we see that when the forefathers of Israel were stubborn and rebellious, their heart was not set aright, and their spirit was not steadfast. The spirit is not steadfast whenever the heart is not set aright. This verse indicates how close the heart is to the spirit.

Matthew 5:3 speaks of the spirit, and 5:8, of the heart. Verse 3 says, "Blessed are the poor in spirit, for theirs is the kingdom of the heavens." Verse 8 says, "Blessed are the pure in heart, for they shall see God." From these verses we see that we need to be poor in spirit and pure in heart. All these verses indicate that our heart is very close to our spirit and also to our soul.

We have pointed out a number of times in the past that our heart is a composition of all the parts of our soul—the mind, the emotion, and the will—plus one part of our spirit, the conscience. Hence, the heart is a composition of all the parts of the soul and one part of the spirit. Our soul is our personality, our person, our self. The English word psychology is derived from *psuche,* the Greek word for soul. The soul is the base of all psychological matters. The psuche, the soul, is the "I"; it denotes our being as humans, that is, our personality. This is the reason that in the Bible the number of persons is often given as the number of souls. For example, we are told that seventy souls of the house of Jacob went down to Egypt (Exo. 1:5). This indicates that a person is a soul, for the soul is one's person.

As human beings, we have an outward organ, the body, to contact the physical, visible world. We also have an inward organ, the spirit, to contact God and the spiritual realm. The soul, located between these two organs, is our person, our self.

THE FUNCTION OF THE HEART

The soul is the person himself, but the heart is the person in action. This means that whenever you act, you act by your heart. Therefore, we may say that our heart is our representative in action. We have something in our inner being that represents us, and this representative is our heart. When a brother says to his wife, "Dear, I love you," this means that his heart loves her. Likewise, whenever we hate something, it is our heart that does the hating. Whenever we enjoy something or dislike something, it is our heart that enjoys or dislikes. Thus, our heart is our representative, the acting commissioner or ambassador, of our inner being.

Because the heart is our representative, Solomon says in Proverbs 4:23, "Keep thy heart with all diligence; for out of it are the issues of life." To keep our heart is actually to guard it. The Hebrew word rendered "keep" means guard. We should guard our heart above all because out of it are the issues of life. "Issues" here implies sources and springs as well as issues. Thus, the heart is related to the sources of life, the springs of life, and the issues of life. First we have the source, then the spring, and then the issue.

Out of the heart come all the issues of our daily life. As human beings, we have life, and this life acts through our heart. Using the illustration of electricity and a switch, we may say that the heart is the switch of our inner being, of our human life. As the flow of electricity depends on the switch, so our daily living is dependent on what our heart switches on and off. Our heart is the switch of our human life, of our daily life, of our being. The word "life" in Proverbs 4:23 implies an organic element, the element of life; it also implies our daily living and activities, in fact, our entire human life. Hence, the word life in this verse is inclusive. As human beings, we have a human life, and this human life has an organic element and also a daily living. The switch of this life is the heart.

Suppose as a brother is studying the Bible he is disturbed by the barking of a dog. Bothered by this sound, he shouts at the dog. The thought and intent of shouting at the dog has its source in his heart. It also springs from the heart and issues from it. As he is reading the Bible and is disturbed by the dog's barking, something within this brother's heart motivates him to shout at the dog. This shouting is an issue that springs out from the source of the heart. This is an illustration of the heart as the acting representative of our entire being.

The activities and movements of our physical body depend on our physical heart. In like manner, our daily living depends on our psychological heart. The way we act and behave depends on the kind of heart we have.

A RENEWED HEART

Because we are fallen and sinful, our psychological heart is corrupt and deceitful. According to Jeremiah 17:9, our heart is deceitful above all things and desperately wicked. A better translation of the Hebrew would say "incurable" instead of desperately wicked. Our heart is corrupt, rotten, to such an extent that it is incurable. This is the condition of the psychological heart of all descendants of Adam.

Turning to God

But God in His salvation promises to give us a new heart. Ezekiel 36:26 says, "A new heart also will I give you, and a new spirit will I put within you: and I will take away the stony heart out of your flesh, and I will give you a heart of flesh." The new heart in this verse does not refer to another heart; it refers to a renewed heart. The first characteristic of this renewed heart is that it turns to God. The turning of our heart to God is a very healthy sign that He has renewed it. A corrupt heart is always away from God. If our heart is away from Him, that is an indication that our heart is still corrupt. Some may ask how they can know if their heart has been renewed. The sign of a renewed heart is that it turns toward God. The sign of a corrupt heart is that it turns away from Him. Therefore, we can know if our heart has been renewed by whether it is turned to God or away from Him.

In God's salvation the renewing of the heart is once for all. However, in our experience our heart is renewed continually because it is changeable. Perhaps when you were saved, your heart turned to God in a very strong way. But after a period of time, your heart may turn away from Him somewhat. To a certain extent at least, your heart may turn away. Then by God's mercy your heart may turn fully to Him once again. Through fellowship with a saint, through coming to the meetings, or by some other gracious means, your heart may turn to the Lord once again. When your heart was turned away from Him, it became somewhat corrupt. But when your heart came back to the Lord, it was renewed. We need to say, "Lord, I thank You that in Your mercy You have visited my heart and turned it back to You." This turning to the Lord is the first characteristic of a renewed heart.

Seeking Purity

The second characteristic of a renewed heart is that it seeks purity. First Timothy 1:5 speaks of love out of a pure heart. In 2 Timothy 2:22 Paul encourages Timothy to be "with those who call on the Lord out of a pure heart." What does it mean for the heart to seek purity? According to the Bible, to have a pure heart is to have a heart with a single motive. Purity, therefore, is a matter of motive. If we do something with a double motive, our heart is not pure. Whatever we do must be with a single purpose, a single motive, for God Himself. We should not have any other purpose. We love God, and because we love Him we do certain things for Him without any other motive. If this is our situation, then our heart is pure.

In Matthew 5:8 the Lord Jesus tells us, "Blessed are the pure in heart, for they shall see God." To be pure in heart is to be single in purpose, to have the single goal of accomplishing God's will for God's glory. According to this verse, those who are pure in heart shall see God. In order to see something clearly, we need to focus on it. This is to be pure in our seeing. In like manner, to be pure in heart is to have a single aim. Our goal, our aim, should be God Himself, and we should not have any other motive.

If you read all the verses in the Bible concerning the heart, you will see that these two characteristics of a renewed heart—turning to the Lord and being pure—are the basic matters in the Bible with respect to the heart. If we turn to God and seek purity, we shall have the proper way to "switch on" our heart toward God. By turning our heart to Him and by being pure in our motive toward Him, the switch of our heart will be turned on and the divine electricity will flow within us. Otherwise, the switch of the heart will be turned off, and God will be cut off in a practical way from our daily living. Then evil things will come out of our heart. It is the source, the spring, and the issue of all manner of evil things. According to Matthew 12:34 and 35, both good and evil things may flow out of our heart: "For out of the abundance of the heart the mouth speaks. The good man out of the good treasure brings forth good things, and the evil man out of the evil treasure brings forth evil things." Furthermore, in Matthew 15:8 the Lord speaks of those whose heart is far away from God. Then in verses 18 and 19 He goes on to say, "But the things which go out of the mouth come out of the heart, and those defile the man. For out of the heart come evil thoughts, murders, adulteries, fornications, thefts, false witnessings, blasphemies." From these verses we see that out of the heart flow the springs of human life.

Turning to God and being pure toward God are the two matters that govern our heart. Psalm 73:1 speaks of a clean heart: "Truly God is good to Israel, even to such as are of a clean heart." We have already pointed out how both the Lord Jesus and Paul stressed the importance of a pure heart. We need a heart turned to God and a heart that is pure toward Him.

A HEART ESTABLISHED BLAMELESS IN HOLINESS

Now we are ready to see what it means for our heart to be established blameless in holiness. Not only should our heart turn to God and be pure, but it also needs the element of holiness added to it. To be holy is to be separated unto God and fully occupied by Him and saturated with Him. For our heart to be holy means that it is separated unto Him, occupied by Him, possessed by Him, and saturated with Him.

Once again we may use the illustration of making tea. Suppose you have a cup of plain water. This water does not contain any tea. But when the element of tea is added to the water, the water is tea-ified. The water is separated unto the tea, it is possessed and occupied by the tea, and it is even saturated with the tea. As a result, it becomes tea-ified water. After the water has been fully tea-ified, it is in a state of tea-ification, a state of having been tea-ified. This illustrates what it means for our heart to be established blameless in holiness.

One version of 3:13 says "in the state of being holy." The word holiness indicates a state; it does not indicate a process. A process would be indicated by the word sanctification. Therefore, it is correct to speak of holiness here as the state of being made holy.

When we were away from the Lord, our heart also was turned away from Him. Instead of being occupied by the Lord, our heart was occupied by many other things. Furthermore, our heart certainly was not saturated with the Lord. Thus, our heart was away from the Lord, it was not occupied by the Lord, and it was not saturated with the Lord. However, we can praise the Lord that, through His mercy and grace, we are now on the way to being separated fully unto the Lord, to being occupied wholly by Him, and to being saturated thoroughly with Him. When this process has been completed, our heart will be in the state of being holy, in the state of holiness.

For our heart to be established blameless in holiness includes much more than simply for our heart to turn to the Lord and to be pure toward the Lord. This is to have our turned and pure heart separated unto the Lord, occupied by the Lord, and saturated with the Lord. Such a heart not only has turned to the Lord but it also has a pure motive. It is separated unto Him, fully occupied by Him, and thoroughly saturated with Him. It is here in such a state that our heart will be established. Once our heart has been established, it will be set, and it will be no longer movable or changeable. Furthermore, when our heart is in such a condition, it will become blameless.

To be blameless is not the same as to be perfect. When something is perfect, it is without blemish or defect. This goes beyond blamelessness. In other words, to be without blame is not as good as to be without blemish. In 3:13 Paul does not require perfection. Rather, he requires only that our heart be blameless. The way for our heart to be blameless is for it to be established by the Lord. If our heart is established by Him, we shall be those whose heart has been separated unto the Lord, occupied by Him, and saturated with Him. Then our heart will be set, established, built up, in holiness. Here, in this state of holiness, the state of being made holy, our heart will become blameless.

LIFE-STUDY OF FIRST THESSALONIANS

MESSAGE TWENTY-TWO

OUR HEART TO BE ESTABLISHED BLAMELESS IN HOLINESS AND OUR BODY TO BE PRESERVED CLEAN IN SANCTIFICATION

Scripture Reading: 1 Thes. 3:13; 4:3-8; Heb. 12:14; Rom. 12:1-2; Eph. 3:17-19; Mark 12:30; Phil. 2:5

In reading the Scriptures we need to touch the burden in the spirit of the writer. In particular, we need to know the burden in Paul's spirit when he was writing 1 Thessalonians. Paul concludes chapter three of 1 Thessalonians with a word of blessing: "That He may establish your hearts blameless in holiness before our God and Father at the coming of our Lord Jesus with all His saints" (v. 13). Paul's desire was that the readers of this Epistle would be established in their hearts blameless in holiness.

In chapter four Paul goes on to charge the saints to abstain from the defiling sin of fornication: "For this is the will of God, your sanctification; that you abstain from fornication." In what way does Paul charge the saints to abstain from this sin? He charges them in the way of sanctification. First he tells them that the will of God is our sanctification. The will of God is that we would be sanctified, kept, preserved, and guarded in sanctification. The best way to abstain from fornication is to be sanctified, preserved, in God's holiness.

In 4:3, 4, and 7 Paul uses the word "sanctification" three times. In verse 3 he says that the will of God is our sanctification; in verse 4, that we should know how to possess our vessel, our body, in sanctification and honor; and in verse 7, that God has called us in sanctification. According to 4:4, we should possess our body in sanctification and honor. Sanctification is before God, and honor is before man. Every fornicator loses his honor before man. In every society fornicators are despised; they have lost their honor before man. Therefore, we need to keep our body from such a sin, and the way to do so is in sanctification.

OUR RESPONSIBILITY IN BEING SANCTIFIED

In 5:23 Paul gives a concluding word concerning sanctification: "And the God of peace Himself sanctify you wholly, and may your spirit and soul and body be preserved complete, without blame, at the coming of our Lord Jesus Christ." Here we see that our entire being—spirit, soul, and body—needs to be sanctified. We need to be sanctified by the God of peace not only in our soul and body, but also in our spirit.

According to 5:23, we bear some responsibility for being wholly sanctified. On the one hand, God will sanctify us wholly. On the other hand, our spirit, soul, and body need to be preserved. Although God preserves us, we need to bear a certain amount of responsibility to be preserved.

We may regard the words "be preserved" as an active-passive verb. This means that although we are being preserved, we need to take the responsibility, the initiative, to be preserved. Thus, "be" implies something active, and "preserved" implies something passive.

God intends to preserve us, but are we willing to be preserved? We may use the matter of giving medicine to children as an illustration of our need to bear responsibility to be preserved. Sometimes a child may need medicine, but he may not be willing to take it. In fact, he may resist the attempt of his parents to give it to him and even make it necessary for them to hold him down. Parents do this in order that the health of the child may be preserved. Sometimes we do not cooperate with the Lord to be preserved. This forces Him to do certain things to subdue us or restrict us so that we may take in what is necessary to be sanctified and preserved.

In 1 Thessalonians, a book on a holy life for the church life, we are told that different parts of our being need to be preserved. Our heart needs to be sanctified, our body needs to be preserved in sanctification, and eventually even our spirit, the most hidden part of our being, also needs to be sanctified.

OUR ACTING AGENT

In the foregoing message we pointed out that our heart is our acting representative. Now I would like to make this matter a little more clear. Perhaps the term "acting agent" is better than representative. Every one of us is a being, a human being. The word "being" is a modern expression. The biblical term for a human being is "soul." This means that each one of us is a soul. The soul, as a being, has two organs: the inward organ, the spirit, and the outward organ, the body. We contact the physical world through the five senses of our body. Likewise, through the spirit, an organ which has senses of its own, we contact God.

Whether or not we are able to contact a certain thing depends upon the organ we use. For example, if you close your eyes, you will not be able to see anything. However, you cannot use your eyes to substantiate sound. For this, you must use your ears. Because atheists do not exercise their spirit, they say there is no God. We cannot substantiate God unless we use our spirit. John 4:24 tells us that God is Spirit and that those who worship Him must worship Him in spirit. If we exercise our spirit, we shall immediately sense that there truly is a God. Deep within, an atheist may say to himself, "Suppose there is a God after all—what will you do?" With the mouth an atheist may say that there is no God, but in the depths of his being, in his spirit, he may sense that there is a God.

ACTIVE IN HEART

Our soul must act. When our soul, our being, acts, that is the heart. But when we keep ourselves at a standstill, this means that our heart does not act.

We all have two hearts: a physical heart and a psychological heart. We know where our physical heart is located, but we do not know the location of our psychological heart. The actions or activities of our physical body depend on the beating of our physical heart. According to medical doctors, the death of the physical body takes place when the heart stops beating. A person who does not have any pulse is dead, for his heart has stopped beating. The point of this illustration is that the death of the body takes place when the heart stops beating. This is also true of the psychological heart.

Both our physical heart and our psychological heart have arteries. The main arteries of the psychological heart are the mind, emotion, and will. Heart attacks are often due to the blockage of the arteries. Recently I read that doctors who examined the bodies of young men who died in the Vietnam War discovered that in many cases their arteries were blocked even though they were quite young. Realizing the danger of blocked arteries, many watch their diet and are careful to exercise in order to cleanse their blood vessels. The problem of the physical heart is an illustration of the problem of the psychological heart. Today there are millions of Christians. But how many of these Christians are truly living? Most of them are not living. The reason they are not living is that the arteries of their psychological heart have been blocked. This blockage has caused them to die spiritually.

We all need to ask ourselves if we are spiritually healthy. To be healthy physically we need a strong heart. We also need a strong heart if we are to be spiritually healthy. All spiritual diseases are of the psychological heart. Our psychological heart may be wrong in different ways. We may be wrong in our thinking, in our loving or hating, or in the way we use our will.

If our psychological heart is healthy, it will be very active in thinking, loving, hating, and deciding. Our heart is our acting agent. This means that if we are active, our heart will be active in mind, emotion, and will. However, if a person is not active in his heart, we may wonder if he is spiritually alive. If he is alive, why is there no activity in his heart?

Why does his heart not function in a normal way, since it is his acting agent?

I can testify that, even though I am elderly, I am very active in my heart. I am full of thought, feeling, and intention. My entire being—spirit, soul, and body—is active. However, the agent of this activity is not the spirit, the soul, or the body; the acting agent is the heart with the three main arteries of mind, emotion, and will.

A RENEWED MIND

In Romans 12:2 Paul speaks of the renewing of the mind. As the body represents our outward being, so the mind represents our inward being. According to Romans 12:1, our body needs to be presented to God as a sacrifice, and our mind needs to be renewed. To be renewed is to be saturated with God. This is sanctification. To be renewed actually is to be sanctified, and to be sanctified is to be transformed. Our mind needs to be renewed, sanctified, transformed.

AN EMOTION TOUCHED WITH THE LOVE OF CHRIST

In Ephesians 3:17 Paul says, "That Christ may make His home in your hearts through faith, that you, having been rooted and grounded in love." Love is a matter of the emotion. According to this verse, Christ makes His home in our hearts, and we ourselves become rooted and grounded in His love. This indicates that our emotion is touched by His love and that we grow in this love. To have our emotion filled with the love of Christ surely is an aspect of sanctification. Furthermore, when we are rooted and grounded in love, we can "know the knowledge-surpassing love of Christ" (Eph. 3:19). This is also related to the sanctification of our heart, in particular of the emotion. To have our emotion filled with the love of Christ is to be saturated with Christ. No doubt, this is the sanctification of our emotion.

LOVING THE LORD WITH OUR WHOLE BEING

Mark 12:30 says, "And thou shalt love the Lord thy God with all thy heart, and with all thy soul, and with all thy mind, and with all thy strength." Here we have the heart, the soul, and the mind, with the soul mentioned in between the heart and the mind. The three parts of the soul—the mind, the emotion, and the will—are also parts of the heart. But why in Mark 12:30 is there no mention of the emotion or the will? The reason is that the emotion and the will are included in the soul. But why, then, is the mind mentioned? The mind is mentioned because it is the leading part of both the heart and the soul. Therefore, we need to love the Lord our God with all our heart, with all our soul, and with all our mind.

Mark 12:30 also tells us to love the Lord with all our strength. The word "strength" here refers to our physical body. Therefore, we need to love the Lord with all our physical strength and with all our heart, soul, and mind. This indicates that our entire being, our inner being and our outer being, should be occupied with the Lord our God and saturated with Him. This is to be sanctified, made holy.

THE SPIRIT AND THE HEART

I am burdened to point out that, as Christians, believers in Christ, we must be living. To be a living believer involves both our spirit and our heart. Doctrinally, we may say that we can become living by exercising our spirit. But in practice often it seems that the exercise of our spirit does not work. Many of us can testify that we have exercised our spirit, but still this did not always work to make us living. The reason the exercise of the spirit may not work is that the heart does not act. This means that there is something wrong in the heart. Perhaps the mind is not renewed, sanctified, transformed; it may not be saturated with the Lord and occupied by Him. Instead, it may be filled with worldly things. We may exercise our spirit and say, "Praise the Lord!" However, this exercise may not work to make us living. The exercise of the spirit works only when our heart is active.

If our heart is dormant or asleep, exercising our spirit to call on the name of the Lord will not be effective. This exercise cannot work if our acting agent, our heart, is dormant.

This is the reason we need to deal thoroughly with our heart. This dealing must include our mind, emotion, and will. Our mind must be the mind of Christ, our emotion must be saturated with the love of Christ, and our will must be one with His will. If this is the condition of our heart, our heart will be active and functioning. Then if we call on the Lord when our heart is active, this calling will be very effective.

We all need to look to the Lord to have mercy on us. We need to pray, "Lord, have mercy on me. I want to have my mind renewed. I want to have my emotion filled with Your love. I want to have a will that is truly one with Your will." If we have such a heart, then the heart as our acting agent will be established blameless in holiness, blameless in the state of being made holy.

POSSESSING OUR BODY IN SANCTIFICATION AND HONOR

As Paul was writing chapter three of 1 Thessalonians, he must have had the intention to go from the inner being, the heart, to the outer being, the body. This is the reason he gives the charge concerning abstaining from fornication and concerning possessing our body in sanctification and honor.

Fornication is a gross sin. According to the Bible, Satan's purpose is to use sin to defile the man God created for Himself. Any kind of vessel is defiled when it becomes dirty. Furthermore, the function of a dirty and defiled vessel is annulled. For example, we do not use a cup that is dirty. Before a dirty cup can be used, it must first be cleansed. God created man as a pure vessel, but Satan injected sin into man with the intention of defiling him and spoiling him. The most defiling sin is fornication. Stealing is sinful and unclean, but it is not as defiling as fornication. Fornication damages God's purpose, it damages the human body, and it damages the family and society. Nothing else damages humanity as seriously as fornication does. Therefore, after speaking concerning the sanctification of the heart, the inward being, Paul could not forget to speak concerning the outward being.

Fornication always comes from a changing heart, a heart that has not been established. If your heart has been established, it will be difficult for Satan to seduce you to commit fornication. But it is easy for those who are changeable and fickle to fall into the snare of fornication.

As Paul was writing chapter three, he probably had the thought of going on to write concerning the believers' outward being. He may have said to himself, "Paul, you are speaking concerning the inward being. Faith is a matter of the heart, and love is a matter of the emotion. Both are related to the inward being. But what about the body outwardly?" Paul was an excellent writer. When he writes about a matter, he writes about it to the uttermost. Thus, when he comes to the matter of outward sanctification, he deals with the most defiling sin, the sin of fornication.

Stay away from fornication. If you become involved in fornication, you will open the door wide to all kinds of corruption. Believers and unbelievers have been damaged by the gross sin of fornication. Therefore, Paul commands the believers to abstain from fornication. He tells them that sanctification is God's will. Because God's will is to keep us always in sanctification, we should abstain from everything that is unclean so that the body may be preserved.

At this point I would like to say a word to the young people. As Christians, we may need to read the newspapers to know the world situation. I read a newspaper nearly every day, but certain pages I would never read, for they are defiling. Once your mind has been defiled by looking at a certain picture, it will be very difficult for you to remove this defiling element. Furthermore, we should not listen to certain kinds of conversations or touch things that are unclean. But most important we should abstain from fornication. We must keep, preserve, safeguard, our vessel clean in sanctification before God. It must be holy, separated, and saturated with God and also kept in honor before man.

Man was created by God with honor, for man was made in God's image. Therefore, we are to express God and represent Him. We have been assigned a most honorable position. Marriage is a holy and honorable matter, and it is for the fulfillment of God's purpose. This is the reason the Bible tells us to honor marriage. But fornication destroys mankind and causes the one who falls into it to lose his honor. Therefore, we must preserve our body clean in sanctification and honor.

A HOLY LIFE FOR THE CHURCH LIFE

I believe we have touched the burden in Paul's spirit as he was writing chapters three and four of 1 Thessalonians. First he dealt with the inward being represented by the heart and then with the outward being represented by the body. Inwardly, our heart must be established in holiness; outwardly, our body must be preserved in sanctification and honor. This is to have a holy life, and this holy life is for the church life. If we have a heart established blameless in holiness and a body preserved clean in sanctification and honor, then, in a practical way, we shall have a holy life for the church life.

LIFE-STUDY OF FIRST THESSALONIANS

MESSAGE TWENTY-THREE

TO BE SANCTIFIED WHOLLY WITH OUR SPIRIT, SOUL, AND BODY PRESERVED COMPLETE

(1)

Scripture Reading: 1 Thes. 4:9, 13; 5:8, 16-24; 2 Cor. 7:1; 1 John 1:6; 1 Tim. 1:5; Rom. 6:6, 19; 7:24; 8:10-11; 12:1; 1 Cor. 6:13b, 15a, 19-20

A BRIEF SURVEY

In 5:23 Paul says, "And the God of peace Himself sanctify you wholly, and may your spirit and soul and body be preserved complete, without blame, at the coming of our Lord Jesus Christ." In order to understand this verse, we need to have a brief review of the entire book of 1 Thessalonians. Chapter one indicates that the holy life for the church life is constructed of faith, love, and hope. Such a life surely turns to God from idols, serves the living God, and waits for the coming of the Lord. This is the main point revealed in chapter one. Chapter two tells us that the apostles did their best as nursing mothers and exhorting fathers to foster such a life. They cared for this life and nourished it so that it would result in a walk worthy of God's kingdom and glory.

How can such a life become worthy of God's kingdom and God's glory? There is no way other than to be sanctified. Thus, chapter three says that this life needs to be perfected in faith and also needs to increase and abound in love in order that the Lord may establish our hearts, the acting agent of our being, blameless in holiness. This is the establishment of our inward being, of our heart, our acting agent.

In chapter four Paul goes on to point out that not only should our heart inwardly be established in holiness, but also that our body outwardly needs to be preserved in sanctification, the process of being made holy. Furthermore, the physical body needs to be preserved not only in sanctification before God, but also in honor in the sight of man. In this chapter Paul also speaks concerning the saints who have died, who are sleeping. He deals with this matter in the scope of hope. In chapter three Paul says that the holy life for the church life should be perfected in faith and should increase and abound in love, and then in chapter four he shows that the resurrection of the dead saints is a matter of hope.

In 5:8 Paul covers the three matters of faith, love, and hope: "But we who are of the day, let us be sober, putting on the breastplate of faith and love, and a helmet, the hope of salvation." In warfare two crucial parts of our body—the head and the breast—need to be guarded. The breast must be covered, and the head must be protected. Hence, we have the breastplate of faith and love to cover our breast, and the helmet of the hope of salvation to cover our head. In our study of the Song of Songs we pointed out that the breasts of the seeking one signify faith and love in Christ. For this reason, the breastplate is of both faith and love. Our head, our mind, the thinking organ with its thoughts, needs to be protected by the helmet of God's salvation. Therefore, in chapter five we see that when we are fighting the spiritual warfare, we need to be covered by the armor of God that includes the breastplate of faith and love and the helmet of the hope of salvation. In chapter five the three basic elements of the Christian life—faith, love, and hope—are all included.

Eventually, in 5:23, Paul expressed his desire that the God of peace would sanctify us wholly, not only in heart or in body. Inwardly we have a heart, and outwardly we have a body. The heart and the body form the main structure of a living, acting person.

As living persons, we have a heart within and a body without. The heart is the directing agent, for it directs our actions, activities, and motions. The body is the means, the organ, by which we act outwardly. Hence, through our body our heart moves, and our body acts under the direction of our heart. This is the reason chapter three deals with the sanctification of the heart and chapter four, with the sanctification of the body.

What, then, about our spirit and our soul? Even though the soul is very much like the heart in its components, there is still a difference between the soul and the heart. As far as the composition of our being is concerned, we have a spirit, a soul, and a body. But in our acting, our living, we have a heart and a body. Thus, when speaking of our being, we should refer to the spirit, the soul, and the body. But in speaking of our living and our actions, we should refer to the heart and the body. Our daily living is a matter of our heart and our body. For this reason Paul in 1 Thessalonians differentiates what we are from how we act. In action, we have a heart with a body. But in our being, that is, with respect to what we are, we have a spirit, a soul, and a body.

In chapter three of 1 Thessalonians sanctification is a matter of our inner part, our heart. In chapter four sanctification is a matter of our outward part, our body. Then in chapter five, as a conclusion of the book, sanctification includes our entire being. This is the reason Paul speaks of the God of peace sanctifying us wholly. By "wholly" Paul means our whole spirit and soul and body. Therefore, he expresses the desire that the saints' spirit and soul and body would be preserved complete. This is to be sanctified wholly.

The adverb "wholly" in 5:23 indicates quantity. It points to the fact that every part of our being—spirit, soul, and body—needs to be sanctified and preserved. Furthermore, the adjective "complete" refers to quality. Thus, Paul, an excellent writer, indicates in a brief way that quantitatively we need to be sanctified wholly, and qualitatively we need to be preserved complete. We need to be preserved not partially or superficially but completely, even absolutely and perfectly. I hope that this brief survey of 1 Thessalonians will help you to understand what we shall cover in this message and in the message following.

A TRIPARTITE BEING

God certainly aspires to sanctify us wholly. He wants to preserve us in the three parts of our being—to preserve our spirit, our soul, and our body. According to 5:23, we are tripartite beings; that is, we have three parts: spirit, soul, and body.

When I was a young Christian, I learned the truth concerning man's tripartite being, and I contended for this truth. In theology this is known as trichotomy. There is also the school of dichotomy, which teaches that man is of two parts, body and soul. First Thessalonians 5:23 proves strongly that the school of dichotomy is not correct. In this verse there is a conjunction between the words spirit and soul and also between the words soul and body. This indicates that the spirit, the soul, and the body are different and distinct. Nevertheless, some teachers of the Bible claim that the words spirit and soul are synonyms. This can be compared to saying that the different members of our physical body, for example, the stomach and the liver, are the same. It is a very serious misunderstanding to claim that the soul and the spirit are synonymous.

Years ago, a missionary who believed in dichotomy came to Hong Kong to attend a conference I was holding there. After one of the meetings, he asked for a time to have fellowship with me. He told me that the conference was wonderful. Then he went on to say, "You teach that man is of three parts. I don't believe this. Man has just two parts—the visible part and the invisible part." I replied, "Brother, to say that man is of three parts is not my teaching; it is the teaching in the Bible. What would you say about 1 Thessalonians 5:23? In this verse Paul speaks of the spirit and the soul and the body, three nouns with two conjunctions. How can you say that man is of only two parts?" He answered, "I know this verse, but I don't believe that the spirit and the soul are two different things." Then I said to him, "Brother, this means that you don't believe the Bible." He then claimed that he believed the Bible to the uttermost and that no matter what I would say, he would continue to believe that the spirit and the soul are synonyms. At that point I said, "If you think that the spirit and the soul are synonymous, this is like saying that the nose and the mouth are the same. If you want to believe this, I won't argue with you. But to me, the mouth is the mouth, and the nose is the nose. Do you say things with your nose, or do you smell things with your mouth?"

I relate this incident to point out that there is a big difference between the spirit and the soul. The spirit and the soul are not synonymous. Rather, the spirit is the spirit, and the soul is the soul. Just as the nose and the mouth are different organs with different functions, so the spirit and the soul are different organs and have different functions. First Thessalonians 5:23 speaks of the spirit and the soul and the body. This indicates clearly that we are of three parts.

It is easy to understand what it means for the body to be preserved. In chapter four Paul commands the believers to abstain from fornication. To abstain from fornication is to preserve our body in sanctification. But what does it mean to preserve our soul and our spirit? We need to be able to explain in a practical way how to preserve our spirit and our soul.

A SHORTCOMING IN READING THE BIBLE

We Christians have a shortcoming in the way we read the Bible. This shortcoming is that we take things for granted and assume we understand them. For example, in reading 5:23 we may say, "Oh, I know what 1 Thessalonians 5:23 says. It tells us that our spirit and soul and body should be preserved complete. From this verse we know that we should not believe in dichotomy, that man is of only two parts, but should believe in trichotomy, that man is of three parts. I, therefore, believe that man is of three parts." This is good, but it is not adequate, because it does not render much help in a practical way. Instead of taking this verse for granted, we need to seek to understand how to preserve our spirit and our soul.

Can you give me the name of a Christian book that explains how to preserve our spirit and our soul? I do not know of any Christian writing that speaks concerning this matter. I believe that if there were such a writing, we would have learned of it during the course of the last fifty years. As we have pointed out, some Bible teachers do not believe that our spirit and soul are different parts. How could they tell us how to preserve our spirit and our soul? Therefore, my burden in this message is related to the preserving of the spirit and the soul.

SANCTIFIED AND PRESERVED

God not only sanctifies us wholly, but also preserves our spirit, soul, and body complete. "Wholly" is quantitative; "complete" is qualitative. In quantity God sanctifies us wholly; in quality God preserves us complete; that is, He keeps our spirit, soul, and body perfect. Through the fall our body has been ruined, our soul has been contaminated, and our spirit has been deadened. In God's full salvation, our entire being is saved and made complete and perfect. For this, God is preserving our spirit from any deadening element (Heb. 9:14), our soul from remaining natural and old (Matt. 16:24-26), and our body from the ruin of sin (1 Thes. 4:4; Rom. 6:6). Such a preservation by God and His thorough sanctification sustain us to live a holy life unto maturity that we may meet the Lord in His *parousia*.

EXERCISING OUR SPIRIT TO CONTACT GOD

Our spirit is composed of three parts: the conscience, the fellowship, and the intuition. Our spirit is mainly for us to have fellowship with God. When we have fellowship with God, we contact Him. This contact with God spontaneously gives us a sense of God, a consciousness of God. Intuition denotes the direct sense and consciousness that come from God. Through this intuition we can know whether we are right or wrong. If we are wrong, we shall be condemned by our conscience. But if we are right, we shall be justified by our conscience. Our conscience, therefore, either accuses and condemns or excuses and justifies. The way to preserve our spirit is first to exercise it to have fellowship with God. If we fail to exercise our spirit in this way, we shall leave it in a deadened situation.

Whenever we Christians come together in a church meeting, we need to function. We need to pray, praise, or give a word of testimony. This is to exercise our spirit and not allow it to remain dormant or in a deadened condition. But sorry to say, many saints do not preserve their spirit by exercising it in this way. Instead, they allow their spirit to remain dormant. It seems that they leave their spirit in a tomb.

However, there are some brothers who disturb the meeting by functioning too frequently without any real riches of Christ. Again and again they stand up to speak without having anything to say. I would encourage brothers such as these to be silent for a period of time until they have the assurance that some of the riches of Christ have truly become their portion. If they stand up to release these riches, all the saints will be happy with them because their testimony will be helpful.

Although some saints may function too much without the riches of Christ, the need of most of the saints is to function much more with the exercise of their spirit.

KEEPING OUR SPIRIT LIVING

Certain verses in chapter five of 1 Thessalonians help us to see that the first way to preserve our spirit is to keep it living through proper exercise. Verses 16 through 19 say, "Always rejoice; unceasingly pray; in everything give thanks; for this is the will of God in Christ Jesus for you. Do not quench the Spirit." To rejoice, pray, and give thanks are to exercise our spirit. When we exercise our spirit in this way, we cause it to be living. Exercising the spirit to keep it living is the first way to preserve it.

No one likes to have any kind of illness or disease in his physical body. If you become ill, you certainly will not want your body to remain in a sick condition. On the contrary, you will do everything possible to bring your body out of such an unhealthy situation. Likewise, we should not leave our spirit in a deadened condition. We should struggle to have our spirit freed from that kind of condition.

How can we release our spirit from a situation of deadness? We can do it through exercising our spirit by rejoicing, praying, and thanking. Do you realize that to be quiet is to keep your spirit in a deadened condition? If you allow your spirit to remain in a situation of death, this means that you do not cooperate with the sanctifying God to preserve your spirit.

Because of the fall, our spirit has been deadened. Our spirit, therefore, must overcome the problem of deadness. Many times the saints attend the church meetings in death. When they attend the meeting, they sit in their chair with a deadened spirit. But other parts of their being may be very active. For example, in their thoughts they may criticize the testimonies given by others; they may think that some testimonies are not real and that others are full of oldness. Although these saints criticize others, they do not preserve their own spirit. Instead of preserving their spirit, they allow it to remain in a deadened condition.

I wish to emphasize strongly the fact that to preserve our spirit is first of all to exercise it in order to pull it out of death. The spirit of an unbeliever is absolutely dead. Most of those around you at school, at work, or in your neighborhood are utterly dead in their spirit. Many of your relatives, perhaps members of your immediate family, are also dead in the spirit. Have you been sanctified, separated, from a spirit-deadening situation? Many saints have not been separated in this way. This is the reason they never pray or praise the Lord in the meetings. They do not rejoice or give thanks. Instead of praising the Lord with the exercise of the spirit, they prefer to save their face by leaving their spirit in a deadened condition. Some may say to themselves, "I am a cultured person. I must cause others to realize that I am refined and have a high education. Thus, I shall sit quietly in the meeting in a cultured way. Let the young people and those who are not well educated shout praises in the meetings. I don't care to behave in such a way." If this is your attitude, your spirit will remain deadened. Furthermore, as far as the condition of your spirit is concerned, you are not sanctified. You are common, for you keep company with those who are dead in the spirit.

This habit of allowing our spirit to remain in death has even invaded the church meetings in the recovery. I am not encouraging anyone to behave in an unruly manner in the meetings. My point is that we need to pull our spirit out of death and cooperate with the operation of the Triune God in sanctifying us. He wants to separate all of us from those whose spirits are deadened. Because we have been regenerated, we need to be different. We need to show that our spirit is living, that it is not deadened. Thus, our spirit should rejoice, pray, and give thanks to the Lord.

KEEPING OUR SPIRIT FROM DEFILEMENT

Another way to preserve our spirit is found in 2 Corinthians 7:1. In this verse Paul says, "Having these promises, beloved, let us cleanse ourselves from all defilement of flesh and spirit, perfecting holiness in the fear of God." This verse indicates that we should abstain from all defilement of both flesh and spirit. We need to stay away from anything that contaminates our spirit. This is the reason we should keep our eyes from looking at evil things, such as defiling pictures. Such pictures defile not only our eyes; they also defile our spirit. This is something I have learned from experience. In 1933 I visited Shanghai the first time. The church had two meeting halls then, one in western Shanghai and the other in northern Shanghai, quite far from each other. For transportation we often used the streetcar. The ride from western Shanghai to northern Shanghai took more than an hour. The first few times I took this ride in the streetcar I looked around at the various sights on the main street. But when I arrived at the meeting hall, I realized that my spirit was deadened. It had been deadened by my looking at so many things on the street. From this I learned to close my eyes and pray when taking the ride by streetcar. This preserved my spirit. Because I learned to preserve my spirit in this way, when I arrived at the meeting hall in northern Shanghai, my spirit was living. I had truly been sanctified in my spirit.

If you become contaminated by looking at certain kinds of pictures, your spirit will be defiled, contaminated, and deadened. As a result, you will not be able to pray unless you first ask the Lord to cleanse you from all defilement. I offer this as an illustration of our need to cooperate with the sanctifying Triune God to have our spirit preserved from deadness and contamination.

LIFE-STUDY OF FIRST THESSALONIANS

MESSAGE TWENTY-FOUR

TO BE SANCTIFIED WHOLLY WITH OUR SPIRIT, SOUL, AND BODY PRESERVED COMPLETE

(2)

Scripture Reading: 1 Thes. 4:9, 13; 5:8, 16-24; 2 Cor. 7:1; 1 John 1:6; 1 Tim. 1:5; Rom. 6:6, 19; 7:24; 8:10-11; 12:1; 1 Cor. 6:13b, 15a, 19-20

In 1 Thessalonians 5:23 Paul says, "And the God of peace Himself sanctify you wholly, and may your spirit and soul and body be preserved complete, without blame, at the coming of our Lord Jesus Christ." In the foregoing message we pointed out that the way to preserve our spirit is first to exercise it to have fellowship with God. According to 5:16-18, we need to rejoice, pray, and give thanks. If we do this, our spirit will be pulled out of a condition of deadness and will be living. Second, we preserve our spirit by keeping it from all defilement and contamination. In this message we shall go on to consider how to preserve our soul and our body.

CLEARING THE ARTERIES OF OUR PSYCHOLOGICAL HEART

Our psychological heart has three main arteries. These arteries, which are also the three parts of the soul, are the mind, the will, and the emotion. It is important to know how in a practical way to have these arteries unclogged. For the unclogging of the arteries of our physical heart, doctors may prescribe medication. But in many cases surgery is required to remove the blockage. The way to unclog the three main arteries of our psychological heart is to make a thorough confession to the Lord. From experience I have learned that we need to stay with the Lord for a period of time to confess our defects, failures, defeats, mistakes, wrongdoings, and sins.

Concerning the Mind

We may begin by confessing all the sinfulness and uncleanness that is in our mind, in our thinking. The artery of our mind can be compared to a ditch that is clogged with dirt and needs to be dug out so that water can flow through it. Our mind is filled with dirt. As a result, this artery is clogged. In order to unclog the artery of our mind, we need to confess everything that is sinful in our thoughts and in our way of thinking. By confessing our thoughts one by one, we shall remove the blockage from this artery.

As we are making confession in this way, we may confess to the Lord how natural our understanding is concerning many matters. Perhaps you do not feel that your understanding of so many things is natural. This is the reason you need to go to the Lord and say to Him, "Lord, enlighten me and expose my mind. Expose all my thoughts. Lord, bring my mind fully into Your light." Then you should follow the enlightenment and exposure to confess the problems in your thinking one by one. For example, the Lord may show you that in your married life and family life your understanding is very natural. You may understand your spouse, your children, and your family affairs in a natural way, not at all in a spiritual way. If the Lord exposes this in you, you should immediately confess and say, "Lord, forgive me. Although I love You, my understanding of married life is altogether natural. Lord, deliver me from this natural understanding and take it out of me." This is an illustration of the kind of confession we need to make concerning our mind. For this kind of exposure and confession it may be necessary for us to stay with the Lord for a long time.

Concerning the Will

What, then, about our will? If we go to the Lord

concerning our will, He will expose it in a thorough and detailed way. It may seem as if we are being examined under a divine microscope, for one by one there will be brought to light all the germs in our will. In particular, we shall realize that we are very rebellious, that we do not know what it means to be submissive to the Lord. One by one, we need to confess the germs of rebellion in our will. The Lord may show you that, a few years ago, you were wrong in a particular matter. Then He may go on to show you how you were wrong with a certain brother or a certain sister. Each time you will need to confess. You should thank the Lord that you are under His light, under His exposure. By confessing all that the Lord exposes in our will, we unclog the artery of our will.

Concerning the Emotion

The artery of the emotion also needs to be unclogged. When we realize how serious is the problem we have with our emotion, we may be deeply sorrowful. We may despair and feel utterly ashamed of the condition of our emotion. We shall realize that in many cases we hate what we should love, and love what we should hate. When we come into the light of the sanctuary, we shall see that the most ugly aspect of our being is our emotion, for we do not use it properly. Both our joyfulness and our sorrow may be altogether natural. As the Lord exposes us, we may feel ashamed of the way we have expressed joy and sorrow, for that expression often was natural, fleshly, even fleshy. No wonder our psychological heart does not function normally.

If we take the time necessary to unclog the three main arteries of our psychological heart, we shall have the sense that our entire being has become living. Our mind, will, and emotion will all be in a very healthy condition. All the "dirt" in these "ditches" will then be dug away.

No one can do this unclogging for you. I can speak to you concerning it, but you must do it yourself. Thus, you need to go to the Lord day by day and ask Him to expose everything wrong in your mind, will, and emotion. Then in the light of what He exposes, you need to confess.

Perhaps you do not feel that you are wrong in your thoughts, in your decisions, or in your emotion. This is the reason you need to go to the Lord for His enlightening. As an illustration, sometimes we may have a physical problem that we are not aware of. Even after the doctor discovers our problem and prescribes the proper medication, we may not feel the medication is necessary. However, when we take the medication and it does its work to cleanse and heal our bodies, we shall be convinced that the doctor's advice was right. In like manner, even though we may not feel that we are wrong in our mind, emotion, and will, we need to go to the Lord and take the "medication" He gives us. If we take it, the arteries of the psychological heart will be kept clean and unclogged.

PRESERVING OUR BODY

In addition to knowing how to preserve our spirit and our soul, we must also know how to preserve our body. Sin has damaged and ruined our body. For this reason, Romans 6:6 says that our body is a "body of sin." Furthermore, we have presented the members of our fallen body to sin, to evil, to lawlessness. Romans 6:19 says, "You presented your members as slaves to uncleanness and lawlessness unto lawlessness." For instance, in gambling a person presents his hands to things that are sinful and unclean.

In Romans 7:24 Paul goes on to say that our body is a body of death: "Wretched man that I am! Who will deliver me from the body of this death?" Then in Romans 8:10 Paul points out that although the spirit is life because of righteousness, "the body is dead because of sin."

If we would preserve our body, we should live a life that never follows the old man, that never follows our soul. Romans 6:6 says, "Knowing this, that our old man has been crucified with Him that the body of sin might be made of none effect, that we should no longer serve sin as slaves." If we do not follow the old man, the body of sin will be made of none effect. This means that the body of sin will lose its job and become unemployed. But if we live according to the soul, we shall use our body to serve the old man. Therefore, to preserve our body first requires that we do not live according to our soul.

Second, to preserve our body requires that we not present any member of our body to anything that is sinful. For example, we should keep our eyes away from evil pictures and our ears from unclean things. Many things that are broadcast over the radio are defiling. A number of saints have testified that they cannot bear to listen to certain talk among those at school or at work because that talk is so evil. Many people of the world are able to speak concerning sinful things without any sense of shame. Thus, we need to keep our body from seeing and hearing things that will contaminate and ruin it. This is to preserve our body in sanctification.

Paul illustrates the importance of preserving our body in this way by giving in chapter four the charge to abstain from fornication. To abstain from fornication is to preserve our vessel, our body, in sanctification and honor. Therefore, in order to preserve our body, we should not present our members to anything sinful.

Today's world is full of contamination and defilement. This makes it very difficult for us to preserve our body. Wherever we go there are defiling elements. Parents need to train their children, even those in elementary school, to keep away from these contaminating elements. Any parent who thinks that children should be allowed to be tested in order to develop resistance is seriously mistaken and in the future will regret this course of action. The parents who follow this way in caring for their children surely will reap the harvest of what they have sown.

As an elderly person, I can testify that we need to preserve our body. Do not think that as you grow older you will not need to guard yourself from lust and defilement. As long as we have not been transfigured and still remain in the old creation, we need to preserve our body.

To preserve our body is actually very difficult. It is much easier to preserve our spirit and our soul than to preserve our body. The most difficult thing for us to do in this defiling, contaminating world is to preserve our body. We need to be careful not to look at anything, listen to anything, or touch anything that will defile our body.

OUR COOPERATION WITH GOD'S OPERATION

In 5:12-24 we see the cooperation of the holy life with the divine operation. In verses 12 through 22 we have the believers' cooperation in living a spiritual and separated life. In verses 23 and 24 we have God's operation in sanctifying and preserving the believers. God desires to sanctify us wholly and to preserve our spirit, soul, and body complete. However, we need to cooperate with Him. The way to cooperate is to rejoice, pray unceasingly, give thanks to Him in everything, not quench the Spirit, and not despise prophesying in the church meetings. If we cooperate in this way, our spirit will be preserved from deadness, our soul will be preserved from pollution in mind, will, and emotion, and our body will be preserved from the defilement of this age. Then in a practical way we shall have a holy life for the church life. Paul's aim in writing 1 Thessalonians, a book for new believers, was that they would live such a sanctified and holy life for the church life.

LIFE-STUDY OF SECOND THESSALONIANS

MESSAGE ONE

A WORD OF ENCOURAGEMENT

Scripture Reading: 2 Thes. 1:1-12

The opening of 2 Thessalonians is very much like that of 1 Thessalonians. In 1:1 and 2 Paul says, "Paul and Silvanus and Timothy to the church of the Thessalonians in God our Father and the Lord Jesus Christ: Grace to you and peace from God our Father and the Lord Jesus Christ." This Epistle and the First Epistle of Paul to the Thessalonians were both addressed to the local church in Thessalonica, a city of the Roman Empire in the province of Macedonia, north of the province of Achaia. This church was composed of all the believers in Christ in that city. Such a local church is of the believers and is in God the Father and the Lord Jesus Christ. This indicates that such a local church is born of God the Father with His life and nature and is united with the Lord Jesus Christ organically in all He is and has done. On the one hand, it is of human beings, in this case the Thessalonians; on the other hand, it is in God and in the Lord Jesus Christ. The organic union in the divine life and nature is the vital base for the believers to live a holy life for the church life, which is the theme of the two Epistles to the Thessalonians.

In chapter one of 1 Thessalonians we see the structure of a holy life for the church life. This structure is composed of faith, love, and hope. As we shall see, 2 Thessalonians also has the same structure.

ENCOURAGEMENT AND CORRECTION

Second Thessalonians is a book of encouragement and correction. The young believers in Christ at Thessalonica needed further encouragement; they also needed some correction. Paul encouraged these believers in his first Epistle. Nevertheless, in the second Epistle he gives them a further word of encouragement. While he is encouraging them, he also corrects them in certain matters.

Actually, 2 Thessalonians is more a book of correction than a book of encouragement. Paul was wise, gentle, and kind. Therefore, he does not directly give a word of correction. Rather, first he encourages the believers and then goes on to correct them. If we read this Epistle carefully, we shall see that a word of encouragement is followed by a word of correction. Then there is some further word of encouragement and after that another word of correction. This book, therefore, is composed of two sections of encouragement and two of correction, in addition to the introduction and the conclusion. In this message let us consider Paul's first word of encouragement to the believers at Thessalonica.

FAITH, LOVE, AND HOPE

In 1:3 Paul says, "We ought to thank God always concerning you, brothers, even as it is fitting, because your faith grows exceedingly, and the love of each one of you all to one another is increasing." We have emphasized the fact that the basic structure of the genuine Christian life is constituted of faith, love, and hope. Such a life does not originate from the ability of the believers' natural being; it originates from the infusion of what God is into the believers. It is carried out by their sacrificial love toward their Lord, who loved them and gave Himself for them, and toward His members, whom He has redeemed through His death in love. This life lasts and stands unchanging by the sustaining power of the hope that looks for their beloved Lord, who promised that He would come to take them to Himself. Such a life is the content of 1 and 2 Thessalonians.

In 1:3 Paul mentions the Thessalonians' faith and love. In the first Epistle faith and love are regarded as part of the structure of the believers' life for the church. Here, in the second Epistle, faith and love are growing and increasing in their Christian life.

In verse 4 Paul continues, "So that we ourselves boast in you in the churches of God for your endurance and faith in all your persecutions and the afflictions which you are bearing." The endurance spoken of here issued from the hope of the Lord's coming back and was supported by this hope. Such endurance of hope is always accompanied by faith. Hence, it says here "your endurance and faith." Both are needed in persecutions and afflictions.

SUFFERING FOR THE KINGDOM

In verse 5 Paul goes on to say, "A plain indication of the righteous judgment of God, that you may be accounted worthy of the kingdom of God, for which also you are suffering." God's judgment is righteous and just upon all men. It will be finalized in the future (Rom. 2:5-9; Rev. 20:11-15). How God deals in this age with different people is an indication, a token, a proof, of the future execution of His righteous judgment.

The believers have been called into the kingdom of God and glory (1 Thes. 2:12). To enter into this kingdom we need to pass through sufferings (Acts 14:22). Hence, the persecutions and afflictions are a plain indication of God's righteous judgment that we may be accounted worthy of the kingdom.

THE GOAL OF THE CHRISTIAN LIFE

The kingdom is the goal of the Christian life. Today we are living in the church life with the goal that one day we shall enter into the kingdom of God. The New Testament emphasizes the cross, the church, and the kingdom. The cross produces the church, and the church ushers in the kingdom. As we are living in the church life, our goal is to enter into God's kingdom.

This goal is neglected by many Christians. If you were to ask certain Christians what the goal of their Christian life is, they would probably say that their goal is to go to heaven. This kind of answer is very poor. The church life does not usher the believers into heaven; it ushers us into the kingdom. Actually, the church life is preliminary to the kingdom.

It is a preliminary stage of the kingdom. This is the reason that, in a very real sense, the New Testament considers the church life to be the kingdom. Romans 14:17 says, "For the kingdom of God is not eating and drinking, but righteousness and peace and joy in the Holy Spirit." Because Romans 14 speaks concerning the church life, the kingdom of God in this verse signifies the church life. According to Paul's understanding, the church life is the kingdom. Of course, the church life today is not the kingdom in full. Rather, it is the kingdom in a developmental stage, a preliminary stage. We are in this preliminary stage of the kingdom with the kingdom in full as our goal. We are proceeding from the preliminary stage to the stage of fullness. This is the correct understanding of the proper goal of the church life.

Many Christians, including us, are dull in understanding the genuine revelation of the New Testament. For this reason, though many read the Bible, they do not see anything. Their situation can be compared to that of the Israelites, who, in the words of Paul, have a veil upon them whenever they read the Old Testament (2 Cor. 3:14-15). Because they are veiled, they do not see anything when they read the Bible. Because many Christians are veiled, they do not understand what Paul means when he says that God has called us into His kingdom and glory. Some Christians interpret the kingdom to mean a heavenly mansion. According to their understanding, to enter into the kingdom is to go to heaven. They hold this concept of the kingdom because they are veiled. They read the Bible, but they do not see God's revelation.

In His mercy, the Lord has removed at least a great part of the veil from our eyes. We surely have seen something of God's revelation, and we shall not be cheated any longer. We know that to go to heaven is not our goal. There is not such a thing revealed in the Bible. God's goal is that we live a church life that will usher us into the kingdom. This means that we should live a life in the preliminary stage of the kingdom that will lead us into the full manifestation of the kingdom.

In 1:5 Paul speaks of being "accounted worthy of the kingdom of God." This implies that some believers may not be accounted worthy of the kingdom. In order to be accounted worthy of the kingdom, we need our faith to grow, our love to increase, and our endurance to be maintained. For the church life we need to have a life composed of the basic structure that includes a growing faith, an increasing love, and a lasting endurance. If we have such a life, we shall be accounted worthy of the kingdom of God.

In verse 5 Paul also tells the Thessalonians that they are suffering for the kingdom. This word corresponds to that in Acts 14:22, which says, "We must through much tribulation enter into the kingdom of God." Paul admonished the saints to bear suffering because we need to suffer in order to enter into the kingdom of God.

GOD'S JUDGMENT

In verse 6 Paul says, "Since it is just with God to repay with affliction those afflicting you." This verse indicates that God is judging and that He will judge in the future. We should not think that God is not judging today. There may be times when it seems that our God is not active. For this reason, atheists may say, "Where is God? It seems to us that there is no God in this universe. If there is a God, then He must be sleeping or retired." No, God is now judging.

More than fifty years ago, I devoted much time to the study of the prophecies in the Bible. In particular, I paid attention to the prophecies concerning the return of the Jews to their own land and to the re-formation of the nation of Israel. As I studied world history and observed the world situation, I wondered how it would be possible for the Jews, who have been scattered over the earth for centuries, to return to their own land and once again be formed into a nation. However, in 1948 the nation of Israel was formed and was even recognized by the United Nations. From that time onward, and especially since 1967, the Middle East has been the focal point of the world situation. How happy I have been to see the fulfillment of prophecies concerning the nation of Israel! God is fulfilling prophecy. Furthermore, He is actively carrying out His judgments. Therefore, instead of being troubled by any kind of opposition, we need to stand with God, with the One who judges those who afflict His people. As Paul says in 1:6, it is just with God to repay with affliction those who afflict His people.

RESTING AT THE UNVEILING OF THE LORD

Verse 7 says, "And to you who are being afflicted, rest, with us at the unveiling of the Lord Jesus from heaven with the angels of His power, in flaming fire." The Greek word translated "rest" also means relief, ease, repose, liberty. In this age the believers suffer persecutions and troubles for the Lord. At the Lord's coming back they will be relieved of their sufferings and enter into the Lord's rest and enjoy its liberty.

In this verse Paul speaks of the unveiling of the Lord Jesus. The Lord is here today; however, He is veiled. His coming back will be His unveiling. Although the universe is immeasurably vast in its dimensions, with the Lord there is no such thing as distance. He is everywhere. One day, at His coming, He will be unveiled, and everyone will see Him.

We thank the Lord that we are not shortsighted. Through His grace, we have both insight and foresight. We are able to see through the veil. Unbelievers, however, do not know what is behind the veil. But we, the believers, know that the Lord Jesus will be unveiled.

At the unveiling of the Lord Jesus from heaven with the angels of His power, we shall rest. The time has not yet come for us to rest. Our rest will be at the Lord's coming, at His unveiling.

DEALING OUT VENGEANCE

In verse 8 Paul continues, "Dealing out vengeance to those who do not know God and to those who do not obey the gospel of our Lord Jesus Christ." This verse covers two conditions and two stages. It speaks of God's dealing out vengeance to those who do not know God and to those who do not obey the gospel of Christ. Certain people do not know God; others do not obey the gospel.

There is no excuse for not knowing God. Some may say, "The gospel was never preached to me. I lived before the gospel was preached." Those who reason in this way will not be able to excuse themselves for not knowing God. According to the Bible, God is made known through His creation (Rom. 1:20). Furthermore, God is made known to man's conscience. Man can know God through creation and by means of his conscience. Our conscience tells us that there is a God. For this reason, no one can say that he does not have a way to know God. Anyone who does not know God will suffer punishment. Those who heard the gospel but did not accept it and obey it will also be punished. Therefore, God will deal out vengeance to two categories of people—to those who do not know God and to those who do not obey the gospel.

ETERNAL DESTRUCTION

Verse 9 continues, "Who shall pay the penalty of eternal destruction from the presence of the Lord and from the glory of His strength." Those who do not know God and those who do not obey the gospel will pay the penalty of eternal destruction. This is eternal perdition.

CHRIST GLORIFIED IN THE SAINTS

In verse 10 Paul speaks of Christ coming to be glorified in His saints: "Whenever He comes to be glorified in His saints, and to be marveled at in all those who have believed (because our testimony to you was believed) in that day." The Lord is the Lord of glory (1 Cor. 2:8). He has been glorified in His resurrection and ascension (John 17:1; Luke 24:26; Heb. 2:9). Now He is in us as the hope of glory (Col. 1:27) to bring us into glory (Heb. 2:10). At His coming back, on the one hand, He will come from the heavens with glory (Rev. 10:1; Matt. 25:31), and on the other hand, He will be glorified in His saints. For Him to be glorified in His saints means that His glory will be manifested from within His members. It will transfigure their body of humiliation into His glory like His glorified body. He will be marveled at, admired, wondered at, in us, His believers, by the unbelievers.

From Colossians 1:27 we know that we have Christ in us as our hope of glory. This indwelling Christ is the coming glory. Christ will come from the heavens, but He will also come out from within us. Therefore, the coming of the Lord is both from the heavens to the earth and also from within us. For Christ to come from within us is for Him to be glorified in us. Christ is now within us as glory. But this Christ of glory is concealed in us; He has not yet been manifested. At His coming back, the Christ of glory within us will be glorified in us. This means that He will come out of us and will be made manifest from within us. Thus, His coming will be a marvel. This is the reason that Paul says that when Christ comes, He will be glorified in His saints and marveled at in all those who believe.

As believers, we all may have the assurance that we have Christ in us and that this Christ is the Christ of glory. However, our unbelieving relatives, friends, and neighbors do not know that we have Christ in us. But when Christ comes, not only from the heavens but also from within us to be manifested, then our unbelieving relatives, neighbors, and friends will marvel.

The Christ who is glorified in us will be marveled at by unbelievers. Someone may say, "Aren't you my son-in-law? What has happened to you?" Then that one may respond, "I testified to you a number of times about Christ living in me. But instead of believing me, you mocked me and despised me. But now you marvel because my Christ has come out from within me to be manifested in glory." One day this will be our situation.

We have Christ in us, and we are in the process of being filled with Christ. But our Christ is veiled, even to us. When the Christ of glory comes out from within us and is manifested, others will marvel at us.

Sometimes even we may find it hard to believe that the glorious Christ is within us right now. Doctrinally, we may believe that Christ is in us. However, we may have some doubts. In the past I wondered if I really had Christ in me. I said to myself, "Is Christ really in you as the hope of glory? Look at how poor you are. It seems that you were better years ago than you are today." Perhaps you also have doubted that Christ is in you. But the day will come when the Christ in you, the hidden Christ, will be made manifest. That manifestation will actually be the glorification of Christ in us. When He comes out from within us, He will be marveled at by all the unbelievers.

WORTHY OF THE CALLING

Verse 11 says, "For which also we pray always concerning you, that our God may count you worthy of the calling, and may fulfill every good pleasure of goodness and work of faith in power." To call us into the heavens is not God's calling; it is to call us into His kingdom and glory.

The Greek word rendered "good pleasure" also means delight. The apostles prayed that God would fulfill the delight, the good pleasure, of the Thessalonians in goodness.

THE NAME OF THE LORD GLORIFIED IN US

In verse 12 Paul concludes, "So that the name of our Lord Jesus may be glorified in you, and you in Him, according to the grace of our God and the Lord Jesus Christ." The grace of our God and the Lord Jesus Christ is the Lord Himself within us as our life and life supply that we may live a life that will glorify the Lord and be glorified in Him.

In verse 12 Paul speaks of the name of the Lord Jesus being glorified in us and of our being glorified in Him. Such a glorification will be according to the grace of our God and the Lord Jesus Christ. This grace is something far more than unmerited favor. Grace is the processed Triune God becoming the all-inclusive life-giving Spirit for our enjoyment. It is according to such a grace that the name of the Lord Jesus will be glorified in us and that we shall be glorified in Him.

As we enjoy this grace, it will cause the Lord Jesus to be glorified in us and us to be glorified in Him.

When we read these verses in chapter one of 2 Thessalonians, we see that they are truly a word of encouragement. In 1:1-12 we have encouragement concerning the basic structure of a holy life for the church life. We have encouragement for our faith, love, and hope.

LIFE-STUDY OF SECOND THESSALONIANS

MESSAGE TWO

A WORD OF CORRECTION OF THE MISCONCEPTION CONCERNING THE DAY OF THE LORD'S COMING

(1)

Scripture Reading: 2 Thes. 2:1-12

In this message we shall consider 2:1-12. Here Paul gives the Thessalonians a word of correction of the misconception concerning the day of the Lord's coming. Because the misconception corrected by Paul is common among many Christians today, Paul's correcting word is needed as much today as when it was first written, if not more so. Before we consider 2:1-12 verse by verse, I would like to speak briefly about the different schools of teaching regarding the Lord's coming.

THREE SCHOOLS OF TEACHING CONCERNING THE LORD'S COMING

Apart from teachings that are definitely heretical, there are among fundamental believers three main schools concerning the Lord's coming and the rapture of the believers. One of these schools is called the pretribulation school. This is the teaching that the coming of the Lord Jesus will take place before the great tribulation. The word "tribulation" is a special term in the study of prophecy. It denotes a period of time at the end of the church age. At the end of the church age there will be a period of seven years, the last of the seventy weeks prophesied in Daniel 9. Daniel 9 speaks of seventy weeks of years concerning the history of Israel. First we have seven weeks, then sixty-two weeks, and finally, after a long interval, the last week, the last seven years.

Just before the beginning of these seven years, a powerful man will rise up—the Antichrist. Here in 2 Thessalonians 2 Antichrist is called the man of lawlessness. According to prophecy, this powerful person will restore the Roman Empire and will become the last Caesar of that empire. Then Antichrist, the man of lawlessness, will make a covenant, an agreement, with the Jews. This agreement will be intended to last for seven years. Because Antichrist will be so powerful, the Jews will be afraid of him; they will fear that he will persecute them in the practice of their religion. For this reason, the Jews will make an agreement with him, and in that agreement he will promise them freedom of worship. The Jews will be very pleased with this agreement, happy to have the freedom to worship the God of their fathers. However, after three and a half years, in the middle of the last seven years of the church age, the man of lawlessness will break his agreement with the Jews and begin to persecute them.

The last seven years may be divided into two periods, each three and a half years in length. In the Bible the second period of three and a half years is also called forty-two months, or 1260 days (Rev. 11:2-3; 13:5). From our study of the Bible we can say strongly and definitely that these last three and a half years will be the time of the great tribulation. This means that the great tribulation will be the second half of the last week; it will last three and a half years, or forty-two months, or 1260 days.

Many teach that the Lord's coming will take place before the great tribulation. However, when they speak of the tribulation, they usually mean the entire last seven years. According to their understanding, the whole of the last week of Daniel's seventy weeks will be the period of the great tribulation. They teach that Christ will come back to rapture the believers before this time of tribulation, that is, before the last seven years of this age. For this reason, this school of teaching is called the pretribulation school.

A second school is the school of post-tribulation. This is the teaching that Christ's coming will be after the great tribulation. Those who teach that the coming of Christ will be after the tribulation use many verses from the Bible as a strong basis for their teaching. Those of this school teach that Christ will come back at the very end of the tribulation. Therefore, their teaching is called the post-tribulation school.

A third school of teaching, represented by Bible teachers such as Pember, Govett, and Panton, teaches in a more detailed way concerning the Lord's coming back than those in either the pretribulation or post-tribulation schools. Those in this third school say that neither the pretribulation school nor the post-tribulation school is fully correct. Rather, each of these schools is only partially correct. The teaching of the first two schools can be compared to a city map that shows only main streets, whereas the teaching of the third school can be compared to a city map that shows not only main streets but also small streets, lanes, and alleys. Therefore, the teaching of those in the third school is more detailed and more accurate.

According to the third school, Christ's *parousia* (presence) will probably begin a little before the middle of the last seven years and will last nearly to the end of this period. Christ will leave the throne in the third heaven and descend to the air concealed in a cloud and remain there for about three and a half years. During this period of time, a number of things will happen. The manchild in Revelation 12 will be raptured just before Antichrist begins to persecute every kind of religion, including Judaism and Catholicism, and he will exalt himself above every object of worship. The manchild will be raptured not to the air but to the throne of God. Furthermore, according to Revelation 14, the one hundred forty-four thousand will also be raptured during this time as the firstfruit, before the second half of the last seven years. We should not make the mistake of regarding the one hundred forty-four thousand in Revelation 14 as identical to the manchild in Revelation 12. These are two different groups of overcomers. The manchild and the one hundred forty-four thousand will be raptured to the throne of

God. Then the Lord Jesus will begin His *parousia;* He will descend from the throne of God to the air. It seems certain that the manchild and the one hundred forty-four thousand will descend with Him. Then at the end of the last seven years, the Lord Jesus will come to earth. Second Thessalonians 2:8 refers to this: "And then the lawless one shall be revealed (whom the Lord Jesus will slay by the breath of His mouth and bring to nothing by the appearance of His coming)." The Greek word rendered "coming" is *parousia,* presence. The appearing of the Lord's *parousia* will be at the end of the last seven years, after Antichrist, the lawless one, has been revealed.

THE LORD'S COMING AND OUR RAPTURE

Let us now consider 2:1-12 verse by verse. In verse 1 Paul says, "Now we ask you, brothers, with regard to the coming of our Lord Jesus Christ and our gathering together to Him." As in verse 8, the Greek word for coming here is *parousia.* Two matters are covered in this verse: the Lord's *parousia* (presence) and our gathering together (rapture) to Him.

The Lord's *parousia* will last for a period of time. It will begin with His coming from the heavens to the air (Rev. 10:1) at the time of the great tribulation, which will occur in the last three and a half years of this age, the second half of the last week of Daniel 9:27 (Matt. 24:21; Rev. 11:2), and it will end with its appearing, "the appearing of His *parousia*" (2 Thes. 2:8; Matt. 24:30). During the Lord's *parousia,* the majority of believers will be raptured to meet the Lord in the air (1 Thes. 4:17). "The day of the Lord" in 2 Thessalonians 2:2 refers, according to the context, to the period of time of the Lord's *parousia* (coming), in which the rapture of the majority of the believers will take place. Verse 3 tells us definitely that before this period of time Antichrist will be revealed to play the greatest role in the great tribulation (v. 4; Rev. 13:1-8, 12-15). This reveals clearly and definitely that the Lord's coming *(parousia)* and the rapture of the majority of believers cannot take place before the great tribulation.

NOT SHAKEN OR ALARMED

Verse 2 says, "That you be not quickly shaken in mind nor alarmed, neither by spirit, nor by word, nor by a letter as by us, as that the day of the Lord is present." According to Darby, "in mind" (lit. from the mind) denotes "a steady and soberly judging mind." Paul did not want the believers at Thessalonica to be shaken in mind or alarmed with respect to the Lord's coming and our rapture. The phrase "by spirit" refers to the pretending of a speaking spirit that claims to have the authority of divine revelation. Someone may claim that he has the spirit to speak concerning the Lord's coming. Paul warns the believers not to hastily listen to such a one. He also warns them not to be shaken "by word, nor by a letter as by us." This may indicate that someone pretended to write a letter using the name of the Apostle Paul. Here Paul seems to be saying, "Brothers, if anyone by spirit, by word, or by a letter as from us, says that the day of the Lord is present, you should not listen to him. Do not be shaken, and do not be alarmed."

THE APOSTASY AND THE MAN OF LAWLESSNESS

Verse 3 says, "Let no one deceive you in any way; because it will not come unless the apostasy comes first and the man of lawlessness is revealed, the son of destruction." The Greek word translated "deceived" may also be rendered "beguiled," not only making a false impression, but actually leading astray.

In verse 3 the pronoun "it" refers to the day of the Lord's coming. This day will not come unless the apostasy comes first. This apostasy will be a falling away from the straight way of God's economy as revealed in the Scriptures. There is a strong prophecy in the Bible that before the Lord's coming back there will be a great apostasy among His people, a falling away from the path of God's economy. Even today there is a tendency among some Christians to leave the straight way of the New Testament.

Verse 3 also indicates that the day of the Lord will not come before the man of lawlessness is revealed. This man of lawlessness is the Antichrist, as prophesied in Daniel 7:20-21, 24-26; 8:9-12, 23-25; 9:27; 11:36-37; Revelation 13:1-8, 12-18; 19:19-20. He will be the man of lawlessness, casting down the truth to the ground, changing laws, destroying and corrupting many to an extraordinary degree, blaspheming God, and deceiving men. Hence, the Lord will utterly destroy him, and he will become the son of destruction.

Verse 3 indicates strongly that the Lord's coming back will not precede the tribulation. Before the Lord's coming there will first be the apostasy and also the revealing of the man of lawlessness. This means that prior to the Lord's coming one matter—the apostasy—and one person—Antichrist—must appear first.

Paul told the Thessalonians that since the apostasy and the revealing of the man of lawlessness must come before the day of the Lord's coming, they should not be shaken by anything or anyone that would claim that the day of the Lord has already come. The apostasy must take place, and the Antichrist must be revealed. Antichrist will be fully revealed during the great tribulation. This indicates that the Lord's coming back will be after the tribulation, not before it. Second Thessalonians 2:3 is a verse used by those who follow the school of post-tribulation to say that the coming of Christ will be after the tribulation.

Among the Brethren, the leading teacher of the school of pretribulation was J. N. Darby. Darby was an excellent teacher of the Word, and we have learned much from him. However, we do not follow him in his teaching concerning pretribulation. The school of post-tribulation is more accurate. Concerning the Lord's coming, there is too much guesswork in Darby's teaching. For instance, he says that in Revelation 4 John was raptured and that this rapture was a type of the rapture of the church before the tribulation. According to Darby's concept, the tribulation begins in Revelation 4. Darby claims that in Revelation 4 John was a representative of the church and that his rapture indicates the rapture of the church before the tribulation. In this matter Darby infers, or guesses, too much.

Benjamin Newton disagreed with Darby's interpretation. He pointed to the second chapter of 2 Thessalonians, where Paul says clearly that the Lord's coming will not take place unless the apostasy comes first and the man of lawlessness, that is, Antichrist, is revealed. As we have pointed out, this means that the Lord's coming back will be after the tribulation.

Neither those who hold to the pretribulation school nor those who follow the post-tribulation school have seen the full truth concerning the Lord's *parousia.* Those who see one aspect of the *parousia* teach the pretribulation coming, but those who see another aspect teach the post-tribulation coming. We consider the *parousia* as a whole and therefore do not stand with either the pretribulation or the post-tribulation school.

ANTICHRIST IN THE TEMPLE OF GOD

In verse 4 Paul gives a further description of Antichrist: "Who opposes and exalts himself above all that is called God or an object of worship, so that he seats himself in the temple of God, proclaiming himself that he is God." This fulfills the prophecy concerning Antichrist in Daniel 11:36 and 37. This will take place in the midst of the last week, as prophesied in Daniel 9:27.

The temple of God mentioned in verse 4 is "the holy place" in Matthew 24:15. Verse 4 indicates that the temple of God will be rebuilt before the Lord comes back. The temple was destroyed more than nineteen centuries ago. But this verse says that Antichrist will seat himself in the temple of God. Therefore, the temple must be rebuilt. The nation of Israel has been formed again, and the city of Jerusalem has been returned to Israel. However, the temple has not yet been built. Some Jews are deeply stirred concerning the rebuilding of the temple. One day, this temple will be rebuilt, and, according to the prophecy of Daniel, Antichrist will seat himself in it.

In verse 5 Paul says, "Do you not remember that, when I was yet with you, I said these things to you?" Although Paul had been with the Thessalonians for only three weeks, he had spoken to them concerning these things.

THE MYSTERY OF LAWLESSNESS

In verse 6 Paul goes on to say, "And now you know that which restrains, that he might be revealed in his own time." This verse indicates that some power hinders the revelation of the man of lawlessness, Antichrist. The words "in his own time" denote the time appointed by God, which will be the last of the seventy weeks, as prophesied in Daniel 9:27; 7:24-26; and Revelation 13:1-8.

In verse 7 Paul continues, "For the mystery of lawlessness is already operating; only there is one who restrains now until he comes out of the midst." The lawlessness that will characterize Antichrist is already operating in this age mysteriously. It is the mystery of lawlessness working today among the nations and in human society. Even now there is a tendency for lawlessness to be prevailing.

Antichrist will be the totality of lawlessness. No one can have unlimited power unless he is lawless. A lawful person cannot have unlimited power, because he is limited by the law. Those who are lawless, who are not limited by the law, but do whatever they please, may become very powerful. Hitler, an example of lawlessness, was such a one.

According to God's sovereignty, "there is one who restrains now until he comes out of the midst." This probably means that the restraining factor will be taken out of the way. Although the mystery of lawlessness is already operating, this lawlessness is at the present time restrained, restricted. But one day this restrainer will be taken away. We need to realize from the prophecy of the Bible that one day the restraining factor will be removed, and then Antichrist will be unrestricted.

In a democratic country such as the United States, even the President is limited by laws. He is not free to do whatever he pleases. But if the limitation of law were to be removed, the one in power could become lawless and do whatever he wants. In such a case, the ruler of a country could become extraordinarily powerful. Today lawlessness is operating, but the restraining factor still exists. Because of this restraining factor, no one can be lawless and become so powerful. But when the restraining factor is removed, someone will rise up to be lawless and do whatever he desires. Then he will become extraordinarily powerful. That man of lawlessness will be Antichrist.

Verse 8 says, "And then the lawless one shall be revealed (whom the Lord Jesus will slay by the breath of His mouth and bring to nothing by the appearing of His coming)." This will be fulfilled in Revelation 19:19-20. This verse indicates that the Lord's coming *(parousia)* is hidden before it appears openly. This also indicates that the Lord's coming involves a period of time. It will remain in secret, and then it will appear to the public.

THE OPERATION OF SATAN

In verse 9 Paul says, "The coming of whom is according to the operation of Satan, with all power and signs and wonders of a lie." This verse reveals that the coming of Antichrist is according to the operation of Satan. The reason Antichrist will be so lawless is that he will be under Satan's operation. Due to the motivation of Satan, he will become extremely powerful. The operation of Satan is with power and signs and wonders of a lie. The entire operation of Satan to deceive people (vv. 9-10) is in its totality a lie, just as he is a liar and the father of it (John 8:44).

This operation of Satan is seen in Revelation 13. At that time, people will be deceived by lying signs and wonders. One of these signs will be that an idol, the lifeless image of Antichrist, will be able to speak.

NOT RECEIVING THE LOVE OF THE TRUTH

Verse 10 continues, "And with all deceit of unrighteousness among those who are perishing, because they did not receive the love of the truth that they might be saved."

A large number of people will follow Antichrist. They will accept his deceit because they do not receive the love of the truth in order to be saved.

In verse 11 Paul goes on to say, "And because of this, God sends to them an operation of error that they might believe the lie." Because the perishing ones did not receive the love of the truth, which God intended to give them that they might be saved, God sends to them an operation of error, an active power of misleading, that they might believe the lie.

In verse 12 Paul concludes, "That all might be judged who have not believed the truth, but have had pleasure in unrighteousness." The believers have the pleasure of goodness (1:11); the perishing sinners who reject the truth of God have pleasure in unrighteousness. To sin is a delight to them (Rom. 1:32).

We all need to be clear regarding the Lord's coming and not be shaken or alarmed by strange teachings concerning it. Today some teach that Christians will not pass through the tribulation, but will be raptured before the tribulation. This candy-coated teaching is not accurate. Do not listen to such teachings concerning the Lord's coming and our being gathered unto Him. The word in 2:1-12 is brief, but it is very sound and clear. I would encourage you to read the Life-studies on Matthew and Revelation for more details.

We should not simply know about the Lord's coming. We need to live a life to match the Lord's requirements so that we may be counted worthy to be in the manchild, or to be among the one hundred forty-four thousand, or to be the living ones who are raptured according to Matthew 24. Those believers who are watchful and ready will be raptured before the tribulation. However, those who are not watchful and ready will pass through the tribulation.

LIFE-STUDY OF SECOND THESSALONIANS

MESSAGE THREE

A WORD OF CORRECTION OF THE MISCONCEPTION CONCERNING THE DAY OF THE LORD'S COMING

(2)

Scripture Reading: 2 Thes. 2:1-12; Dan. 9:24-27

In the foregoing message we considered the three main schools of teaching concerning the coming of the Lord Jesus, His *parousia,* and our gathering together, our rapture, to Him. These are the schools of pretribulation, post-tribulation, and the school that considers the entire *parousia* in detail. We also saw that in 2:1-12 Paul gives a word of correction of the misconception concerning the day of the Lord's coming.

In 2:1 Paul speaks of the coming of our Lord Jesus Christ and our gathering together to Him. In 2:2 and 3 Paul tells the believers not to be quickly shaken in mind nor alarmed, neither by spirit, by word, or by letter, as from the apostles, that the day of the Lord is present. He also charges them not to allow anyone to deceive them. Then Paul goes on to say that the day of the Lord will not come unless the apostasy comes first and the man of lawlessness, Antichrist, is revealed in his own time. At present, although the mystery of lawlessness is already working, there is a restraining factor, but one day this factor will be removed. Then the lawless one will be revealed. However, the Lord Jesus will slay him by the breath of His mouth and bring him to nothing by the appearing of His coming *(parousia,* v. 8). The coming of the lawless one will be according to the operation of Satan, with all power, signs, and wonders of a lie and with all deceit of unrighteousness among those who are perishing, because they did not receive the love of the truth that they might be saved. Because of this, God will send them an operation of error that they might believe the lie.

THE SEVENTY WEEKS

In the foregoing message we pointed out that the man of lawlessness, Antichrist, will be manifested in the middle of the last of the seventy weeks mentioned in Daniel 9. In this message I would like to give a further word regarding the seventy weeks in Daniel 9 in relation to Paul's word of correction in 2 Thessalonians 2:1-12.

Determined upon Israel and Jerusalem

Daniel 9:24 says, "Seventy weeks are determined upon thy people and upon thy holy city, to finish the transgression, and to make an end of sins, and to make reconciliation for iniquity, and to bring in everlasting righteousness, and seal up the vision and prophecy, and to anoint the Most Holy." In this verse a week equals seven years. Seventy weeks, therefore, are seventy times seven years or four hundred ninety years. Daniel was told that these seventy weeks are determined upon "thy people and upon thy holy city." This means that the seventy weeks are related to Daniel's people, the children of Israel, and to the holy city, Jerusalem. This verse also speaks of finishing the transgression, making an end of sins, making reconciliation for iniquity, bringing in everlasting righteousness, sealing up the vision and the prophecy, and anointing the Most Holy. If we read this verse carefully, we shall see that it speaks of the ending of this age. The bringing in of everlasting righteousness refers to the millennium, to the thousand-year kingdom, when there will be righteousness on earth. Therefore, this one verse indicates that the seventy weeks will reach unto the end of this age and will bring in the thousand-year kingdom.

Unto Messiah the Prince

Daniel 9:25 says, "Know therefore and understand, that from the going forth of the commandment to restore and to build Jerusalem, unto the Messiah the Prince, shall be seven weeks, and threescore and two weeks: the street shall be built again, and the wall, even in troublous times." The seven weeks in this verse denote forty-nine years. If you study the books of Ezra and Nehemiah, you will see that from the time that the king of Persia gave the commandment to rebuild Jerusalem unto the completion of this rebuilding was forty-nine years. Verse 25 also speaks of a period of threescore and two weeks, or sixty-two weeks. This is equal to four hundred thirty-four years. The first seven weeks and the sixty-two weeks yield a total of four hundred eighty-three years. This leaves the last week, a period of seven years, for the future. The first forty-nine years go from the commandment to rebuild Jerusalem to the completion of the rebuilding. The four hundred thirty-four years extend from the building of Jerusalem to Messiah the Prince. The last part of verse 25 says that the "street shall be built again, and the wall, even in troublous times." This refers to the building that took place during the first seven weeks, that is, during the first period composed of forty-nine years.

The Prince That Shall Come

Verse 26 says, "And after threescore and two weeks shall Messiah be cut off, but not for himself: and the people of the prince that shall come shall destroy the city and the sanctuary; and the end thereof shall be with a flood, and unto the end of the war desolations are determined." The words "cut off" refer to the crucifixion of Christ, the Messiah. Christ was cut off not for Himself but for us. He was crucified for us.

The "people of the prince that shall come" is a reference to the people of Titus, a prince of the Roman Empire. In A. D. 70 the Roman army under the leadership of Titus thoroughly destroyed Jerusalem and the temple, the sanctuary. The history written by Josephus describes this terrible destruction.

Verse 27 says, "And he shall confirm the covenant with many for one week: and in the midst of the week he shall cause the sacrifice and the oblation to cease, and for the overspreading of abominations he shall make it desolate, even until the consummation, and that determined shall be poured upon the desolate." In this verse the pronoun "he" refers to "prince" in verse 26. However, this "he" will actually be the coming Antichrist. In typology, Titus was a prefigure of Antichrist. What he did in A. D. 70, Antichrist will repeat in the future. Hence, the prophecy here in Daniel 9 regards the two as one: the first, Titus, is the prefigure; the second, Antichrist, is the fulfillment.

The Antichrist, the one typified or prefigured by Titus, will according to verse 27 "confirm the covenant with many for one week." This covenant will be an agreement that is intended to last for a period of seven years. This seven years is the last of the seventy weeks mentioned in Daniel 9:24. In the midst of the last week, the last seven years, Antichrist will "cause the sacrifice and the oblation to cease." This means that he will stop the Jews from offering sacrifices on the altar in the temple and will begin to persecute every kind of religion.

The Church Age as an Insertion

From the time the commandment was given to rebuild the city of Jerusalem until the completion of this rebuilding was forty-nine years, or seven weeks. Then the time from this completion to the crucifixion of Christ was sixty-two weeks, or four hundred thirty-four years. After the crucifixion of Christ, the seventy weeks were suspended. This suspension will continue until the beginning of the last seven years of this age.

In the four Gospels the Lord Jesus said that because of His crucifixion God would give up the children of Israel. Therefore, their history was suspended at the cross, and from that time onward they have been forsaken by God. God has temporarily set them aside, put them away. The divine history then comes to the church. This means that the history of the church occupies the period of time between the end of the sixty-ninth week and the beginning of the seventieth week. In other words, the church age is equal to the time during which the seventy weeks are suspended. We may also say that the age of the church, the entire history of the church, is an insertion wedged in between two parts of the history of the children of Israel.

This understanding corresponds fully to what is revealed in certain of the parables uttered by the Lord Jesus in the Gospel of Matthew. For instance, the parable in Matthew 21:33-46 speaks of the transfer of the kingdom of God. In this parable the vineyard is the city of Jerusalem, and the husbandmen are the leaders of the Israelites. Matthew 21:41 says, "They say to Him, He will miserably destroy those evil men, and will lease the vineyard to other husbandmen, who will render the fruits to him in their seasons." This was fulfilled when the Roman prince, Titus, and his army destroyed Jerusalem in A. D. 70.

In the parable of the marriage feast the Lord Jesus says, "And the king was angry; and he sent his troops and destroyed those murderers and burned their city" (Matt. 22:7). These were the Roman troops under Titus which destroyed Jerusalem. Matthew 22:9 indicates that the preaching of the New Testament has turned to the Gentiles: "Go therefore to the thoroughfares, and as many as you find, call to the marriage feast."

The Seventieth Week, the Millennium, and Eternity

These parables indicate that after the crucifixion of the Lord Jesus, God gave up the children of Israel and focused His attention on the church. Therefore, at the time of Christ's crucifixion, the history of the children of Israel was suspended. This suspension will continue until the end of the church age, when God will once again visit the children of Israel. Then the last of Daniel's seventy weeks will begin. After this seventieth week, there will be the millennium, the thousand-year reign of Christ on earth. The millennium will be followed by the new heaven and the new earth with the New Jerusalem. That will be eternity.

The Breaking of the Covenant

Antichrist will be extraordinarily powerful. For this reason, the Jews will be afraid of him and will be compelled to make an agreement, a covenant, with him that is intended to last for seven years. According to that covenant, Antichrist will promise the Jews that he will not persecute their religion. However, in the middle of the last week, the last seven years, Antichrist will break this covenant. He will force the Jews to stop offering the sacrifices, and he will seat himself in the temple of God, claiming that he is God. Speaking of Antichrist, the man of lawlessness, 2 Thessalonians 2:4 says, "Who opposes and exalts himself above all that is called God or an object of worship, so that he seats himself in the temple of God, proclaiming himself that he is God."

In the Bible the last of the seventy weeks is divided into two parts. What divides this week in half is Antichrist's breaking his covenant with the Jews, forbidding the continuation of the sacrifices, and seating himself in the temple. The Bible does not say much about the first half of the seventieth week; however, it has much to say about the second half. This second half is called "time, times, and half a time," that is, three and a half years; it is also described as forty-two months and twelve hundred sixty days (Rev. 11:2-3; 13:5).

THE LORD'S DESCENT FROM THE THRONE TO THE AIR

While Antichrist is moving on earth, the Lord Jesus will begin to move from the heavens to the air. We are not clearly told at what time the Lord will begin this move. As a result of careful study, I would say that this will begin very close to the middle of the last seven years. Revelation 12 indicates that the manchild will be raptured to the throne of God. From the book of Revelation we also know that the last three and a half years will begin after the manchild is raptured. At the time of the rapture of the manchild, the Lord Jesus will still be on the throne in heaven.

Furthermore, the one hundred forty-four thousand, first-fruit to God and the Lamb, in Revelation 14 will also be raptured to the throne of God. These one hundred forty-four thousand firstfruit will not be taken to the air; rather, they will be taken to the heavens, even to the heavenly Mount Zion. The rapture of the firstfruit to the heavens is typified by the firstfruit in Exodus 23:19 being brought into the house of the Lord for God's enjoyment: "The first of the firstfruits of thy land thou shalt bring into the house of the Lord thy God." According to Revelation 14, the harvest, the majority of the believers, will be left on earth to pass through the second half of the last seven years, which will be the period known as the great tribulation. Shortly after the manchild and the firstfruit are raptured to the throne, probably the Lord Jesus will begin His descent from the throne to the air, concealed in a cloud.

THE REAPING OF THE HARVEST

Where does 1 Thessalonians 4 fit into this picture? The rapture in 1 Thessalonians 4 must correspond to the reaping of the harvest in Revelation 14. This harvest will be reaped, raptured, probably at the end of the last three and a half years. This means that the harvest will be reaped toward the very end of the great tribulation.

In 2 Thessalonians 2:3 Paul says, "Let no one deceive you in any way; because it [the day of the Lord] will not come unless the apostasy comes first and the man of lawlessness is revealed, the son of destruction." After the apostasy and the revealing of the man of lawlessness, there will be the appearing of the Lord's *parousia.* The revelation of the Antichrist will be completed during the last seven years. This revelation of Antichrist must be first, and then there will be the appearing of the Lord's *parousia.*

In verse 8 Paul says, "And then the lawless one shall be revealed (whom the Lord Jesus will slay by the breath of His mouth and bring to nothing by the appearing of His coming)." This indicates that the Lord's coming *(parousia)* will first be hidden and then will appear openly. This also indicates that the Lord's coming involves a period of time. It will remain in secret for a period of time, and then will appear to the public. The Lord's *parousia* will take place secretly during the last three and a half years. Then when the Lord Jesus slays Antichrist, His *parousia* will appear. Therefore, the Lord's *parousia* will begin with His coming from the heavens to the air and will be completed with its public appearing.

LIFE-STUDY OF SECOND THESSALONIANS

MESSAGE FOUR

A FURTHER WORD OF ENCOURAGEMENT

Scripture Reading: 2 Thes. 2:13—3:5

In this message we come to 2:13—3:5, a portion of 2 Thessalonians that contains a further word of encouragement. In these verses Paul covers a number of very precious matters. In 2:13 Paul says, "But we ought to thank God always concerning you, brothers beloved by the Lord, because God chose you from the beginning unto salvation in sanctification of the Spirit and belief of the truth." God loved us (v. 16), chose us from the beginning, and called us through the gospel (v. 14). He chose us unto His salvation, which is by sanctification of the Spirit, and He called us to the obtaining of the Lord's glory. Now He is taking us on with eternal encouragement and good hope in grace.

GOD'S CHOICE

In his word of encouragement Paul reminds the young believers of God's selection, God's choice. He tells them that from the beginning, that is, from eternity past (see Eph. 1:4), God chose them. It certainly is encouraging to know that before time began God chose us. This means that our being saved did not begin in time; rather, it began in eternity. In eternity past God considered us and selected us. From the beginning God chose us unto salvation.

SALVATION IN SANCTIFICATION OF THE SPIRIT

The salvation unto which we were chosen by God is salvation in sanctification of the Spirit. Sanctification of the Spirit is the divine transformation. By this we are thoroughly saved from all old and negative things and made a new creation to obtain the Lord's glory.

Sanctification is a matter of transformation, and transformation involves a process. Now, as saved ones, we are all in the process of being sanctified, transformed.

We may use cooking to illustrate the process of sanctification. The church life can be compared to a kitchen. When God called us and saved us, He purchased us as "groceries" from a large "supermarket." In His "shopping" God called us. Now we are undergoing the process of being "cooked" in the "kitchen" of the church. This process of cooking is sanctification, transformation.

Because the church life is a kitchen for God's cooking, the church will not always have an appearance that is neat and orderly. This is usually the situation in a kitchen when a good meal is being prepared. Do not expect your local church to be perfect. A kitchen is a place of process. Because of this process, many things are not ready, but they are in the process of being made ready. Sometimes I am asked how I can tolerate the situation in the church. I reply, "Why should I not tolerate it? The church is a kitchen. Wait for another period of time and you will see the results of the work that is taking place now in the kitchen."

According to 2:13, salvation is in sanctification. This means that salvation does not immediately result in our going to heaven. No, God's salvation is now in sanctification. God is sanctifying us. This should remind us of Paul's word in 1 Thessalonians 5:23, where he says, "And the God of peace Himself sanctify you wholly." At present we are all undergoing the process of sanctification in the kitchen of the church life. We know what it means to be cooked in this kitchen. However, those outside the kitchen do not understand what we mean when we speak of the process of being cooked.

Do not expect that everything in the church life will be marvelous and orderly. This is not the situation of any local church on earth. Furthermore, we should not think that the local churches at Paul's time were better than the churches today. On the contrary, because our cooking has been improved, the local churches in the Lord's recovery today may be better than the churches in Paul's day.

Often the messy condition of a kitchen indicates that an excellent meal is being prepared. The kitchen may be messy, but the food that is being cooked will be very tasty. If you want the food in your local church to be flavorful, you must be willing for your kitchen to be messed up.

Suppose you invite me to your home for a meal. If I see that everything in your kitchen is neat and orderly, I may be disappointed, for I shall realize that there may not be much to eat. But if I see that your kitchen is messy because of all the preparations for the meal, I shall know a feast is being prepared. When no one is cooking, the kitchen may be neat. But when a good meal is being prepared, the kitchen will not be so orderly. If everything in a church is neat and orderly, this may indicate that no one is doing any cooking. This means that there is a shortage in the process of sanctification.

I can testify that the kitchen of the church in Anaheim is messy. This proves that in Anaheim we are in the process of sanctification. God, according to His selection, has placed us into the process of sanctification. In the church in Anaheim we are experiencing a great deal of cooking; we are being sanctified and transformed. Sometimes when I am being cooked, I may wonder what is happening. Then the Lord reminds me that I have prayed for transformation and have ministered concerning it. In Anaheim I may say that I cook the elders, and the elders cook me. Furthermore, the elders are being cooked by the saints. Certain brothers and sisters seem to be especially given to cooking the elders. Actually the cooking in the kitchen of the church life is not done by any human hand. Rather, it is done by the Lord according to His wisdom and sovereignty.

God has selected us unto salvation in sanctification and not merely to have our sins forgiven. There is no need to be cooked in order to experience the forgiveness of sins. We simply need to pray, "Lord Jesus, I repent. I confess that I am a sinner. But, Lord, I believe in You, and I thank You for dying on the cross for my sins." A person who prays in this way can be saved and have the forgiveness of sins. But this is not sanctification. After we experience forgiveness, we need to undergo the process of sanctification.

The Lord intends to sanctify us, to transform us. Transformation is a process that is not necessarily enjoyable. Nevertheless, we need to learn how to enjoy the Lord even when we are being cooked.

In verse 13 Paul tells us that sanctification is of the Spirit. Do you know where the Spirit is? You need to realize that the Spirit is in you to sanctify you. In 1 Thessalonians 4 Paul speaks of sanctification, and this sanctification is of the Spirit. The indwelling of the Spirit is actually our sanctification. The Spirit indwells us with just one goal—to sanctify us, to transform us, to change us metabolically. This is sanctification of the Spirit.

BELIEF OF THE TRUTH

In verse 13 Paul also speaks of belief of the truth. In this verse the word "belief" actually means faith. The faith of the truth comes before salvation in sanctification of the Spirit. God chose us from the beginning unto the faith of the truth and unto salvation in sanctification of the Spirit.

CALLED UNTO THE OBTAINING OF THE GLORY OF THE LORD JESUS CHRIST

In verse 14 Paul goes on to say, "To which also He called you through our gospel unto the obtaining of the glory of our Lord Jesus Christ." The words "to which" refer to salvation in sanctification of the Spirit and belief of the truth, as mentioned in verse 13. In eternity God chose us unto salvation in sanctification of the Spirit and belief of the truth, and then in time He called us unto the obtaining of the glory of our Lord. Salvation in sanctification of the Spirit and belief of the truth are the procedures. Obtaining the glory of our Lord is the goal.

First God chose us and then He called us. He chose us unto the faith of the truth and unto the salvation in sanctification of the Spirit. Then through the gospel He called us unto the obtaining of the glory of the Lord Jesus Christ. The glory of the Lord is that He is the Son of God the Father, possessing the Father's life and nature to express Him. To obtain the Lord's glory is to be in the same position as sons of God to express Him.

I doubt that the majority of today's Christians understand what it means to be called unto the obtaining of the glory of our Lord Jesus Christ. In verse 14 Paul does not say that God has called us unto the obtaining of forgiveness, justification, or reconciliation. He says that God has called us unto the obtaining of the glory of the Lord Jesus. In John 17:22 the Lord said in His prayer to the Father, "And the glory which You have given Me I have given to them, that they may be one, even as We are one." The glory which the Father has given the Son is the sonship with the Father's life and divine nature (John 5:26) to express the Father in His fullness (John 1:18; 14:9; Col. 2:9; Heb. 1:3). This glory the Son has given to His believers that they also may have the sonship with the Father's life and divine nature (John 17:2; 2 Pet. 1:4) to express the Father in the Son in His fullness (John 1:16). I doubt that many Christians have this understanding regarding the glory of the Lord Jesus.

The glory of the Lord Jesus is that the Father has given Him the Father's life and nature for Him to express the Father. This is the glory the Son has given to us. This means that the Son has given us the Father's life and nature so that we may be able to express God the Father. What a glory! God has called us unto the obtaining of this glory, the glory of the divine life and the divine nature to express the divine Being. Although you may never have considered this before, this is the truth according to the revelation in the New Testament. Hallelujah for such a marvelous glory!

HOLDING THE TRADITIONS

In 2:15 Paul goes on to say, "So then, brothers, stand firm and hold to the traditions which you were taught, whether by word or by our letter." We should not think that tradition is always bad. The traditions to which Paul refers here are excellent. We need to stand firm and hold to these traditions.

ETERNAL ENCOURAGEMENT AND GOOD HOPE IN GRACE

Verse 16 says, "Now our Lord Jesus Christ Himself, and God our Father, who has loved us and given us eternal encouragement and good hope in grace." According to this verse, what we have is not temporary and transitory comfort and strengthening, but eternal encouragement. This eternal encouragement is by the divine life. It is sufficient for any kind of environment and situation. Therefore, it is with good hope.

Eternal encouragement is related to the divine life. Whenever you are disappointed, you need to be reminded that the divine life is within you. If you consider even a little that the divine life is inside of you, you will be encouraged. Do you know what kind of life you have? You have God's life. The very life of God has been given to you. Eternal encouragement, therefore, is actually eternal life.

We can be encouraged simply by considering a little about the eternal life we have received. If you feel weak, be reminded that you have eternal life. In this way you will be strengthened and encouraged. This eternal encouragement is sufficient for any environment and situation. God has loved us and has given us eternal encouragement.

God has also given us good hope in grace. This hope is the hope of glory (Col. 1:27), which is the hope of the Lord's coming (1 Thes. 1:3), when we shall be either resurrected or transfigured into glory (1 Thes. 4:13-14; Phil. 3:21; Heb. 2:10). This good hope is in grace, and grace is nothing less than the Triune God processed to become the all-inclusive life-giving Spirit. In this grace we have a good hope. We may say that grace is God Himself in Christ for us to enjoy that we may be sanctified by His Spirit and encouraged and established with eternal encouragement and good hope.

Some saints have said to me, "Brother Lee, we have heard your ministry for many years. It seems that actually you are ministering just one thing. It is marvelous that you can give thousands of messages on the same thing." This is not my way of ministering; it is the biblical way and the way practiced by Paul. Have you noticed that in Romans Paul speaks in one way, but in 1 Corinthians he talks about the same matter in another way? Now we see that in 2 Thessalonians 2 he speaks regarding the same thing in yet another way.

I especially like the last part of chapter two, verses 13 through 17, for in these verses Paul presents important matters to new believers. His writing here is simple, but the content is profound. First Paul says that God chose us from the beginning unto salvation in sanctification of the Spirit. Then he says that God has called us through the gospel unto the obtaining of the glory of our Lord Jesus Christ. In verse 16 Paul says that we have been given eternal encouragement and good hope in grace. Paul does not use the expression "eternal encouragement" in any of his other books. John speaks about the same thing, but he uses different terms. In 2:16 Paul refers to eternal life as eternal encouragement. In this verse the relative pronoun "who" may refer both to the Lord Jesus Christ and to God the Father, yet "has loved us and given us" is singular. This indicates that Paul regarded the Lord and the Father as one.

We need to learn to use the expressions Paul used, such as eternal encouragement. If you see that a brother is weak or disappointed, you may say to him, "Brother, have you not received eternal encouragement? Eternal encouragement is the eternal life that is within you."

Suppose a person who is very unhappy has a diamond in his pocket. Simply by looking at the diamond, he may be encouraged and become happy. We have the real diamond, and this diamond is the eternal life as our eternal encouragement. Do you realize that you have such a diamond in your pocket? Why, then, do you look at your troubles and sufferings instead of at this diamond? Oh, praise the Lord for the diamond of eternal encouragement! This encouragement is eternal life and good hope in grace.

ENCOURAGED AND ESTABLISHED

In verse 17 Paul says, speaking of the Lord Jesus Christ and God the Father, "Encourage your hearts and establish you in every good work and word." If we want God to encourage us, we need to encourage ourselves. If we help ourselves, God will help us. But if we do not help ourselves, God will not help us. If you are not willing to eat the food on the dining table, others cannot help you. But if you eat, everyone will be willing to help you. This is an illustration of the fact that we need to encourage ourselves and establish ourselves, and then God will encourage and establish us.

PRAYING FOR THE MINISTERS OF THE WORD

In 3:1 Paul says, "For the rest, brothers, pray concerning us, that the word of the Lord may run and be glorified, even as it is also with you." For the word of the Lord to be glorified is for the divine riches contained in the word of the Lord to be released and expressed in the believers' living. We all need to learn how to let the word of the Lord run and how to cause the word of the Lord to be glorified in us.

Verse 2 says, "And that we may be delivered from improper and evil men; for not all hold the faith." The ministers of the word of God need such a prayer for them by the saints.

GUARDED FROM THE EVIL ONE

In verse 3 Paul declares, "But the Lord is faithful, who will establish you and guard you from the evil one." We are guarded by eternal encouragement and good hope (2:16-17). Only the eternal life can guard us from the evil one. The whole world lies in the evil one (1 John 5:19), but the divine life with which we have been born of God keeps and guards us from him (1 John 5:18, 4; 3:9). We have a part within us that has been regenerated, born of God. That part, which is actually the Lord Himself, always guards us.

THE APOSTLES' CONFIDENCE

In verse 4 Paul goes on to say, "We have confidence in the

Lord concerning you, that what we charge, you both are doing and will do." The charge here is like those in 1 Thessalonians 4:2-4, 9-12; 5:11-22; 2 Thes. 2:2, 15; 3:6, 10, 12-15.

THE LORD DIRECTING THE BELIEVERS' HEARTS

In verse 5 Paul concludes, "And the Lord direct your hearts into the love of God and into the endurance of Christ." The Lord directs our hearts by the leading of the Spirit, through whom the love of God has been poured out into our hearts (Rom. 8:14; 5:5). The love of God in this verse is our love toward God that issues from the love of God (1 John 4:19) that has been poured out into our hearts. On the positive side, we need to enjoy the love of God so that we may love Him in order to live for Him. On the negative side, we need to participate in the endurance of Christ so that we may endure the sufferings as He did to stand against Satan, the enemy of God.

In 2:13—3:5 Paul once again touches faith, love, and hope. This indicates that 2 Thessalonians is a continuation of 1 Thessalonians. This portion of 2 Thessalonians is a conclusion of Paul's writings to new believers concerning the basic structure of the Christian life for the church life. As we have pointed out, this basic structure includes faith, love, and hope. By faith we have been saved into sanctification. We have been called unto the obtaining of the Lord's glory, and we have eternal encouragement, which is eternal life, and also good hope in grace. Now according to 3:5, we need the Lord to direct our hearts into the love of God and into the endurance of Christ.

LIFE-STUDY OF SECOND THESSALONIANS

MESSAGE FIVE

CHOSEN BY GOD UNTO SALVATION IN SANCTIFICATION OF THE SPIRIT

(1)

Scripture Reading: 2 Thes. 1:3-5, 10-11; 2:13-14, 16

A HOLY LIFE FOR THE CHURCH LIFE

The books of 1 and 2 Thessalonians contain a total of eight chapters. All these chapters are on the same subject: a holy life for the church life. Whenever we read 1 and 2 Thessalonians, we should not be distracted by other matters. No doubt, in the eight chapters of these two books a number of other points are covered. We need to be careful in our reading not to be distracted by these points. As we read 1 and 2 Thessalonians, we need to keep in mind that the central thought of these Epistles is a holy life for the church life.

This holy life for the church life is constructed of faith, love, and hope. The way to carry out such a life is to be sanctified wholly. In 1 Thessalonians 5:23 Paul says, "And the God of peace Himself sanctify you wholly, and may your spirit and soul and body be preserved complete, without blame, at the coming of our Lord Jesus Christ." If we would be sanctified wholly, we need to have our heart established blameless in holiness, and we need to preserve our vessel, our body, in sanctification and honor. Furthermore, all the parts of our being—our spirit, our soul, and our body—need to be preserved complete. This is to sanctify our entire being to have a holy life for the proper church life.

In 2 Thessalonians Paul repeats much of what he has said in 1 Thessalonians. Like a father with a loving heart toward his children, Paul is repetitious. This is characteristic of parents, especially as they grow older. Again and again, they may say the same thing to their children. Therefore, 2 Thessalonians is a repetition and a further development of 1 Thessalonians. It is a repetition with warnings and corrections. In 2 Thessalonians 2 Paul warns the believers not to be misled. He also corrects them in order to bring them back to the right track. Nevertheless, the main subject—the holy life for the church life—is the same in both books. Furthermore, in both 1 Thessalonians and 2 Thessalonians we see the basic structure of the Christian life, a structure that includes faith, love, and hope.

FAITH GROWING AND LOVE INCREASING

In 2 Thessalonians 1:3 and 4 Paul says, "We ought to thank God always concerning you, brothers, even as it is fitting, because your faith grows exceedingly, and the love of each one of you all to one another is increasing, so that we ourselves boast in you in the churches of God for your endurance and faith in all your persecutions and the afflictions which you are bearing." In verse 3 Paul speaks of the believers' faith and love. He says that their faith is growing and that their love is increasing. In 1 Thessalonians 3:2 Paul says that he sent Timothy to establish and encourage the Thessalonians for the sake of their faith. From 1 Thessalonians 3:10 we learn that Paul was eager to see them again in order to perfect what was lacking in their faith. In 1 Thessalonians 3:12 Paul also urged the believers to increase in love: "And the Lord cause you to increase and abound in love to one another and to all, even as we also to you." In 1 Thessalonians 4:9 Paul goes on to tell the believers that they have been taught of God to love one another. Therefore, in 1 Thessalonians Paul was concerned that the believers' faith would be perfected and that their love would increase and abound. Now in 2 Thessalonians 1:3 Paul encourages the new believers at Thessalonica by saying that the apostles thank God because their faith grows exceedingly and because their love is increasing. This indicates that, as Paul repeats the matter of faith and love, he adds a word of encouragement.

ENDURANCE OF HOPE

But where does Paul speak of hope in 2 Thessalonians? Paul's first reference to the believers' hope is in 1:4, where Paul says that he boasts of their endurance and faith in all their persecutions and afflictions. Hope is implied by the word "endurance." Their endurance issued from the hope of the Lord's coming back and was supported by it. Such endurance of hope is always accompanied by faith. For this reason, Paul speaks of their endurance and faith. In 2:16 Paul again speaks of hope: "Now our Lord Jesus Christ Himself, and God our Father, who has loved us and given us eternal encouragement and good hope in grace." Paul, an excellent writer, could not forget the basic structure of his Epistles to the Thessalonians with the elements of faith, love, and hope.

HOLINESS AND SANCTIFICATION

In 1 Thessalonians 3 Paul speaks of holiness; in chapter four of sanctification; and in chapter five, of being sanctified. In 1 Thessalonians 3:13 he says, "That He may establish your hearts blameless in holiness before our God and Father at the coming of our Lord Jesus with all His saints." Then in 1 Thessalonians 4:3 he says, "This is the will of God, your sanctification," and in verse 4, "That each one of you know how to possess his own vessel in sanctification and honor." Then in 1 Thessalonians 5:23 Paul says, "And the God of peace Himself sanctify you wholly, and may your spirit and soul and body be preserved complete, without blame, at the coming of our Lord Jesus Christ." This is the holiness and sanctification spoken of in 1 Thessalonians for the carrying out of a holy life for the church life with the three elements of faith, love, and hope.

In 2 Thessalonians 2:13 Paul gives a further word concerning sanctification: "But we ought to thank God always concerning you, brothers beloved by the Lord, because God chose you from the beginning unto salvation in sanctification of the Spirit and belief of the truth." God has chosen us unto salvation in sanctification, and this sanctification is of the Spirit. Paul's word about sanctification here implies all that he has said regarding holiness and sanctification in 1 Thessalonians. This means that it implies what Paul has said about having our heart established blameless in holiness, about preserving our body in sanctification, and about being sanctified wholly by the God of peace.

THE BRIDGE OF SALVATION

In 2:13 neither sanctification nor salvation is a simple matter. When I was young, I regarded God's salvation as something that was very simple. First I was eager to know definitely whether I had been saved. Eventually I came to know for sure that I had been saved. After that, I made salvation a major subject in my conversation with others. Whenever I met a person, I was eager to find out whether or not he was saved. Gradually I came to realize that salvation is not such a simple matter. Now if you would ask me if I have been saved, I would reply, "I have been saved, I am still being saved, and I shall be saved. Eventually, I shall be wholly, fully, and thoroughly saved."

Another way to ask about my experience of salvation would be to say something like this: "Brother Lee, you said that you have been saved, that you are now being saved, and that you will be saved thoroughly. Please tell us how much you have been saved. Also, how much are you being saved day by day? We know that you have been a Christian for more than fifty years. Please tell us how much of you has been saved and how much still needs to be saved." I use these questions as an illustration of the fact that salvation is not a simple matter.

If someone asks you if you have been saved and how much you have been saved, you should say, "I know that I have been saved. However, I cannot tell you how much I have been saved. But I do know that I need to be saved much more. I have participated in God's salvation to some degree, but I need to participate in it to a far greater degree."

In 2:13 Paul says that God chose us *unto* salvation. This salvation has a long span. According to what we are able to understand, this span begins with regeneration and ends with glorification. Although we were fallen, sinful, and deadened, God came to regenerate us. Through regeneration, we began to participate in God's salvation. However, regarding this salvation we have a long way to go.

We may liken the span of God's salvation to a long bridge. This bridge of salvation begins in time and reaches to eternity. If you were to ask me where I am today on this bridge, I would have to answer that I do not know. I know definitely that I have not crossed all the way over this bridge. I know that I am somewhere on the bridge of salvation, but only God knows exactly where this is.

Although we do not know where we are on the bridge of God's salvation, we can know with assurance that we shall never lose our salvation or our regeneration. Once we have been regenerated, we are regenerated for eternity. Regeneration is a once-for-all matter. Regeneration can be compared to our birth as human beings. Once a person has been born as a human being, he will never cease to be a human being, a person. In the same principle, regeneration is a matter once for all, even for eternity.

THE DEGREE OF OUR SALVATION AND THE EXTENT OF OUR SANCTIFICATION

The degree of our salvation depends on the extent of our sanctification. The more we are sanctified, the more we are saved. Perhaps yesterday you were further along on the bridge of salvation than you are today. The reason may be that you lost your temper with your husband or wife, and this caused you to move backwards somewhat on the bridge. You backslid and lost a little of your sanctification. Therefore, you are not as sanctified now as you were yesterday.

Suppose an old friend visits you and asks you to participate with him in a certain kind of worldly entertainment.

If you accept his invitation, you will lose even more sanctification and move back farther on the bridge of salvation. However, if you refuse his invitation and instead preach the gospel to him and encourage him to become a Christian, you may recover the sanctification you have lost and even progress further on the bridge. As a result, you are more sanctified and more saved. The point here is that how much we have been saved is determined by how much we have been sanctified. We need to be impressed that God's salvation is not simple and that it is related to sanctification.

Suppose a young brother becomes weary of attending the church meetings. Therefore, one day instead of attending the meeting, he decides to go to the beach. The next time he comes to a meeting, he may feel that he is in death. The reason is that he has lost some of his sanctification. He did not preserve his spirit, soul, and body.

SANCTIFICATION AND JUSTIFICATION

Martin Luther fought a great battle for the truth of justification by faith. Because he was involved in this battle, we should not blame him for failing to see other aspects of God's full salvation. Luther taught that justification is by faith. According to this, if we believe in the Lord, we shall be justified. However, there is a sense in which justification is also a matter of degree. On the one hand, the Bible speaks of justification before sanctification (Rom. 6:19). But on the other hand, there is a sense in which sanctification comes first and justification follows (1 Cor. 6:11). In this sense, God's justification must go according to the standard of sanctification. If we are not sanctified, then we cannot be justified.

THE PROCESS OF GOD'S SALVATION

God's salvation of us involves a process. It has a beginning, and it will have a consummation. Once again, we may use human life as an illustration. Life begins at birth. But after birth there is a long process of growth. I have been growing in human life for many years, and still I have not yet reached the consummation. The principle is the same with God's salvation. However, many Christians regard salvation in too simple a way. Moreover, in systematic theology salvation may be presented as if it were simple and clear cut. But God's salvation is not simple, and in a certain sense it is not clear cut. On the contrary, it has a beginning, a process, and a consummation. Not even our human life is simple. Why, then, should we expect God's full salvation to be so simple?

We need to have the proper concept concerning God's salvation. If we have the right understanding of this, we shall realize that the extent to which we are saved is determined by the degree we have been sanctified. According to Paul's word in 2:13, salvation is in sanctification of the Spirit.

In our actual experience of God's salvation, we move back and forth on the bridge. Perhaps you yield to a certain temptation, and move backward on the bridge of salvation. But even then the sanctifying Spirit is working in you. As a result, that step backward may cause you to move even farther ahead than you were before. For example, a brother may lose his temper with his wife and exchange words with her. No doubt, this failure causes him to move backward on the bridge of salvation. However, when he repents and returns to the Lord, he will once again move ahead, further than he was before.

In our experience none of us moves steadily ahead on the bridge of salvation. On the contrary, we all move ahead in the way of going backward and forward. Even though this may not be clearly revealed as a doctrine in the Bible, we know from our experience that this is the way we advance on the bridge of God's salvation.

LIFE-STUDY OF SECOND THESSALONIANS

MESSAGE SIX

CHOSEN BY GOD UNTO SALVATION IN SANCTIFICATION OF THE SPIRIT

(2)

Scripture Reading: 2 Thes. 1:3-5, 10-11; 2:13-14, 16

The books of 1 and 2 Thessalonians were written in an elementary way because they are letters to young saints, to new believers. These two Epistles can be compared to writings that are for students in elementary school. However, even in elementary writings there may be certain basic elements.

In 2 Thessalonians 2:13 Paul speaks of salvation in sanctification of the Spirit. Here we have three basic elements: salvation, sanctification, and the Spirit. All these terms refer to basic elements of God's salvation.

According to Paul's word in 2:13, God has chosen us unto salvation. The word "unto" means with a view to. Here Paul is saying that God has chosen us with a view to salvation; He has chosen us so that we may enter into salvation. In the foregoing message we pointed out that salvation here can be compared to a long bridge, to a bridge with a very long span. The bridge of God's salvation reaches from time to eternity; it brings us out of this present age into eternity. God has chosen us with a view of bringing us onto this bridge.

CHOSEN FROM THE BEGINNING

In order to understand these elementary writings to the Thessalonians, let us analyze some of the words and expressions used by Paul. Second Thessalonians 2:13 says, "But we ought to thank God always concerning you, brothers beloved by the Lord, because God chose you from the beginning unto salvation in sanctification of the Spirit and belief of the truth." The phrase "from the beginning" in this verse refers to eternity past. God's choosing is His selection. God the Father chose us, selected us, in eternity past. Paul speaks of this selection in Ephesians 1:4: "According as He chose us in Him before the foundation of the world that we should be holy and without blemish before Him, in love." God the Father in eternity had a plan, a purpose. For the fulfillment of this purpose He has selected us. We all have been selected by God. We have been chosen according to His foreknowledge. Long before we were born, even before the foundation of the world, God the Father saw us and knew us. When God saw us, He was happy with us. He may have said to Himself concerning you, "I want this one for My eternal purpose."

Jacob and Esau

The case of Esau and Jacob is an illustration of God's selection. Romans 9:13 says, "As it is written, Jacob I loved, but Esau I hated." As God considered the twins, Esau and Jacob, He could say to Himself, "I don't like Esau, the first one. I am not happy with him. I prefer the second one, Jacob, the supplanter."

If you ask me to explain why God loves Jacob and hates Esau, I would have to answer that I am not able to explain it. I do not know why God loves Jacob, but hates Esau. Only He knows the reason. God has His own desire. The Bible tells us that God loved Jacob and hated Esau, but it does not give us the reason.

When I was young, I thought that God was unfair. It seemed to me that Esau was much better than Jacob. Jacob was a thief and a deceiver. Eventually, I had no choice but to accept what the Bible says regarding God's loving Jacob and hating Esau.

As those who have been selected by God the Father, we all are Jacobs. None of us is an Esau. Because we are Jacobs, we should not consider ourselves gentlemen. No, like Jacob our forefather, we are supplanters. But we are supplanters who have been selected by God the Father in eternity past.

No Escape

I would like to say a word especially to the young people. Because you were selected by God in eternity past, there is no point in trying to run away from Him. In a very real sense, God is a great fisherman, and He has "hooked" you. God hooked you in eternity. Therefore, there is no way you can get off His hook.

In eternity past God spread many hooks attached to long strings. The hook on which you were caught was floating free until one day the hook came to you, and you were caught. Now you cannot get off the hook. God the Father has chosen you, and you cannot escape.

THE APPLICATION OF THE SPIRIT

After man was created, he fell and became corrupt. Therefore, God the Son came to redeem us and accomplish what God had planned. Following that, God the Spirit came to apply what God had planned and what Christ, the Son of God, had accomplished. This application is sanctification.

We may not have had any thought concerning God or any heart toward Christ. Nevertheless, one day we were caught by the Spirit, and the Spirit began to apply what the Father has planned and what the Son has accomplished. As a result, for no apparent reason, we came to believe in the Lord Jesus.

Even though our friends, neighbors, schoolmates, and associates may not believe in Christ, we cannot help believing in Him. I can testify of this from my own experience. One day I began to love the Lord Jesus. I have never seen Him, but I love Him. He is so good to me! Others may say that this is superstitious and regard Jesus as nothing. To them I would say, "You may not care for the Lord Jesus, but I love Him." This is not any kind of superstition. It is the application of the Spirit.

As we have pointed out, the application of the Spirit is what Paul means in 2:13 by sanctification. When we receive the application of the Spirit, we are separated to the Lord.

My friends and classmates could not understand what had happened to me, and I myself could not explain it. I only know that, at the age of nineteen, I suddenly lost my interest in other things and cared only for the Lord. I loved to pray, call on the Lord's name, read the Bible, go to meetings, and tell others how lovable the Lord Jesus is. Certain people wondered who hired me to do this. I told them, "I have not been hired by anyone. Rather, I am willing to spend as much money as possible to print tracts that I myself have written." This was my early experience of the sanctification of the Spirit.

When I was a young person, I loved to play soccer. One day, after I was saved, I was playing soccer. At a certain time, when the ball came to me, something within said, "Stop! Don't play any longer. Leave the soccer field." All the players were shocked; they did not know what had happened to me. Then I walked off the field and told them that I would not play soccer any longer. That was an experience of the sanctification of the Spirit.

Many of us can give testimonies concerning the Spirit's sanctification. Even though you may be very young in the Lord, the Spirit is nevertheless being applied to you. Whatever the Spirit applies to you is an aspect of your sanctification.

Because we have experienced the application of the Spirit, we do not have the freedom to do certain things that others are able to do. This is not a matter of teaching; it is a matter of God the Spirit living within us.

God the Father loves us and has chosen us. God the Son died for us and accomplished redemption for us. Now God the Spirit has come to apply all this to us.

I believe that many of the sisters can testify that being sanctified by the Spirit affects their shopping. Because they have been sanctified by the Spirit, their shopping has become different. As they are considering the purchase of a particular item, the Spirit within them may say, "Don't touch that." The Spirit may say no much more than He says yes. No one teaches the sisters to change their way of shopping. The different way of shopping is the result of the sanctification of the Spirit. It is in this sanctification of the

Spirit that we are saved. This is salvation in sanctification of the Spirit.

It is very easy for a husband and wife to exchange words. This is extremely common in married life. But I can testify that in the sanctification of the Spirit I have been saved from exchanging words with my wife. If I did not have the sanctification of the Spirit, I would probably exchange words with my wife every day. However, I can testify before the Lord that in my married life I have been saved in sanctification of the Spirit from exchanging words with my wife.

A SUBJECTIVE SANCTIFIER

Every day, even every minute, we are being sanctified. The One who sanctifies us is the Spirit. This is the reason the Bible speaks of the sanctification of the Spirit. All day long the Spirit, the third of the Trinity, is sanctifying us, applying to us what the Father has planned and what the Son has accomplished. Oh, we have such a practical, living, and subjective Sanctifier!

Even while we are sinning, the Spirit is sanctifying us. You may be committing a sin, but even then the Spirit is working to sanctify you. How gracious this is!

In Hebrews 10:29 the Spirit is even called the Spirit of grace. As believers in Christ, we all have received the Spirit of grace. The Spirit of grace sanctifies us unconditionally, that is, without any conditions or terms. The Spirit has been commissioned to sanctify us. He has been given to us for the purpose of completing the work of sanctification.

THE MARK OF THE TRIUNE GOD

Sanctification separates us unto God by putting a mark on us. This mark is actually the Triune God Himself. Whenever we are sanctified, we are marked with the Triune God. As a result, others can see the Triune God in us. Furthermore, this mark is increasing and becoming more intensified. Year after year, this mark has been wrought deeply into my life. This is the work of the Spirit's sanctification. By the sanctifying work of the Spirit we are being saved. Furthermore, this is the way we live a holy life for the church life.

LIVING A HOLY LIFE FOR THE CHURCH LIFE

Our Spirit Preserved

To live a holy life for the church life is to have our spirit, soul, and body preserved. Paul speaks of this in 1 Thessalonians 5:23: "May your spirit and soul and body be preserved complete, without blame, at the coming of our Lord Jesus Christ." We need to have our spirit preserved from deadness. This means that we should be living in our spirit. We should contact God all the time and serve Him in a living way. We need always to have a direct sense from Him. Furthermore, we need to have a conscience that is without offense. This means that we keep our conscience, the leading part of our spirit, good and pure. To preserve our spirit is to keep it from deadness, contamination, and offenses. If our spirit is preserved in this way, we shall have a living spirit with a direct sense of God. We shall also have peace in our conscience. This is to preserve our spirit.

Our Soul Preserved

We also need to have our entire soul preserved. Our mind needs to be renewed, transformed, and sobered. Our will should be submissive and flexible, yet strong. Our emotion should always be properly adjusted. If our emotion is proper, we shall love what we ought to love and hate what we ought to hate. This is to have an emotion according to God's desire. If our mind, will, and emotion are in such a condition, our soul is preserved. We are not biased in any way, but every aspect of our soul is upright.

Our Body Preserved

We also need to be preserved in our body. In order to have our body preserved, we should no longer live by our old man. If we do not live by our old man, our body will be a slave to righteousness instead of a slave to sin. Positively, we preserve our body by presenting it to God a living sacrifice

(Rom. 12:1). Then our body will even become a member of Christ (1 Cor. 6:15) so that we may live Christ, express Christ, magnify Christ. Furthermore, our body will then be the sanctuary of the Holy Spirit for God's dwelling (1 Cor. 6:19). God dwells in our body to move and to express Himself, to glorify Himself. In this way our spirit, soul, and body will be preserved in the Triune God. This is a holy life, and this is to be saved in the sanctification of the Spirit. This is the kind of life that is for the church life. The church life depends on such a holy life.

In the two Epistles to the Thessalonians Paul wrote to new believers about basic matters. I hope that we shall all pay our attention to what Paul says in these books so that day by day we may be sanctified and that our spirit, soul, and body may be preserved, with our heart, the acting agent and representative of the soul, established blameless in holiness. Praise the Lord that it is possible for us to live such a holy life for the church life!

LIFE-STUDY OF SECOND THESSALONIANS

MESSAGE SEVEN

A CONCLUDING WORD

Scripture Reading: 2 Thes. 3:6-18

In this message we shall consider 3:6-18. In 3:6-15 we have Paul's word of correction of the disorderly walk, and in 3:16-18, we have Paul's conclusion.

A CORRECTION OF THE DISORDERLY WALK

The concluding sections of this book surely sound like a word spoken to young believers. After speaking concerning profound matters in 2:13—3:5, Paul goes on to give a word concerning correction of the disorderly walk. In 3:6 he says, "Now we charge you, brothers, in the name of the Lord Jesus Christ, that you keep away from every brother walking disorderly and not according to the tradition which you received from us." A disorderly walk is not only according to the flesh (Rom. 8:4), but is also against the building up of the church life (1 Thes. 5:11; Rom. 14:19; 1 Cor. 10:23).

It may seem that walking disorderly is a small point. Nevertheless, it certainly is practical. I believe that the disorderliness in Thessalonica came from the misconception regarding the Lord's coming back. Some believers thought that the Lord Jesus would be coming back soon, and therefore it was not necessary for them to work. Their concept may have been that as long as they had something to eat and could survive, that was adequate. Those who have such a concept become "superbelievers." They go above the level of proper spirituality.

Several years ago, a number of the young people thought that as long as they loved the Lord Jesus and were living the church life, it was not necessary for them to have a higher education. They thought it was adequate to do some kind of simple work. I came to know the situation and realized that this concept is absolutely wrong. We live in an age when it is necessary to have an education. In order to live properly in this age, we need a good education. Without the right kind of education, it would not be easy for us to make a living. I gave a strong word to the young people encouraging them to complete college and, if possible, to go on to graduate school. Furthermore, I encouraged them to study subjects such as medicine or law. I am thankful that this word was widely accepted by the young people. During the years that followed, many completed their education. Now they can testify how much help they received from that word.

Do not think that as long as we are spiritual, seek the Lord, and are for the Lord's testimony and recovery, there is no need for us to be prepared for work through good education. We live in an age of education, knowledge, science, and industry. If the young people do not have a proper education, it will be difficult for them to have a proper human living. Therefore, I encourage all the young people to gain a good education.

In verse 6 Paul charges the believers to keep away from any brother who walks disorderly. This indicates that Paul considers it a serious matter to walk disorderly, for this is a damage to the church life.

At this point I would like to say that it is better not to do anything with which the brothers would not agree. If you want to do a certain thing and the brothers do not feel good about it, you should hesitate and reconsider. The fellowship of the brothers is a protection and a safeguard. It will preserve you in the church life. Perhaps you think that you know more than the brothers. This may actually be the situation. Nevertheless, it is always safe to listen to the brothers. This is a good protection and safeguard.

Paul tells us not to keep company with one who is disorderly. If you keep company with such a one, you may encourage him to continue in his disorderly living. Staying away from him will serve as a warning to him. It will also help to keep you from making the same kind of mistake.

Walking disorderly is upsetting to the church life. If we would have a proper church life, we need to learn to walk in an orderly way and to stay away from anyone who walks disorderly.

THE PATTERN OF THE APOSTLES

In verses 7 through 9 Paul reminds the Thessalonians that, in the matter of orderly living, the apostles were a pattern to them: "For you yourselves know how you ought to imitate us, because we were not disorderly among you; nor did we eat bread as a gift from anyone, but in labor and hardship we worked night and day that we might not be burdensome to any of you; not that we do not have the right, but that we might give ourselves to you as a pattern to imitate us." The apostles were for the building up of the church in all things (2 Cor. 12:19). They were absolutely not disorderly among the believers, but were a pattern for the believers to imitate.

Because of the influence of the religious background, Christians often say, "We do not follow a man. We are following the Lord. You should not imitate any man. Instead, you need only to imitate the Lord." In a sense, this is right. However, it is not easy to follow the Lord directly, since none of us has ever met Him physically. Some who insist on following only the Lord may reply, "We should study the four Gospels and see how the Lord Jesus walked. Then we shall be able to follow in His footsteps." However, in many things related to our human living, there are not any footsteps of the Lord to follow. For example, He was never married. How, then, can you follow Him in your married life? We can follow Him indirectly by following other believers. There were practical reasons for Paul to charge the Corinthian believers to follow him as he followed the Lord (1 Cor. 11:1). Because Paul was an imitator of Christ, we should be imitators of Paul.

Of course, following another believer depends on the situation. Suppose an archbishop comes to us and tells us to follow him. We would have to say, "Dear archbishop, we cannot follow you or imitate you in being an archbishop."

Many believers today are confused concerning whom to follow and whom not to follow, whom to imitate and whom not to imitate. But in the Lord's recovery we have been enlightened through the Lord's speaking. I would not encourage you to follow any particular person. Using Paul's word, I would encourage you to follow "the tradition which you received from us" (2 Thes. 3:6). By tradition Paul means teachings and instructions, given verbally or in writing. We cannot deny that in the Lord's recovery we have His speaking, teaching, and instruction. Although I would not ask you to imitate a particular person, I would urge you to pay heed to all of the speaking, teaching, and instruction you have received. These are the traditions from the Lord, and we should follow them. Because these traditions are free from the influence of the religious background, it is safe for anyone to follow them.

In this chapter, Paul encourages the believers not simply to follow his walk, but especially to follow his instructions, his teachings. This is to walk according to the tradition the believers received from the apostles.

THE MEANING OF WALKING DISORDERLY

Verses 7 and 8 indicate what it primarily means to walk disorderly. According to the context, to walk disorderly here is not to work and yet to still eat. If anyone does not work and yet eats, he walks disorderly. But because the apostles were not disorderly, they did not eat bread as a gift from anyone. Rather, they worked night and day in order not to be burdensome to the believers.

In verse 10 Paul goes on to say, "For even when we were with you, we gave you this charge, that if anyone does not want to work, neither let him eat." It is disorderly not to work and yet to eat. However, a brother would be walking orderly if he did not work and also did not eat. It is not working and yet eating that causes one to be disorderly.

Verse 11 says, "For we hear of some walking among you disorderly, working at nothing, but busybodies." They were busy but "working at nothing," busy only with what was not their own business. Busybodies are nobody, and with them there is no Body of Christ. None of us should be busybodies. We all must learn to be busy, that is, to do our own work properly.

In verse 12 Paul continues, "Now such we charge and entreat in the Lord Jesus Christ, that working with quietness they may eat their own bread." Here we see that we should work without gossiping and eat our own bread. Do not invite those who do not want to work to have dinner with you. As long as they are not willing to work, you should not invite them to eat with you. To invite them to eat free of charge is to show love for them in a way that is not proper.

In verses 13 through 15 Paul tells the believers not to lose heart doing good; not to associate with anyone who does not obey the apostle's word in this letter; and to admonish him as a brother, not to count him as an enemy. The main point in this portion is that we all must learn to live in an orderly way. Let us walk orderly so that the brothers will agree with what we do.

PEACE FROM THE LORD OF PEACE

Verse 16 says, "Now the Lord of peace Himself give you peace continually in every way. The Lord be with you all." To keep the charge in verses 12 through 15 is to have peace from the Lord in every way. As long as disorder exists in a certain church, there cannot be peace there. In the church life we need to be at peace in everything, in every way, and with everyone. For this, we need the Lord of peace to give us peace continually in every way.

ENJOYING THE LORD AS GRACE

In verses 17 and 18 Paul concludes, "The greeting is by my hand, Paul, which is a sign in every letter. The grace of our Lord Jesus Christ be with you all." It is only when the Lord is enjoyed by us as grace that we can keep the church life from any kind of misleading and disorderliness. Both to live a proper church life and to keep it in order, we need the enjoyment of the Lord as the supplying grace. Only by grace can we live a proper life for the church life.

A CLOSING WORD ON THE HOLY LIFE FOR THE CHURCH LIFE

We have emphasized the fact that the books of 1 and 2 Thessalonians are on a holy life for the church life. In these Epistles the words holy, sanctification, and sanctified are used repeatedly. In 1 Thessalonians 4:3 Paul says, "For this is the will of God, your sanctification." It is God's will that we be sanctified. In 1 Thessalonians 4:7 Paul goes on to say, "For God has not called us for uncleanness but in sanctification." Then in 1 Thessalonians 5:23 Paul expresses the desire that the God of peace would sanctify us wholly. Verses such as these indicate that 1 Thessalonians is concerned with the believers' living a holy life.

In 2 Thessalonians 2:13 we are told that God has chosen us unto salvation in sanctification of the Spirit. Here we see that salvation is carried out in sanctification. This means that to be sanctified is to experience God's salvation in a practical way.

Both 1 and 2 Thessalonians are concerned with such a holy life, a life that is separated unto God and sanctified wholly by God and for God. This holy life is for the church life.

Some may wonder how we can prove from 1 and 2 Thessalonians that the holy life is for the church life. This can be proved by the fact that both of these Epistles are addressed to the church of the Thessalonians in God the Father and the Lord Jesus Christ. This indicates that Paul wrote to the Thessalonian believers on the subject of the holy life with the intention that they would live this kind of life for the church life.

The two Epistles to the Thessalonians also emphasize the basic structure of the Christian life, a structure composed of faith, love, and hope. Faith is the foundation, love is the building, and hope is the topstone. Again and again in these books, Paul speaks of faith, love, and hope. He encourages the believers to be established in these things. He also wants to foster their faith, love, and hope and to encourage the saints to grow in these things.

In order to experience the carrying out of salvation in sanctification and grow in the basic structure of the holy life for the church life, we need the eternal life as the eternal encouragement. We also need the Spirit as grace, and we need the grace itself. Therefore, it is by the eternal life as the eternal encouragement, by the Spirit as grace, and by grace itself as the processed Triune God that we live a holy life for the church life. This is the revelation in 1 and 2 Thessalonians.

LIFE-STUDY OF FIRST TIMOTHY

MESSAGE ONE

GOD'S DISPENSATION VERSUS DIFFERING TEACHINGS

Scripture Reading: 1 Tim. 1:1-17

With this message we begin a series of Life-study Messages on 1 Timothy, 2 Timothy, Titus, and Philemon. In previous Life-studies we have covered six books written by Paul: Romans, Hebrews, Ephesians, Colossians, Galatians, and Philippians. In these six books the basic and crucial truths concerning Christ and the church are revealed. The other four Epistles written by Paul are 1 and 2 Corinthians and 1 and 2 Thessalonians.

Of the fourteen Epistles written by Paul, Galatians, Ephesians, Philippians, Colossians, Romans, and Hebrews are very basic and may be regarded as a group. First Timothy, 2 Timothy, Titus, and Philemon may also be considered a group. We believe that the arrangement of the books in the New Testament is according to the Lord's sovereignty. In this sovereign arrangement, the four books of 1 Timothy, 2 Timothy, Titus, and Philemon are put together as a group.

Perhaps you are wondering how the other four of Paul's Epistles—1 and 2 Corinthians and 1 and 2 Thessalonians—relate to the first two groups of writings. The first group, composed of six books, contains the basic revelation concerning Christ and the church, whereas the second group, composed of four books, deals with God's economy regarding the church. This group covers the dispensation of God with respect to the church. First and 2 Corinthians strengthen both of these groups of Epistles. In these two books we see some further and richer revelation concerning Christ and the church. On the one hand, in 1 and 2 Corinthians we have further riches of Christ; on the other hand, these books strengthen the economy of God concerning the church. Then what about 1 and 2 Thessalonians? In these Epistles Paul shows us our hope, the hope of glory, that is, the appearing of our dear Lord Jesus Christ.

I. THE PURPOSE OF THE FOUR EPISTLES

A. First Timothy—to Unveil God's Dispensation concerning the Church

First Timothy unveils to us God's dispensation concerning the church. It is not easy to present such a brief yet all-inclusive summary of this book. Only when we dig into the depths of this Epistle do we realize that this is the subject. If we get into the depths of this book, we shall see that it can be summarized as a book which speaks of God's dispensation, His New Testament economy, concerning the church.

In 1:4 Paul uses the marvelous term "God's dispensation." This dispensation is an economical administration. Hence, it refers to God's economy. God's economy is revealed in four expressions found in 1 Timothy 3: Great is the mystery of godliness; God was manifested in the flesh; the church is the house of the living God; the church is the pillar and base of the truth. God's dispensation is related to the great mystery of godliness, to the manifestation of God in the flesh, and to the church as both the house of the living God and the pillar and base of the truth. When God's dispensation is put together with these four matters, we see that 1 Timothy does in fact reveal God's economy concerning the church.

B. Second Timothy—to Inoculate the Church against the Decline

The purpose of 2 Timothy is to inoculate the church against the decline. On the one hand, an inoculation is positive; on the other hand, it is negative, for it indicates that we need to be protected from a disease that could kill us. Paul's purpose in writing 2 Timothy was to inoculate the church against decline, degradation, and deterioration.

C. Titus—to Maintain the Order of the Church

The purpose of the book of Titus is to maintain the order of the church. It was written to assure that a local church would have a proper order.

The unveiling of God's dispensation concerning the church in 1 Timothy, the inoculation against the decline of the church in 2 Timothy, and the maintaining of the order of the church in Titus are three aspects of one purpose: that is, to preserve the church as the proper expression of the Triune God, as symbolized by the golden lampstands in the ultimate portion of the divine revelation (Rev. 1:12, 20). For the accomplishment of this purpose, the following basic and crucial things are stressed repeatedly in these three books:

1) The faith, the contents of the complete gospel according to God's New Testament economy; hence, it is objective, as mentioned in 1 Timothy 1:19; 2:7; 3:9; 4:1, 6; 5:8; 6:10, 12, 21; 2 Timothy 2:18; 3:8; 4:7; Titus 1:13.

2) The truth, the reality of the contents of the faith, as mentioned in 1 Timothy 2:4, 7; 3:15; 4:3; 6:5; 2 Timothy 2:15, 18, 25; 3:7, 8; 4:4; Titus 1:1, 14.

3) Healthy teaching, in 1 Timothy 1:10; 2 Timothy 4:3; Titus 1:9; 2:1; healthy words, in 1 Timothy 6:3; 2 Timothy 1:13; healthy speech, in Titus 2:8; healthy in the faith and in faith, in Titus 1:13; 2:2. All these are related to the condition of life.

4) Life, the eternal life of God, in 1 Timothy 1:16; 6:12, 19; 2 Timothy 1:1, 10; Titus 1:2; 3:7.

5) Godliness, a living that is the expression of God, as mentioned in 1 Timothy 2:2, 10 (godly); 3:16; 4:7, 8; 5:4; 6:3, 5, 6, 11; 2 Timothy 3:5, 12 (godly); Titus 1:1; 2:12 (godly). The opposite, ungodliness, is mentioned in 1 Timothy 1:9 (ungodly); 2 Timothy 2:16; Titus 2:12.

6) Faith, our act of believing in the gospel, in God, and in His word and deed; hence, it is subjective, as mentioned in 1 Timothy 1:2, 4, 5, 14, 19; 2:15; 3:13; 4:12; 6:11; 2 Timothy 1:5, 13; 2:22; 3:10, 15; Titus 1:1, 4; 2:2; 3:15.

7) Conscience, the leading part of our spirit, which justifies or condemns our relationships with God and with man, as mentioned in 1 Timothy 1:5, 19; 3:9; 4:2; 2 Timothy 1:3; Titus 1:15.

The faith equals the economy, the household administration, the dispensation, of God. The truth is the contents, the reality, of the faith according to God's economy. Healthy teachings, healthy words, and healthy speech are the ministry of the truth, ministering to people the reality of the divine truths. Eternal life is the means and power to carry out the divine realities of the faith. Godliness is a living that expresses the divine reality, an expression of God in all His riches. Faith (subjective) is the response to the truth of the faith (objective), receiving and participating in the divine realities. Conscience is a test and check to preserve us in the faith.

D. Philemon—an Illustration of the Believers' Equal Status in the New Man

Philemon does not seem to be related to 1 and 2 Timothy and Titus. According to many Bible teachers, these three books are called pastoral Epistles, books that give instructions on how to pastor, shepherd, a church. Because the term pastoral as applied to these books is too shallow, I prefer not to use it. I admit, however, that there is an element of pastoring, of shepherding, in these books. But it is altogether too superficial to speak of them as pastoral Epistles. If we look into the depths of these books and realize that they speak respectively of God's dispensation concerning the church, inoculation against the decline of the church, and the maintenance of the order of the church, we shall realize that Philemon should be put together with them.

In Philemon we have an illustration of the believers' equal status in the new man. Although Philemon was a master, and Onesimus was a slave, they shared an equal status in the new man. As we shall see, Onesimus ran away from his master, but was saved through Paul in prison. Then Paul sent him back to Philemon not as a slave, but as a dear brother in Christ. Therefore, here we see an illustration of the equal status of all believers in the new man. If we put this Epistle together with 1 and 2 Timothy and Titus, we shall know how to have a proper local church life.

The title of this message is "God's Dispensation versus Differing Teachings." Very few Bible readers have seen this point in chapter one of 1 Timothy. But in this chapter there is the matter that God's dispensation is versus differing teachings. What is the focus of God's revelation, the focal point of God's economy, His dispensation? God's economy is to dispense Himself in Christ through the Spirit into His chosen people so that they may have the divine life and nature to be Christ's Body, the new man, the church, to express God in the universe. This is the crucial point.

The problem among Christians throughout the centuries has always been the differing teachings versus God's revelation. Some may argue that when they teach people to be immersed, they teach according to God's revelation. Although this may be true, immersion is not the main point of the divine revelation. The crucial point is not related to immersion, to whether we use wine or grape juice at the Lord's table, or to whether we believe in a rapture that is pretribulation, post-tribulation, or mid-tribulation. Neither is the focal point of God's economy the huge image in Daniel 2 or the beasts in Revelation 13. How pitiful that Christians have argued over the type of water used in baptism, but have altogether neglected God's dispensation! It is vital for us to see that God's economy is God's dispensing of Himself as the wonderful Triune God—the Father, the Son, and the Spirit—into His chosen ones so that, having His very life and nature, they may become His many sons, the members of Christ, to manifest Him in the universe. This is the central revelation in the Scriptures; it is what the Bible speaks of as God's dispensation.

There were some during Paul's time who were teaching differently, just as there are today. They were teaching things that were versus God's dispensation. However, Peter, John, James, Paul, and the rest of the apostles preached the same thing—Christ and the church. Although the apostles were many, their ministry was one. We should never think that Peter, John, James, and Paul taught differently from one another. No, they all taught Christ and the church.

In the four Gospels one Person is revealed through four biographies. These biographies are written from different angles, but they do not reveal more than one Person. All four reveal the same Person, the Lord Jesus Christ. Because this wonderful Person has a Body, beginning with Acts and continuing through to the end of the New Testament, we see the Body of this Person. Again I say, all the apostles preached and taught the same thing, Christ and the church.

Because the apostles taught and preached Christ and the church, they all had one ministry. For this reason, Paul could say, "We have this ministry" (2 Cor. 4:1). The apostles were many, but they had received just one ministry. In chapter one of Acts there is a further indication that all the apostles were in one and the same ministry (v. 17). Any so-called ministry that is different from the ministry of Paul and the other apostles is actually not a ministry at all; it is a different teaching. According to the New Testament, the one ministry is to minister Christ to God's chosen people so that the church may be formed. This is God's economy, and it is versus all manner of differing teachings. God's economy certainly is not a matter of head covering, foot-washing, and regulations about eating or the keeping of days. God's dispensation is versus these differing teachings.

II. INTRODUCTION

A. Paul, an Apostle of Christ Jesus

Paul opens 1 Timothy with the words, "Paul, an apostle of Christ Jesus, according to the command of God our Savior and of Christ Jesus our hope." It was according to the command of God and of Christ that Paul became an apostle. In his earlier Epistles, he told us that he was an apostle through the will of God (1 Cor. 1:1; 2 Cor. 1:1; Eph. 1:1; Col. 1:1). The command of God is a definite expression, a further direction, of the will of God.

God our Savior (1 Tim. 1:1; 4:10; Titus 2:13) and our Savior God (1 Tim. 2:3; Titus 1:3; 2:10; 3:4) are titles particularly ascribed to God in these three books, which take God's salvation as a strong base for the teachings concerning God's New Testament economy (1:15-16; 2:4-6; 2 Tim. 1:9-10; 2:10; 3:15; Titus 2:14; 3:5-7). It was according to the command of such a saving God, a Savior God, not according to the command of the law-giving God, a demanding God, that Paul became an apostle.

In 1:1 Paul speaks of "Christ Jesus our hope." Christ Jesus is not only God's Anointed (Christ) to be our Savior (Jesus) that we may be saved to gain the eternal life of God, but also our hope to bring us into the full blessing and enjoyment of this eternal life. The hope of eternal life revealed in Titus 1:2 as the base and condition of Paul's apostleship, and the blessed hope revealed in Titus 2:13, which is the appearing we are waiting for of the glory of the great God and our Savior, are all wrapped up with the Person of God's Messiah, our Savior. Hence, He Himself is our hope, the hope of glory (Col. 1:27). It was according to the command not only of our Savior God, but also of the One Who has saved us with eternal life and will bring us into the glory of this life, that Paul became an apostle. His command is of the eternal life and is to be fulfilled by the eternal life, in contrast to the command of the law-giving God, which was of letters and which was to be fulfilled by human effort, without the supply of eternal life.

B. To Timothy, Genuine Child in Faith

In verse 2 Paul continues his word of introduction: "To Timothy, genuine child in faith: grace, mercy, peace, from God the Father and Christ Jesus our Lord." In Greek the name Timothy is *timotheos,* composed of *time,* meaning honor, and *theos,* meaning God. Thus, it means to honor God. Timothy became a genuine child of Paul, not by natural birth, but in faith, that is, in the sphere and element of faith; not naturally, but spiritually.

III. GOD'S DISPENSATION VERSUS DIFFERING TEACHINGS

A. Differing Teachings

In verse 3 Paul says, "Even as I urged you, when I was going into Macedonia, to remain in Ephesus in order that you might charge certain ones not to teach differently." Paul's word about "going into Macedonia" must refer to his travels after his liberation from the first imprisonment in Rome. Probably he wrote this Epistle from Macedonia, which is made up of what is today northern Greece and southern Bulgaria.

In verse 3 Paul refers to "certain ones." These were dissenting ones, as mentioned in verse 6 and in Galatians 1:7; 2:12.

To teach differently was to teach myths, unending genealogies (v. 4), and the law (vv. 7-8), all of which were vain talking (v. 6) and differed from the apostles' teaching centered upon Christ and the church.

Paul's Epistles are the completion of the divine revelation concerning God's eternal purpose and economy (Col. 1:25). His ministry completes the revelation concerning the all-inclusive Christ and His universal Body, the church as His fullness to express Him. Concerning the church as the Body of Christ, there are two sides: life and practice. From Romans through 2 Thessalonians, a full revelation is given concerning the life of the church, including its nature, responsibility, and function. Now, from 1 Timothy through Philemon, a detailed revelation concerning the practice of the church is presented. This pertains to the administration and shepherding of a local church. For this the first thing needed is to terminate the differing teachings of the dissenters, which distract the saints from the central line and ultimate goal of God's New Testament economy (vv. 4-6). The differing teachings in 1:3-4, 6-7; 6:3-5, 20-21, and the heresies in 4:1-3, are the seed, the source, of the church's decline, degradation, and deterioration dealt with in the second book.

1. Myths

In verse 4 Paul continues, "Nor to occupy themselves with myths and unending genealogies, which give occasion for questionings rather than God's dispensation which is in faith." The Greek word rendered "myths" in this verse is *muthos.* The same word is translated tales in 4:7 and fables in 2 Timothy 4:4. It refers to words, speeches, and conversations concerning such things as rumors, reports, stories (true or false), and fictions. It might include Jewish stories of miracles and rabbinical fabrications. They were the profane and old-womanish tales (4:7) and Jewish myths (Titus 1:14). The Jewish myths may have been the seed of Gnostic mythologies.

2. Unending Genealogies

The "unending genealogies" mentioned in this verse probably refer to Old Testament genealogies adorned with fables (Titus 3:9).

3. Giving Occasion for Questions

The myths and unending genealogies give occasion for questionings and vain talking rather than God's dispensation.

4. Vain Talking

The myths and the unending genealogies give rise to vain talking and cause people to misaim from the goal of the charge of love. In verses 5 and 6 Paul says, "But the goal of the charge is love out of a pure heart, and a good conscience, and unfeigned faith; from which things some, having misaimed, have turned aside to vain talking." The charge in verse 5 refers to the charge mentioned in verse 3. The differing teachings of the dissenting ones in verse 3 caused envy and discord among the believers. Such envy and discord were contrary to love, the goal of the apostle's charge. To carry out the apostle's charge, love, which is out of a pure heart, a good conscience, and unfeigned faith, is needed.

A pure heart is a single heart without mixture, seeking the Lord only and taking the Lord as the unique goal. A good conscience is a conscience without offense (Acts 24:16). Unfeigned faith, connected with faith in verse 4, is faith without pretense or hypocrisy, that purifies the heart (Acts 15:9) and works through love (Gal. 5:6). In order to deal with the differing teachings when the trend of the church is toward decline, all these attributes are required. They are necessary if we are to have a pure, true, and genuine love.

5. The Law

In verse 7 Paul refers to law teachers: "Desiring to be law teachers, understanding neither what they are saying, nor concerning what they confidently affirm." Law teachers, teaching people what to do and what not to do, are different from the minister of Christ (4:6), who ministers His riches to others. According to this verse, those who desire to be law teachers confidently affirm certain things. The Greek for confidently can also be rendered strongly or emphatically. The same word is used in Titus 3:8.

According to verses 8 through 10, the law is good if used lawfully. Paul says that the "law is not enacted for a righteous man, but for the lawless and unruly, for the ungodly and sinners, for the unholy and profane, for smiters of fathers and smiters of mothers, for manslayers, for fornicators, homosexuals, kidnappers, liars, perjurers, and if there be any other thing opposed to healthy teaching."

The words "healthy teaching" imply the matter of life. Anything that is healthy refers to the health of life. The sound teaching of the apostles, which is according to the gospel of the glory of God, ministers healthy teaching as the supply of life to people, either nourishing them or healing them. In contrast, the differing teachings of the dissenting ones in verse 3 sow the seeds of death and poison into others. Any teaching that distracts people from the center and goal of God's New Testament economy is not healthy.

B. God's Dispensation

In Greek the words "God's dispensation" in 1:4 also mean God's household economy (Eph. 1:10; 3:9). This is God's household administration to dispense Himself in Christ into His chosen people, that He may have a house, a household, to express Himself, which household is the church, the Body of Christ (1 Tim. 3:15). The apostle's ministry was centered upon this economy of God (Col. 1:25; 1 Cor. 9:17), whereas the differing teachings of the dissenting ones were used by God's enemy to distract His people from this. This divine economy must be made fully clear to the saints in the administration and shepherding of a local church.

My burden is altogether centered on God's economy. This has been my burden for more than forty years. During the years I have been in this country, I have not taught anything other than God's dispensation.

1. God's Household Economy

God's dispensation is His household economy. According to the Bible, God does not first want to have a kingdom. Rather, He first wants a house, a family. Once He has a family, His family will spontaneously become His kingdom. If He is not able to secure a family, a household, a house, He will not be able to have a kingdom. Thus, God's dispensation is first a matter of His household economy, or family economy.

2. God's Household Administration

Second, God's dispensation is His household administration to dispense Himself in Christ into His chosen people that He might have a house, a household, the church, the Body of Christ, to express Himself.

3. The Focus of the Apostle Paul's Ministry

God's dispensation was the focus of the Apostle Paul's ministry (Col. 1:25; 1 Cor. 9:17).

4. In Faith

In verse 4 Paul tells us that God's dispensation is in faith. The dispensing of God into us is altogether by faith. The dispensation of God is a matter in faith, that is, in the sphere and element of faith, in God through Christ. Faith may be in contrast to questionings. God's economy to dispense Himself into His chosen people is not in the natural realm, nor in the work of law, but in the spiritual sphere of the new creation through regeneration by faith in Christ (Gal. 3:23-26). By faith we are born of God to be His sons, partaking of His life and nature to express Him. By faith we are put into Christ to become the members of His Body, sharing all that He is for His expression. This is God's dispensation according to His New Testament economy, carried out in faith.

We need to be deeply impressed with the meaning of faith in the New Testament. We have spoken much about this in our Life-studies of Romans, Hebrews, and Galatians. Faith is firstly God being the Word spoken to us. We have God and then God as the Word spoken. Through the Word of God and by the Spirit of God we are infused with God in Christ. As a result, something rises up within us. This is faith. Faith then works in us to bring us into an organic union with the Triune God. Through this organic union, God is continually transfused and infused into us. As a result, we have the divine life and the divine nature to become God's sons, members of Christ, and parts of the new man. As a totality we become the house of God, the Body of Christ, and the new man. This is God's dispensation in faith.

5. According to the Gospel of the Glory of the Blessed God

God's dispensation is "according to the gospel of the glory of the blessed God" (v. 11). Have you heard this expression before? Many have heard of the gospel of grace, the gospel of forgiveness, the gospel of justification, and the gospel of regeneration, but not the gospel of glory. This gospel not only brings good news concerning forgiveness of sins and justification by faith; the gospel of glory is the gospel of God's dispensation. Glory is God expressed. Thus, the gospel of glory is the gospel of the expressed God; it is a gospel which expresses God's glory.

The "gospel of the glory of the blessed God" is an excellent expression. It refers to God's dispensation mentioned in verse 4. The gospel with which Paul was entrusted is the effulgence of the glory of the blessed God. This gospel, by dispensing God's life and nature in Christ into His chosen people, shines forth His glory, in which He is blessed among His people. This is the commission and ministry the apostle received of the Lord (v. 12). This should be commonly taught and preached in a local church.

In verse 12 Paul says, "I give thanks to Him Who empowers me, Christ Jesus our Lord, because He has counted me faithful, appointing me to the ministry." The Lord not only appointed the apostle to the ministry and commissioned him with the dispensation of God outwardly, but also empowered him inwardly to carry out His ministry and fulfill His commission. This is altogether a matter of life in the Spirit.

6. A Pattern under God's Dispensation

In 1:13-17 we see a pattern under God's dispensation.

a. The Foremost Sinner

Paul says that he was a foremost sinner (vv. 15-16). He was a blasphemer of God, a persecutor of man, and an insulting, destructive person with respect to the church. In verse 13 he says of himself, "Who formerly was a blasphemer and a persecutor and an insulting destructive person; but I obtained mercy because being ignorant I acted in unbelief." A blasphemer is one who blasphemes God, and a persecutor is one who persecutes man. Saul of Tarsus, a strict Pharisee (Acts 22:3; Phil. 3:4-5), could never have blasphemed God. But he had spoken evil of the Lord Jesus. Now he confesses that this was blaspheming. This indicates that he believed in the deity of Christ.

Saul of Tarsus persecuted the church in an insulting, destructive way (Acts 22:4; Gal. 1:13, 23), just as the insulting Jews persecuted the Lord Jesus.

Paul also says that he was ignorant and acted in unbelief. To be ignorant means to be in darkness, and unbelief comes from blindness. Saul of Tarsus was in darkness and acted in blindness when he opposed God's New Testament economy.

b. Having Obtained Mercy

In verse 13 Paul testifies that he obtained mercy. Saul, a blasphemer and persecutor, first obtained mercy and then received grace (v. 14). Mercy reaches farther to the unworthy one than grace. Because Paul was a blasphemer of God and a persecutor of man, God's mercy reached him first rather than the Lord's grace.

c. Favored with the Lord's Grace

Verse 14 continues, "And the grace of our Lord superabounded with faith and love in Christ Jesus." The Lord's grace, following God's mercy, visited Saul of Tarsus and not only abounded, but superabounded in him with faith and love in Christ. Faith and love are the product of the Lord's grace. Mercy and grace come to us from the Lord; faith and love return to the Lord from us. This is a spiritual traffic between the Lord and us. Faith is for us to receive the Lord (John 1:12), and love is for us to enjoy the Lord whom we have received (John 14:21, 23; 21:15-17).

d. Saved by Christ Jesus

In verse 15 Paul declares, "Faithful is the word and worthy of all acceptance, that Christ Jesus came into the world to save sinners, of whom I am the foremost." Christ came into the world to be our Savior by incarnation (John 1:14). He was God incarnated that He may save us through His death and resurrection in His human body. This should be constantly announced as the gospel, the glad tidings, in a local church.

e. Believing on Christ unto Eternal Life

In verse 16 Paul speaks of believing on Christ unto eternal life. The uncreated life of God is the ultimate gift and topmost blessing given by God to those who believe on Christ.

f. To Display All the Longsuffering of Christ and to Be a Pattern to All the Believers

In verse 16 Paul says, "But because of this I obtained mercy, that in me, the foremost, Jesus Christ might display all His longsuffering for a pattern to them who are about to believe on Him unto eternal life." Saul of Tarsus as the foremost among sinners became a pattern to sinners, who can be visited by God's mercy and saved by the Lord's grace.

7. Honor and Glory to the King of the Ages

In verse 17 Paul says, "Now to the King of the ages, incorruptible, invisible, the only God, be honor and glory unto the ages of the ages, Amen!" This word needs to be understood in relation to the decline of the church. When Paul was in prison, the churches began to decline, and the situation was very disappointing. Many were discouraged. Even some of Paul's co-workers left him. But he had a strong faith with an absolute assurance that the very God in whom he believed, the One who had entrusted him with the gospel of glory, is the King of the ages. He never changes. No earthly king can be called the King of the ages. Caesar was a temporary ruler, but how different is our God! The God whom Paul served truly is the King of the ages. This means that He is King of eternity. He never changes; He always remains the same.

Everything except God is corruptible. The church may decline, deteriorate, and become degraded, but God is incorruptible. Paul also says that God is invisible. God is powerful, everlasting, incorruptible, and also invisible. We cannot see Him. Certain terms ascribed to God in this verse are used only in this book. With Paul, we need to use these words to praise God. I would encourage someone to write a suitable melody for the singing of this verse. In a living, released way, we need to declare, "Now to the King of the ages, incorruptible, invisible, the only God, be honor and glory unto the ages of the ages, Amen!"

LIFE-STUDY OF FIRST TIMOTHY

MESSAGE TWO

FAITH AND A GOOD CONSCIENCE NEEDED FOR THE KEEPING OF THE FAITH

Scripture Reading: 1 Tim. 1:18-20

In the foregoing message we saw from 1:1-17 that God's dispensation is versus differing teachings. In this message we shall consider 1:18-20, verses which indicate that faith and a good conscience are needed for the keeping of the faith.

I. A CHARGE COMMITTED BY THE APOSTLE TO HIS CHILD TIMOTHY

In 1:18 Paul says, "This charge I commit to you, child Timothy, according to the prophecies previously made concerning you, that in them you might war the good warfare." To what charge is Paul referring here? In answering this question we must observe the principle that in understanding a sentence, a phrase, or even a word of the Bible, we need to consider the context, not only of the paragraph in which the verse is found, but sometimes of the entire book or even of the whole Bible. With this principle as our basis, we need to consider Paul's use of the word charge in verse 18 in the context of the chapter as a whole. The charge here covers the main points presented in the previous seventeen verses. On the positive side, the main point of these verses is God's dispensation; on the negative side, it is the differing teachings. Hence, the charge given by the apostle to his spiritual son concerns the dispensation of God positively and the differing teachings negatively.

A. According to the Prophecies Previously Made concerning Timothy

In verse 18 Paul says that he committed the charge to Timothy "according to the prophecies previously made" concerning him. It may be that some prophetic intimations were made concerning Timothy when he was admitted into the ministry (Acts 16:1-3). Perhaps the elders in the church which recommended Timothy to Paul laid hands on him. At that time prophecies might have been spoken concerning him.

B. To War the Good Warfare

Speaking of these prophecies, Paul tells Timothy, "In them you might war the good warfare." To war the good warfare is to war against the differing teachings of the dissenters and to carry out God's dispensation (v. 4) according to the apostle's ministry concerning the gospel of grace and eternal life for the glory of the blessed God (vv. 11-16).

C. In the Prophecies

Paul charged Timothy to war the good warfare in the prophecies. This means in the sphere, support, and confirmation of the prophecies.

At this point we need to see something concerning the grouping and the timing of Paul's Epistles. Although Philemon is grouped with 1 and 2 Timothy and Titus, it was actually written earlier, during Paul's first imprisonment. Paul was imprisoned the first time because of the Jews, not because of persecution carried out by the Roman Empire. We know from Acts that Paul appealed to Caesar and this caused him to be sent to Rome, where he was imprisoned. During his first imprisonment, Paul wrote four books: Ephesians, Philippians, Colossians, and Philemon. Thus, according to the time it was written, Philemon should be grouped with Colossians, Philippians, and Ephesians; however, in content it should be grouped, not with these Epistles, but with 1 and 2 Timothy and Titus. Philemon was written not long before Paul's release from prison. In the book of

Philippians he expressed his expectation that soon he would be released and visit the churches. Not long afterward, Paul's expectation was fulfilled. Having been released, he traveled to Ephesus, where Timothy was, and from Ephesus he went into Macedonia. From Macedonia Paul wrote the first Epistle to Timothy. Then from Macedonia he went to Nicopolis, where he wrote the Epistle to Titus. First Timothy and Titus, therefore, were written after Paul's release from his first imprisonment. After approximately a year, Caesar Nero suddenly began to persecute Christians. At that time, Paul was accused of being the outstanding leader among the Christians. He was arrested and imprisoned again, this time due to Nero's persecution. From prison, he wrote the second Epistle to Timothy. In chapter four he indicates to his dear child Timothy that he was ready to depart, to be martyred, to be poured out as a drink offering.

During Paul's first imprisonment, the churches were tested. This test showed that decline and degradation had set in. This decline was altogether due to differing teachings, teachings that were different from the ministry. This was the reason Paul charged Timothy to war a good warfare.

Throughout the centuries, the degradation and decline of the church has had one source: teachings which differ from the ministry of the apostles. In Acts 2:42 we see that at the beginning of the church life, the believers continued in the teachings of the apostles. These teachings were *the* ministry. What the apostles taught and preached was nothing other than Christ and the church. They preached a Christ who had been incarnated, crucified, resurrected, and ascended in order that, as resurrection life, He might be imparted into His believers to produce the church. This is the focal point of the teaching of the apostles, and it is crucial for us to see it. No doubt, in the Bible there are teachings concerning many things. However, the focus of the ministry of the apostles was the incarnated, crucified, resurrected, ascended, and glorified Christ to be our Savior, our life, and everything to us so that we may become His Body, the church. This is the vital focus of the New Testament revelation, and this is God's economy.

We need to contact the Word and receive God by the Spirit through the Word. Then we shall have faith. By coming to the Word, we are infused with God, and spontaneously faith operates within us to bring us into an organic union with God. The more we enjoy God's infusion, the more we become one with Him. However, this vital matter has been lost for centuries. Knowing the importance of this, Paul charged Timothy to fight a good fight, to war a good warfare.

On the one hand, Timothy was to war against the differing teachings of the dissenters. On the other hand, he was to carry out God's dispensation according to the apostle's ministry. If we wish to carry out God's dispensation, we must do it not according to the teachings of traditional Christianity nor according to systematic theology, but according to the apostle's ministry.

Furthermore, God's dispensation concerns the gospel of grace and eternal life. These are two basic elements in the gospel. This gospel is for the glory of the blessed God; it is for the expression, the manifestation, of the blessed God.

When Paul was in prison the first time, dissenters rose up to teach differently. These differing teachings were the seed of the church's decline. Paul realized the situation even while he was in prison. We know this by the contents of books such as Colossians and Philippians. Especially in Colossians we see that certain isms—Judaism, Gnosticism, asceticism—had crept into the church life. These differing teachings caused dissension and decline. Thus, Paul charged his faithful co-worker to fight the good fight against the differing teachings and fight for God's dispensation.

Today we also must be on the alert for differing teachings. Throughout the centuries, the church has been poisoned and corrupted by such teachings. If we are not on guard, differing teachings may also cause damage to the Lord's recovery. In the past we have seen the damage caused by differing teachings propagated in a subtle, hidden way. This has helped the leading ones in many churches to learn the important lesson of being watchful for differing teachings. We must not allow any differing teachings to come into the Lord's recovery. The recovery is strictly for the carrying on of *the* ministry. By this I do not mean my ministry, but the ministry of the apostles, which began with Peter and is still being carried on today. All true apostles teach and preach the same thing, even the one thing—God's New Testament economy. The focus of our preaching and teaching is Christ and the church. To teach and preach God's economy concerning Christ and the church is to war a good warfare.

II. HOLDING FAITH AND A GOOD CONSCIENCE

In verse 19 Paul continues, "Holding faith and a good conscience, which some thrusting away have become shipwrecked regarding the faith." This verse tells us how to war the good warfare. In order to war a good warfare, we must hold faith and a good conscience.

A. Faith, Our Believing Act

The word faith in the expression "holding faith" refers to our believing act; hence, it denotes subjective faith. As we have indicated, this faith rises up in us when we come to the Word and are infused with God through the Word and by the Spirit. The subjective faith moves within us to bring about an organic union between us and the Triune God. In this union we receive the divine life and nature to become God's many sons and the many members of the Body of Christ, the new man, to be the corporate expression of the Triune God for eternity. We must war the good warfare by this kind of faith, not by trying to keep the law.

B. A Good Conscience

Along with faith, we also need a good conscience, a conscience without offense (Acts 24:16). A good conscience is a safeguard of Christian faith and life. Faith and a good conscience go together. Whenever there is an offense in our conscience, there will be a leakage, and our faith will leak away. A good conscience accompanying faith is needed for warring the good warfare against the dissenting teachings in a troubled local church.

C. Shipwrecked

It is difficult to say whether the relative pronoun "which" in verse 19 refers just to conscience or to both faith and conscience. It may refer to both, since subjective faith is closely related to the conscience. As we have pointed out, if we do not have a good conscience, we cannot have living faith. Likewise, if we do not have a living faith, we cannot have a good conscience. Faith and a good conscience can be compared to a married couple: faith is like a husband, and conscience is like a wife. Since subjective faith and a good conscience go together, I prefer to regard the relative pronoun here as having both faith and conscience as the antecedent. Faith comes from our contact with God and brings us into the organic union with God; conscience is the organ touched by God after we contact Him by faith.

By thrusting away faith and a good conscience, some "have become shipwrecked regarding the faith." This shows us the seriousness of thrusting away a good conscience. To keep faith and a good conscience is a safeguard for our Christian faith and life. The word shipwrecked implies that the Christian life and the church life are like a ship sailing on a stormy sea, needing to be safeguarded by faith and a good conscience.

Those who thrust away faith and a good conscience become shipwrecked regarding *the* faith. In this verse Paul speaks both of subjective faith, our act of believing, and of objective faith, those things in which we believe. In speaking of those who are shipwrecked regarding the faith, Paul has in mind the objective faith, the contents of the complete gospel according to God's New Testament economy.

In verse 20 Paul goes on to name two of those who have become shipwrecked regarding the faith: "Of whom is Hymenaeus and Alexander, whom I have delivered to Satan that they may be disciplined not to blaspheme." Hymenaeus was a heretical teacher (2 Tim. 2:17), and Alexander was an opposer, an attacker, of the apostle (2 Tim. 4:14-15).

It is worthy of note that here Paul mentions names. Being more careful or "spiritual" or "heavenly" than Paul, we may not be willing to mention names under any circumstances. God took the lead to mention the name of His enemy—Satan. God has never said, "My people, I have an enemy. But because I am so merciful, patient, and all-embracing, I don't want to expose him or mention his name, in hope that one day he will repent." As God has singled out the name of His enemy, Paul mentioned the names of Hymenaeus and Alexander.

Furthermore, Paul does not tell us in verse 20 that he has been praying for Hymenaeus and Alexander. He does not charge Timothy, "Timothy, learn of me to pray for those who injure you as I have been praying for Hymenaeus and Alexander." On the contrary, in 2 Timothy 4:14 Paul says, "Alexander the coppersmith did many evil things to me; the Lord will repay him according to his works."

Paul tells Timothy that he has delivered Hymenaeus and Alexander to Satan "that they may be disciplined not to blaspheme." How utterly different this is from saying that he committed them to the Lord's gracious hand that they may receive His mercy. Paul expected Satan to work for him to discipline Hymenaeus and Alexander.

First Timothy 1:20 is a most unusual verse dealing with a negative matter. Two people are named not by a backslidden brother but by the leading apostle. Furthermore, they are delivered not to God, nor to the church, nor to a spiritual person, but to Satan.

Paul delivered Hymenaeus and Alexander to Satan "that they may be disciplined not to blaspheme." Paul does not say "punished"; rather, he speaks of being disciplined. Discipline is somewhat different from punishment. When parents deal with their children, they may tell them that they are punishing them. However, that is not actually punishment; it is loving discipline. The discipline in verse 20 may refer to the destruction of the physical body (see 1 Cor. 5:5).

Through the carrying out of a certain discipline Hymenaeus and Alexander would learn not to blaspheme God, slander God's economy, nor damage the apostle's ministry. To deliver persons like Hymenaeus and Alexander to Satan is to exercise the authority that the Lord has given to the apostle and the church (Matt. 16:19; 18:18) for the administration of the church against Satan's evil plot.

LIFE-STUDY OF FIRST TIMOTHY

MESSAGE THREE

PRAYER TO CARRY OUT GOD'S DESIRE FOR MAN'S SALVATION

Scripture Reading: 1 Tim. 2:1-7

A PROPER PRAYER LIFE FOR A PROPER CHURCH LIFE

In the first chapter of 1 Timothy Paul lays a good foundation to speak of the church life in a positive way. In 2:1 he goes on to say, "I exhort therefore, first of all, that petitions, prayers, intercessions, thanksgivings be made on behalf of all men." If we would have a proper church life, we must first have a prayer life. The leading ones, those who minister the Word in the church, should take the lead to have such a prayer life. A prayer ministry is the prerequisite for the administration and shepherding of a local church. Thus, Paul exhorts Timothy that petitions, prayers, intercessions, and thanksgivings be made on behalf of all men. This is the first word concerning the positive aspect of the church life Paul gives after speaking of God's economy and after charging Timothy to war the good warfare for God's economy. Timothy had to take the lead to have a prayer life.

A prerequisite for having a proper church life in the Lord's recovery today is to have a prayer life. A proper church is a praying church. A church that is without prayer is pitiful. Prayerlessness is a sin. All in the Lord's recovery must be prayerful and stand against the sin of prayerlessness. The elders in the churches must take up Paul's charge to "first of all" pray.

Of the fourteen Epistles written by Paul, ten were written to churches and four to individuals. Romans was written to all the believers in Rome, and Hebrews was written not to individuals, but to believing Hebrews addressed corporately. Ephesians, Philippians, Galatians, Colossians, 1 and 2 Corinthians, and 1 and 2 Thessalonians were all written to churches. However, the four Epistles of 1 and 2 Timothy, Titus, and Philemon were written to individuals. Some may think that these Epistles are not related to us because they were written to individuals. However, we should be today's Timothy, Titus, and Philemon. In particular, each individual saint needs to be a Timothy.

If we would be a Timothy, we must take the lead not to argue, gossip, or criticize, but to pray. Whenever we hear some news, good or bad, concerning a particular church, we should pray. Do not discuss the situation, do not gossip about it, and do not criticize. Just pray! Likewise, if you hear something about a saint or about an elder, pray for that one. The first requirement to have a proper church life is to pray. Oh, we all need to practice this! If we exercise ourselves to have a prayer life, the church will be living and uplifted. If some would be today's Timothys to take the lead to pray, the others will follow. This can be illustrated by the way a flock of sheep follows the few who take the lead. If you, as a Timothy, take the lead to pray, the congregation in your locality will follow.

Instead of talking so much and even instead of working so much, we should pray more. Should you hear that a saint is weak or backsliding, do not talk about that person, and do not criticize him. Moreover, do not immediately go to visit him. Instead, pray for him. Whether or not you should visit him depends on the Lord's leading. After you pray about the matter, if the Lord leads you to visit that one, simply follow the Lord and visit him. But do not do anything presumptuously. If the Lord does not lead you to visit a backsliding saint, you should not visit him on your own. It is possible that even in visiting the saints we may be presumptuous. Yes, visiting a backsliding saint is a presumptuous sin if it is done in ourselves apart from prayer and the Lord's leading. But if through our prayer the Lord definitely leads us to visit a certain one, that visitation will be effective.

We should also pray whenever we hear of problems among the saints. We should not presume that we are experienced and qualified to solve problems. Such an attitude is not only presumptuous; it is also blasphemous, for it is to consider ourselves as God. If we learn about a problem between brothers, we should bring this matter to the Lord in our prayer.

The first thing the elders should do in caring for the church is pray. Do not make decisions without praying. Do not either criticize someone or praise him without first praying for him. Before doing anything, we need to pray. Furthermore, our prayers should not be light or superficial; they must be thorough. Only after we have prayed for a matter thoroughly should we make a decision concerning it, not by ourselves independently, but in oneness with the Lord and according to His leading. If the elders practice in this way the church life in our locality will be uplifted and proper.

Brother Nee often told us that in reading the Bible we need to touch the spirit of the writer. The Bible in black and white letters can be likened to a human body, and the writer's spirit can be likened to the life, or to the spirit, in the body. Within the "body" of the Bible, there is the writer's spirit. If we touch Paul's spirit in 2:1-7, we shall sense his burden that those who take the lead in the church life must have a prayer life. In these verses Paul seems to be telling Timothy, "I have shown you a clear picture of God's economy and how it is versus different teachings. I have also pointed out to you that, in His mercy, the Lord has made me a pattern of His economy. I have also charged you solemnly to war the good warfare on behalf of God's economy. Now deep in my spirit is the burden to exhort you to pray. I exhort that petitions, prayers, intercessions, thanksgivings be made on behalf of all men. Do not think that teaching comes before prayer. No, prayer must be first, and teaching, second."

In 2:1 Paul mentions petitions, prayers, intercessions, and thanksgivings. Prayer is general, with the essence of worship and fellowship. Petitions are special and are for particular needs. The Greek word rendered "intercessions" means approach to God in a personal and confiding manner, that is, intervening, interfering, before God in others' affairs for their benefit. In addition, we must offer thanksgiving. Often when we hear good news about certain churches, elders, or saints, we praise them instead of giving thanks to God for them. If the situation in a certain church is good, it is because of God, not because of the church. Likewise, if a particular elder or saint is doing well, it also is because of God's grace. Therefore, instead of praising a church or a person, we should give thanks to God.

In mentioning petitions, prayers, intercessions, and thanksgivings, Paul's spirit was very burdened concerning the importance of prayer. He wanted his dear spiritual children to pray. Again and again I would emphasize the fact that we can have a proper church life only if we have a prayer life. I can testify that I have never prayed more than I have during the past several years. I can also testify that I have seen definite answers to my prayers. Recently, my activity was limited for a time so that I could rest and care for my health. When I heard about certain needs, I prayed for them. Perhaps the Lord limited me that He might impress me with the fact that prayer is more important than work. May we all learn the lesson that the way to have a good church life is to pray. This is crucial. If our talking is turned into praying, the church in our locality will be transformed.

GODLINESS AND GRAVITY

After pointing out that we should pray on behalf of all men, Paul goes on to say that we should pray "on behalf of kings and all who are in high position, that we may lead a tranquil and quiet life in all godliness and gravity." A tranquil and quiet life is one that is peaceable, still, and without disturbance, not only outwardly in circumstances, but also inwardly in our heart and spirit, that we may have an enjoyable church life in godliness and gravity. Godliness is God-likeness; it is to be like God and to express Him.

The Christian life should be a life which expresses God and bears God's likeness in all things. Gravity is a qualification of human character which is worthy of utmost respect; it implies dignity and inspires and invites honor. Godliness is the expression of God; gravity is toward man. Our Christian life should express God toward man with an honorable character that invites man's utmost respect.

OUR SAVIOR GOD

Verse 3 says, "This is good and acceptable in the sight of our Savior God." In this Epistle Paul emphasizes the Savior God. Hence, in this verse he speaks not of the God of grace, nor of the God of mercy, but of the Savior God, the God who saves us.

GOD'S DESIRE

In verse 4 Paul says that God desires all men to be saved and come to the full knowledge of the truth. We should pray on behalf of all men because God our Savior desires all men to be saved and know the truth. Our prayer is required for the carrying out of God's desire.

God desires all men not only to be saved, but also to have the full knowledge of the truth. Truth means reality, denoting all the real things revealed in God's Word, which are mainly Christ as the embodiment of God and the church as the Body of Christ. Every saved person should have a full knowledge, a complete realization, of these things.

The object of the two Epistles to Timothy is to deal with the church's decline. In the first Epistle the decline crept in subtly through differing teachings (1:3), and in the second, it developed openly and became worse through the heresies (2:16-18). To deal with such a decline the truth must be maintained. The first Epistle emphasizes that God desires all His saved ones to have the full knowledge of the truth and that the church is the pillar and base of the truth (3:15). The second Epistle stresses that the word of the truth should be rightly unfolded (2 Tim. 2:15), and that the deviated ones should return to the truth (2 Tim. 2:25).

ONE MEDIATOR

In 1 Timothy 2:5 Paul continues, "For there is one God and one Mediator of God and men, the Man, Christ Jesus." In this verse Paul explicitly says that there is one God. Although God is Triune—the Father, the Son, and the Spirit—He is still the one God, not three Gods, as mistakenly realized and believed by many Christians.

In this verse Paul also tells us that there is one Mediator of God and men. A mediator is a go-between. The one Mediator is the Man, Christ Jesus. The Lord Jesus was God from eternity (John 1:1). In time He became a man through incarnation (John 1:14). While He was living on earth as a man, He was also God (1 Tim. 3:16). After resurrection He was still man as well as God (Acts 7:56; John 20:28). Hence, He is the only One qualified to be the Mediator, the go-between, of God and men.

THE TESTIMONY BORNE IN ITS OWN TIMES

Verse 6 says, "Who gave Himself a ransom on behalf of all, the testimony to be borne in its own times." Christ gave Himself a ransom for the accomplishment of redemption for all men. This was necessary in order for Christ to be our Mediator. The Greek word for ransom means payment in recompense. He is qualified to be the Mediator between God and man, not only in His divine and human Person, but also in His redemptive work. Both His Person and work are unique.

In this verse Paul speaks of "the testimony to be borne in its own times." This is in apposition to the preceding clause; that is, the fact that Christ gave Himself a ransom for all men becomes the testimony to be rendered in its own times. Whenever this fact is proclaimed, it is a testimony to be rendered to men in its own times. For example, when this fact was preached in Africa, that automatically became a testimony rendered to men in Africa in its own times. The preaching of the fact is always spontaneously a testimony of the fact. When Paul preached in Asia Minor, that was the testimony borne in its own times. The same was true when he received the Macedonian call and began to preach in eastern Europe. That was the proper time for the testimony to be declared there. Whenever the facts of Christ's incarnation and death on behalf of all are proclaimed, that is the preaching, the testimony, borne in its own times.

PAUL'S TRIPLE STATUS

In verse 7 Paul concludes, "For which I was appointed a herald and an apostle (I speak the truth, I do not lie), a teacher of the nations in faith and truth." A herald is a proclaimer of the gospel of Christ, an official reporter of God's New Testament economy; an apostle is one sent by God with a divine commission to set up churches for God, an ambassador from God to the world for the carrying out of His purpose; and a teacher is a tutor who defines, explains, and teaches the contents of God's eternal purpose and His New Testament economy. Paul had such a triple status and commission for the nations, the Gentiles.

FAITH AND TRUTH

Paul had such a status in faith and truth. Faith here refers to the faith in Christ (Gal. 3:23-26), and truth refers to the reality of all the things revealed in the New Testament. This corresponds to 4:3, those who believe and "have fully known the truth." It is in the sphere and element of this faith and truth, not of the law, types, and prophecies of the Old Testament, that Paul was appointed a herald, an apostle, and a teacher of the New Testament.

THE PRINCIPLE OF INCARNATION

The title of this message is "Prayer to Carry Out God's Desire for Man's Salvation." Although God has such a desire, a heart, to save people, He can fulfill His desire only through the principle of incarnation. This means that He cannot save people directly; He must do it through us. Not even the angels have been appointed by God with such a commission for the carrying out of God's desire. This commission has been entrusted only to man. For the carrying out of this commission, we need to pray. According to Acts 10, both Peter and Cornelius were praying. Peter was praying on the housetop, and Cornelius was praying in his house. From both sides, prayer ascended to the throne of God for the carrying out of God's desire. By means of this prayer, God could accomplish His desire to save the Gentiles. The first Gentile household to be saved was that of Cornelius. This one example shows that our prayer is crucial for the carrying out of God's desire for man's salvation.

LIFE-STUDY OF FIRST TIMOTHY

MESSAGE FOUR

THE NORMAL LIFE OF THE BROTHERS AND SISTERS IN THE CHURCH

Scripture Reading: 1 Tim. 2:8-15

In this message we shall consider from 2:8-15 the normal life of the brothers and sisters in the church. After Paul charges Timothy to take the lead to have a prayerful life, he goes on to speak of this matter. In 2:8-15 Paul devotes one verse (v. 8) to the brothers and seven verses to the sisters (vv. 9-15). This indicates that if we are to have a proper church life, the sisters must bear a sevenfold burden, a sevenfold responsibility.

I. THE BROTHERS

A. Praying in Every Place

Concerning the brothers, Paul says in verse 8, "I will therefore that men pray in every place, lifting up holy hands, without wrath and reasoning." In a local church the leading ones must have a prayer life, as they were charged in verses 1 and 2, to set an example of prayer for all the members to follow by praying always in every place. In Ephesians 6 Paul tells us to pray at every time, but here he says to pray in every place. Although it is possible for us to pray at every time, morning, afternoon, evening, and night, it may not be possible for us to pray in every place. The requirement to pray in every place is more demanding than that to pray at every time. If we can pray in every place, we can surely pray at every time. But even if we are able to pray at every time, it still may not be possible for us to pray in every place. For example, it is not possible to pray in certain worldly places. Since you cannot pray in those places, you should not go there. If you can pray in a particular place, it is permissible for you to be there. But if you cannot pray in a certain place, you should not be there. According to verse 8, the brothers must bear the unique burden to pray in every place. Pray at work, at home, and in your car. As men, we should be those who pray.

It is significant that Paul opens verse 8 with the words, "I will." This expression is stronger than "I wish" or "I exhort." Paul's use of the word "therefore" indicates, as we pointed out in the previous message, that the elders, the leading ones, are to take the lead in prayer and pave the way for others to follow them to have a prayerful life. In the first message of this Life-study we covered some very important matters related to God's dispensation. But no matter how important these matters are, they cannot be carried out without the prayer of the brothers. Knowing this, Paul said, "I will therefore that men pray in every place."

As I am speaking about this matter of praying in every place, I am deeply burdened. I would beg you all, especially the leading ones, from now on to have another kind of life—a life of praying in every place. If you pray in every place, your living will be transformed, and the church in your locality will be transformed also. Some brothers may not be entirely satisfied with the church in their locality. The only way for the church in your locality to be satisfying to you is for you to pray at every time and in every place. Instead of discussing the situation of the church, pray for the church. The normal life of the brothers in the church is to pray in every place.

B. Lifting Up Holy Hands

When we pray in every place, we should lift up holy hands. Hands are a symbol of our doings. Hence, holy hands signify a holy living, a living sanctified and separated unto God. Such a holy life strengthens our prayer life. When our hands are not holy, our living is not separated unto God. We then have no supporting strength to pray, no holy hands to lift up in prayer.

In prayer, we should not lift up our eyes to observe others, but lift up holy hands. If you are watchful over the elders and the saints in a critical way, your prayer life will be killed. But if you lift up holy hands, your prayer will be strengthened.

C. Without Wrath and Reasoning

In verse 8 Paul also urges the brothers to pray "without wrath and reasoning." Wrath and reasoning kill our prayer. Wrath is of our emotion, and reasoning is of our mind. To have a prayer life and pray unceasingly, our emotion and mind must be regulated to a normal condition under the control of the Spirit in our spirit.

The Greek word for reasoning means disputatious reasoning. What Paul is speaking of here is not normal or ordinary reasoning, but a reasoning filled with disputation. We must avoid this if we are to pray properly.

Paul's word about not having disputatious reasonings is related to his admonition to lift up holy hands. If we close our eyes and lift up our hands, we shall be able to pray. But if we open our eyes to consider others and reason about their situation, we shall not be able to pray. Instead of lifting up our hands, we may clasp them behind our back. Who can pray with his hands clasped behind his back? But if we lift up our hands and refrain from disputatious reasoning, we shall be able to pray in a proper way.

From experience I have learned that our prayer life can be affected by our mood. If I do not keep myself in a proper mood, my prayer life is put to death. Anger always destroys our prayer life for a period of time. If a brother loses his temper with his wife, he may find that he cannot pray properly for a few days. If we are to have a prayer life, we must learn not to be moody or angry with others. By the Lord's grace that is with our spirit, we must exercise a strict control over our emotion.

II. THE SISTERS

In verse 9, Paul turns to the sisters. He begins this verse with the word "similarly." This refers to "I will" in verse 8. It may also indicate that Paul's word about praying in every place applies to the sisters as well as to the brothers.

A. Adorning Themselves

Verse 9 says, "Similarly, that women adorn themselves in proper clothing with modesty and sobriety, not with braided hair and gold or pearls or costly clothing." Proper clothing denotes what is fitting to the sisters' nature and position as saints of God. Clothing in Greek implies deportment, demeanor. Clothing is the main sign of a sister's demeanor, and it must befit her saintly position.

The Greek word rendered modesty literally is shamefastness, that is, bound or made fast by an honorable shame (Vincent), implying not forward or overbold, but moderate, observing the proprieties of a woman.

Sobriety denotes sober-mindedness, self-restraint. It means to restrict oneself soberly and discreetly. The sisters in a local assembly should clothe themselves with these two virtues—shamefastness and self-restraint—as their demeanor.

In verse 10 Paul continues, "But, what befits women professing godly reverence, by good works." Godly reverence is reverence toward God; it is the revering and honoring of God as those who worship Him should.

B. Learning

In verse 11 Paul says, "Let a woman learn in quietness in all subjection." Quietness means silence. For a sister to learn in silence and in all subjection is to realize her position as a woman. This safeguards the sisters from the presumption of overstepping their position in the local assembly.

Verse 12 continues, "But I do not permit a woman to teach or to exercise authority over a man, but to be in quietness." To teach here means to teach with authority, to define and decide the meaning of doctrines concerning divine truth. For a woman to teach in this way or to exercise authority over a man is to leave her position. In God's creation man was ordained to be the head, and woman was to be in subjection to man (1 Cor. 11:3). This ordination should be kept in the church. The word quietness in verse 12 refers to silence from speaking.

In verse 13 Paul offers a word of explanation, "For Adam was formed first, then Eve." This brings us to the beginning. God always wants to bring us back to His beginning (Matt. 19:8).

In verse 14 Paul goes on, "And Adam was not deceived, but the woman being quite deceived was in transgression." Verse 13 gives the first reason that a woman should subject herself to man. Here is the second. Eve was deceived by the serpent (Gen. 3:1-6) because she did not remain in subjection under the headship of Adam, but overstepped her position to contact the evil tempter directly without her head being covered. This is the strong ground for the apostle not to permit the sisters in a local assembly to teach with authority or to exercise authority over men, but to learn in silence and remain in all subjection. Man's headship is woman's protection.

C. Their Salvation

In verse 15 Paul concludes, "But she shall be saved through childbearing, if they remain in faith and love and holiness with sobriety." Childbearing is a suffering. Suffering restricts and protects the fallen one from transgression.

The grammar in verse 15 is rather unusual. At the beginning of the verse Paul says, "She shall be saved"; then he goes on to say, "if they remain in faith and love and holiness with sobriety." The pronoun "she" refers to Eve in verse 13. The reason Paul changes from a singular to a plural pronoun was that in referring to Eve he was including all women. Not all women are included in the pronoun "she," but none can deny that they are included in the pronoun "they." Paul's use of pronouns in this verse makes it clear that in speaking of Eve he is speaking of all women.

In verse 15 Paul mentions faith, love, and holiness. Faith is to receive the Lord (John 1:12), love is to enjoy Him (John 14:21, 23), and holiness is to express Him through sanctification. By faith we please God (Heb. 11:6), by love we keep the Lord's word (John 14:23), and by holiness we see Him. (Heb. 12:14).

In this message I am especially burdened concerning modesty, the leading female virtue. In some families there is not adequate stress on modesty. Rather, both boys and girls are brought up and instructed in the same way. Modesty is a virtue which emphasizes the difference between male and female. As we have pointed out, the Greek word rendered "modesty" in 2:9 is literally shamefastness, that is, bound and made fast by an honorable shame.

A word related to the virtue of modesty is shamefacedness. To be shamefaced is to be modest and have a sense of shame and know how to show shame. When a sister speaks in a church meeting, she should do so with modesty, with a certain amount of shamefacedness.

Modesty is a great safeguard and protection to a female. It is a mistake to teach girls in the same way as boys. Boys may expose themselves in certain situations; girls, however, should not. Otherwise, they will be without protection. This lack of protection can open the way for fornication. If the women working in an office have the virtue of modesty, they will be free from any improper involvement with the men who work there. A woman working in an office may easily become involved with a man if she does not have the proper covering, the necessary modesty, shamefacedness, which causes her to keep a proper distance.

All the sisters in the church life should have the virtue of modesty. The sisters should dress according to the principle of modesty. This principle does not allow the exposure of one's body. For a woman to expose her body is to go against the principle of modesty. A sister needs to have a head covering, not only physically, but also psychologically, ethically, morally, and spiritually. This is the modesty spoken of in the Bible. To be modest simply means that a female is fully covered in every way.

In the church life the brothers and sisters have quite a lot of contact with one another in fellowship. In such fellowship it is necessary for the sisters to wear a moral, ethical, and spiritual covering known as modesty. In all their contact with the brothers, the sisters should be covered with an "overcoat" of modesty. This is a great safeguard and protection.

The sisters should never forget that they are females. This must be true especially of young unmarried sisters. They should be careful not to allow any evil thing to defile their holy body, which has been separated unto God and which is the temple of the Holy Spirit. For a young woman to preserve her body in this way requires modesty. I advise all the young sisters to wear a heavenly cloak to cover themselves from the influence of this evil age. Then they will be preserved for God's purpose. At the time appointed by God, He will arrange for the right brother to marry a young sister as a virgin. Again and again I would remind the sisters to wear a cloak of modesty. The sisters must always remember that they are females. As females it is necessary for them to be covered. This is modesty.

Along with modesty, the sisters need sobriety (2:9). As a sister is practicing modesty, she needs to be sober. Far from being foolish, she should be sober-minded and discreet. She should be clear about things and have a keen discernment. A sister should be quiet, but she should not be without sobriety and discernment. A sister should be quiet soberly, not foolishly. As a sister exercises herself to be quiet and not to overstep her position, she needs a keen discernment within. Her spiritual sky should be clear, without clouds or smog. Then she will be clear, careful, and discreet.

The two virtues of modesty and sobriety are of great importance in the church life. The sisters should attend the church meetings in order to gain the full knowledge of the truth. This knowledge will cause them to be sober in their understanding. Then, along with their modesty, they will have what Paul calls "holiness with sobriety" (2:15). They will not be holy in a foolish way, in a way devoid of knowledge. On the contrary, they will be holy in a way that is full of knowledge, understanding, and discernment.

In the first two chapters of 1 Timothy Paul gives practical instructions to have a proper local church: (1) terminate the distraction of differing teachings (1:3-11); (2) emphasize God's dispensation, making it the central line and goal of the Christian life (1:4-6); (3) preach Christ to save sinners (1:12-17); (4) war a good warfare for God's New Testament economy by holding faith and a good conscience (1:18-19); (5) deal with the heretical teachers and the opposers of the apostle (1:20); (6) let the leading ones take the lead to have a prayer life, interceding for all men that Christ's redemption may be testified in due time (2:1-7); (7) let the brothers follow the pattern of prayer, praying all the time (2:8); and (8) let the sisters adorn themselves in proper deportment and subject themselves to the brothers, remaining in quietness, faith, love, and holiness with sobriety.

LIFE-STUDY OF FIRST TIMOTHY

MESSAGE FIVE

OVERSEERS AND DEACONS FOR THE CHURCH'S ADMINISTRATION

Scripture Reading: 1 Tim. 3:1-13

In 3:1-13 Paul speaks of overseers and deacons for the church's administration. In verses 1 through 7 he covers the overseers, and in verses 8 through 13, the deacons.

I. OVERSEERS

A. Aspiration for Oversight

In verse 1 Paul says, "Faithful is the word: If anyone aspires to oversight, he desires a good work." Paul begins with the expression, "Faithful is the word." This expression indicates that what he is about to say is very important.

In verse 1 Paul speaks of oversight, and in verse 2, of overseers. The Greek word rendered oversight is *episkope,* from *epi* meaning over and *skope* meaning sight; hence, oversight, denoting the function of an overseer. The Greek word translated overseer is *episkopos* from *epi* and *skopos* meaning seer; hence, overseer (bishop, from Latin *episcopus*). An overseer in a local church is an elder (Acts 20:17, 28). The two titles refer to the same person: elder, denoting a person of maturity; and overseer, denoting the function of an elder. It was Ignatius in the second century who taught that an overseer, a bishop, is higher than an elder. From this erroneous teaching came the hierarchy of bishops, archbishops, cardinals, and the pope. This teaching is also the source of the episcopal system of ecclesiastical government. Both the hierarchy and the system are abominable in the eyes of God.

In verse 1 Paul tells us that if anyone aspires to oversight, he desires a good work. Aspiration with a pure motive differs from ambition with an impure motive. It is the Lord's desire that many brothers have the aspiration spoken of here. For the Lord's recovery and for the building up of the local churches, there is the need of the proper leading ones. Hence, aspiration for oversight is not only justifiable, but even admirable. On the one hand, we condemn ambition; on the other hand, we appreciate the fact that many brothers have the aspiration for oversight. A brother with this kind of aspiration truly desires a good work.

B. Qualifications of an Overseer

1. Without Reproach

In verse 2 Paul says, "The overseer then must be without reproach, husband of one wife, temperate, of a sober mind, orderly, hospitable, apt to teach." Paul first mentions the qualification of being without reproach. This does not denote perfection in the eyes of God, but an irreproachable condition in the eyes of man. An overseer must be one with a good reputation. There should be no ground for others to speak evil of him.

2. Husband of One Wife

An overseer should be the husband of one wife. This implies the restraint of the flesh, which is necessary for an elder. It keeps an elder in a simple and pure married life, free from the tangle of a complicated and confused marriage.

3. Temperate

An overseer should be temperate. Temperate here means self-controlled, moderate.

4. Of a Sober Mind

To be of a sober mind is not only to be sensible, but also to be discreet in understanding. In 1 and 2 Timothy and Titus Paul uses the words sober and sobriety a number of times. All the saints in the church life need to be sober in their understanding. All must have the virtue of sobriety. If we have the Christian virtue of sobriety, we shall be very discerning and full of insight. However, we shall be quiet, not talkative. A talkative person is not a sober person. One who is sober is keen in his understanding, but slow to speak.

In our fellowship as Christians, it is very important that we understand others. Should someone come to you for fellowship, you should not say very much. Instead, listen while the other party does the talking. However, many have the habit of interrupting the other party and speaking too quickly. If we are to have the proper fellowship with others, we need to be inwardly like a calm lake. Talkativeness, however, stirs up the water and causes the lake to become muddy.

The elders should take the lead in all positive aspects of the church life. They should take the lead in prayer and in exhibiting the virtue of sobriety. If a brother is able to be silent for fifteen minutes while someone is having fellowship with him, he is able to meet this qualification to be an elder. When anyone is speaking to him, the elder should be a calm, tranquil lake, clear and transparent. This is one of the qualifications of an overseer. Talkativeness disqualifies a brother from being an elder. A proper elder is one who is quiet, calm, keen in understanding, and very discerning.

5. Orderly

The Greek word rendered orderly in 3:2 also means decorous. To be orderly, decorous, is to have behavior that always fits the situation. It is to be neither too fast nor too slow, neither too bold nor too timid. A decorous person is one who always does what is fitting. One who is decorous talks when talk is necessary and is silent when silence is required. He can also laugh when laughter is appropriate.

This one qualification shows how difficult it is to be an elder. It is not too much to say that being an elder is the most difficult task on earth. How difficult it is to meet even the one qualification of being orderly or decorous! Even in the way he uses the telephone an elder should be decorous. On the one hand, he should not talk too long; on the other hand, if his conversation is too brief, he may offend others. It is possible to go to an extreme even in the matter of the way we use the telephone. One extreme is that a brother takes the telephone off the hook, refusing to talk to anyone. Another extreme is that his telephone conversations are too long. Neither is orderly.

Elders should also be orderly in the way they speak to others. Sometimes they need to speak loudly; at other times, they should speak softly.

Furthermore, they should be orderly in the way they have their hair cut. To have hair that is either too long or too short is not orderly. By these few examples we can see that the requirements of eldership are virtually without limit.

Because the requirements of an elder are so many and so difficult, it is surely vain for anyone to be ambitious for eldership. Those who have this ambition simply do not know how difficult it is to be an elder. If a brother does not have a genuine aspiration with a pure motive for the Lord's recovery, he should not desire to be an elder. He should seek to fulfill his ambition outside the church, not in pursuing the eldership. The church is not an arena for a brother to satisfy his ambition.

The eldership is very demanding, and the requirements are extremely high. For this reason, I sympathize with the elders. From experience I know that they will receive telephone calls even in the middle of the night. They have no choice but to answer the telephone and take care of the situation of the one who calls.

At this point I would like to speak a word of comfort and encouragement to those who are children of elders. An elder's children may be troubled by the fact that their father gives so much of his time to the church. If an elder fails to give adequate time to the church life, he cannot fulfill his responsibility properly. However, because the church takes so much of his time, he has relatively little time to devote to his children. I would encourage the children of elders to realize that for their father to give his time to the church is very acceptable to God. Temporarily the children may have some hardship. But the Lord will reward them. Instead of being disappointed by their situation, they should be glad that their father has consecrated his life and time to the Lord's recovery. Eventually, the children of an elder will enjoy the Lord's reward.

To be an elder is a great blessing to one's family and to the church. It is surely worthwhile for a brother to aspire to oversight. Although being an elder is a most difficult job, it is a great blessing.

Those who are elders in the churches in the Lord's recovery are burdened by the Lord and chosen according to the insight, oversight, and foresight of the spiritual eyes of the church. They are not elected, and they are very different from those who may be called elders in different denominations.

6. Hospitable

Another qualification of an overseer is that he must be hospitable. Hospitality requires love, care for people, and endurance. All these virtues are required if one is to qualify to be an elder.

Nothing is more bothersome than giving hospitality. Hospitality tests the qualifications of elders. The principle of hospitality is giving without receiving; it is suffering without requiring anything in return. Hospitality means sacrifice with joy, but without recompense. An elder must have a heart and a spirit for such hospitality.

7. Apt to Teach

In verse 2 Paul says that an elder should be apt to teach. To teach here is similar to parents teaching their children. An elder must be apt to render this kind of home teaching to the members of the local church.

If a parent has not received a proper education, it will be difficult for him to teach his children. Likewise, if the elders would be apt to teach, they need to be knowledgeable. For example, an elder should be able to explain what the mystery of Christ is. If a brother is not knowledgeable concerning the truth, he is disqualified from the eldership. An elder should be able to teach the saints like a parent helps a child with his homework. However, this does not mean that every elder should be a teacher. It is not necessary for parents to be teachers in order to help their children with homework. Similarly, not all elders are teachers, but they all should be apt to teach.

8. Not an Excessive Drinker

In verse 3 Paul lists other qualifications: "Not an excessive drinker, not a striker, but forbearing, not contentious, not fond of money." When Paul says that an elder should not be an excessive drinker, he, of course, has in mind not an excessive drinker of wine. However, the principle here is that an elder should not be excessive in anything. This requires strong self-control. In the matters of food and clothing, for example, an elder should not be excessive. This tests his ability to exercise self-control.

9. Not a Striker

The next requirement, "not a striker," is related to the control of one's temper. This implies a strong restraint of the temper. An elder should be one who does not lose his temper.

10. Forbearing

To be forbearing is to be yielding, gentle, mild, reasonable, and considerate in dealing with others. It is to deal with people without strictness.

11. Not Contentious

An elder should not be contentious. He should not be quarrelsome; rather, he should be peaceable and not debate with others or contend with them. Even if someone comes to fight with him, he should not fight back, but should learn not to be contentious.

12. Not Fond of Money

An elder should not be fond of money. Money is a test to all men. An elder must be pure in money matters, especially since the church fund is under the elders' management (Acts 11:30). An elder must realize that the money which passes through his hands is not for his personal gain. He should not have even the thought of monetary gain.

13. Managing Well His Own Household

In verses 4 and 5 Paul goes on to say, "One who manages well his own household, having his children in subjection with all gravity; (but if anyone does not know how to manage his own household, how will he take care of the church of God?)" Managing well his own household is a proof that one is qualified to take the oversight of a local church. An elder should exercise to manage his household well and maintain it in good order. It is clear that anyone who does not know how to manage his own household cannot take care of the church of God.

14. Not a New Convert

Verse 6 says, "Not a new convert, lest being blinded with pride he fall into the judgment of the Devil." The Greek word rendered blinded literally means beclouded with smoke. Pride here is likened to smoke that beclouds the mind, making it blind, besotted with the self-conceit of pride. One who is blinded with pride may fall into the judgment of the Devil. This judgment refers to that to which Satan was sentenced due to his pride in his high position (Ezek. 28:13-17). The Devil was judged because of his rebellion which came from pride. The Devil was proud, blind, and rebellious. For this, he received God's judgment.

15. Having a Good Testimony from Those Outside

In verse 7 Paul concludes, "And he also must have a good testimony from those outside, that he may not fall into reproach and the snare of the Devil." An elder must be right with himself, with his family, with the church, and with those outside—the society. And, according to the context, an elder must be right in intention, in motive, in character, in attitude, in words, and in deeds.

To fall into the judgment of the Devil is due to the pride of the elder himself; to fall into the snare of the Devil is occasioned by the reproach of outsiders. An elder should be alert not to be proud on the one hand, and not to be reproachable on the other, that he may avoid the Devil's entanglement.

II. DEACONS

A. Qualifications of a Deacon

In verse 8 Paul says, "Deacons must similarly be grave, not double-tongued, not addicted to much wine, not seeking gain by base means." Deacons are serving ones. The overseers take care of the church; the deacons serve the church under the direction of the elders. These are the only two offices in a local church.

1. Grave

Deacons are to be grave. This virtue inspires and invites honor and respect. A person who is grave is neither loose nor light.

2. Not Double-tongued

A serpent is double-tongued. A deacon in a local church rendering service to all the saints may easily be double-tongued in contacting them. In that case, he practices the nature of the Devil and brings death into the church life.

Today we often use the expression two-faced instead of double-tongued. A two-faced person is hypocritical. He may speak one way to a brother in his presence and another way about the brother in his absence. Deacons should be neither double-tongued nor two-faced. If you do not have the Lord's leading to speak frankly to a brother about his situation, simply be quiet. Do not say anything to please him. Furthermore, you should not speak negatively about him behind his back.

The deacons should fulfill their duty without talking too much. However, there is a great temptation to talk excessively. In their contact with the elders, the deacons may acquire information about certain matters. It is tempting to pass on this information. When a deacon behaves in this way, he becomes the information center of the church. The deacons should not be informers. Restricting the circulation of needless information will kill the germs of death in the church life.

3. Not Addicted to Much Wine

Deacons should not be addicted to much wine. Being addicted to much wine is a sign of being unable to control oneself. A deacon in the service of a local church must exercise self-control in a full way.

4. Not Seeking Gain by Base Means

A deacon also should not seek gain by base means. He should not seek gain from rendering service to the saints. This is seeking gain by base means (see 6:5b). A deacon, therefore, should not be fond of money.

5. Holding the Mystery of the Faith in a Pure Conscience

Verse 9 says, "Holding the mystery of the faith in a pure conscience." The faith here, as in 1:19 and 2 Timothy 4:7, is objective. It refers to the things we believe in, the things which constitute the gospel. The mystery of the faith is mainly Christ as the mystery of God (Col. 2:2) and the church as the mystery of Christ (Eph. 3:4). A deacon in a local church should hold this mystery with full understanding in a pure conscience for the Lord's testimony.

If the deacons know the mystery of the faith, the standard of their service will be uplifted. Whenever the deacons are asked by the elders to do a certain thing or to help others in a particular way, they should realize that they are serving the saints in the mystery of the faith. This will uplift their service. It makes a tremendous difference if the deacons' contact with others is based on God's New Testament economy.

Years ago, I visited the royal palace in London. I noticed that every aspect of the service of the palace, from the changing of the guard to the work of the janitors, was done with a high standard and with dignity. Even the janitors conducted themselves with dignity and gravity, in a way which invited others' respect. How much more true this should be of the service of the deacons in a local church! Even the cleaning of the rest rooms should be done with gravity. Those who serve in this way should realize that they are not cleaning in a worldly place. Rather, they are serving the church, the house of God.

In verse 9 Paul speaks of a pure conscience. A pure conscience is a conscience purified from any mixture. To hold the mystery of the faith for the Lord's testimony, we need such a purified conscience.

In order to have a pure conscience, the deacons need to behave according to their knowledge of the mystery of the faith. We may know this mystery, but not live according to it. As a result, instead of having a pure conscience, we have a conscience that condemns us. A deacon should consider how he deals with his wife, his children, and the other saints. He then may realize his shortage, that he does not live according to the mystery of the faith. A deacon must be justified in the first place by his own conscience. He should have a conscience which testifies even to the demons that he lives according to the standard of the mystery of God's New Testament economy. Then he will truly hold the mystery of the faith with a pure conscience.

6. Unreprovable

In verse 10 Paul continues, "And let these also first be proved; then let them minister, being Unreprovable." Unreprovable here means blameless. The word that the deacons should first be proved may imply a period of apprenticeship. The word minister in this verse means to serve. This is the function of a deacon.

7. Husband of One Wife

Verse 12 says, "Let deacons be husbands of one wife." The requirement here is the same as that of the overseers, as mentioned in verse 2.

8. Managing His Children and His Own Household Well

In verse 12 Paul also says that deacons should manage "their children and their own households well." Managing the children and the household well proves the capability of a brother to serve the church.

B. Blessing on a Good Deacon

1. Obtaining a Good Standing

In verse 13 Paul mentions the blessing on a good deacon: "For those who have ministered well obtain for themselves a good standing and much boldness in faith which is in Christ Jesus." The word ministered here means served. The expression "a good standing" refers to a firm and steadfast standing as a believer and a saint before God and man. To serve the church well as a deacon strengthens one's Christian standing.

2. Obtaining Much Boldness in Faith Which Is in Christ Jesus

By serving well, a deacon will also be blessed with much boldness in faith which is in Christ Jesus. The word boldness also means confidence. To serve the church well strengthens the boldness, the confidence, of the Christian faith. Faith here is subjective and refers to our act of believing.

III. DEACONESSES

Verse 11 says, "Women similarly must be grave, not slanderers, temperate, faithful in all things." The word women in this verse refers to deaconesses (Rom. 16:1), not to the wives of the deacons. Sisters who are serving ones in the church are deaconesses. Such ones must be grave. Furthermore, they should not be slanderers. This corresponds to "not double-tongued" in verse 8. The Devil is a slanderer (Rev. 12:10). To slander is to practice the nature of the evil slanderer. A sister who is a deaconess, a serving one in a local church among many other sisters, should flee slander, the evil act of the Devil.

Deaconesses must also be temperate and faithful in all things. We have pointed out that to be temperate is to be self-controlled, moderate. The charge to be "faithful in all things" corresponds to "not seeking gain by base means" in verse 8. A sister as a deaconess needs to be faithful, trustworthy in all things, especially in things concerning gain.

LIFE-STUDY OF FIRST TIMOTHY

MESSAGE SIX

THE FUNCTION OF THE CHURCH

Scripture Reading: 1 Tim. 3:14-16

First Timothy 3:14-16 is the most crucial portion in the four books of 1 and 2 Timothy, Titus, and Philemon. Paul has covered the matters of the differing teachings, the dispensation of God, the need for the leading ones to have a prayer life so that all the other brothers may follow, and the charge to the sisters to remain in faith, love, and holiness with sobriety. Furthermore, the elders have been established and the deacons have been appointed. A church that has all these characteristics is certainly wonderful. Now in verse 15 Paul tells us that the church is the house of the living God, the pillar and base of the truth. Then in verse 16 he goes on to declare: "And confessedly, great is the mystery of godliness, Who was manifested in the flesh, vindicated in the Spirit, seen by angels, preached among the nations, believed on in the world, taken up in glory." In these verses Paul presents an extremely high standard for the church.

Among Christians today the standard of the church is far below God's standard revealed in 3:15 and 16. In order to reach this standard, the church must have all the characteristics described in the first two and a half chapters of 1 Timothy. There must be no differing teachings, and God's economy must be practiced continually. The leading ones must have a prayer life, and all the other brothers must follow them to pray in every place. Furthermore, the sisters should remain in faith, love, and holiness with sobriety. Then the government of the church must be established with the two offices of elders and deacons. It is our expectation to practice this kind of church life. We praise the Lord that in His recovery we have seen such a church life at least to a certain extent. Whenever God's standard for the church is attained as outlined in 1 Timothy, the church will function as the house of the living God and the pillar and base upholding the truth. This is also the great mystery of godliness, the manifestation of God in the flesh. Not only was the Lord Jesus the manifestation of God in the past; the church today should also be the manifestation of God. This is the goal, the aim, of these four Epistles written by Paul.

Even though Paul witnessed the beginning of the decline of the church, he was not disappointed or discouraged. Because he had both insight and foresight, he could be encouraged. He knew that some day and somehow the church would reach God's standard. The majority of the believers may decline, but a small number at least would be chosen, preserved, and established to practice the church life according to the divine standard.

We in the Lord's recovery can testify of the great difference between the recovery and today's organized Christianity. Reconciliation between the two is impossible. All the saints should be encouraged that the situation in the Lord's recovery is heading toward God's standard. This standard is that the church should function as the house of the living God, the pillar and base of the truth, and as the great mystery of godliness, God manifest in the flesh. The church life today must be the manifestation of God in the flesh. When visitors, including those who have not yet believed in the Lord, come to the meetings and behold such a manifestation, they will no doubt be greatly surprised. They may say, "What is this? It is different from anything we have seen elsewhere. It is even different from the church services in religion." Yes, the church is different; it is the house of the living God, the pillar and base of the truth, and the manifestation of God in the flesh. Every local church must reach this standard and continue according to it. There should be no decline; rather, we should maintain God's standard until the glorious appearing of our Head, the Savior, Jesus Christ.

In 3:14 Paul says, "These things I write to you, hoping to come to you shortly." By "these things" Paul means all he has covered thus far in this Epistle. When he wrote this book, he was hoping to come shortly to see Timothy.

I. THE HOUSE OF THE LIVING GOD

Verse 15 continues, "But if I delay, that you may know how one ought to conduct himself in the house of God, which is the church of the living God, the pillar and base of the truth." The words "know how one ought to conduct himself" indicate that in this book Paul gives instructions concerning how to take care of a local church.

According to Paul's word in verse 15, the church is the house of God. The Greek word rendered house may also be translated household. The same word is used in 3:4, 5, and 12. The household, the family, of God is the house of God. The house and the household are one thing—the assembly of the believers (Eph. 2:19; Heb. 3:6). The reality of this house as the dwelling place of the living God is in our spirit (Eph. 2:22). We must live and act in our spirit so that God can be manifested in this house as the living God.

As God's dwelling place, the church is both God's house and His household, His family. In the Old Testament, the temple and God's people, His family, were two separate things. But in the fulfillment in the New Testament, the dwelling place and the family are one. The family is God's dwelling place, and God's dwelling place is His family. As we have indicated, the Greek word for house may be translated either as house or household. According to God's New Testament economy, God's family is His house. These are not two separate things; they are actually one. We are God's family and also His temple, His dwelling place.

In speaking of the church as the house of God, Paul specifically refers to God as the living God. The living God who lives in the church must be subjective to the church rather than merely objective. An idol in a heathen temple is lifeless. The God who not only lives but also acts, moves, and works in His living temple, the church, is living. Because He is living, the church is also living in Him, by Him, and with Him. A living God and a living church live, move, and work together. The living church is the house and the household of the living God. Hence, it becomes the manifestation of God in the flesh.

II. THE PILLAR AND BASE OF THE TRUTH

Speaking metaphorically, Paul goes on to say that the church is "the pillar and base of the truth." The pillar supports the building, and the base holds the pillar. The church is such a supporting pillar and holding base of the truth.

The truth here refers to the real things which are revealed in the New Testament concerning Christ and the church according to God's New Testament economy. The church is the supporting pillar and holding base of all these realities. A local church should be such a building that holds, bears, and testifies the truth, the reality, of Christ and the church.

The church as the house of the living God is both the pillar which bears the truth and the base which upholds the pillar. As we have pointed out, the truth is the reality and the contents of God's New Testament economy. This economy is composed of two mysteries: Christ as the mystery of God (Col. 2:2) and the church as the mystery of Christ (Eph. 3:4). Christ and the church, the Head and the Body, are the contents of the reality of God's New Testament economy.

III. THE MYSTERY OF GODLINESS

Verse 16 begins with the words, "And confessedly, great is the mystery of godliness." The conjunction "and" in verse 16 indicates that Paul has not finished speaking about the church in verse 15. Oh, the church is a great matter! It is the house of the living God and the pillar and base of the truth. Paul's use of the conjunction at the beginning of verse 16 indicates that the church is something even more than the house of the living God and the pillar and base of the truth. The church is also the mystery of godliness. The church is the house, the pillar and the base, and the mystery of godliness.

According to the context, godliness in verse 16 refers not only to piety, but to the living of God in the church, that is, God as life lived out in the church. This is the great mystery confessed universally by believers in Christ.

The church as the house of the living God and as the pillar and base of the truth is not so mysterious. But the church as the manifestation of God in the flesh certainly is a mystery. A mystery always goes beyond our understanding. It refers to something which cannot be explained. If we are able to explain a certain matter, it is not a mystery.

The church is not only the house of the living God and the pillar and base of the truth, but also the mystery of godliness. Godliness refers to God expressed. What are we doing in the church life? We are expressing God. Human beings may not realize this adequately, but the angels recognize it and appreciate it. On the one hand, the good angels rejoice when they behold the expression of God in the church. On the other hand, the evil angels and the demons tremble in fear. They realize that eventually those in the church life will condemn them to the lake of fire.

When the Lord Jesus was born, a host of angels praised God (Luke 2:10-14). If the angels rejoiced at the birth of the Lord Jesus in Bethlehem, the city of David, will they not also rejoice to see God manifested in the church, which is Christ's increase and enlargement? Furthermore, when the Lord Jesus, living out God and manifesting Him on earth, confronted the demons, the demons cried out. In at least one case they begged the Lord Jesus not to send them into the abyss (Luke 8:31). If the demons trembled at the presence of the Lord Jesus, will they not also tremble at the manifestation of the living God in the church? No doubt when the church is living out God and manifesting Him, the demons and the evil angels will be terrified. Every local church must be a place where Christ is born anew in the saints. Furthermore, every local church must live out God in such a way that the Devil's time is shortened. On the one hand, when the churches come up to God's standard, the angels will sing and rejoice; on the other hand, the demons and the evil angels will tremble.

It may come as a surprise that in verse 16 Paul suddenly uses the relative pronoun "who," when he says, "Who was manifested in the flesh." In Greek the antecedent of this relative pronoun is omitted, but easily recognized, that is, Christ who was God manifested in the flesh as the mystery of godliness. The transition from "the mystery..." to "Who" implies that Christ as the manifestation of God in the flesh is the mystery of godliness (Col. 1:27; Gal. 2:20). This mystery of godliness is the living of a proper church, and such a living is also the manifestation of God in the flesh. The portion of verse 16 from "Who was manifested" to "taken up in glory" may have been a church song in the early days.

The first part of verse 16 speaks of a matter—the mystery of godliness. Hence, we would expect Paul to use the relative pronoun "which" to refer to the mystery of godliness as a matter. However, the fact that he uses the relative pronoun "Who" implies that the mystery of godliness is a person and not merely a matter. As we shall see, this person is Christ as the Head with His Body.

Through incarnation and human living (John 1:1, 14), God was manifested in the flesh. "In the flesh" means in the likeness, in the fashion, of man (Rom. 8:3; Phil. 2:7-8). In the form of man Christ appeared to people (2 Cor. 5:16), yet He was God manifested in a man.

Christ was also "vindicated in the Spirit." The Greek word also means justified. The incarnated Christ in His human living was not only vindicated as the Son of God by the Spirit (Matt. 3:16-17; Rom. 1:3-4), but was also justified, proved, and approved as right and righteous by the Spirit (Matt. 3:15-16; 4:1). He was manifested in the flesh, but vindicated and justified in the Spirit. He appeared in the flesh, but He lived in the Spirit (Luke 4:1, 14; Matt. 12:28) and offered Himself to God through the Spirit (Heb. 9:14). His transfiguration (Matt. 17:2) and His resurrection are all vindications of the Spirit. Furthermore, in resurrection He even became the life-giving Spirit (1 Cor. 15:45; 2 Cor. 3:17) to dwell and live in us (Rom. 8:9-10) for the manifestation of God in the flesh as the mystery of godliness. Hence, now we know Him and His members no longer according to the flesh, but according to the Spirit (2 Cor. 5:16). Since the manifestation of God in the flesh is vindicated in the Spirit, and the Spirit is one with our spirit (Rom. 8:16), we must live and behave in our spirit that this vindication may be accomplished.

Paul also says "seen by angels." Angels saw the incarnation, human living, and ascension of Christ (Luke 2:9-14; Matt. 4:11; Acts 1:10-11; Rev. 5:6, 11-12).

Christ was also preached among the nations. Christ as God's manifestation in the flesh has been preached as the gospel among the nations, including the nation of Israel, from the day of Pentecost (Rom. 16:26; Eph. 3:8).

Furthermore, Christ has been "believed on in the world." Christ as the embodiment of God in the flesh has been believed on, received as Savior and life, by people in the world (Acts 13:48).

Paul concludes verse 16 with the phrase "taken up in glory." This refers to Christ's ascension into glory (Mark 16:19; Acts 1:9-11; 2:33; Phil. 2:9). According to the sequence of historical events, Christ's ascension preceded His being preached among the nations. However, it is listed here as the last event of Christ being the manifestation of God in the flesh. This seems to indicate the church taken up in glory. Hence, it implies that not only Christ Himself as the Head, but also the church as the Body, is the manifestation of God in the flesh. When a church is well taken care of according to the instructions given in the first two chapters, with the oversight of the elders and the service of the deacons fully established, as revealed in chapter three, the church will function as the house and household of the living God for His move on the earth and as the supporting pillar and holding base of the truth, bearing the divine reality of Christ and His Body as a testimony to the world. Then the church becomes the continuation of Christ's manifestation of God in the flesh. This is the great mystery of godliness—Christ lived out of the church as the manifestation of God in the flesh!

I wish to emphasize the fact that although Christ was taken up in glory (Acts 1) before the preaching of Him began in Acts 2, Paul mentions this last, not only after the preaching, but even after being believed on in the world. This indicates that "taken up in glory" may include not only the ascension of Christ, but also the rapture of the church. The Head, Christ, was taken up before the preaching of Him began; however, the Body, the church, will be taken up only after Christ has been preached and believed on in the world. Therefore, in verse 16 there is a definite indication that this verse refers not only to the Head as the manifestation of God in the flesh, but also to the Body as the continuation of this manifestation. This is indeed logical, for how can a person's head function in isolation from his body? The Head, Christ, has been taken up in glory, and the Body, the church, will also be taken up in glory. Both the Head and the Body are the mystery of godliness. This is the manifestation of God in the flesh.

LIFE-STUDY OF FIRST TIMOTHY

MESSAGE SEVEN

THE PREDICTION OF THE DECLINE OF THE CHURCH

Scripture Reading: 1 Tim. 4:1-5

In this message we shall consider the prediction of the decline of the church as presented in 4:1-5.

I. THE SPIRIT'S PREDICTION

In 4:1 Paul says, "But the Spirit says expressly that in later times some will depart from the faith, giving heed to deceiving spirits and teachings of demons." The fact that this verse begins with the word "but" indicates that what follows is in contrast to what is mentioned in 3:15 and 16. At the end of chapter three, Paul reached the high point of the four Epistles of 1 and 2 Timothy, Titus, and Philemon, presenting a glorious picture of the church. However, in 4:1-5, he describes something very dark, something much in contrast to the situation in 3:15 and 16.

In 4:1 Paul uses the expression "the Spirit says expressly." This is the Spirit who dwells in our spirit and speaks to us there (Rom. 8:9-11, 16). We need to exercise our spirit that it may become keen and clear to listen to the Spirit's speaking and be kept from the deceiving spirits and teachings of demons.

Many in today's Pentecostal movement follow the Old Testament way of prophesying and say, "Thus saith the Lord." This expression cannot be found in the New Testament. In the New Testament we see the principle of incarnation. According to this principle, God does not speak directly. Rather, He speaks through man. First, in Jesus Christ God became incarnated and mingled with man. Now after the death and resurrection of Christ, it is possible for

Him to be one spirit with those who believe in Christ. In 1 Corinthians 6:17 Paul declares, "He that is joined unto the Lord is one spirit." This refers to the mingled spirit, the divine Spirit mingled with the regenerated human spirit. In the New Testament it is this mingled spirit which does the speaking. For this reason, 4:1 does not say, "The Spirit of God says," nor, "The Holy Spirit says." Instead, this verse reads, "The Spirit says...." According to the principle of incarnation revealed in the New Testament, this implies our spirit. We have seen that the principle of incarnation means that divinity is brought into humanity and works with humanity. Hence, when the Spirit speaks, He speaks within our spirit, through our spirit, and out from our spirit. If there were no one who was truly one spirit with the speaking God, there would be no way, according to the New Testament principle, for God to speak.

Paul took the lead to be one spirit with the Lord. Because he was one with Him in this way, Paul was able to speak a great deal for the Lord. In 1 Corinthians 7 Paul says definitely that concerning a particular matter he does not have a word from the Lord, but that he gives his opinion, his judgment, as one who has received the mercy of the Lord to be faithful (v. 25). But as we read this portion of the Bible today, we see that Paul's word is in fact the word of the Lord. When Paul spoke, the Triune God, who has been processed to become the Spirit and who was mingled with Paul's regenerated spirit, spoke from within him. We also have such a mingled spirit within us today. It is in and through this mingled spirit that the Spirit speaks expressly.

First Timothy 4:1 is a continuation of 3:15 and 16. No doubt, these latter verses were Paul's words. Now in 4:1 Paul says that the Spirit speaks expressly. Where was the Spirit speaking? There can be no doubt that the Spirit was speaking from within Paul. As Paul was writing to Timothy about the church as the house of God, the pillar and base of the truth, and the great mystery of godliness, the Spirit was speaking in his spirit. This is not the Spirit who suddenly descends upon us and causes us to prophesy, "Thus saith the

Lord." The speaking of the Spirit in 4:1 is according to the way of incarnation. The Spirit spoke from within Paul's spirit.

If we would hear the speaking of the Spirit, we need to exercise our spirit. Only our spirit can listen to the speaking of the Spirit. The mind is not qualified for this; it lacks the ability to listen to the Spirit's speaking. The Spirit speaks to our spirit, and our spirit responds to the Spirit. Therefore, as we read 1 Timothy, we must exercise our spirit to listen to the Spirit speaking from within the spirit of the Apostle Paul.

II. DEPARTING FROM THE FAITH

According to 4:1, the Spirit says that in later times some will depart from the faith. The later times, or after times, refer to times after the writing of this book. This differs from the last days in 2 Timothy 3:1, which denote the closing period of this age.

As he was writing this Epistle, Paul realized that in time to come some would depart from the faith. In this verse the faith is objective and refers to the contents of our belief. On the one hand, Paul was bold and encouraged, not in the least disappointed. He believed that the church was the house of the living God, the pillar and base of the truth, and even the mystery of godliness. On the other hand, deep within his spirit, he knew that certain so-called believers would depart from the faith, from God's New Testament economy. Paul could know this because the Spirit who was mingled with his spirit revealed it to him. This departure from God's New Testament economy would be the beginning of the decline of the church life.

Paul says that those who depart from the faith will give heed to deceiving spirits and teachings of demons. Many Christians do not realize that, according to the Bible, there are two categories of evil spirits. The deceiving spirits in 4:1 are in contrast to the Spirit, as mentioned in 1 John 4:1, 3, and 6. These are the fallen angels who followed Satan in his rebellion and became his subordinates, who work for his kingdom of darkness (Matt. 25:41; Eph. 6:12). Demons are the unclean and evil spirits (Matt. 12:22, 43; Luke 8:2) of the living creatures on earth in the pre-adamic age who joined Satan's rebellion and were judged by God (see Life-study of Genesis, Message Two). After being judged, they became demons, working on earth for Satan's kingdom. The demons differ from the deceiving spirits, the fallen angels. The fallen angels are in the air, whereas the demons are active on earth.

In verse 1 Paul speaks of both the deceiving spirits in the air and the demons on earth. Among Christians today there are deceptive doctrines which come from the deceiving spirits in the air and also teachings which originate with demons. The history of the church has proved that Paul was right in saying that such teachings and doctrines would come in and that those who depart from the faith would give heed to them.

In verse 2 Paul continues, "In the hypocrisy of men who speak lies, seared in their own conscience as with a branding iron." The phrase "in the hypocrisy of men who speak lies" modifies teachings of demons in verse 1. The teachings of demons are carried out in the hypocrisy of those who lie. This indicates that demons and lying speakers collaborate to deceive people. These hypocrites work together with evil spirits and demons to bring in deceitful teachings and demonic doctrines.

The conscience of hypocritical liars has lost its sense as if seared with a hot branding iron, an iron used to brand the slaves and cattle of a certain owner. This book strongly stresses the conscience. In the church life the love which is contrary to envy and discord is of a good conscience (1:5). Those who thrust away a good conscience become shipwrecked regarding the faith (1:19). The serving ones in the church must hold the mystery of the faith in a pure conscience (3:9). To keep a good and pure conscience is to keep the conscience sensitive in its function. This will safeguard us from the demonic and hypocritical teachings of deceiving liars.

When I was young, I had confidence in anyone who testified that he was a Christian. One day, Brother Nee pointed out the fact that some Christians lie. I wondered how a Christian could be a liar. The Bible says that Satan is the father of lies (John 8:44). Eventually I learned from experience that Christians can lie. In the case of these lying Christians, it seems as if their conscience has been seared and has lost its function. Today many lies have been spread about us by Christians. Some have even gone so far as to put these lies into print. But our conscience testifies that we in the Lord's recovery surely believe the truth revealed in the Bible, perhaps more than other Christians.

We in the Lord's recovery should not only know God's dispensation, but should also know Satan's evil plot. We must see the sharp contrast between the situation at the end of chapter three and that described at the beginning of chapter four. We need to be discerning, sober-minded, and clear concerning the difference between today's Christianity and the Lord's recovery. We must also know what the Devil is doing through evil spirits, demons, and those who speak lies in hypocrisy.

Verse 3 says, "Forbidding to marry, commanding to abstain from foods which God has created to be partaken of with thanksgiving by those who believe and have fully known the truth." Marriage and eating were ordained by God. Eating is for the existence of mankind, and marriage for the continuation and multiplication of mankind. Satan, on the one hand, causes men to abuse these two things in the indulgence of their lustful flesh; on the other hand, he causes men to be unbalanced in the way of asceticism by forbidding marriage and the eating of certain foods. This is a demonic teaching!

Marriage was ordained by God for the carrying out of God's purpose with man. Food is necessary to sustain mankind to exist on earth for the fulfillment of God's purpose. But Satan, through the deceiving spirits and the teachings of demons with the collaboration of hypocrites and liars, seeks to destroy these things, either causing people to abuse them through indulgence or to practice asceticism.

III. THE TRUTH CONCERNING FOOD

In verse 3 Paul speaks of "foods which God has created to be partaken of with thanksgiving." All edible things were created by God for men to live on. We should partake of them with thanksgiving to God out of a grateful heart.

Because all food is God's gift to us, we should receive it with thanksgiving. As we partake of our food, we should say, "Lord, thank You." However, we do not have to follow the traditional ritual of saying a so-called word of grace. On the one hand, I do not agree with the practice of such a ritual; on the other hand, I do not agree with neglecting to thank the Lord for the food He has given us. I can testify that I thank the Lord again and again for my food. I even thank Him for a glass of water and say, "Lord, this water is a gift from You, and I thank You for it." Those who practice saying "grace" usually do so before they start eating. But we should thank the Lord for our food not only before we eat it, but also while we are partaking of it and when we have finished our meal. Furthermore, we may express our thanks for each particular item we eat.

The foods God has created should be partaken of with thanksgiving "by those who believe and have fully known the truth." To believe is to be saved and thus begin in the spiritual life. To have fully known the truth is to realize God's purpose in His economy and to grow unto maturity in the spiritual life. God desires all men to be saved and to come to the full knowledge of the truth (2:4). The truth here is God's New Testament economy. As those who are saved by believing in the Lord Jesus for salvation and who know the content, the reality, of God's economy concerning Christ as the mystery of God and the church as the mystery of Christ, we should be thankful for all the food we eat. Those who believe and who know the truth are qualified to receive their food with thanksgiving. We know that we are living on earth for God and for His purpose. Thus, we receive what He has prepared for our sustenance, and we thank Him for it all.

In verses 4 and 5 Paul goes on to say, "For every creature of God is good, and nothing is to be rejected, being received with thanksgiving; for it is sanctified through the word of God and intercession." The statement that "every creature of God is good" is contrary both to Gnosticism, which teaches that some created things are evil, and to ascetic teachings that command men to abstain from certain foods. Some insist that we should eat only vegetables and not meat. But according to Paul's word, every creature of God is good.

Furthermore, Paul says that "nothing is to be rejected." In the past, I politely said, "No, thank you," when I was served certain foods at Cantonese feasts. In particular, I declined to eat turtle, snake, or frogs. I simply was unable to eat those things. But according to Paul's word, we should not reject anything created by Him, but receive all things with thanksgiving.

In verse 5 Paul concludes, "For it is sanctified through the word of God and intercession." All the food we eat can be sanctified, separated unto God for His purpose, through the word of God and intercession. Here the word of God refers to the word of our prayer addressed to God, of which part may be quotations from the Scriptures, or part, messages we hear and read. In this verse intercession refers to our prayer to God for the food we eat. Such prayer separates our food from being common and sanctifies it unto God for His purpose, that is, to nourish us that we may live for Him.

Many versions do not have the boldness to use the word intercession, even though this is the meaning of the Greek word. Instead, they render the Greek word as prayer. But here Paul is definitely saying that we should make intercession for our food. We may pray for ourselves, but we intercede either for someone else or for something. According to Paul's word in this verse, we need to intercede for our food and ask the Lord to sanctify it. Whenever we sit down to eat, we should pray for the food and make intercession for it, saying, "Lord, sanctify this food for Your purpose that it may nourish Your servant. Lord, I believe, and I know the truth. I am here on earth for You and for Your economy. I need this food, and I ask that it be sanctified, separated, to Yourself for the fulfillment of Your economy." In the eyes of God, after intercession has been made for our food in this way, the food becomes holy. This is the proper way to receive our God-given food with thanksgiving.

LIFE-STUDY OF FIRST TIMOTHY

MESSAGE EIGHT

A GOOD MINISTER OF CHRIST

Scripture Reading: 1 Tim. 4:6-16

In 4:6 Paul uses the expression "a good minister of Christ Jesus." A minister of Christ is one who serves others with Christ, ministering Christ as Savior, life, life supply, and every positive thing. He differs from a teacher of the law and of other things (1:7, 3).

I. LAYING THESE THINGS BEFORE THE BROTHERS

A minister of Christ does not mainly denote a minister who belongs to Christ, but a person who ministers Christ to others. He is one who serves people with Christ. For example, if we say that a man is a serving one of a particular meal, we do not mean, of course, that he belongs to the meal. We mean that he serves others with that meal. In like manner, although it is true that a minister of Christ belongs to Christ, the main thought here is that he serves others with Christ, ministering Christ to them. Not only does he belong to Christ, but he serves Christ to others.

In today's Christianity there are a great many ministers who belong to Christ, but very few of them minister Christ to others. To be a minister of Christ does not primarily mean to preach Christ, teach Christ, or tell others about Christ. The main significance of this term is ministering Christ to others.

Verse 6 confirms this understanding of the expression "a good minister of Christ." Here Paul says, "Laying these things before the brothers, you will be a good minister of Christ Jesus, being nourished with the words of the faith and of the good teaching which you have closely followed." By "these things" Paul means all he has covered thus far in this Epistle. Just as a steward lays different courses of food before guests at a dinner, so a good minister of Christ should lay "these things" before the believers. Furthermore, Paul's use of the term "being nourished" indicates that his concept is that of supplying life to others. It is significant that here Paul does not say "being taught," but "being nourished" with the words of the faith. If we would minister Christ to others, we ourselves must first be nourished. Being nourished with Christ, we shall have Christ as food, as life supply, to minister to others. The words "being nourished" give us the ground to say that a good minister of Christ does not merely teach others about Christ, but ministers Christ into others as food. Others should be able to testify of us that we have nourished them with Christ.

Throughout the years, my aim in the ministry has been to nourish the saints. No doubt I have passed on a good deal of knowledge. But I can testify that in every message, I exercise my spirit not just to pass on knowledge, but, while I am giving forth a certain kind of knowledge, to supply something nourishing to the Lord's people. My desire is to minister the riches of Christ as food that the saints may be nourished. Recently, many have written me letters telling how they have been richly fed with Christ through the messages.

If you have a heart to care for others in the Lord's recovery, you should not give them mere teaching. Whenever you fellowship with others concerning Christ, you may give them some knowledge. But while you are teaching them, you need to exercise your spirit to minister spiritual food that they may be nourished. If you do this, you will be a good minister of Christ.

With Paul and Timothy we see an excellent pattern. As we have pointed out, Paul told Timothy to lay "these things before the brothers," referring to the things which he was writing in this Epistle. However, before Timothy could lay these things before others, he first had to feed on them himself. He had to digest them, assimilate them, and allow them to saturate his inner being. Then he would be able to lay them before the brothers. Today we should follow Timothy's example and lay before the saints the things with which we have been nourished by the Lord through the ministry. How wonderful the church life would be if we all did this! However, if we turn from the ministry and seek to produce something different, we may give place to differing teachings. It was not Timothy's intention to teach anything different from what Paul taught. Rather, he would lay before the brothers what he had received from Paul.

At this point, I would like to say a word concerning my burden in putting out the Life-study Messages. The aim of these messages is to produce groceries for the local churches. My burden is not mainly to "cook" these spiritual groceries; it is to produce them and supply them to the churches that every local church may be a well-stocked supermarket, filled with a variety of nourishing foods. If the leading ones in a local church lay before the saints the riches contained in the Life-studies, the saints will be abundantly nourished. I have received many letters testifying that this has happened.

It is a fact of history in the Lord's recovery that any church which follows the ministry is strong and blessed. But those churches which neglect the ministry and try instead to do something on their own have become a failure. However, in saying these things, I wish to make it very clear that I by no means insist that the churches or the saints read the Life-study Messages. To repeat, my burden is to produce groceries. The churches and the saints are free either to use them or to disregard them. But if the saints cast away the nourishment found in these messages, I wonder what they will feed on. We are what we eat. If we eat the "groceries" produced in today's religion, we shall be part of religion. Let me say in frankness and honesty that the leading ones need to take "these things" and lay them before the saints that they may be nourished.

Paul's expression "laying these things before the brothers" is very significant. We need to be impressed with the fact that this also is part of the Bible, the Word of God. I do not charge anyone to lay my words before the saints. It is not my practice to charge the churches to do anything. Representatives of hundreds of churches can testify that I do not charge them to do things. I do not even know many of the things that take place in the church in Anaheim, where I live. I am very glad that the elders take action regarding many things without letting me know. This is a strong proof that I am not a pope. Very much to the contrary, I am a little servant of the Lord, a farmer burdened to produce groceries for the saints. Far from charging the churches to do anything, I simply long that they feed on the spiritual riches the Lord has given us. Do not lay Witness Lee's teaching before the brothers. Instead, present them the riches, the groceries, the Lord has shown us from the Word.

I am deeply burdened by the fact that many who love the Lord Jesus and seek Him have been deceived and frustrated. We must find a way to share with them the spiritual riches the Lord has provided us. Many who truly love the Lord are starving. We must take up the burden to supply them with food. We all need to be good ministers of Christ, serving others with His riches. Let us first be nourished ourselves and then minister this nourishment to all the people of God.

We would emphasize that being nourished is for the growth in life. This is a matter of life and it differs from merely being taught, which is a matter of knowledge. To minister Christ to others requires that we ourselves first be nourished with the words of life concerning Christ.

II. BEING NOURISHED

In verse 6 Paul specifically speaks of "being nourished with the words of the faith and of the good teaching." The words of the faith are the words of the full gospel concerning God's New Testament economy. The focus of God's economy is not the image in Daniel 2 or the four beasts in Daniel 7. If you want to see the focal point of God's economy, study the book of Galatians, Ephesians, Philippians, and Colossians. We need to be nourished with the words of the faith, God's economy, found in these books.

According to verse 6, we should also be nourished with the good teaching which we have closely followed. The words of the good teaching are the sweet words that contain and convey the riches of Christ to nourish, edify, and strengthen His believers. Actually, the words of the faith and the words of the good teaching refer to the same thing. If we would teach others, we ourselves must first follow these words closely. Following them closely and being nourished with them, we shall then be able to feed others. For example, if a mother does not know how to nourish herself properly, she will not know how to feed healthy food to her children. Through her own experience of being nourished, she will know what food is best for her children. This illustrates the fact that as good ministers of Christ, we must first be nourished ourselves with the words of the faith and of the good teaching which we have closely followed, and then we shall be able to nourish others.

III. REFUSING PROFANE AND OLD-WOMANISH TALES

In verse 7 Paul goes on to say, "But the profane and old-womanish tales refuse, and exercise yourself unto godliness." The Greek word for profane means touching and being touched by worldliness, contrary to being holy. If we would exercise ourselves unto godliness, we must refuse profane and old-womanish tales. Much of the teaching and preaching in Christianity today falls in the category of old-womanish tales. We should forget these tales and come back to the pure word of the Bible. In the so-called services among Christians today, there is a great deal of profane, secular, and worldly talk. People discuss politics and how to be successful in business. All this is profane talk, comparable to old-womanish tales.

IV. EXERCISING UNTO GODLINESS

Refusing the profane and old-womanish tales, we should exercise unto godliness. Such exercise is like gymnastics. The words "unto godliness" mean with a view to godliness. Godliness is Christ lived out of us as the manifestation of

God. This very Christ is today the Spirit dwelling in our spirit (2 Cor. 3:17; Rom. 8:9-10; 2 Tim. 4:22). Hence, to exercise ourselves unto godliness is to exercise our spirit to live Christ in our daily life.

In verse 7 Paul uses a Greek term referring to gymnastic exercise with respect to exercise unto godliness. We know from 3:16 that the mystery of godliness, God manifest in the flesh, is great. By our spirit with the indwelling Spirit we must exercise ourselves unto this goal, unto the expression of God.

In verse 8 Paul continues, "For bodily exercise is profitable for a little, but godliness is profitable for all things, having promise of the present life and of the life which is coming." The words "a little" denote a few things to a small extent of our being, in contrast with all things. "All things" refer not only to one part of our being, but to all parts—physical, psychological, and spiritual—both temporal and eternal. The promise of the present life which is in this age is like that in Matthew 6:33; John 16:33; Philippians 4:6-7; and 1 Peter 5:8-10. The promise of the coming life which is in the next age and in eternity is like that in 2 Peter 1:10-11; 2 Timothy 2:12; Revelation 2:7, 17; 21:6-7. A promise like that in Mark 10:29-30 is both of the present life and of the coming life.

Once again, I would urge you to refuse all profane and old-womanish tales. Even talk about doctrines such as eternal security can be nothing more than an old-womanish tale. People may come to us after a meeting and say, "I have been to the meetings of the church a number of times. But I have not yet heard a message on eternal security. What do you think about this?" Others may want to discuss the seventh-day Sabbath. This also is to talk of old-womanish tales.

In applying the matter of old-womanish tales to the talk common among today's Christians, I am following the principle established by Paul. Here in 1 Timothy the old-womanish tales probably refer to Jewish tales. Those with a background in Judaism were familiar with many tales. In the same principle, those who have spent years in Christianity also know many tales. Some come to us and ask about healing, speaking in tongues, prophesying, and even the lengthening of legs. I have known many persons who spoke in tongues but who did not exhibit godliness in their daily living. We must be a living testimony of those who refuse the old-womanish tales and who continually exercise themselves unto godliness.

It is of crucial importance that we exercise unto godliness. Inwardly we need nourishment, and outwardly, we should have godliness. From within we should be nourished with Christ, and then we should have a living which is the expression of God.

V. A PATTERN TO THE BELIEVERS

In verse 10 Paul goes on to say, "For to this end we labor and strive, because we have set our hope on the living God, Who is the Savior of all men, especially of those who believe." Because our God is living, we can set our hope on Him.

In verse 12 Paul says to Timothy, "Let no one despise your youth, but be a pattern to the believers in word, in conduct, in love, in faith, in purity." Although Timothy was young, he was charged by the apostle to bear the responsibility of caring for the building up of a local church and appointing elders and deacons. For such a responsibility, he was charged not to be childish, but to be a pattern to the believers. He was to be an example in word, in conduct, in love, in faith, and in purity. He was to be pure, without mixture, in motive and act.

Verse 13 says, "Until I come, attend to reading, to exhortation, to teaching." Here Paul does not refer to reading in the sense of study, but to reading aloud in public. According to the context, this kind of public reading may be for exhortation and teaching.

VI. NOT NEGLECTING THE GIFT

Verse 14 continues, "Do not neglect the gift which is in

you, which was given to you by means of prophecy with the laying on of the hands of the elders." Here Paul speaks not of the gift which was upon Timothy, but of the gift which was in him. This was probably a teaching gift, according to the context of verses 11, 13, and 16. This may also be confirmed by 1 Timothy 1:3; 4:6; 5:7; 6:2, 12, 20; 2 Timothy 1:13-14; 2:2, 14-15, 24-25; 4:2, 5.

Paul's word about the gift being "in you" indicates that the gift mentioned here is not an outward endowment, but the inward ability of life to minister to others. It is not a miraculous gift, such as speaking in tongues or healing (1 Cor. 12:28), but the gift of grace, such as teaching and exhorting (Rom. 12:7-8).

This gift was given by means of prophecy with the laying on of the hands of the elders. Laying on of hands has two functions: one for identification, as in Leviticus 1:4, and the other for impartation, as here. Through the laying on of the hands of the elders and the Apostle Paul (2 Tim. 1:6), the gift of grace was imparted to Timothy.

Literally the Greek word for elders should be rendered presbytery, meaning the body of elders, the eldership. The elders, who are the overseers (3:2), represent a local church, which is the expression of the Body of Christ. The laying on of the hands of the elders signifies that the Body of Christ participated with God in imparting the gift of grace to Timothy. This was not a personal matter; it was a Body matter.

LIFE-STUDY OF FIRST TIMOTHY

MESSAGE NINE

DEALING WITH THE SAINTS OF DIFFERENT AGES

Scripture Reading: 1 Tim. 5:1-16

THE DIVINE STANDARD AND THE HUMAN LEVEL

At the end of chapter three Paul comes to the high point of God's economy. In 3:15 and 16 we see the divine standard. But in 5:1-16 Paul comes down to the human level. On the one hand, in the church life we must have the divine standard; on the other hand, we must care for matters on the human level. In 5:8, for example, Paul speaks of providing for our own relatives. All the instructions in this chapter are very human, normal, and ordinary. Nothing is special, miraculous, or supernatural. The whole book is written in the same principle. This is necessary for the church life.

The principle of presenting both the divine standard and the human level is found not only in 1 Timothy, but also in the Epistles of Ephesians and Colossians. In Ephesians Paul first writes concerning the church according to the divine standard. Afterward, on the human level, he writes about husbands, wives, parents, children, slaves, and masters. In like manner, in Colossians Paul first writes about Christ according to the divine standard. Then he speaks on a human level about family matters. In 1 Timothy Paul does not come to the human level directly. Rather, he comes to this level by giving instructions to Timothy. In 5:1-16 Paul tells Timothy how to deal with the saints of different ages. My burden in this message is to cover four points from 5:1-16.

LIVING A NORMAL HUMAN LIFE

First, all the instructions given here are presented in a very human way. We should never think that if we reach

God's standard, we no longer need to be human. Some believers have been influenced by the false teaching that Christians should be like angels, that it is no longer necessary for them to lead a normal human life. Many monks and priests in Catholicism have a living that is abnormal. Furthermore, the requirement that priests and nuns not be married not only is contrary to humanity, but has its source in demons. According to Paul's word in 4:1-3, forbidding others to marry is a demonic teaching.

We all need to learn to be human. In fact, the more spiritual we are, the more human we shall be. If we would live Christ, we must learn to be human in a genuine way. When the Lord Jesus was on earth, He was very human.

To damage humanity is to ruin both the means and the channel created by God for His economy. The reason demons and fallen angels forbid marriage and command people to abstain from foods is that their intention is to destroy mankind. Thus, we in the church must be human and follow the standards of normal human living. Some have falsely accused us of not being human. We utterly repudiate these allegations. In the church life we definitely emphasize the proper humanity. I can testify that I myself live in a normal human way. If you examine my living, you will find me to be very human. I am not a "saint" or an angel; I am simply a human being. Furthermore, I encourage all the elders to be human. The elders should not help the saints in their locality to be like angels. We appreciate the angels, but we do not want to imitate them. Instead, we prefer to be human.

We should be human Christians. On the one hand, we have the divine nature (2 Pet. 1:4); on the other hand, we are normal human beings. The fact that we have the divine nature with the divine life does not mean that we shall ever be deified. Rather, we are to live a genuinely human life by the divine life and nature. In this way we shall be able to live the highest human life, a life like that of the Lord Jesus. When He was on earth, He lived a human life by means of the divine life and the divine nature. The Lord's human living was by the divine life. Our human living should be the same. Thus, we all must learn to be human.

In 5:1-16 we see that Paul instructed his young co-worker Timothy to contact the saints in a human way. Verse 1 says, "Do not upbraid an elderly man, but entreat him as a father." To entreat an elderly man as a father is surely to behave in a very human manner. In relation to brothers who are a generation older than they, the younger brothers should deal with them as fathers.

Paul also tells Timothy to entreat "younger men as brothers; elderly women as mothers; younger women as sisters." Timothy was not to assume an elevated position as a bishop, regarding himself as superior to others. On the contrary, he was to behave as a brother to younger brothers and sisters, as a son to a father, and as a son to a mother. In the church life there are many fathers, mothers, brothers, and sisters. To deal with the saints as such is to behave humanly.

Our contact with the saints must be in a proper atmosphere and with the right attitude and spirit. The atmosphere, attitude, and spirit in our contact with others mean a great deal. If a young brother assumes some kind of elevated position in relation to an elderly man, the relationship between them will be damaged. But if he would contact him as a son speaking to a father, their fellowship will be intimate, loving, touching, and even inspiring.

Suppose that in my relationship with the saints I conduct myself as a teacher and treat the saints as my pupils. If this is my attitude, my contact with the saints will be quite poor. But if I am very human in my relationships with the saints and regard myself as a brother among brothers and sisters, mothers and fathers, the contact will be loving and intimate. What a difference it makes when we are truly human in our relationships to one another! I repeat, in the church life we all must be human.

EXERCISING WISDOM

In 5:1-16 we see in the second place that Paul instructed Timothy to exercise wisdom. His word not to upbraid an elderly man, but to entreat him as a father is a word of wisdom. It is a matter of wisdom not to rebuke sharply an elderly man. In dealing with saints of different ages, we need not only love, but also wisdom. We need to realize whom we are contacting. Are we speaking to an elderly brother or sister? Then we must speak to them as a son to a father or mother. Are we contacting a younger brother or sister? Then we must speak to them as a brother to a brother or a brother to a sister. Furthermore, we should speak one way to a father, another way to a mother, and in other ways to brothers and sisters. For example, in our human family we do not speak in the same way to all members of the family. We do not talk to our father in the same way as we do to our mother. If we speak the same way to all members of our family, we are indeed foolish. In all our relationships with saints of different ages we need wisdom.

If we exercise wisdom, we shall speak differently to saints of different ages. The brothers will talk to brothers in a way appropriate to brothers, but they will speak to sisters in a way appropriate to sisters. This is wisdom. We must not speak to a young sister in the same way as we do to an elderly man. Furthermore, one sister may embrace another. But a young sister should not show her love for a brother, young or old, by embracing him. Do not love the saints in a foolish way. Instead, always exercise wisdom, realizing whom you are contacting.

IN ALL PURITY

Third, all our dealings with the saints must be "in all purity" (5:2). Every contact with the brothers and sisters in the church life must be pure in every way. We need to be pure in our motive and intention.

In the contact between brothers and sisters there is especially the need for all purity. For this reason, a brother and sister who are close to the same age should not talk privately in a closed room. Either another brother or another sister should be present. Consider the example of the Lord Jesus. He spoke to Nicodemus in a house alone at night, but

He talked to the Samaritan woman out in the open during the day. This indicates that the contact between brothers and sisters must be in all purity.

In the church life the traffic in fellowship between brothers and sisters cannot be avoided. If we do not exercise all purity, we may fall into some kind of snare. Many have fallen into a snare because they were careless and failed to exercise purity in their contact with others. Therefore, we would emphasize again and again that the contact between brothers and sisters must be in all purity.

As we have indicated, our contact with all the saints, brothers and sisters, elderly and young, must be pure in every way. In speaking to an elderly sister as a mother, you need to be pure in your motive. It is evil to have impure motives. To have an impure motive means to seek gain for ourselves, to seek some kind of advantage or promotion. In our contact with all the saints in the church life we should have just one motive—to minister Christ to them that they may grow in the Lord.

DOING OUR DUTY

The fourth point I would bring out in this message is the matter of our duty. We need to be human, we need to exercise wisdom, we need to have all purity, and we need to do our duty. In the church life everyone must have certain duties to perform. No one should be idle or a busybody. In 5:4 Paul says, "But if any widow has children or grandchildren, let them first learn to show godliness toward their own household and to render a return to their parents; for this is acceptable in the sight of God." Return here denotes requital, recompense. To render such a return is to show gratitude to one's parents.

In verse 13 Paul speaks of those who "learn to be idle, going around from house to house; and not only idle, but also gossips and busybodies, speaking things which they ought not." Some are idle, seemingly having nothing to do. But their idleness causes them to become busybodies. They go around from house to house gossiping and "speaking things which they ought not." No one in the church should be idle, and no one should be a gossip or a busybody. Instead, everyone should have something to do, some proper duty to perform.

Realizing the need for all the saints to do their duty, Paul tells Timothy not to allow a widow to be enrolled who is under sixty years old (v. 9). He then tells Timothy to refuse younger widows, for they may set aside their first pledge, or faith (vv. 11-12). Setting aside "their first pledge" means to break a pledge or promise. This indicates that some younger widows promised, pledged, to devote themselves in their widowhood to some service of the church.

In verse 14 Paul goes on to say, "I will therefore that younger widows marry, bear children, rule the house, give no occasion to the opposer for reproach." Childbearing and house affairs are a rescue and safeguard to idle busybodies. This is God's ordination to restrict and protect women since the fall (Gen. 3:16).

Paul's word in verse 14 about younger widows marrying is somewhat of a contrast to what he says in 1 Corinthians 7:8. The word in 1 Corinthians was Paul's wish in his earlier ministry. In 5:14 we have his advice in his later ministry, according to his experiences concerning young widows. The difference here indicates that even in his God-inspired teachings, Paul was not legal. On the contrary, he could be very flexible. This indicates that, in the New Testament, concerning some matters there is no legality. In certain cases, the way we take may vary according to the actual situation.

LIFE-STUDY OF FIRST TIMOTHY

MESSAGE TEN

DEALING WITH THE ELDERS

Scripture Reading: 1 Tim. 5:17-25

In 5:17-25 Paul instructs Timothy concerning how to deal with the elders. The elders are the authority, or the government, of a local church. Thus, to deal with the elders is to deal with the authority, the government, the administration, of the church. For centuries there has been a debate among Christians over the kind of administration there should be in the church. In 5:17-25 Paul touches the crucial matter of the church's administration.

I. ELDERS COUNTED WORTHY OF DOUBLE HONOR

Verses 17 and 18 say, "Let the elders who take the lead well be counted worthy of double honor, especially those who labor in word and teaching. For the Scripture says, You shall not muzzle a threshing ox, and, The workman is worthy of his pay." According to verse 18, the expression "double honor" includes material supply. Especially those who labor in word and teaching should receive this necessary supply. All the elders should be able to take the lead in a local church, but some, not all, have a special capacity in teaching. The word in verse 17 denotes the general speaking of doctrines, and teaching denotes instructions concerning particular things. Those who labor in word and teaching may be fully occupied, devoting all their time to this. Therefore, the church and the saints should care for their living. For this reason, in verse 18 Paul refers to what the Scripture says about not muzzling a threshing ox and about the workman being worthy of his pay.

II. AN ACCUSATION AGAINST AN ELDER

In verse 19 Paul goes on to say, "Against an elder do not receive an accusation, except on the word of two or three witnesses." According to the Greek here, the accusation made against an elder should not merely be verbal; rather, it should be put in writing. To make an accusation against an elder is a very serious matter. For the sake of accuracy, it should be put in writing and not merely be spoken. Furthermore, it should not be received except on the word of two or three witnesses.

Verse 19 is simple, but it implies something very important. The fact that Timothy was charged by Paul to receive an accusation against an elder indicates that the apostles have authority to deal with the elders after they have been appointed by the apostles to be elders. There is no doubt that the written accusation against an elder was to be presented to Timothy. Who, then, was Timothy? According to those who are in favor of a hierarchical system in which the bishops are over the elders, Timothy is regarded as a bishop. But as we have previously pointed out, according to the New Testament, bishops are elders, and elders are bishops. These terms are synonymous and refer to the same people. We know from 1 Thessalonians 1:1 and 2:6 that Timothy was an apostle. Furthermore, in the book of 1 Timothy we see that Timothy was the representative of the Apostle Paul. Therefore, for an accusation to come to Timothy was for it to come to an apostle. We would expect such an accusation to come to the apostles because they were the ones who had appointed the elders.

Some have had the concept from reading Brother Nee's book *The Normal Christian Church Life* that once apostles have appointed elders in a particular local church, the apostles do not under any circumstances have the right to interfere with the affairs of that church. This, however, is a misunderstanding of Brother Nee's word. In another book, *Church Affairs,* Brother Nee points out that after the elders have been appointed by the apostles, they should take the lead in the church according to the apostles' teaching. If the elders lead others astray or if they are wrong in some way, accusation against them can be made by the saints to the apostles.

However, an apostle is not a pope. If we read the New Testament carefully, we shall see that the elders are not appointed by anyone who is a dictator or who exercises autonomous authority. On the contrary, elders are appointed in the way of life. As the saints in a particular locality meet together to worship God and to serve the Lord, it will be manifested that certain brothers have a greater degree of maturity than others. Although no one will be fully mature, some will be comparatively mature. Not even in Philippians 3 did Paul regard himself as matured in full. Because maturity is relative, the qualifications of an elder are not absolute. In other words, an elder's qualifications are comparative. Among all the saints in a local church, certain brothers, by comparison, are more qualified and mature than others. These brothers are manifested as such before the eyes of the church, and all the saints clearly realize that these are the ones who should be appointed elders. This appointment does not come either by a vote of the congregation or by the exercise of autonomous authority. Instead, elders are selected according to the insight and foresight of the saints. Based upon the saints' insight and foresight, the apostles then appoint certain ones to be elders. The apostles minister the Word, bring others to the Lord's salvation, and edify them after they are saved; they also establish these believers as a local church. Therefore, they have the standing and the position to say that those who have been manifested as relatively more mature than others should be appointed elders.

In verse 20 Paul continues, "Those who sin reprove before all that the rest also may be in fear." The fact that apostles can rebuke elders who sin indicates that the apostles have authority over the elders. The expression "before all" refers to the whole church. A sinning elder should receive public reproof because of his public position. If an elder is reproved publicly, the rest of the elders will be "in fear."

Verse 21 says, "I solemnly charge you before God and Christ Jesus and the chosen angels that you guard these things without prejudice, doing nothing by way of partiality." The elders in a local church are God's deputy authority. Dealing with them is a solemn thing before God. Hence, the apostle solemnly charged Timothy before God, Christ, and the angels to do it in such a way that the chosen angels, the good angels with God's authority, may see that His authority is established and maintained among His redeemed people on earth.

Paul's use of the term "chosen angels" indicates that here he is dealing with administration, government, authority. The book of Daniel indicates that the chosen angels are authorities, representatives of God's administration. Paul deliberately uses the term "chosen angels" to indicate that here his instructions are related to administration, government, and authority in the church. Paul not only charged Timothy before God and Christ Jesus, but also charged him before the chosen angels.

Paul's charge to Timothy in verse 21 was to "guard these things without prejudice, doing nothing by way of partiality." To guard is to observe and keep. Prejudice refers to prejudgment, condemnation, before hearing the case, and partiality refers to inclination, favor, or bias. The words "without prejudice" imply without prejudgment to the credit of the accuser, whereas "doing nothing by way of partiality" implies no perverted favor to the accused elder. On the one hand, Timothy was not to take sides with those who made an accusation against an elder. To give them credit in a hasty way would be to show prejudice. On the other hand, Timothy was not to be partial, not to show perverted favor, to the elder against whom the accusation was made. Therefore, in handling an accusation against an elder, three matters should be observed: first, there must be the word of two or three witnesses; second, there should be no prejudice; and third, nothing should be done by partiality. No credit should be given privately to the accusers, and there should not be any perverted favor toward the one accused.

III. LAYING HANDS ON ELDERS

In order to follow these instructions, Timothy was charged not to act in haste. Verse 22 says, "Lay hands quickly on no man, nor participate in others' sins; keep yourself pure." We have seen that laying on of hands has two functions, identification and impartation. According to the context of the previous verses, here the laying on of hands refers primarily to laying hands on the elders. This should not be done hastily.

In verse 23 Paul goes on to say, "No longer drink water, but use a little wine for the sake of your stomach and your frequent weaknesses." According to the context, this verse implies that the condition of one's physical health may affect his spiritual dealing with others.

In verses 24 and 25 Paul says, "The sins of some men are manifest beforehand, going before to judgment, and some also they follow after. Likewise also, the good works are manifest beforehand, and those that are otherwise cannot be hidden." The word sins in verse 24 indicates that this verse continues verse 22. It explains that some people's sins are manifest earlier and others', later. Hence, we should not lay hands on anyone in haste. What is mentioned here concerning the judging of sins is a principle applicable both to man's judgment and God's. The words "some also they follow after" refer to the sins of others now being hidden, but later manifest, going to judgment later.

The implication of the apostle's charge in these two verses is that Timothy should not approve a person hastily because sins have not been manifested, nor condemn a person in haste because good works have not been manifested. Often a person's wrongdoings are concealed. It takes time for them to be exposed. However, sometimes a person's good deeds are also hidden, possibly covered by false accusations and rumors. Time is also necessary for the falsehood to be dispelled and the real situation to be brought to light. Thus, we should not make a quick decision whether an elder is right or wrong. Instead, we should wait and allow time to expose the situation.

It is easy for us to make quick decisions and hasty judgments. But even though it is difficult to take time in matters such as these, we need to learn not to be hasty. The elders should follow this principle in caring for the church. They should not judge anything or anyone hastily. What they do should be with witnesses and without prejudice, partiality, or haste.

A number of times saints have come to me with accusations against an elder. My response always has been to say, "Let me pray and then have fellowship with some co-workers about this situation." Because an accuser sometimes wanted a hasty judgment, he rebuked me and claimed that I took sides with the one accused. However, I did not take sides with anyone. Instead, I wanted to pray and have fellowship with others in order not to act in haste.

The church is very different from any worldly organization and also different from organized Christianity. The church is according to the Lord's mercy and grace and under His authority. In dealing with the administration of the church, we must observe the four points of having witnesses and of acting without prejudice, partiality, or haste. Do not show prejudice in receiving an accusation, and do not show partiality in defending anyone against accusation. Instead, take time, pray, have fellowship with those who possess spiritual insight, and wait for the Lord's leading.

Often elders have told me of the need for more elders in their locality. Usually they would recommend someone to be appointed to the eldership. Then I would ask how long the brother has been saved, how long he has been in the church life, and how much he has grown in the Lord. Then I would encourage the brothers to wait for another period of time and also to pray. As a result, many have learned that my practice is always to tell others to wait and pray. Actually, this is not my policy; it is the instruction of the Apostle Paul. After a period of time has passed and the leading ones in a certain place still feel that a brother should be appointed to the eldership and that, comparatively speaking, there is no one more qualified than he, I may recommend that he serve as an apprentice in order to be proved. This means that he will share the responsibility of an elder, but yet not occupy the position of an elder.

In dealing with the administration of a local church, we follow neither the way of dictatorship nor democracy. Elders are not appointed by a dictator; neither are they elected by a vote of the congregation. In the Lord's recovery there is no such thing as an autonomous dictator. We do not practice dictatorship, but we do recognize the divine authority, the divine life, and the divine light. The administration of a local church is not according to the way of worldly government or organization. But in the church we have the Lord's headship with the divine nature, life, light, wisdom, and grace. Therefore, we pray and wait on Him as we watch and observe the growth of the saints. In those very rare cases where there is ground for accusation against an elder, we do not act in haste. On the contrary, we wait and pray. We know from verses 24 and 25 that eventually a person's sins or good works will be manifest. As the snow melts and exposes the rocks hidden beneath it, so either a person's sins or his good deeds will eventually be brought to light. For this reason, we neither receive an accusation against an elder nor justify an elder in a hasty way. Rather, we would make sure that the accusation is substantiated by two or three witnesses and then we would act without prejudice, partiality, or haste. Furthermore, we acknowledge the Lord's sovereignty and wait for Him to make the situation clear.

Many have accused me of being a pope and of acting like an autonomous dictator to control the local churches. In the Lord's recovery today, there are approximately four hundred churches in addition to those in mainland China. About three hundred seventy of these churches have been established directly by the ministry in the past thirty-one years. I certainly do not control all these churches. Some people, however, may ask why the churches and the saints pay attention to what I say in the ministry. They listen simply because I feed them and minister Christ to them. We thank the Lord that, in His mercy, He has opened His Word to us and established the ministry of the Word among us so that all the churches may be supplied and that all the saints may be nourished. The Lord's way to care for the churches is the way of supply and nourishment.

Very rarely is there any exercise of authority among us in the Lord's recovery. I avoid the exercise of authority whenever possible. Even though I may have the standing in the Lord to say something, my practice is not to exercise authority. In like manner, rarely do the elders in the local churches exercise authority. Our desire is to care for the saints, to love them, feed them, comfort them, and encourage them. This is the proper way for elders to function, for we are not an organization, but we are an organic entity, the Body of Christ.

LIFE-STUDY OF FIRST TIMOTHY

MESSAGE ELEVEN

DEALING WITH SLAVES AND MONEY LOVERS

Scripture Reading: 1 Tim. 6:1-10

In 6:1-10 Paul deals with slaves and with money lovers. In verses 1 and 2 he speaks concerning slaves. Then in verse 3 he suddenly refers to teaching differently and not consenting to healthy words. Then in verse 7 he begins to talk about the love of money. Apparently the dealing with slaves has nothing to do with different teachings, and the different teachings are not related to the love of money. Nevertheless, in 6:1-10 Paul put these things together. This is indicated by the word "if" at the beginning of verse 3 and the word "for" at the beginning of verse 7. The use of these words at the beginning of these verses indicates that they are a continuation of the foregoing verses.

In studying the Bible we should not be careless. Even little words such as "if" and "for" deserve our attention. Paying attention to words such as these often can bring in light. These words not only enable us to see the continuation in thought; they also afford a way for light to come in. Because by the Lord's mercy we have received so much light from the Word, we can say that in the recovery we know the Bible in the way of life, light, and spirit.

In the United States today there are different kinds of theology. Certain seminaries teach modernistic theology, which denies the authority of the Bible and teaches that Jesus was merely a man, that His death on the cross was not for redemption but was merely an act of martyrdom, and that He did not rise from the dead. In the theology departments of some secular colleges and universities, religion and theology are regarded merely as part of man's culture.

However, in other seminaries fundamental theology is taught. Nevertheless, the standard concerning the truth is not very high. The highest standard of theology found among Christians today in the United States is that which has its source in the teachings of the Brethren, especially as those teachings were made popular by Dr. C. I. Scofield and his famous Reference Bible and correspondence courses. Although Scofield adopted nearly all the teachings of the Brethren, he rejected the Brethren way to practice the church life. The leading teacher among the Brethren was J. N. Darby. Anyone who calls himself a theologian but who is not familiar with the writings of Darby is not a theologian of the highest caliber.

In 1925 I wrote to Brother Nee asking him which book, according to his knowledge, would be the best to help me understand the Bible verse by verse. As a young believer, I was eager to obtain a thorough knowledge of the Word of God. I wanted to understand every verse of the Bible, from the first verse in Genesis to the last verse in Revelation. Brother Nee told me that the best help in knowing the Bible in this way was Darby's *Synopsis of the Books of the Bible*. Eight years later he gave me a copy of this five volume work.

J. N. Darby and his contemporaries were great teachers of the Bible. According to history, the Bible was opened more to the Brethren teachers than to anyone who had gone before them. These Brethren teachers did not know the Word merely according to tradition or according to letters in black and white; they knew the Bible according to fresh light which came directly from the Lord. Having been enlightened by the Lord, they received the vision and the revelation of many truths in the Word.

Christians today often talk about the Bible in dead letters. Some are familiar with Bible geography and history; they also know certain elementary teachings. However, they may not have any light or revelation.

We have pointed out that it is possible for Christians to speak of certain Bible doctrines as if they were nothing more than old-womanish tales. For some, even the doctrine of justification by faith is a "tale." For example, a particular Lutheran pastor in China fifty years ago taught justification by faith. Nevertheless, he himself was an opium smuggler. As far as he was concerned, justification by faith was nothing more than a "tale." Concerning this matter, he was altogether without light or revelation. One day an elderly lady evangelist from Norway, who was very prevailing in the preaching of regeneration, stopped this Lutheran pastor after a meeting and asked him if he had been regenerated. When he tried to tell her that he had been regenerated, she said that simply by looking at his face, she knew that he had not been regenerated. This Lutheran pastor was insulted and so much filled with hatred for this lady evangelist that he plotted that night to murder her. But at that very hour the Holy Spirit enlightened him and rebuked him, and he repented and cried to the Lord. The next morning when this lady evangelist saw him, she looked at his face and said, "Praise the Lord, you have been regenerated!" Then in the meeting this pastor gave his testimony with great impact. This influenced hundreds of young people to be saved. The case of this Lutheran pastor illustrates the difference between knowing the Bible merely according to the black and white letters and knowing the Word according to the shining of the divine light.

Among Christians today there are many old-womanish tales. Not only are there "tales" about doctrine, but also "tales" having to do with so-called miracles. A certain Pentecostal pastor once told me about teeth that were supposedly filled miraculously with gold. Another Pentecostal minister claimed that in a certain meeting a person in the congregation miraculously spoke in Chinese. Both stories, however, were nothing more than "tales."

The apostle's teaching in 1 Timothy is far superior to old-womanish tales. Furthermore, in this Epistle there is no mention of miraculous things. On the contrary, in 5:23 Paul tells Timothy, "No longer drink water, but use a little wine for the sake of your stomach and your frequent weaknesses." Here Paul does not exercise a miraculous gift to heal his co-worker. Instead, he encourages Timothy to be human, not religious, and to care for his health in a human way.

Many of those who teach the Bible do not have any light or revelation. They merely teach the Word according to the black and white letters, perhaps also giving out information about geography or history. Where can you hear a message from 1 Timothy 1:4 on the subject of God's dispensation in the New Testament? By the Lord's mercy, He has shined upon us and made known His truth. For this reason, I hope that reputable theologians and professors will study the Recovery Version and the Life-study Messages, even study them in a critical way. I believe that if they study our writings, they will receive light.

I. WITH SLAVES UNDER THE YOKE

Let us now consider the logical connection between 6:2 and 3 and between 6:6 and 7. In 6:1 and 2 Paul charges those who are slaves under the yoke to count their masters worthy of all honor so that "the name of God and the teaching be not blasphemed." The word blasphemed means ill spoken of, reproached. Furthermore, Paul charges the slaves who have believing masters to serve them in a proper way. Paul concludes verse 2 with the words, "These things teach and exhort."

II. WITH MONEY LOVERS

A. Teaching Differently

Then in verses 3 and 4 Paul goes on to say, "If anyone teaches differently and does not consent to healthy words, those of our Lord Jesus Christ, and the teaching which is according to godliness, he is blinded with pride." To teach differently is to teach things that differ from the apostles' teaching centered on Christ and the church. The "healthy words" here refer to the health of life. The sound teaching of the apostles ministers healthy teaching as the supply of life to people. The words of our Lord Jesus Christ are words of life (John 6:63); hence, they are healthy words. The healthy words of the Lord are the source of the teaching according to godliness. When the Lord's words of life are taught, particularly in certain aspects, they become the teaching according to godliness. The living words of the Lord always bring forth godliness—a life that lives Christ and expresses God in Christ.

Paul's word in 6:3 concerning teaching differently indicates that even his teaching concerning slaves was according to the healthy words of the Lord Jesus. Paul's teaching was according to godliness. However, because some did not consent to healthy words, they taught differently. They did not teach according to godliness. Thus, there is definitely a connection between verses 2 and 3.

All our teaching must be according to the healthy words of God's economy. Even those who care for the children in the children's meeting should teach the children in principle according to the healthy words of the Lord Jesus. This means that the children should receive teaching which is according to godliness.

B. Blinded with Pride

In 6:4 and 5 Paul says that the one who teaches differently and who does not consent to healthy words is "blinded with pride, understanding nothing, but is sick with questionings and contentions of words, out of which come envy, strife, revilings, evil suspicions, perpetual wranglings of men corrupted in mind and deprived of the truth, supposing godliness to be a means of gain." Teachings differing from the healthy words of the Lord always issue from people's pride with self-conceit which blinds them. Paul and his co-workers taught in a certain way. But some who were blinded with pride deliberately taught differently. To them, it was humiliating to teach the same as others. I can testify that when I was in China, I was very happy to teach the same thing as Brother Nee. As much as possible, I even used the same terms Brother Nee used, for I realized that in this way I was carrying out the Lord's ministry.

In verse 4 Paul uses the expression "sick with questionings." To question and contend about words is a sickness. "Sick" here is in contrast to "healthy" in verse 3.

The word revilings in 6:4 literally means blasphemies. As in Colossians 3:8, it refers here to revilings, railings toward man, not blasphemies toward God.

We have seen that in verse 5 Paul speaks of "perpetual wranglings of men corrupted in mind and deprived of the truth, supposing godliness to be a means of gain." The Greek for "perpetual wranglings" can also be rendered "incessant quarrels." These wranglings are carried on by men corrupted and depraved in mind and deprived, bereft, destitute, of the truth. The Greek word for "deprived" implies that these are ones who once possessed the truth, but now it has been put away from them. Hence, they are destitute of the truth.

In verse 5 Paul refers to those who suppose "godliness to be a means of gain." They make godliness a way of gain—material profit, a gain-making trade. The desire for material gain is another reason certain ones teach differently. Thus, because of pride and the desire for profit, for riches, some today are teaching differently. Pride is related to wanting a name and a good reputation, and gain is related to money and material profit.

C. Godliness with Contentment

In verse 6 Paul says, "But godliness with contentment is great gain." Concerning the expression "contentment," Vincent says, "An inward self-sufficiency, as opposed to the lack or the desire of outward things. It was a favourite Stoic word." The expression "great gain" means great means of gain. It mainly denotes the blessings in this age—godliness plus self-sufficiency and the ability to be free from greediness and the cares of this age.

Paul's mention of gain in verses 5 and 6 brings him to the matter of dealing with money lovers in verses 7 through 10. For this reason, he uses the conjunction "for" to join verses 6 and 7.

Once again I would point out that because we pay

attention to these details, we have come to know the Bible in the way of life, light, and spirit. We do not claim to know the Bible more than others do in geography or history. Neither do we claim the ability to recite more verses. But we can testify that by the Lord's mercy and through the help of great Bible teachers who have gone before us, the Lord has shown us much light. The Lord has given us light, life, and spirit through the Word. The Psalmist once declared, "The entrance of thy words giveth light" (119:130). Furthermore, the Lord Jesus said, "The words which I have spoken unto you are spirit and are life" (John 6:63). We praise the Lord for giving us light, life, and spirit!

The Lord Jesus was raised in a carpenter's home in Nazareth and was regarded as one who was unlearned. But there can be no doubt that He had tremendous light, life, and spirit. To have light, life, and spirit does not depend on one's scholarship or degrees. On the contrary, our confidence in our education can hinder us from receiving light, life, and spirit through the Word.

In 6:7 Paul goes on to say, "For we have brought nothing into the world; it is evident that neither can we carry anything out." This has been wisely ordained by God that we may trust in Him for our needs and live by Him in order to express Him without preoccupation or distraction.

Verse 8 continues, "But having food and covering, with these we shall be satisfied." Although the word covering refers to clothing, it may include dwelling. To be satisfied is to have sufficient provision for our needs.

D. The Desire to Be Rich

In verse 9 Paul says, "But those who resolve to be rich fall into temptation and a snare and many foolish and harmful desires, which plunge men into ruin and destruction." The resolve mentioned here is related to the strong desire to be rich. This is the love of riches, not the possession of them, that leads the avaricious into temptation. Some are actually rich; others have only a strong desire for riches. This evil desire ruins and destroys them. Ruin here implies destruction, and destruction implies perdition, both temporal and eternal. Those who resolve to be rich fall into a snare, as into a net, and also into many foolish and harmful lustful desires, which cause men to drown or sink into ruin and destruction.

In verse 10 Paul concludes, "For the love of money is a root of all evils, which some having aspired after have wandered away from the faith and pierced themselves with many sorrows." Paul says that the love of money is a root of all evils. He does not say that it is the only root. The Greek word rendered aspired after means craved for, longed for. Those with this craving have wandered away from the faith; they have been led astray from the contents of our belief, from the truth of God's New Testament economy.

LIFE-STUDY OF FIRST TIMOTHY

MESSAGE TWELVE

A MAN OF GOD

Scripture Reading: 1 Tim. 6:11-21

In 1:4 we read of God's dispensation, and in 6:11 Paul uses the expression "man of God." Hence, this book begins with God's dispensation and concludes with the charge to a man of God. God's desire is to produce men of God by dispensing Himself into those who believe in Christ. A man of God is one who partakes of God's life and nature (John 1:13; 2 Pet. 1:4) and thus becomes one with Him in His life and nature (1 Cor. 6:17) and thereby expresses Him. This corresponds to the mystery of godliness, which is God manifest in the flesh (1 Tim. 3:16).

FLEEING AND PURSUING

First Timothy 6:11 says, "But you, O man of God, flee these things, and pursue righteousness, godliness, faith, love, endurance, meekness." On the one hand, Paul charges Timothy to flee certain things and, on the other hand, to pursue certain other things. Timothy must flee the negative things previously mentioned in this Epistle. He should pursue righteousness, godliness, faith, love, endurance, and meekness. It is significant that Paul does not tell Timothy to pursue power, gifts, miracles, and theological training. Furthermore, as we shall see, in verse 12 Paul does not charge him to fight for his theology or to lay hold on the doctrinal knowledge he has accumulated. However, many Christians today pursue power, fight for doctrines, and lay hold on theological knowledge, and they charge the younger generation to do the same. They also promote natural gifts, talents, and abilities. But in 1 Timothy very little is said of man's ability. Concerning the eldership, Paul tells Timothy that an elder should be apt to teach. This refers to the ability to instruct others like a parent helping a child with homework. Paul's emphasis in 1 Timothy definitely is not on power, gifts, or natural ability.

Paul charges Timothy to pursue righteousness, godliness, faith, love, endurance, and meekness. Righteousness is a matter of being right with people before God according to God's righteous and strict requirements. If we would be those who carry out God's dispensation for the building up of local churches as the expression of Christ, we must pursue righteousness. We must seek to be right with God and man.

In the second place, we should pursue godliness, the expression of God. In 4:7 Paul told Timothy to exercise himself unto godliness. A man of God should not pursue power or miraculous gifts. Instead, he should pursue righteousness and godliness; he should seek to be right with God and man in order to be a living expression of God in every way. This is to live a daily life which manifests God.

In verse 11 Paul lists faith after godliness. Faith is to believe in God and His word and to trust in Him and His word. As we have pointed out, faith involves an organic union by contacting God through the Word and in the Spirit. Faith, therefore, denotes a living union. Instead of pursuing a great work, we should pursue the organic union with the Triune God.

In 6:11 Paul goes on to mention love. We should be those who love others by the love of God (1 John 4:7-8, 19-21).

Paul also speaks of endurance and meekness. We should pursue endurance, the ability to bear sufferings and persecutions, and also meekness, which is a proper attitude in facing opposition. It is certain that if we live a godly life, we shall suffer. The world opposes God. If we live God and also live out God, expressing Him, we shall be opposed and attacked by the godless world. Thus, we should pursue endurance, and we should also pursue meekness.

FIGHTING THE GOOD FIGHT OF THE FAITH

In verse 12 Paul continues his charge: "Fight the good

fight of the faith." To fight for the faith means to fight for God's New Testament economy. In particular, it is to fight for Christ as the embodiment of God and for the church as the Body of Christ.

LAYING HOLD ON ETERNAL LIFE

In verse 12 Paul also says, "Lay hold on the eternal life to which you were called and have confessed the good confession before many witnesses." The eternal life here is the divine life, the uncreated life of God, which is eternal. Eternal denotes the nature more than the time element of the divine life. To fight the good fight of the faith in the Christian life, especially in the Christian ministry, we need to lay hold on this divine life and not trust in our human life. Hence, in 1 and 2 Timothy and Titus, the eternal life is stressed again and again (1 Tim. 1:16; 6:19; 2 Tim. 1:1, 10; Titus 1:2; 3:7). To bring forth God's dispensation concerning the church in 1 Timothy, to confront the process of the church's decline in 2 Timothy, and to maintain good order in the church life in Titus, this life is a prerequisite.

We have been called to the eternal life of God. We were born of the human natural life, but we were reborn of the divine eternal life when we were called by God in Christ.

The words "confessed the good confession before many witnesses" may refer to Timothy's confession of the faith at his baptism. At that time Timothy probably confessed a good confession of the eternal life before many witnesses, as we all should do, believing and being assured that he had received the life of God.

Verses 11 and 12 are a marvelous summary of nearly the whole New Testament. A man of God should pursue righteousness, godliness, faith, love, endurance, and meekness; he should fight for God's New Testament economy and lay hold on eternal life. All these matters are essential aspects of the New Testament. In contrast, the beasts in Revelation 13 and the lake of fire in Revelation 20 cannot compare with these essential aspects. We today must fight the good fight of the faith. This means that we must fight for Christ as the embodiment of God and for the church as the Body of Christ. Furthermore, we must not merely fight objectively, but fight subjectively by laying hold on eternal life. We should not do anything apart from this life. We should speak to our husband or wife and to our children not by the natural life, but by the eternal life. Even in the matter of buying a pair of shoes, we should live according to the eternal life to which we have been called. As today's Timothys, we need to lay hold on eternal life.

In verse 12 Paul specifically says that we have been called to eternal life. No other book in the New Testament speaks of "the eternal life to which you were called." This is a particular characteristic of 1 Timothy. Do you realize that you have been called to eternal life? This eternal life does not mainly refer to blessings in the future. To be called to eternal life does not mean that we have been called to enjoy blessings in heaven. Eternal life should be our life today, a life for our present daily living. By our first birth, the physical birth, we received the Adamic life. But because we have been called to eternal life, we should no longer live the Adamic life, the natural life. Yes, we must be truly human, even Jesusly human, but not in our natural life. On the contrary, we need to live a human life by the eternal life. We have been called to this life, and now we need to live it.

I am deeply burdened concerning this matter of being called to the eternal life. I am especially concerned for those dear saints who have been distracted from the eternal life to which we have been called and who have become preoccupied with other things. We have been called uniquely to eternal life. This life, the divine life, is actually the Triune God Himself. Having been called to eternal life, we now should lay hold on this life, live this life, and have our whole being according to this life.

THE CHARGE TO A MAN OF GOD

In verse 13 Paul goes on to say, "I charge you before God, Who gives life to all things, and Christ Jesus, Who witnessed before Pontius Pilate the good confession." Here Paul describes God as the One who gives life to all things. This indicates that we must focus our attention on life. Every aspect of our Christian walk must be something to which God can give life.

Paul's concept in verse 13 is that God gives life and that when Christ was on earth, He lived the eternal life. He lived by the very God who gives life to all things. Then at the end of His journey on earth, He stood before Pontius Pilate and made a good confession. The Lord's confession before Pilate was related to His living by the divine life. Now we can understand why Paul charges Timothy before God and before Christ Jesus. He charges Timothy before God because God gives life to all things, and he charges him before Christ Jesus because He lived the eternal life and confessed it before Pontius Pilate. Therefore, Paul indicates that Timothy must be such a person; that is, he must be a man of God. Christ was truly a man of God, living righteousness, godliness, faith, love, endurance, and meekness. Now Paul charges Timothy to be the same kind of person, a man of God living by the divine life.

In verse 14 Paul continues, "That you keep the commandment spotless, without reproach, until the appearing of our Lord Jesus Christ." The commandment must refer to the charge in verses 11 and 12. The word appearing refers to the Lord's second coming. Paul charges Timothy to live the life of a man of God until the coming of the Lord Jesus. Then the Lord could speak well of Timothy as one who lived on earth as the continuation of Himself. I hope that at the time of the Lord's appearing, He will be able to say to us, "Faithful child, you have been part of My continuation. I lived on earth as a man of God. You were My continuation because you also lived the life of a man of God. You did not live by the natural life, but you lived by the eternal life."

In verses 15 and 16 Paul goes on to say, "Which in its own times He will show, the blessed and only Sovereign, the King of those who reign as kings and Lord of those who rule as lords, Who alone has immortality, dwelling in unapproachable light, Whom no man has seen nor can see, to Whom be honor and eternal might. Amen." The relative pronoun "which" refers to "appearing" in verse 14. The personal pronoun "He" in verse 15 refers to God the Father, according to Acts 1:7. Although the Father dwells in unapproachable light, we not only can approach Him in Christ, but we also can have fellowship with Him. We can approach the Father because we are no longer in darkness. He is in the light, and we are in the light also (1 John 1:5, 7).

A CHARGE TO THE RICH

In a very real sense, 1 Timothy concludes with 6:16. However, in verses 17 through 19 Paul gives an additional charge to the rich. Verse 17 says, "Charge those who are rich in the present age not to be high-minded, nor to set their hope on the uncertainty of riches, but on God Who affords us all things richly for our enjoyment." This word may be regarded as a supplement to 6:7-10.

The rich are often a source of trouble to the church. However, many Christian leaders today like to have rich people in their congregations. But we should not have any preference for the rich. The poor may burden the church somewhat, but they do not damage the church or ruin it. Rich people damage God's economy much more than do the poor. The New Testament even says that those who are poor, either spiritually or materially, are blessed (Matt. 5:3; Luke 6:20). Because Paul deals with God's dispensation concerning the church, he cannot avoid speaking about the problems of rich people. He charges them not to be high-minded, nor to set their hope on the uncertainty of riches.

In their fund-raising activities, many Christian leaders give glory to those rich people who donate large sums of money. But they often neglect those who give only a small amount. The leading ones in the churches and the co-workers should not have this appreciation of rich people. Brother Nee even had the practice of not spending time with the wealthy. He preferred to be invited to the home of a poor brother. In this matter Brother Nee's attitude no doubt was right.

Verses 18 and 19 continue, "To do good, to be rich in good works, ready to distribute, willing to communicate, laying away for themselves as a treasure a good foundation for the future, that they may lay hold on that which is really life." Doing good here refers to the ready distribution of material things to the needy and the willing communication with such needs. To be rich in good works is to be rich according to God's pleasure (Eph. 2:10), not only in material things. The expression "a good foundation for the future" refers to the next age (compared with the present age in verse 17), the kingdom age, when the overcoming saints will enjoy the Lord's reward. For this we all need to lay a good foundation in the present age as a treasure for us to enjoy in the future. Those who are rich in this age should use their riches in such a way that they lay away as a treasure a good foundation for the future.

In verse 19 Paul charges Timothy to encourage the rich to "lay hold on that which is really life." This life is the eternal life referred to in verse 12. Material riches are for the human natural life in this age, which is temporal and hence not real. If we do good with material things, we accomplish something for the real life, laying away a treasure for our enjoyment in the eternal life in the next age. This requires us to lay hold on God's eternal life, which is the real life. Otherwise, we shall lay hold on our human natural life in laying away a treasure of material riches for a life in this age, a life that is not real. We should care for the eternal life rather than for the natural life.

Both verse 12 and verse 19 stress the eternal life of God. This indicates that the divine life is the vital and crucial factor in our Christian life.

GUARDING THE DEPOSIT

Verses 20 and 21 say, "O Timothy, guard the deposit, turning away from profane, vain babblings and oppositions of what is falsely called knowledge, which some professing have misaimed concerning the faith." The deposit was that which was committed to Timothy and entrusted to him: the healthy words which he received from Paul not only for himself, but also for others. By "what is falsely called knowledge" Paul means the teachings of the false teachers, teachings which were called knowledge (probably referring to Gnostic knowledge). This false knowledge replaced the genuine knowledge of the healthy word of God which was entrusted to Timothy. Those who profess what is falsely called knowledge have misaimed concerning the faith. Concerning the objective contents of our belief, they have missed the mark, as in shooting. They have misaimed concerning God's New Testament economy. After giving this further word, Paul concludes by saying, "Grace be with you."

LIFE-STUDY OF SECOND TIMOTHY

MESSAGE ONE

THE DIVINE PROVISIONS FOR THE INOCULATION AGAINST THE DECLINE OF THE CHURCH

Scripture Reading: 2 Tim. 1:1-14

Second Timothy, the last Epistle written by Paul, opens with the words, "Paul, an apostle of Christ Jesus through the will of God, according to the promise of life which is in Christ Jesus, to Timothy, beloved child: Grace, mercy, peace, from God the Father and Christ Jesus our Lord." This book was written at a time when the churches established through the apostle's ministry in the Gentile world were in a trend of degradation, and the apostle himself was confined in a remote prison. Many had turned away from him and forsaken him (1:15; 4:16), including even some of his co-workers (4:10). It was a discouraging and disappointing scene, especially to his young fellow-worker and spiritual child, Timothy. Due to this, in the opening of this encouraging, strengthening, and establishing Epistle, he confirmed to Timothy that he was an apostle of Christ, not only through the will of God, but also according to the promise of life which is in Christ. This implies that the churches may become degraded, and many of the saints may backslide in unfaithfulness, but the eternal life, the divine life, the uncreated life of God, promised by God in His holy writings and given to the apostle and all the believers, remains forever the same. With and upon this unchanging life the firm foundation of God has been laid and stands unshaken through all the tide of degradation (2:19). By such a life those who seek the Lord out of a pure heart are able to stand the trial of the church's decline. This life, on which the apostle in his first Epistle charged Timothy and others to lay hold (6:12, 19), should be an encouragement and strengthening to him in perilous times.

Only in the two Timothys did the apostle include God's mercy in the opening greeting of his Epistles. God's mercy reaches farther than His grace. In the degraded situation of the churches, God's mercy is needed.

I. THE SUBJECT OF THE BOOK: INOCULATION AGAINST THE DECLINE OF THE CHURCH

When Paul was writing this Epistle, he was fully aware that the churches were declining. However, because he was one who laid hold on the promise of eternal life, he was not discouraged or disappointed. He had something within him which never changed—the eternal, uncreated, incorruptible life of God. No matter how the environment may change, this eternal life remains the same. Because he himself was encouraged in the life of God and not disappointed by the situation, Paul wrote the Second Epistle to Timothy not only as an encouragement and strengthening to a younger co-worker, but also as an inoculation for the entire Body of Christ against the decline of the church.

We should not regard 2 Timothy merely as a so-called pastoral book. If we have the proper insight, we shall realize that the divine thought within Paul was to inoculate the believers against the decline of the church. Paul foresaw this decline. However, deep within he was encouraged, not because he could understand matters according to logic, but because he laid hold of the eternal life promised by God in His holy writings. The very life promised by God in the Scriptures dwelt within Paul. Paul's burden in writing this Epistle was both to encourage and to strengthen Timothy and also to inject a divine substance into the church in order to inoculate the church against the germ of decline. We praise the Lord that this inoculation has been effective. Yes, the church throughout the centuries has been ruined to a certain extent, but it has not been exterminated. Paul had the foresight to inoculate the church against decline. Even today we in the Lord's recovery are enjoying the benefit of this inoculation.

My burden in this message is to consider eight basic elements of this inoculation. These divine provisions for the inoculation include a pure conscience, unfeigned faith, the divine gift, a strong spirit, eternal grace, incorruptible life, healthy words, and the indwelling Spirit. These ingredients of the marvelous dose administered by Paul are found in 1:1-14.

II. INTRODUCTION

Verses 1 and 2 are an introductory word. In verse 1 Paul says that he was an apostle not only through the will of God, but also according to the promise of life which is in Christ Jesus. The expression "the promise of life" does not mean that we have only the promise and not the life. It means that we have received the promised life. A similar term, "the promise of the Spirit," is used in Galatians 3:14. This term does not mean that we have received only the promise and have not received the Spirit. It means that we have received the Spirit who has been promised. In the same principle, the words "the promise of life" denote the promised life. Paul was an apostle according to the life which God had promised, which Paul had received, and which dwelt within him. Paul became an apostle by this life.

The eternal life according to which Paul became an apostle is incorruptible and unchanging, for this life is actually the processed Triune God Himself. Because Paul was indwelt by this life, not even the whole Roman Empire was able to prevail over him in its dealings with him. Paul was strengthened by the processed Triune God as life.

Nowhere else but in the opening of this Epistle does Paul say that he was an apostle according to the promise of life. Elsewhere he tells us that he was an apostle through the will of God (Eph. 1:1). Not many Christian teachers emphasize the fact that Paul's apostleship was not only through the will of God, but also by the promise of eternal life. The reason Christians emphasize the will of God but not the promise of life is that they themselves do not see this matter of life. Whatever we do and whatever we are in the Lord's recovery today must be according to eternal life and by this life. Praise the Lord that we are in His recovery by this life!

III. THE DIVINE PROVISIONS FOR THE INOCULATION

The life mentioned in verse 1 includes all the eight basic elements of the inoculation. This means that eternal life includes a pure conscience, unfeigned faith, the divine gift, a strong spirit, eternal grace, the element of incorruption, healthy words, and the indwelling Spirit. If we have this life, which is actually the processed Triune God, we have a pure conscience, unfeigned faith, and all the other provisions of the divine inoculation. Let us now consider these provisions one by one.

A. A Pure Conscience

In verse 3 Paul says, "I thank God, Whom I serve from my forefathers in a pure conscience, how unceasingly I have remembrance concerning you in my petitions night and day." To serve here is to serve God in His worship (Acts 24:14; Phil. 3:3). Paul followed in the footsteps of his forefathers to serve God in a pure conscience. In a time of degradation, a pure conscience, a conscience purified from any mixture, is needed if we are to serve God.

I have the assurance that all the saints who are so honest, truthful, and faithful to the Lord in His recovery have not only a good conscience, but also a pure conscience. In this matter we should not accept the lie of the enemy. The more we doubt that we have a pure conscience, the more we shall feel that our conscience is not pure. We need to declare, "Satan, get away from me! I have a pure conscience. Satan, don't you know that I am for the Lord and not for anything else? I am for the Lord, for His recovery, for His church, and for His interests." The more we testify in an honest way that we have a pure conscience, the stronger will be our realization that our conscience is in fact pure. The way for us to have a pure conscience is to declare by faith, honestly, truthfully, and steadfastly, that we have a pure conscience toward the Lord. Do not listen to your doubts, and do not believe the lies of the enemy. The Lord's blood prevails against him. Do not believe the enemy when he says that you are weak, or when he accuses you of being impure and not having a good conscience. Do you not love the Lord? Are you not for the Lord and His church? Learn to tell the enemy, "Satan, you have been cheating me long enough. I will not believe you any longer, and I will not allow you to hold me back. I am for the Lord, and I have a pure conscience."

It is the eternal life which strengthens us to make such a declaration to the enemy. This is why I say that a conscience that is pure and good is included in eternal life. Because we have eternal life within us, we can be strengthened to declare that we have a pure conscience.

B. Unfeigned Faith

Verse 5 says, "Having been reminded of the unfeigned faith in you, which dwelt first in your grandmother Lois and your mother Eunice, and I am persuaded dwells also in you." Here Paul reminds Timothy of the unfeigned faith which is in him. This faith first indwelt Timothy's grandmother and then his mother. Now it dwells in him. We today may praise the Lord that this faith is also in us. Because we have eternal life, we have unfeigned faith.

Faith refers to the organic union with the Triune God in which we receive God's infusion through His Word and in His Spirit. The more we touch the Word by exercising our spirit, the more we shall contact the Lord and be infused with Him. As a result, our faith will be strengthened. This faith is actually the reflection of the eternal life we have received. Therefore, to repeat, faith refers to the organic union between us and the Triune God in which we contact the living God through His Word and by His Spirit to receive His infusion.

C. The Divine Gift

In verse 6 Paul goes on to say, "For which cause I remind

you to fan into flame the gift of God which is in you through the laying on of my hands." This word was written to encourage and strengthen Timothy in his ministry for the Lord, that his ministry not be weakened by Paul's imprisonment and the degraded situation of the churches. Here Paul seems to be saying to Timothy, "Timothy, I charge you to fan into flame the gift of God which is in you. Something in you is burning. However, it is not sufficient for it just to be burning—you need to fan this gift into flame. You have something in you which is a gift of God. Since you have unfeigned faith, I remind you to fan this gift into flame."

It is rather difficult to define what Paul means by the gift of God in verse 6. It may refer to a particular spiritual function or ability, something burning within Timothy that enabled him to function in a particular way.

All the saints in the Lord's recovery need to fan into flame the gift of God which is in them. However, in the meetings many saints seem to throw away the fan. Especially in the meetings of the church, we need to fan into flame the gift which is in us. Then the flame will grow higher and brighter, and the riches of Christ will be manifest. All the saints need to be encouraged with the fact that they have eternal life, a pure conscience, and unfeigned faith. For this cause, they should fan into flame the gift of God.

D. A Strong Spirit

In verse 7 Paul continues, "For God has not given us a spirit of cowardice, but of power and of love and of a sober mind." The spirit here denotes our human spirit, regenerated and indwelt by the Holy Spirit (John 3:5-6; Rom. 8:16). Fanning into flame the gift of God is related to our regenerated spirit.

Paul says that we have a spirit of power, of love, and of a sober mind. Power refers to our will, love to our emotion, and a sober mind to our mind. This indicates that a strong will, a loving emotion, and a sober mind have very much to do with a strong spirit for the exercise of the gift of God which is in us.

We need to believe that God has given us such a spirit, and we should praise Him for it. We should not say that we do not feel as if we have a spirit of love, power, and a sound mind. In our physical body we usually do not have any feeling with respect to our internal organs unless there is something wrong with them. Under normal circumstances, are you aware of the fact that you have a liver? I may not be conscious of my liver, but I know that I have this organ and that it is functioning. In like manner, we may not feel as if we have the kind of spirit described in verse 7. Nevertheless, we need to believe Paul's word and exercise our spirit.

In verse 8 Paul says, "Therefore do not be ashamed of the testimony of our Lord, nor of me His prisoner; but suffer evil with the gospel according to the power of God." Here we have the reason Paul charged Timothy in the two preceding verses to fan into flame the gift of God which was in him. We need to do this in order not to be ashamed of the testimony of the Lord. Not to be ashamed of the testimony of our Lord is to stand against its downward current in the declining churches. We should also be ready to suffer evil with the gospel. The gospel, which is personified here, was suffering persecution. Therefore, Timothy should expect to suffer evil along with the gospel. Our suffering of persecution along with the gospel must be to the extent of what the power of God can endure, not limited by the endurance of our natural strength.

E. Eternal Grace

In 1:9-10a Paul says, speaking of God, "Who has saved us and called us with a holy calling, not according to our works, but according to His own purpose and grace, which was given to us in Christ Jesus before times eternal, but now has been manifested through the appearing of our Savior Christ Jesus." God has not only saved us to enjoy His blessing, but also called us with a holy calling, a calling for a particular cause, to fulfill His purpose. The purpose here is God's plan according to His will to place us into Christ, making us one with Him to share His life and position that we may be His testimony. Grace is God's provision in life for us to live out His purpose.

The grace given to us in Christ was bestowed upon us before the world began. The phrase "before times eternal" means before the world began. This is a sure and unshakable foundation, standing firmly against the waves of the downward current and exposing the total powerlessness of the enemy's efforts to counter the eternal purpose of God. In order to strengthen Timothy, the apostle identifies their ministry with this eternal grace, the sure foundation.

In verse 9 Paul says that God's grace was given to us before times eternal; in verse 10 he says that this grace has been manifested through the appearing of our Savior Christ Jesus. God's grace was given to us in eternity, but was manifested and applied to us through our Lord's first coming to nullify death and bring life to us. Because this grace was manifested through the appearing of Christ, Old Testament saints like Abraham and David did not experience it. The grace destined to be given to us came with the appearing of the Lord Jesus. This grace is not merely a blessing; it is a Person, the Triune God Himself given to us to be our enjoyment. This grace came when the Lord Jesus appeared, and now it is with us today.

F. The Incorruptible Life

The last part of verse 10 says of Christ, "Who nullified death, and brought life and incorruption to light through the gospel." Christ nullified death, making it of none effect, through His Devil-destroying death (Heb. 2:14) and death-swallowing resurrection (1 Cor. 15:52-54).

The eternal life of God is given to all believers in Christ (1 Tim. 1:16) and is the main element of the divine grace given to us (Rom. 5:17, 21). This life has conquered death (Acts 2:24) and will swallow up death (2 Cor. 5:4). It was according to the promise of such a life that Paul was an apostle (2 Tim. 1:1). This life and its consequent incorruption have been brought to light and made visible to men through the preaching of the gospel.

Life is the divine element, even God Himself, imparted into our spirit. Incorruption is the consequence of life saturating our body (Rom. 8:11). This life and incorruption are able to counter the death and corruption of the decline among the churches.

Second Timothy 1:11 says, "For which I was appointed a herald, and an apostle, and a teacher." The relative pronoun "which" refers to the gospel of divine grace and eternal life. This corresponds to the gospel presented in grace and life by the Apostle John (John 1:4, 15-17). For such a gospel Paul was appointed a herald, an apostle, and a teacher. A herald announces and proclaims the gospel, an apostle sets up and establishes the churches for God's administration, and a teacher gives instructions to the churches with all the saints.

In verse 12 Paul goes on to say, "For which cause also I suffer these things; but I am not ashamed, for I know Whom I have believed, and I am persuaded that He is able to guard my deposit unto that day." The apostle had a cause for his sufferings, a cause on the highest plane—to proclaim the glad tidings of the gospel of grace and life, to establish the churches, and to instruct the saints. Such a cause should also be an encouragement and strengthening to Timothy in facing the deterioration of the declining churches. Since Paul was not ashamed, Timothy should not be ashamed either.

In verse 12 Paul says, "I know Whom I have believed." What the apostle believed was not a thing or a matter, but a living Person, Christ, the Son of the living God, who is the embodiment of divine grace and eternal life. The eternal life in Him is powerful; it is more than able to sustain to the end the one who suffers for His sake and also to preserve him for the inheritance of the coming glory. The grace in Him is more than sufficient to provide His sent one with all he needs for finishing the course of his ministry unto a reward in glory (4:7-8). Hence, He is able to guard that which the apostle has committed unto Him for the day of His return.

Such an assurance should also be an encouragement and strengthening to the weakened and sorrowful Timothy.

The words "my deposit" refer to that which Paul had committed to the Lord. The apostle had committed his entire being with his glorious future unto the One who is able, through His life and grace, to guard his deposit unto "that day," the day of Christ's second appearing.

G. The Healthy Words

In verse 13 Paul continues, "Hold a pattern of healthy words which you heard from me, in faith and love which are in Christ Jesus." The preceding word in verse 12 is a pattern, an example, of healthy words. The words of our Lord Jesus Christ are words of life (John 6:63); hence, they are healthy words. The word healthy here refers to the health of life.

H. The Indwelling Spirit

In verse 14 Paul concludes, "Guard the good deposit through the Holy Spirit Who dwells in us." The Holy Spirit dwells in our spirit (Rom. 8:16). Hence, to guard the good deposit through the Holy Spirit requires us to exercise our spirit.

We have pointed out that the Spirit is the ultimate consummation of the Triune God's contact with man. Praise the Lord that today this Spirit dwells in our spirit!

We thank the Lord for all the divine provisions for the inoculation against the decline of the church. The more we experience these provisions, the more we shall be inoculated against any kind of decline. Having such a marvelous inoculation, we should be able to declare that in the Lord's recovery there is no decline.

LIFE-STUDY OF SECOND TIMOTHY

MESSAGE TWO

THE BASIC FACTOR OF THE DECLINE—FORSAKING THE APOSTLE AND HIS MINISTRY

Scripture Reading: 2 Tim. 1:15-18

In this message we shall consider 1:15-18, verses which show that the basic factor of the decline consists in forsaking the apostle and his ministry. Although this portion of 2 Timothy is short, Paul must have had strong feelings when he wrote these words.

In 1:1-14 Paul covered many positive, encouraging, and strengthening matters. Based on his charge to Timothy in verses 1 through 7, Paul says in verse 8, "Therefore do not be ashamed of the testimony of our Lord, nor of me His prisoner; but suffer evil with the gospel according to the power of God." Here the gospel is personified; it is regarded as a living person that is suffering persecution. Paul encouraged Timothy to suffer evil with the gospel according to the power of God.

In verse 9 Paul goes on to speak of God who "saved us and called us with a holy calling, not according to our works, but according to His own purpose and grace, which was given to us in Christ Jesus before times eternal." The purpose here refers to God's goal, and grace refers to the means of reaching this goal. The grace to reach God's goal was given to us in Christ Jesus "before times eternal," that is, before the world began. Grace "has been manifested through the appearing of our Savior Christ Jesus" (v. 10). Hence, grace did not come until the Lord Jesus came. John 1:17 indicates this: "The law was given through Moses; grace and reality came through Jesus Christ." The grace which came through Jesus Christ is nothing less than the Triune God dispensed into us for our enjoyment. This grace carries out God's purpose and enables us to reach His goal.

Grace works in two ways. It works negatively to nullify death, and it works positively to bring in life and incorruption. This work of grace is still taking place within us. Today, in the church life grace is nullifying death and bringing life and incorruption to light through the gospel. Although we heard the gospel preached in the past, we probably did not hear that the gospel of grace nullifies death and brings in life and incorruption.

On behalf of such a gospel, Paul was "appointed a herald, and an apostle, and a teacher" (v. 11). Paul was a herald to proclaim the gospel, an apostle to establish churches, and a teacher to instruct the churches and the saints in the details of the gospel. For the sake of this gospel, Paul suffered "these things." However, he was not ashamed, for he knew the One whom he had believed and was persuaded that He was able to guard his deposit, to guard what he had committed unto Him (v. 12).

In verse 13 Paul charges Timothy, "Hold a pattern of healthy words which you heard from me, in faith and love which are in Christ Jesus." Paul's foregoing words to Timothy are a pattern of the healthy words which Timothy was to hold. We should hold such a pattern in faith, in the organic union with the Triune God, and in the divine love. Furthermore, according to verse 14, we should "guard the good deposit through the Holy Spirit Who dwells in us." The good deposit here is equal to the healthy words. We should guard this deposit through the indwelling Holy Spirit. The more we consider all the matters covered in verses 1 through 14, the more we realize what riches these verses contain.

I. THE APOSTASY

In 1:15 Paul says, "This you know, that all who are in Asia turned away from me, of whom are Phygelus and Hermogenes." Asia here refers to the province of Asia. In this verse Paul indicates that believers in Asia who had formerly received the apostle's ministry now forsook him. In spite of such desertion, the apostle grew stronger in the grace that was in Christ, who was the same and would never change. Without being discouraged, he exhorted his son in faith to persevere steadily in the ministry in the midst of failure and ruin of the churches.

It is difficult to say to whom the words "all who are in Asia" refer. Does it mean that every believer in Asia turned away from Paul? Paul specifically names Phygelus and Hermogenes, two who must have taken the lead to desert the apostle because of his imprisonment. But what about all the other believers in Asia? We cannot say that every one deserted Paul, for Paul mentions Onesiphorus as one who often refreshed him and who sought him out diligently in Rome and found him (vv. 16-17).

A number of expositors say that these verses point to an apostasy, a departure from the truth. But what was the extent of the apostasy? I believe that "all who are in Asia" points to the general situation among the believers in Asia without including every particular believer. Generally speaking, there was apostasy in Asia.

II. THE FAITHFULNESS

Second Timothy 1:15-18 indicates that we cannot be neutral. We are either a Phygelus or Hermogenes, or we are an Onesiphorus. Onesiphorus was an overcomer who resisted the general trend and stood against the down current to refresh the Lord's ambassador in spirit, soul, and body, one who was not ashamed of Paul's imprisonment for the Lord's commission. Concerning him Paul says, "May the Lord grant him to find mercy from the Lord in that day! And in how many things he served in Ephesus, you know very well." The words "that day" refer to the day of the Lord's victorious appearing to reward His overcomers (4:8; Rev. 22:12).

The principle here is nearly the same as that at the time of Elijah. Elijah said to the Lord, "I have been very jealous for the Lord God of hosts: because the children of Israel have forsaken thy covenant, thrown down thine altars, and slain thy prophets with the sword; and I, even I only, am left; and they seek my life, to take it away" (1 Kings 19:14). The Lord replied, "Yet I have left me seven thousand in Israel, all the knees which have not bowed unto Baal" (v. 18). The principle here is that even during a period of decline, a downward trend when most of God's people are carried away, there are always a number who remain faithful. There will always be an Onesiphorus to stand against the downward trend. Yes, Phygelus, Hermogenes, and others in Asia turned away from Paul. But Onesiphorus, an overcomer, stood against the decline, against the down current.

I am certain that both Phygelus and Hermogenes were believers. Otherwise, Paul would not have said that they turned away from him. Phygelus and Hermogenes were with Paul at one time. Probably they were not ordinary believers; they must have been either co-workers or leading ones among the saints. To be sure, they took the lead to turn away from Paul.

Those who turned away from Paul turned away not only from his person, but also from his ministry. Actually, it is not the person himself who is important; it is the ministry carried on by a person which is of extreme importance. When Paul said that certain ones turned away from him, he did not mean that they merely turned away from him as a person, but that they turned away from his ministry. In perilous times, genuine believers, even leading ones and co-workers, may turn away.

In relation to this matter, I would like to relate certain aspects of the history of the Lord's recovery. During the years I was with Brother Nee in mainland China, I saw many who accepted Brother Nee's ministry for a time and later turned away. Although the number of saints was not large, it happened again and again that some, perhaps just two or three, turned away from Brother Nee's ministry.

We have also had many similar experiences from the time we were sent from mainland China to Taiwan in 1949. In the short period of six years, the number of saints in the Lord's recovery in Taiwan increased from approximately five hundred to more than twenty-five thousand. One year we invited a very spiritual and experienced brother from England to minister to us. His first visit was profitable, for he ministered to us without touching the practice of the church life. But when, at our invitation, he came the second time, he did so with the intention of correcting us with respect to the practice of the church life. Actually, he wanted to convince us to forsake the ground of the church. According to his concept, whenever two or three believers meet in the name of the Lord Jesus, there is the reality of the church. He taught that during the era of what he called organized Christianity there could be in any city a number of groups meeting in the Lord's name and that each would possess the reality of the church to a certain degree. Due to this brother's influence, a small number of young people turned from the practice of the church life, declaring that they had seen a vision of what they called "the full Christ." It is not clear what they meant by this expression. The Bible speaks of the unsearchable riches of Christ and refers to the fullness of Christ, but there is no mention of a "full Christ."

Even though these young people began to undermine the work in Taiwan, I simply waited and prayed. Seven years went by before the issue was settled. At one point I told them frankly that I would follow the way of Christ and the church for eternity. I asked them to consider seriously what would happen if they would only take Christ, but neglect the church life. Furthermore, I told them that as children of light we should conduct ourselves in the light. I declared again that I would forever follow the way of Christ and the church as recovered through Brother Nee. Concerning this, I assured them that I would never change. I went on to tell them that if they preferred to leave the church life and follow their vision of "the full Christ," I would not hinder them. On the contrary, they were certainly free to follow a way which they regarded as better. However, I told them that they should not remain with us pretending to be the same as we are when actually they were undermining the work. They claimed that they had no problem with the ground of the church, and they continued among us for seven years. All that time they were undermining the work in Taiwan.

In His sovereignty, the Lord brought me to this country and burdened me to start the ministry here. Certain of the leading ones in Taiwan wrote me regularly about the situation with the young brothers who were constantly undermining the work there. I answered them by referring to the words of the Lord Jesus in John 2:19: "Destroy this temple, and in three days I will raise it up," a reminder of a message I had given. In that message I said, "If this work on the island of Taiwan is something of man, it should be torn down. But if it is of the Lord, once it has been destroyed, the Lord will raise it up again in resurrection." I encouraged the leading ones to be at peace. Eventually, the dissenting ones left the church life and the work in Taiwan. Shortly thereafter they were divided among themselves. They did not succeed in their attempt to destroy the church life.

Let me now relate several experiences through which we have passed in the Lord's recovery in the United States. At one time a group of Christians who emphasize speaking in tongues wanted to join with us for the practice of the church life. On the one hand, we did not oppose tongues-speaking; on the other hand, we did not encourage it, and we were not willing for the meetings to be dominated by it. After a short period of time, this group left the church.

Others who were once among us recognized that the way of the church is true. However, their preference was for a native American apostle. When I learned of this, I said to myself, "Only the first group of apostles were native apostles, Jews who were apostles to Jews. But Paul became a foreign apostle, an apostle to the Gentiles." To reject a foreigner and to accept only so-called native apostles violates the principle of the Body. The Body of Christ is universal. Nevertheless, we assured those who desired a native apostle that they were free to look for one and find one if they could. Hence, those who desired a native apostle also turned from the church life.

Another case involves a brother who was gifted in speaking. On one occasion he testified publicly that the Lord had told him to commit himself to the way of the recovery. After a certain time, he was distracted from the church life and came to believe that the church ground is too narrow. He had the concept that the recovery was merely something transplanted from China. Therefore, this brother also left the church life.

Yet another case concerns a certain brother who considered the denominations to be the field for our work. He claimed that if we offend those in the denominations, we shall lose the field of our work. This brother admitted that we were the church; however, he counselled us not to make such a statement. We replied that this can be compared to a woman not saying that she is the wife of a certain man. This brother's goal was to bring believers into a halfway shelter for Christians who had left the denominations, but who had not come into the church life. Actually, this is to compromise the truth, to share the teachings about the Christian life but, out of fear, to hold back the truth concerning the church. This brother promotes the books by Brother Nee that do not concern the church, but neglects those books which are related to the church life. He also has turned away.

One brother was in the church life for several years. Then he declared that he had seen a so-called third line. He claimed that Brother Nee had seen the line of Jerusalem and the line of Antioch, but that he had come to see the line of Ephesus. Thus, he turned from the church life to practice this "third line."

Another brother claimed that he knew the best way to practice the church life. According to him, the way to build a local church is with the children both from families in the church and of families in the neighborhood. I visited a Lord's table meeting deliberately to see the situation in his locality. Even though very young children were allowed to partake of the bread, I did not say a critical word. However, I did tell the brother, "As the church, we are all-inclusive; we are not sectarian. Even if you wish to practice the church life according to your way, we do not oppose you. But please do not insist that you have found the best way or the unique way to build the church. Such insistence will be a cause of problems." Eventually, this brother also turned away.

In recent years certain ambitious ones looked upon the Lord's recovery as an opportunity for them to gain power. They realized that in the "field" of the recovery there were no "lions" or "tigers." On the contrary, all the saints were "doves" and "lambs." In other words, the saints in the Lord's recovery seemed to be naive. Although these ambitious ones tried to gain power for themselves, they failed. They came to realize that the naive "doves" and "lambs" had someone standing with them, that it is God Himself who guards His glory in His recovery. Unable to do what they desired, these also left the church life.

My point in relating these facts of history is to say that we should not think that everyone who comes into the Lord's recovery will remain. Because the church life is a test to all, a certain number eventually will turn away. However, we should not be disappointed by this. We should be encouraged just as Timothy was encouraged by Paul's word. Yes, the way of the Lord's recovery is a test and an exposure. But the recovery also proves that, although some turn away like Phygelus and Hermogenes, others like Onesiphorus stand firm. Today in His recovery the Lord has hundreds, even thousands, of such ones.

Paul's desire was that the Lord would grant mercy to Onesiphorus both in the present and on "that day." This indicates a double blessing: a blessing to the whole house of Onesiphorus in this age and blessing to Onesiphorus himself on the day of the Lord's victorious appearing. Do you want to receive this double blessing of the Lord's mercy? If so, then do not be a Phygelus or Hermogenes, but an Onesiphorus. When others turn away, stay with the apostle and his ministry.

After we went to Taipei from mainland China, we built a meeting hall that could accommodate about five hundred people. The first Lord's Day after the building was completed, the new hall was filled, mainly with Christians who had fled the mainland. Realizing the situation of those in the audience, I spoke a frank word. I said, "In Christianity today there are different kinds of churches. Some of these churches will marry you; others will assist you with your medical problems; and still others will help you find employment. Some churches will give opportunities for those who are talented or wealthy. If you have certain abilities, they will give you a position. However, the church here does not afford you this kind of help. Furthermore, there are no positions to satisfy your ambition. If you want such things, you are in the wrong place. As the church here, we care only to preach the pure gospel, to teach the Bible, and to help people receive Christ, love Him, and grow in Him. We are not here for any earthly concern. We care for heavenly things. All those who are truly seeking these heavenly things please continue to meet with us. All the rest should go elsewhere to find the help you are seeking." The next Lord's Day more than half did not return. We realized that those who came back cared for the things of the Lord. Most of them have been gained for the Lord and are in the church life.

Once again I would say that in the Lord's recovery we care only for Christ and the church. This is our battle cry. Our goal is not to help people with earthly pursuits, much less to satisfy their ambition for position. We are here to minister Christ for the church according to God's eternal purpose. If you are seeking Christ and the church, then the church life is the place for you. Those who are seeking something other than Christ and the church will eventually realize that the church life is not the place for what they are seeking, and they will turn away.

LIFE-STUDY OF SECOND TIMOTHY

MESSAGE THREE

THE INOCULATOR

Scripture Reading: 2 Tim. 2:1-15

We have pointed out that the subject of 2 Timothy is inoculation against the decline of the church. In this message we shall consider five specific titles given to the inoculator in 2:1-15. These titles are a teacher, a soldier, a contender (an athlete), a husbandman, and a workman. If we read these verses carefully, we shall see that Paul regarded Timothy and his other co-workers as those who should be teachers, soldiers, contenders, husbandmen, and workmen.

I. A TEACHER

In 2:1 Paul says, "You therefore, my child, be empowered in the grace which is in Christ Jesus." The word "therefore" refers to chapter one. Paul's exhortation in 2:1 is in view of what has been mentioned in the preceding chapter. Based upon what he has just written to Timothy, Paul now goes on to encourage him to be empowered in the grace which is in Christ Jesus. Paul did not charge Timothy here to be empowered in knowledge or in gifts. He charged him to be empowered in grace. The apostle himself had experienced the empowering of grace in life (1:9-12). Now he exhorts Timothy to be empowered in the same grace. This grace is God's provision in life for us to live out His purpose. Instead of being discouraged, Paul was empowered in grace, even though he was in prison. He realized that grace is nothing less than the processed Triune God—the Father embodied in the Son and the Son realized as the indwelling Spirit. Second Corinthians 13:14 indicates that grace is the very Triune God Himself: "The grace of the Lord Jesus Christ, and the love of God, and the fellowship of the Holy Spirit, be with you all" (lit.). Grace is not a thing; it is a unique Person, the living, divine Person of the Triune God processed to be the all-inclusive, life-giving, indwelling Spirit. This Spirit now dwells in us as our grace. We all can be empowered in this grace in the indwelling Triune God processed to be our enjoyment.

The more we are empowered in this grace, the more able we shall be to teach others. Thus, in verse 2 Paul goes on to say, "And the things which you have heard from me through many witnesses, these commit to faithful men, who will be competent to teach others also." The things to which Paul refers here are the healthy words in 1:13. The healthy words, after being committed to faithful men, become the good deposit in them (1:14). This word indicates that if someone in a local church has a deposit of the Lord's healthy words, he should train the faithful ones, the trustworthy ones, that they also may have a good deposit from the Lord, thus making them competent to teach others.

Paul realized that Timothy had received a good deposit, that he had been taught and nourished with the riches of grace. Therefore, he charged Timothy to commit these things to others who would be faithful and competent to carry on the same ministry. This indicates that more than one person is needed to carry on the riches of God's New Testament economy. My hope is that through all these Life-study Messages thousands of saints in the Lord's recovery will receive a good deposit of the riches of grace concerning God's New Testament economy. Then those who have received these riches will be able to commit these things to others. Imagine what the situation would be if the Lord had ten thousand saints filled with His good deposit, spreading the riches of His economy throughout the earth. No doubt, this would hasten the time of His glorious appearing.

There is one God, one Christ, one Spirit, and one church. Because God is one, His way must also be one. Is this way to be found in Catholicism or in the denominations or in the charismatic movement? Certainly not! Neither is God's unique way found among the independent Christian groups.

God's way is in His recovery. Actually, the recovery is the recovery of the unique way. Many saints can testify with a pure conscience from the depths of their being that if they do not take the way of the recovery today, they have no other way. The Lord's recovery is *the* way. I say this, not because I have been used of the Lord in His recovery, but simply because it is a fact. Some who became dissenting and left discovered that they had no way to go back to the denominations. In certain cases the denominations might not even be willing to accept them. This shows that if we touch the recovery and then leave it, we commit spiritual suicide, for we turn away from God's unique way.

In 2:1 and 2 Paul is burdened to charge Timothy, one who had received such a good deposit, to pass on the riches of grace to others. Then there would be many teachers, many ministers of Christ, to spread the riches of God's New Testament economy.

II. A SOLDIER

In verse 3 Paul continues, "Take your share in suffering evil as a good soldier of Christ Jesus." The apostles considered their ministry a warfare for Christ, just as the priestly service was considered a military service, a warfare, in Numbers 4:23, 30, 35 (lit.). Whenever we minister Christ to others, we find ourselves in a battle. Hence, we should not only be teachers committing the deposit to others, but we should also be soldiers fighting for God's interests.

Verse 4 says, "No one serving as a soldier entangles himself with the affairs of life, that he may please the one who enlisted him." The word for life here in Greek is *bios,* indicating the physical life in this age. To fight a good fight (4:7) for the Lord's interests on this earth we must be cleared of any earthly entanglement. The matters of our material, physical life should not entangle us as we are endeavoring to minister Christ to others. This ministry is a fighting, and the fighting requires that we be free from entanglement. On the one hand, the priestly service is a ministry to God; on the other hand, it is a warfare against God's enemies. As the priests were bearing the ark of testimony, they had to be prepared to fight against those who might attack this testimony.

III. A CONTENDER

In verse 5 Paul likens Timothy to an athlete contending in the games: "And if also anyone contends in the games, he is not crowned unless he contends lawfully." At the same time Timothy was to be a teacher and a soldier, he was also to be an athlete. A soldier must fight to win the victory, whereas an athlete must contend lawfully to receive the crown.

It is important for a runner in a race to run fast. That is not the time for him to exercise patience. In a foregoing message I encouraged you to wait and pray. But when it comes to running the race to win the crown, we should not wait. On the contrary, we should run to reach the goal.

IV. A HUSBANDMAN

Verse 6 continues, "The laboring husbandman must be the first to partake of the fruits." Here Paul likens Timothy to a husbandman, a farmer. Just as a soldier must win the victory and an athlete must receive the crown, so a husbandman must partake of the fruits, the food. This requires patience. As athletes we should be quick, but as farmers we need to be patient. If out of impatience a farmer would pluck up the tiny sprouts, his crop would be ruined. Likewise, if he drives his cattle too much, he may hurt them. With both crops and livestock, farmers must learn to have patience.

Verses 7 through 14 are related to Paul's charge to Timothy that he be a husbandman. After telling Timothy to consider what he says and that the Lord will give him understanding in all things (v. 7), Paul goes on to say, "Remember Jesus Christ, raised from among the dead, of the seed of David, according to my gospel." The word "raised" in verse 8 indicates Christ's victory over death by His divine life with its resurrection power. The expression "seed of David" indicates Christ's dignified human nature exalted and glorified along with His divine nature. The words “my gospel” indicate that Paul’s gospel was the glad tidings of the living Person of Christ, who possesses both the divine and human nature, who was incarnated to be the Son of Man and resurrected to be the Son of God, as indicated in the parallel portion, Romans 1:1-4.

Paul says that he suffered evil “unto bonds as a criminal,” but that “the word of God is not bound” (v. 9). In spite of all the opposition by human efforts that were instigated by the enemy, Satan, the bonds of the apostle released the word of God, giving it free course and making it more prevailing.

In verse 10 Paul continues, “Therefore I endure all things for the sake of the chosen ones, that they also may obtain the salvation which is in Christ Jesus with eternal glory.” The “chosen ones” denotes the believers in Christ, who were chosen by God the Father before the foundation of the world (Eph. 1:4) and selected from mankind for salvation. The apostle endured all sufferings for our sake that we also may obtain salvation as he did.

In verse 10 Paul does not speak of salvation *and* eternal glory, but of salvation *with* eternal glory. Eternal glory is the ultimate goal of God’s salvation (Rom. 8:21). God’s salvation leads us into His glory (Heb. 2:10). This encourages us to endure sufferings for the gospel (Rom. 8:17).

Immediately after charging Timothy to be a husbandman, Paul speaks of suffering. This indicates that a husbandman must be one who is able to suffer and endure. As a farmer, he must learn not only to suffer, but also to die.

In these verses Paul not only speaks of his own sufferings, but he also presents the Lord Jesus as a pattern of one who suffered, died, and was resurrected. Verses 11 through 13 may have been a hymn. This passage corresponds to Romans 6:8 and 8:17. Verse 11 says, “Faithful is the word: For if we died with Him, we shall also live with Him.” The expression “died with Him” is related to Christ’s crucifixion, as symbolized by baptism (Rom. 6:3-8). Likewise, the words “live with Him” mean to live Christ in His resurrection (Rom. 6:5, 8; John 14:19).

Verse 12 says, "If we endure, we shall also reign with Him; if we deny Him, He also will deny us." Enduring is related to life in this age, and reigning with Christ, to the coming age. If we deny Him, He will deny us; that is, He will not acknowledge us (Matt. 10:33; Luke 9:26).

Verse 13 continues, "If we are faithless, He remains faithful, for He cannot deny Himself." The word faithful in this verse refers to the Lord's faithfulness to His own word. If we are faithless, the Lord will remain faithful, for He is not able to deny Himself. If we become faithless to Him, although He remains faithful, He cannot accept us as faithful by making Himself unfaithful, that is, by denying Himself, by denying His nature and His being.

In verse 14 Paul says, "Remind them of these things, solemnly charging them before the Lord not to have contentions of words, which are profitable for nothing, to the ruin of those who hear." By "these things" Paul refers to the charge that faithful, competent men, to whom the good deposit has been committed, should be not only teachers, but also soldiers, athletes, and husbandmen. Like the Lord Jesus during His life on earth, they need to be patient and have endurance. The Lord suffered with patience, and He endured. After He was put to death, He was resurrected. Based on this, Paul says that if we die with Him, we shall live and that if we suffer with Him, we shall reign with Him.

V. A WORKMAN

In verse 15 Paul says, "Be diligent to present yourself approved to God, an unashamed workman, cutting straight the word of the truth." Here Paul indicates that the inoculator is to be a workman. As a carpenter, this workman must cut straight the word of the truth. This means to unfold the word of God in its various parts rightly and straightly without distortion. Just as a carpenter has the skill to cut wood in a straight way, so the Lord's workman needs the skill to cut straight the word of truth. This is necessary because in the decline of the church so many truths are twisted and presented in a warped, biased form.

"Contentions of words" (2:14), "profane babblings" (v. 16), the eating word of gangrene (v. 17), and "foolish and ignorant questionings" (v. 23) are often very much used by the Devil (v. 26) in the down current among the churches to produce contentions (v. 23), to ruin the hearers (v. 14), to promote ungodliness (v. 16), and to overthrow people's faith (v. 18). Hence, there is the need of the word of the truth rightly unfolded to enlighten the darkened ones, inoculate against the poison, swallow up the death, and bring the distracted back to the right track.

Among Christians today, only the superficial aspects of the truth are not twisted. Virtually all the deeper things of the truth have been distorted. Concerning these things, many have not cut the word of truth straightly, but cut it in a way that is curved and biased. Therefore, we should be not only teachers, soldiers, contenders, and farmers, but also workmen, carpenters, cutting straight the word of the truth. The truth here does not merely denote biblical doctrine; it refers to the contents and the reality of God's New Testament economy. The main elements of this truth are Christ as the mystery of God and the embodiment of God and the church as the mystery of Christ and the Body of Christ. We all need to learn to cut straight the word of truth with respect to Christ and the church.

Certain of the Brethren teachers interpret Paul's word about cutting straight the word of truth to mean dividing the Bible into various dispensations: innocence, conscience, human government, promise, law, grace, and kingdom. The Bible can be understood according to these dispensations. However, arranging the Word into dispensations is not what Paul means in 2:15 about cutting straight the word of the truth. As used in the three books of 1 and 2 Timothy and Titus, the word truth has a specific significance: it denotes the contents of God's New Testament economy. Not realizing this, many readers of the Bible think that in 2:15 Paul is speaking of truth in a general way. But we need to understand the word truth in this verse according to its usage in the three books of 1 and 2 Timothy and Titus. First Timothy

3:15 says that the church is "the pillar and base of the truth." This truth is the mystery of godliness, God manifest in the flesh. The church should bear, uphold, this truth, this reality. Numerous times in these three Epistles Paul speaks of the truth. For example, in 1 Timothy 2:4 he says that God "desires all men to be saved and come to the full knowledge of the truth." The word of the truth in 2 Timothy 2:15 refers to the healthy words of God's New Testament economy. As workmen, we should learn not merely to divide the Bible into dispensations. This is too superficial. We must learn to unfold the word of the truth concerning God's economy. If we would do this, we need to consider carefully Paul's use of the word truth in these three Epistles. If we consider these books carefully, we shall see that truth here denotes the reality of the contents of the New Testament economy of God. Therefore, to cut straight the word of the truth is to unfold without bias or distortion the reality of God's economy revealed in the New Testament.

LIFE-STUDY OF SECOND TIMOTHY

MESSAGE FOUR

THE SPREAD OF THE DECLINE

Scripture Reading: 2 Tim. 2:16-26

Second Timothy 2:16 is a contrast to Paul's word in verse 15, where he says, "Be diligent to present yourself approved to God, an unashamed workman, cutting straight the word of the truth." The good workman is one who cuts straight not the word of knowledge or doctrine, but the word of truth. Many Christians think that truth in such verses as 2:15 means doctrine or teaching. However, in the New Testament truth does not denote mere doctrine. Concerning Christ in His incarnation, John 1:14 says, "The Word became flesh and tabernacled among us...full of grace and truth." It certainly would be nonsensical to interpret truth here as doctrine. How could we say that the Word became flesh and was full of doctrine? In New Testament usage truth refers to the reality of God's New Testament economy. When Christ came through incarnation, grace and reality also came. Both grace and reality are God Himself. Grace is God in the Son as our enjoyment; reality is God realized by us in the Son. Therefore, grace and reality both refer to God incarnate. When we receive grace, we also receive reality. Then we have God as our reality. This reality is the truth in 2 Timothy 2:15. As we have pointed out, this truth is the reality of the contents of God's New Testament economy. These contents include Christ as the Head and the church as the Body. To cut straight the word of the truth is not simply to divide the Bible into various sections. Rather, it is to cut the healthy word of the reality of the contents of God's economy.

I. AVOIDING PROFANE, VAIN BABBLINGS

A. Advancing to More Ungodliness

As a contrast to verse 15, Paul goes on to say in verse 16, "But avoid profane, vain babblings, for they will advance to more ungodliness." The word profane denotes that which touches worldliness and is touched by it; it refers to what is contrary to being holy. The profane, vain babblings Paul charged Timothy to avoid advance to more ungodliness, to a situation which is contrary to godliness, contrary to the manifestation of God in our daily life and in the church life.

B. Spreading as Gangrene

In verse 17 Paul goes on to say, "And their word will spread as gangrene, of whom are Hymenaeus and Philetus." The Greek word rendered spread may also be rendered feed or eat. Literally it means "will find pasture," as in John 10:9. The word for pasture in Greek is the medical term for the consuming progress of a mortifying disease (Alford). Hence, its meaning in this verse is to spread.

The word gangrene denotes an eating sore, a cancer. Paul uses such a strong word to describe those who teach differently. He tells us that their word not only advances unto more ungodliness, but that it spreads as gangrene which consumes the flesh and causes part of one's body to die. According to our observation, this has been the situation among certain dissenting ones.

C. Hymenaeus and Philetus

1. Having Misaimed concerning the Truth

Speaking of Hymenaeus and Philetus, Paul says in verse 18 that concerning the truth they "have misaimed, saying that the resurrection has already taken place, and overthrow the faith of some." The word misaimed means to miss the mark, swerve, deviate. Paul does not say that Hymenaeus and Philetus misaimed concerning doctrine or teaching; he says that they misaimed concerning the truth, concerning the reality of the New Testament economy. They swerved from the truth by saying that the resurrection had already taken place. This is to claim that there will be no resurrection. This is a serious heresy, for it denies the divine power in life (1 Cor. 15:52; 1 Thes. 4:16; Rev. 20:4, 6).

2. Overthrowing the Faith of Some

In verse 18 Paul also says that by having misaimed concerning the truth Hymenaeus and Philetus overthrew the faith of some. Faith here is subjective and refers to the act of believing. This subjective faith, our believing act, is very much related to the resurrection of Christ (Rom. 10:9). As we have pointed out, this subjective faith involves an organic union between us and the Triune God. For one's faith to be overthrown is to have this inward organic union damaged in some way. Some among us can testify of having had this organic union temporarily cut off by hearing the words of those who taught differently. Inwardly these ones realized that the organic union within them had ceased. That was the overthrowing of their faith.

II. THE FIRM FOUNDATION OF GOD AND ITS SEAL

In verse 19 Paul declares, "However, the firm foundation of God stands, having this seal, The Lord knows those who are His, and, Let everyone who names the name of the Lord depart from unrighteousness." Many Christian teachers claim that the foundation here refers to Christ. It is true that in 1 Corinthians 3:11 Paul says that Christ is the unique foundation. Apart from Him, we do not have any other foundation. Nevertheless, if we consider verse 19 according to the context of the chapter, we shall see that the foundation here does not refer to Christ as the foundation of the church, but refers to the church as the foundation, or base, of the truth. Verses 14 through 18 give instruction concerning how to deal with heresies on the negative side and how to handle the truth on the positive side. According to the context of verses 15, 18, and 25, the foundation here does not refer to Christ as the foundation of the church, but to the church as the foundation of the truth. This corresponds to "the base of the truth," which holds the truth (1 Tim. 3:15), especially the truth of the resurrection of Christ (Acts 4:33).

The church is built with the divine life in Christ, a life which is indestructible, unconquerable (Heb. 7:16; Acts 2:24), and able to withstand decline into death from any source. Hence, the church is the firm foundation of God that stands forever against any heresy. No matter what kind of heresies may come in or how extensively the gangrene may spread, this firm foundation stands.

Certain of those who left the Lord's recovery expected that soon afterwards the recovery would collapse. However, because it is built upon a firm foundation, the recovery did not collapse and it will never collapse. Had the Lord's recovery been founded on something other than the divine life, the eternal life, it would have collapsed long ago. But because the recovery has the firm foundation of the truth, it is not hurt by attack. On the contrary, those who seek to damage the recovery actually damage themselves, and at the same time they strengthen the recovery and expose the firmness of its foundation. The recovery is built on something eternal and divine—God's life with His nature. For this reason, not even the gates of Hades can conquer it. Because it is built on the indestructible and unconquerable eternal life, the firm foundation of the truth stands. In recent years, it has not been necessary for us to protect the Lord's recovery. It has been protected by the unconquerable divine life. Hence, the church is the firm foundation of God standing in the eternal life.

Paul says that this firm foundation has "this seal." The seal has two sides. On the Lord's side it is: "The Lord knows those who are His." This is based on the Lord's divine life, which He has given to all His believers and which has brought them into an organic union with Him, making them one with Him and causing them to become His. On our side it is: "Let everyone who names the name of the Lord depart from unrighteousness." This is the issue of the divine life: it enables us to depart from unrighteousness and keeps us blameless in His holy name. The church as the firm foundation in the divine life bears such a two-sided seal, testifying that the Lord's divine life has made us His and has kept us from things which are contrary to His righteous way.

III. A GREAT HOUSE

Verse 19 indicates definitely that the ones exposed in verses 16 through 18 are not the Lord's. Their evil doings are a strong proof of this.

In verse 20 Paul continues, "But in a great house there are not only gold and silver vessels, but also wooden and earthen, and some unto honor, and some unto dishonor." The word "but" at the beginning of this verse indicates that it stands in contrast to the definition in the preceding verse concerning genuine believers.

What does Paul mean by the expression "a great house"? In this great house there are not only gold and silver vessels, but also wooden and earthen ones, and some unto honor and others unto dishonor. I have spent a great deal of time considering this matter before the Lord. The house of God defined in 1 Timothy 3:15 and 16 is the genuine church in its divine nature and essential character as the foundation of the truth, whereas the great house here refers to the deteriorated church in its mixed character, as illustrated by the abnormally big tree in Matthew 13:31 and 32. In this great house there are not only precious vessels, but also base ones. Thus, we cannot believe that the great house in this verse refers to the church as the house of the living God in 1 Timothy 3:15. The great house is certainly not the house of the living God. The house of the living God is the great mystery of godliness and also God manifest in the flesh. How could such a house contain vessels unto dishonor? Therefore, the great house no doubt refers to Christendom, to Christianity.

Furthermore, this great house is equal to the big tree in Matthew 13. The genuine church today is the house of the living God, whereas abnormal Christianity is the great house. How great today is this abnormal house! Just as many unclean birds lodge in the big tree, so in the great house there are vessels unto dishonor, wooden and earthen vessels. In the genuine church, however, there are only gold and silver vessels.

A. Vessels unto Honor and unto Dishonor

Honorable vessels are of both the divine nature (gold) and the redeemed and regenerated human nature (silver). These, like Timothy and other genuine believers, constitute the sure foundation to hold the truth. Dishonorable vessels are of the fallen human nature (wood and earth). Hymenaeus, Philetus, and other false believers are of these.

B. Cleansed from the Dishonorable Vessels

In verse 21 Paul goes on to say, "If therefore anyone cleanses himself from these, he will be a vessel unto honor, sanctified, useful to the master, prepared unto every good work." To cleanse ourselves is to "depart from unrighteousness" (v. 19), as an outward evidence of the inward divine nature. The word "these" in verse 21 denotes the vessels unto dishonor, including those mentioned in verses 16 through 18. We should not only cleanse ourselves from anything unrighteous, but also from the dishonorable vessels. This means that we must stay away from them. Hence, we must cleanse ourselves from the unrighteous things and from the dishonorable vessels of wood and earth. If we cleanse ourselves from these negative things and negative persons, we shall be vessels unto honor, sanctified, useful to the master, and prepared unto every good work. Unto honor is a matter of nature, sanctified is a matter of position, useful is a matter of practice, and prepared is a matter of training.

IV. PAUL'S CHARGE TO TIMOTHY

A. Fleeing and Pursuing

Verse 22 continues, "But flee youthful lusts, and pursue righteousness, faith, love, peace, with those who call on the Lord out of a pure heart." Timothy should beware not only of outward corruption among the churches, but also of inward lusts within himself. He must avoid the outward corruption and flee the inward lusts. Furthermore, he should pursue righteousness, faith, love, and peace, with those who call on the Lord out of a pure heart. Righteousness is toward self, faith is toward God, and love is toward others. Peace is the consequence of these three virtues.

B. Calling On the Lord

To call on the Lord out of a pure heart is to "name the name of the Lord" in our prayer and praise to Him. The Lord's seekers must be those who call on His name. Today those who call on the Lord out of a pure heart are found in His recovery. Thank the Lord that we are with those who call on Him out of a pure heart. With such believers we may pursue the virtues of righteousness, faith, love, and peace.

C. Refusing Foolish and Ignorant Questionings

In verse 23 Paul says, "But foolish and ignorant questionings refuse, knowing that they produce contentions." The Greek word rendered foolish may also be rendered stupid. The word ignorant denotes that which is uninstructed, undisciplined, untrained, that is, not subject to God, but following one's own mind and will (Darby). The word produce means to engender, to beget. We must refuse such foolish questionings, for they have their source in Satan, the serpent. Many years ago I read that someone suggested that the serpent may have stood up in the form of a question mark when he talked with Eve. He questioned her with the words, "Hath God said?" (Gen. 3:1). All foolish questionings originate with the serpent. Thus, we should refuse foolish and ignorant questionings, questionings which beget contentions. These questionings always arise from an evil, serpentine source.

D. Not Contending

In verse 24 Paul goes on, "And a slave of the Lord must not contend, but be gentle toward all; apt to teach, bearing with wrong." When people wrong you, you should not be troubled. Instead, as a slave of the Lord, you should be gentle and bear with the wrong.

E. Correcting Those Who Oppose

In verse 25 Paul continues, "In meekness correcting those who oppose, if perhaps God may give them repentance unto the full knowledge of the truth." Paul's use of the word repentance indicates that with the opposers of the truth it is the heart and conscience which are in question. The truth is the revelation of the living God and His economy—His heart's desire. To receive the divine revelation, the heart and conscience need to be rightly exercised toward God. The heart should be turned to Him, directed solely to Him, and the conscience must be pure and void of offense before Him. Otherwise, one might be carried away as a captive by the Devil and fall into his snare (v. 26).

In verse 25 Paul again refers to the full knowledge of the truth. Paul does not speak here of the full knowledge of the Bible or the full knowledge of doctrine and teaching. He emphasizes repentance unto the full knowledge of the truth. The inoculator must bear the burden to correct with meekness those who oppose in the hope that they may be enlightened, repent, and return to the full knowledge of the truth.

It is possible that those who repent "may return to soberness out of the snare of the Devil, having been caught by him, unto His will" (v. 26). According to Vincent, to return to soberness means to become sober again, to awake out of a drunken stupor. Paul's use of the expression "the snare of the Devil" indicates that the opposers of the truth, being short of the adequate knowledge of the divine revelation, have been captured and kept in a snare by the Devil. The enemy of God occupies their reprobate mind with error and shuts God out, just as he did with the Pharisees (John 8:42-45). They need to return to God in their heart and have a thorough dealing in their conscience.

The pronoun "him" in the phrase "having been caught by him" refers to the Devil. However, "unto His will," literally translated "unto the will of that One," refers to God, mentioned in verse 25. Hence, it means toward God's will, for God's will, to do God's will.

Suppose some approach you with the intention of arguing about a certain doctrine or practice. Instead of entering into an argument with them, present God's dispensation to them. In order to do this, you need to be familiar with the contents of God's New Testament economy. All the saints should be trained, perhaps by the leading ones in their locality, to present the full knowledge of the truth, to share with others the reality of the contents of God's New Testament economy.

Often we are asked why we say that we are the church. The first time I heard this question in the United States was in 1963. During a time of fellowship, a brother asked me, "Why does your group call itself the church in Los Angeles?" In answer to this very good question I pointed out that in the Bible the saints in a particular locality, such as Jerusalem or Antioch, were regarded simply as the church in that locality. Acts 8:1 speaks of the church in Jerusalem, and 13:1, of the church in Antioch. I went on to point out that in Jerusalem there was just one church. Peter, James, and John were all for the building up of the one church in Jerusalem. However, today's Christians have gone astray and meet in many different denominations. For this reason, in the city of Los Angeles there are different kinds of so-called churches. There are even groups which say they are a Chinese church or a Korean church. Then I asked which of these different kinds of churches we should join. The one who raised the question about the church in Los Angeles admitted that we should not join any of those so-called churches. Then I proceeded to say that if we in Los Angeles do not call ourselves the church in Los Angeles, we shall be another sect. If we are not the church in Los Angeles, then what are we? We have no choice but to call ourselves the church in Los Angeles.

Realizing that some may say that the church in Los Angeles should include all the saints in that city, I went on to say, "It is true that the church in Los Angeles includes all the believers in Los Angeles. However, most of them are not willing to meet simply as the church. This is their responsibility, not ours. For example, the Jones family may have many members. Suppose the majority of the members move away from home and only three remain. Are these three not the Jones family? Are they wrong to put a sign on their house saying 'The Jones Family'? Certainly not. If they are not called Jones, then what should they be called? It certainly would be wrong for them to take the name of Smith or any other name. It is right for them to say that they are the Jones family, even though many of the members of the family have gone away and live elsewhere. Likewise, many of those who are truly members of the church in Los Angeles do not meet as the church. Nevertheless, those who do stand as the church have the right to describe themselves as the church in Los Angeles."

On this occasion I asked, "Why don't those in the denominations call themselves the church? They are bothered by the fact that we claim to be the church in Los Angeles. They need to ask themselves why they take such names as Presbyterian and Lutheran. I hope that they would be willing to drop these names and simply be the local church in their city. To those who are willing to do this in this city I would say, 'Since we are all the same church, the church in Los Angeles, why don't we simply come together and be the church? Let us all meet together for the church life.' " This is one illustration of how we need to learn the full knowledge of the truth and then learn how to present the truth to others, especially to opposers. It is our hope that others may be enlightened and also come to the full knowledge of the truth.

LIFE-STUDY OF SECOND TIMOTHY

MESSAGE FIVE

THE WORSENING OF THE DECLINE

Scripture Reading: 2 Tim. 3:1-13

The subject of 2 Timothy is inoculation against the decline of the church. After a word of introduction (1:1-2), Paul speaks of the divine provisions for the inoculation: a pure conscience, unfeigned faith, the divine gift, a strong spirit, eternal grace, incorruptible life, the healthy word, and the indwelling Spirit (1:3-14). Then he goes on to point out that the basic factor of the decline is the forsaking of the apostle and his ministry (1:15-18). In 2:1-15 Paul speaks of the inoculator, indicating that he must be a teacher, soldier, contender, husbandman, and workman. In the second half of chapter two he tells us of the spread of the decline, a spreading likened to that of gangrene (2:16-26). In chapter three Paul first speaks of the worsening of the decline, showing that it will become grievous times of deceiving (3:1-13), and then speaks of the antidote of the inoculation—the divine word (3:14-17). In chapter four there are three sections: the incentive to the inoculator—the coming reward (4:1-8); the issue of the decline—loving the present age and doing many evil things (4:9-18); and the conclusion (4:19-22). If we consider the outline of 2 Timothy, we shall see that it is not merely a pastoral book, a book for so-called pastors. On the contrary, it is a book written for inoculators, those who would inoculate others against the decline of the church.

I. THE DIFFICULT TIMES

A. Coming in the Last Days

Chapter three opens with the words, "But know this, that in the last days difficult times shall come." Once again Paul uses the word "but" to point out a contrast. The contrast here is with the hope just expressed at the end of the preceding chapter. Toward the end of chapter two Paul declared that "the firm foundation of God stands" (v. 19), and that we should "flee youthful lusts, and pursue righteousness, faith, love, peace with those who call on the Lord out of a pure heart" (v. 22). Furthermore, if in meekness we correct those who oppose, "God may give them repentance unto the full knowledge of the truth, and they may return to soberness out of the snare of the Devil" (vv. 25-26). Paul realized that even though the decline would spread, the firm foundation of God still stands unshakable, bearing a seal which says, "The Lord knows those who are His," and, "Let everyone who names the name of the Lord depart from unrighteousness." At least God would have a remnant of those who call on the Lord out of a pure heart and pursue righteousness, faith, love, and peace. Furthermore, such ones may even dispense the inoculation against the church's decline. Yes, the decline is spreading, but we have a firm standing, we can enjoy the riches of the Lord, and we can do the work of inoculation, even convincing those who oppose to come back to the full knowledge of the truth. This is to bring back those who have been caught by the Devil, and snared by him, to God's will. All this indicates that Paul was not discouraged. Even though the decline is spreading, we can do something positively to inoculate others against it.

Then in contrast to all this Paul says in 3:1, "But know this, that in the last days difficult times shall come." Paul had the foresight and the insight to realize that difficult times would come in the last days. The expression "the last days" denotes the closing period of the present age (2 Pet. 3:3; Jude 18). It began from the end of the so-called apostolic age, in the latter part of the first century, and will last until Christ's second appearing. The long duration of this period was not revealed to the apostles (Matt. 24:36); they expected the Lord to return in their generation.

Many Christians identify "the last days" in 3:1 with the "later times" in 1 Timothy 4:1. This is a mistake. In the Bible there is a dividing line between the Old Testament and the New Testament. The ancient Jews regarded the times of the Old Testament as the early times or early days. With the coming of Christ the period of the Mosaic law was over. Christ's coming began a new period, regarded as the last days, which will continue until Christ's second coming. Concerning Christ's second coming, there is a secret period of time, which was not known by the apostles. They were eager to know the time of the Lord's second coming. But in Mark 13:32 the Lord Jesus said, "But of that day or that hour knoweth no one, not even the angels in heaven, neither the Son, but the Father." Later, after the Lord's resurrection, the disciples asked Him, "Dost thou at this time restore the kingdom to Israel?" (Acts 1:6). To this the Lord replied, "It is not for you to know times or seasons, which the Father hath set within his own authority" (v. 7). It is not easy to explain how the Lord could say that only the Father, not the Son, knows the time of the end. Perhaps in refusing to answer the question about the time of His coming, the Lord Jesus was maintaining the proper position under the headship of the Father. Therefore, He told them that this was something which "the Father hath set within his own authority."

The early disciples thought that the Lord Jesus would come back in their generation. This was Paul's concept when he wrote 1 and 2 Thessalonians. This shows that the length of the last days was a secret unknown by the apostles. We simply do not know the duration of time the Father has set in His administration between the Lord's ascension and His second coming.

In 3:1 Paul says that in the last days "difficult times shall come." The Greek for "difficult times" also means hard times, grievous times, perilous times. This means that these times will be extremely difficult for Christians. In verse 12 Paul says, "All who desire to live godly in Christ Jesus will be persecuted." For those who pursue righteousness, faith, love, and peace and who call on the name of the Lord out of a pure heart, this time will indeed be difficult, grievous, perilous. Here Paul seems to be saying, "Timothy, I am encouraged by the fact that the firm foundation of God stands and that, with others, you can pursue righteousness, faith, love, and peace and call on the Lord out of a pure heart. You can stand together and dispense the inoculation against the decline of the church. Some may even be recovered to the full knowledge of the truth and to the will of God. Nevertheless, I want you to know that the time which is coming will be very difficult for you. This time will be grievous, perilous, for all those who call on the Lord out of a pure heart and who desire to live godly in Christ Jesus."

B. What Men Shall Be

In verse 2 Paul goes on to say, "For men shall be lovers of self, lovers of money, boasters, arrogant, revilers, disobedient to parents, unthankful, unholy." The prophetic picture presented in verses 2 through 5 portrays not the evil condition of non-Christian society, but the corrupted situation of the "great house" mentioned in 2:20, degraded Christianity. This is proved by the phrase, "having a form of godliness" (v. 5). Unbelievers do not have even the form of godliness. Those who have such a form are those who are called Christians. Thus, the men in verse 2 are Christians.

The first thing Paul says about these men is that they will be "lovers of self." Many Christians today are self-lovers. Not only those who indulge in worldly entertainments are selfish; even those who attend the chapels and cathedrals may be selfish.

In the three Epistles of 1 and 2 Timothy and Titus seven kinds of lovers are mentioned: lovers of self, lovers of money (2 Tim. 3:2; 1 Tim. 6:10), lovers of pleasure, lovers of God (2 Tim 3:4), lovers of good (Titus 1:8), lovers of husbands, and lovers of children (Titus 2:4). There are also two kinds of nonlovers: nonlovers of good and nonlovers of God (2 Tim. 3:3-4). Of whatever one is a lover, that is what his whole heart, even his entire being, is set on, occupied, and possessed by. This is crucial! Whether there could be a day of glory in the church's victory or grievous days of the church's decline depends altogether upon what we set our heart upon, what it is we love. History tells us that the root of the church's decline was the loss of her first love toward the Lord (Rev. 2:4). To maintain the victorious standard of the church, we must be lovers of God and lovers of the good which pertains to God's economy.

In verse 2 Paul speaks of those who are boasters, arrogant, revilers, disobedient to parents, unthankful, and unholy. The Greek word for arrogant also means haughty, and the word rendered revilers is literally blasphemers, as in 1 Timothy 1:13. Here, however, it does not refer to blasphemers of God, but to revilers or railers, those who speak evilly and injuriously of men. How much we have been reviled by those who call themselves Christians!

In a foregoing message I mentioned that some brothers in Taiwan who had been under my training for years became dissenting. Some even reviled God's government. They were not only rebellious, but they were also unthankful, ungrateful. It is significant that in verse 2 Paul puts together unthankfulness with disobedience to parents. This may indicate that here unthankful mainly refers to being unthankful to one's parents. We should be thankful to those who have raised us both physically and spiritually, thankful both to our natural parents and to our spiritual parents.

In the 1940s Brother Nee suffered intense opposition and was forced to be out of function for six years. Some of those who were dissenting with him still felt positive toward me because they had received help from me. One day one of them asked me, "Do you believe that Brother Nee has never been wrong?" I answered, "Whether or not Brother Nee has ever been wrong is not my business. I only know that I am indebted to him just as a child to his parents. If it were not for this servant of the Lord, I could not have the life I now have as a Christian. I have learned the lesson of Ham, the son of Noah, and I dare not say anything negative about him. In a real sense, he has been a spiritual father to me. He has raised me up in the Lord. Therefore, I do not dare say anything negative concerning him." I can testify that throughout the years I have seen the blessing which has come from maintaining such an attitude toward my spiritual father. Both to our parents in the flesh and in the spirit we must learn to be thankful. It is a very serious matter to be ungrateful toward our parents. One aspect of today's trend is unthankfulness. This trend, this current, has even swept into Christianity.

In verses 3 and 4 Paul continues, "Without natural affection, implacable, slanderers, without self-control, savage, nonlovers of good, traitors, reckless, blinded with pride, lovers of pleasure rather than lovers of God." To be implacable is to be irreconcilable, to be a traitor is to be a betrayer, and to be reckless is to be headstrong. In the picture presented here there are three kinds of lovers—lovers of self, lovers of money, and lovers of pleasure—and two kinds of nonlovers—nonlovers of good and nonlovers of God.

Verse 5 says, "Having a form of godliness, but having denied its power; from these also turn away." A form of godliness is a mere outward semblance without the essential reality. The power of godliness is the real and practical virtue of a living influence to express God.

In these verses we have a dreadful picture of today's degraded Christianity. By the Lord's mercy and grace, we in His recovery must reject the situation portrayed here and be the very opposite of it.

Verses 6 and 7 speak of those who are "always learning and never able to come to the full knowledge of the truth." This word has been fulfilled among many Christians today. They hear sermon after sermon and study the Bible, but they do not know the reality of the contents of God's New Testament economy. They do not know Christ as the embodiment of the Triune God or the church as the mystery of Christ.

Verse 8 says, "And just as Jannes and Jambres opposed Moses, so these also oppose the truth, men corrupted in mind, disapproved concerning the faith." According to Jewish tradition, Jannes and Jambres were the Egyptian magicians who opposed Moses, as mentioned in Exodus 7:11 and 22.

In the decline among the churches, truth is the target of the enemy's attack. Hence, truth is also the remedy and rescue from the diseased and ruined situation. In verse 8 disapproved means reprobate, and the faith denotes the contents of our belief.

In verse 9 Paul goes on to say, "They shall not advance farther, for their folly shall be completely manifest to all, as also the folly of those became." The word folly refers to the lack of intelligence and the senselessness of their doing. The "folly of those" refers to the folly of Jannes and Jambres, who were defeated and brought to nothing (Exo. 8:18; 9:11).

II. THE INOCULATOR STANDING AGAINST THE TIDE OF THE DECLINE

In verse 10 Paul reminds Timothy, "But you have closely followed my teaching, conduct, purpose, faith, longsuffering, love, endurance." Conduct refers to manner of life, and the Greek word for purpose is used in Paul's Epistles in relation to the purpose of God.

In verse 11 Paul speaks of the persecution and sufferings which he endured in Antioch, Iconium, and Lystra. Lystra was the city where Timothy lived (Acts 16:1-2), near Iconium and Antioch in Pisidia.

Verse 12 says, "And indeed, all who desire to live godly in Christ Jesus will be persecuted." The Greek word rendered desire can also mean determine. To live godly is to live a life of godliness. All those who desire, determine, to live a life of godliness in Christ Jesus will be persecuted. For this reason we should not expect good treatment from today's Christianity. Instead, we should expect persecution for living a godly life in an ungodly situation. As long as we stand for the Lord's recovery, we shall be condemned, opposed, and attacked. Rumors will be spread concerning us, and our names will be smeared and defiled. Such persecution comes not from the worldly people, but from so-called Christians. In John 16:2 the Lord Jesus said that the time is coming when those who kill the disciples will think they are serving God.

Out of their zeal for God, they will kill the followers of the Lord, simply because these do not follow the traditional way.

III. THE WORSENING OF THE DECLINE

In verse 13 Paul concludes, "But evil men and impostors will grow worse and worse, deceiving and being deceived." The word impostors means juggling impostors. This verse indicates that the decline of the church will become worse. Evil men and impostors, those who deceive others by their skill in juggling, will become worse and worse. Being deceived themselves, they will also deceive others.

We thank the Lord that, in His mercy, He has brought us into the recovery where we can hear honest and healthy words.

LIFE-STUDY OF SECOND TIMOTHY

MESSAGE SIX

THE ANTIDOTE OF THE INOCULATION

Scripture Reading: 2 Tim. 3:14-17

We have seen that the subject of 2 Timothy is the inoculation against the decline of the church. In this message we shall consider the antidote of the inoculation, which is the divine Word. In 2:16-26 we have the spread of the decline and in 3:1-13, the worsening of the decline. We praise the Lord that in 3:14-17 we have a wonderful, heavenly, divine, spiritual, and rich antidote. As we shall see, this antidote is the divine word of the Old Testament and the New Testament, the God-breathed Scripture which is profitable for teaching, reproof, correction, and instruction in righteousness and which completes the man of God and fully equips him for every good work.

I. THE DIVINE WORD

A. Of the New Testament

Second Timothy 3:14 says, "But you, continue in the things which you have learned and have been assured of, knowing from whom you have learned." The things which Timothy learned of the apostle and was assured of were the vital portion of the content of the New Testament, which completed the divine revelation (Col. 1:25). Hence, he had the practical understanding of a great part of the New Testament. These were the things he had learned from Paul and which he had been assured of by him.

The word ministered by Paul was the completing word of God's revelation, the main part of the New Testament. Verse 14 indicates that from Paul Timothy received the proper knowledge of the New Testament and became assured of it, even though at that time the New Testament was not complete as a written volume. Timothy was granted the central revelation of the New Testament.

B. Of the Old Testament

In verse 15 Paul goes on to say, "And that from a babe you have known the sacred writings, which are able to make you wise unto salvation through faith which is in Christ Jesus." In addition to the knowledge of the New Testament, Timothy also had, from his childhood, a good foundation in the knowledge of the Old Testament. He was one who was fully perfected and equipped to minister the word of God, not only in caring for a local church, but also in confronting the increasing decline of the church.

Together verses 14 and 15 refer to both the Old Testament and the New Testament. By knowing the sacred writings from childhood, Timothy was familiar with the Old Testament, and from Paul he gained a proper knowledge of the central part of the New Testament. Therefore, Timothy had a proper understanding of the Bible as a whole. Today all the saints in the Lord's recovery, especially the young people, need the understanding of the Word of God, an understanding of both the Old Testament and the New Testament.

II. THE SCRIPTURE

A. All God-breathed

Verse 16 says, "All Scripture is God-breathed and profitable for teaching, for reproof, for correction, for instruction in righteousness." The Greek words rendered, "All Scripture is God-breathed and profitable," may also be translated "Every Scripture God-breathed is also profitable."

To confront the death, corruption, and confusion in the church's decline, the eternal life upon which chapter one is based (vv. 1, 10), the divine truth emphasized in chapter two (vv. 15, 18, 25), and the holy Scripture highly regarded in chapter three (vv. 14-17) are all needed. The eternal life not only swallows up death, but also renders the life supply; the divine truth replaces the vanity of corruption with the reality of all the divine riches; and the holy Scripture not only dispels confusion, but also furnishes divine light and revelation. Hence, in this book the apostle stresses these three things.

The expression "God-breathed" indicates that the Scripture, the Word of God, is the breath of God. God's speaking is God's breathing. Hence, His word is spirit (John 6:63), *pneuma,* or breath. Thus, the Scripture is the embodiment of God as the Spirit. The Spirit is therefore the very essence, the substance, of the Scripture, just as phosphorus is the essential substance in matches. We must "strike" the Spirit of the Scripture with our spirit to kindle the divine fire.

As the embodiment of God the Spirit, the Scripture is also the embodiment of Christ. Christ is God's living Word (Rev. 19:13), and the Scripture is God's written word (Matt. 4:4).

B. Profitable

According to verse 16, all Scripture is profitable for teaching, for reproof, for correction, and for instruction in righteousness. Reproof here means conviction or confutation. Correction denotes setting right what is wrong, turning someone to the right way, or restoring a person to an upright state. Instruction refers to discipline or chastisement in righteousness. This means to discipline or chastise in the element and condition of righteousness.

C. To Complete the Man of God

In verse 17 Paul says, "That the man of God may be complete, fully equipped for every good work." We have seen that a man of God is one who partakes of God's life and nature (John 1:13; 2 Pet. 1:4) and thus becomes one with Him in His life and nature (1 Cor. 6:17) and thereby expresses Him. This corresponds to the mystery of godliness, which is God manifest in the flesh (1 Tim. 3:16). Through the God-breathed Scripture, the man of God may be complete, fully equipped for every good work. Complete here means complete and perfect in qualifications, and equipped denotes being fitted out, furnished, made ready.

We need to know the Bible not merely according to letters in black and white, but also according to the divine revelation and heavenly wisdom. Do not think that having an advanced degree qualifies anyone to understand a book such as Ephesians. If we study this Epistle only in letters, we shall not be able to understand it. For a proper understanding of this book, and for the Bible as a whole, we need a spirit of wisdom and revelation. This was the reason Paul prayed, "That the God of our Lord Jesus Christ, the Father of glory, may give to you a spirit of wisdom and revelation in the full knowledge of Him, the eyes of your heart having been enlightened" (Eph. 1:17-18). We thank the Lord that for more than fifty years we have been receiving such a spirit of wisdom and revelation. As a result, the messages put out in the Lord's recovery always contain something fresh and new. These messages are given not merely according to the black and white letters of the Scripture, but according to the spirit of wisdom and revelation.

We in the Lord's recovery do not treasure theology, tradition, or the councils. We honor, respect, and treasure the holy Word under the shining of the heavenly light which comes by a spirit of wisdom and revelation. Because we depend on God's enlightenment, His Word is opened to us.

Many Christians misuse 3:16 and 17. They point out that the holy Scripture is for teaching, reproof, correction, and instruction in righteousness and that it enables the man of God to be equipped, completed, and perfected. Although all this is true, it neglects the element of life in the Word. Those who regard the Bible as a book of teaching, reproof, correction, and instruction often ignore the life essence of the Word. As human beings we have a physical body outwardly, but inwardly we have a spirit and a soul. Our person is composed not mainly of the outward part, the body, but of the inward parts, the spirit and the soul. The principle is the same with the Bible. The Bible has not only a "body" of letters in black and white; it also has a spirit, because it is

God-breathed. If in reading the Bible we exercise only our mind to study it, we shall not receive the life supply.

Most Christians neglect the spirit and take the Bible as a book of letters. The Lord Jesus once said, "The words which I have spoken unto you are spirit and are life" (John 6:63). Furthermore, we have pointed out that every word of the Bible is part of God's breath. Thus, we should not only study the Word, but also breathe in the divine breath embodied in the Word. If we do not breathe the divine breath by exercising our spirit, we shall not receive life from our study of the Bible. But when we breathe in God's breath, we are enlivened by a divine, heavenly, and spiritual element.

I wish to emphasize the fact that to study the Bible in order to follow its instructions is not sufficient. Often during a wedding ceremony a minister will instruct the bride and groom according to Paul's word in Ephesians 5. The minister will then remind the wife to submit to the husband and the husband to love his wife. Although they may promise to fulfill these requirements, they will not be able to do so unless they receive the divine breath in the Word. The instructions in righteousness given according to the Bible do not work if we do not receive the breath of God, for then, in practice, we shall make these instructions the same as the ethical teachings of Confucius.

We thank the Lord for showing us that in reading the Word we need to exercise our eyes, our mind, and our spirit. We may say that with the eyes we contact the body of the Word, that with our mind we contact the soul of the Word, and through the exercise of our spirit to pray the Word, we contact the spirit of the Word. Then we not only understand the meaning of a certain portion of Scripture; we also inhale the divine breath to receive the life supply.

Many of us can testify that a certain verse of the Bible may be very precious to us as we read it. However, disciples of Confucius may also regard certain statements made by him as precious. But with the teachings of Confucius there is no divine breath. God's Word contains His breath. Within the letters of the Bible there is the Spirit who gives life. This is the reason that in reading the Word we must exercise our spirit in addition to our mind. Then the verses we read will be not only precious to us, but they will nourish, refresh, and water us.

Actually, the function of the Word in teaching, reproof, correction, and instruction is all related to transformation. The Bible corrects us not primarily outwardly, but inwardly in the way of transformation. This means that the word of Scripture works within us in a metabolic way. Just as the food we eat and digest nourishes us from within, metabolically changing and transforming us, so the Word of God transforms us by inwardly teaching, reproving, correcting, and instructing us.

If we would be nourished by the Word, we should not only pray it, but also psalm it and sing it. In Colossians 3:16 Paul says, "Let the word of Christ dwell in you richly, in all wisdom teaching and admonishing one another in psalms, hymns, and spiritual songs, singing with grace in your hearts to God." By praying, psalming, and singing the Word we shall fan our spirit into flame. Furthermore, when we pray, psalm, and sing the Word, we inhale the divine breath and receive more of the element of God. In this way God dispenses Himself into us and infuses us with His element.

We cannot deny the fact that the Lord has shown us much light from His Word. For example, much light has been shed on the Gospel of John. If you read the outline of the Gospel of John printed in the Recovery Version, you will realize that the Lord indeed has opened the Word to us. Many may know the Bible in black and white letters, but, by the Lord's mercy and grace, we know the Bible in life, light, and spirit.

Allow me to testify concerning the light we have received on John 16:8-11. One day in my reading of these verses I saw that sin, righteousness, and judgment are related to the three persons of Adam, Christ, and Satan. Sometime later I was asked to give the message for a gospel meeting in the church in Shanghai. I spoke on these verses and told the people, "As human beings, you were born in Adam. In Adam you have sinned and you have been condemned. But there is another person—Christ—and there is a way for you to get out of Adam and into Christ that you may be justified by God. If you believe in Christ, you will be transferred into Him. But if you do not believe into Christ, you will remain in Adam, the first person, and eventually your destiny will be that of Satan, the third person. Judgment has been prepared for Satan. Do you intend to help Satan suffer judgment for eternity? Will you remain in Adam with sin and eventually share the judgment with Satan, or will you believe in Christ and be transferred into Him in order to receive the gift of righteousness?" That message was very good, full of light. After delivering that message, I was fully nourished. Brother Nee spoke to me sometime later concerning that message and said, "Witness, hardly anyone has seen that in John 16:8-11 sin is related to Adam, righteousness to Christ, and judgment to Satan. I encourage you to continue to teach the Bible in this way." I could never forget Brother Nee's word to me. Today I am still being encouraged, strengthened, and confirmed by that word.

We thank the Lord that over the years the light has been shining upon us, even pouring out upon us. Apart from the Lord's enlightening, we may read 2 Timothy a dozen times without seeing anything related to the inoculation. To see this we need a light. Under the light we can realize that the divine word, the Scripture, is the antidote of the inoculation.

We should not read the Bible in the way the religionists did at the time of the Lord Jesus and Paul. They did not realize that the title of God—the God of Abraham, the God of Isaac, and the God of Jacob—implied resurrection. Probably Gamaliel instructed Paul according to Genesis 12 and 15, but it was not until Paul was enlightened of the Lord and received revelation that he realized that Abraham's wife and his concubine typified two covenants. This shows that it is one thing to be a Bible scholar; it is quite another thing to have the light of God's revelation.

We should not merely study the Word in letter. We need to pray that the Lord would give us a spirit of wisdom and revelation. If we do not have such a spirit but read only the black and white letters of the Bible, we shall not experience life, light, or spirit. There is a great difference between the way the Bible is used among most Christians today and the way it is used among us in the Lord's recovery. The majority of believers use the Word in the way of letters, but we use it in the way of life, light, and spirit. This is the reason we constantly humble ourselves before the Lord, open to Him, and look to Him for light, vision, wisdom, and revelation. May we all learn to come to the Word of God in this way.

LIFE-STUDY OF SECOND TIMOTHY

MESSAGE SEVEN

THE INCENTIVE TO THE INOCULATOR

Scripture Reading: 2 Tim. 4:1-8

In this message we shall consider the incentive to the inoculator (4:1-8). As we shall see, this incentive is the coming reward.

I. THE APOSTLE'S CHARGE

In 4:1 Paul says to Timothy, "I solemnly charge you before God and Christ Jesus, Who is about to judge the living and the dead, and by His appearing and His kingdom." God has given all judgment to Christ because He is a man (John 5:22, 27; Acts 10:42; 17:31; Rom. 2:16). As the righteous Judge (2 Tim. 4:8), He will judge the living from His throne of glory at His second appearing (Matt. 25:31-46), and He will judge the dead at the great white throne after the millennium (Rev. 20:11-15).

In 4:1 Paul speaks of Christ's appearing and His kingdom. Christ's appearing will be for judgment, to reward each one of us (Matt. 16:27; Rev. 22:12), and His kingdom will be for His reigning with His overcomers (Rev. 20:4, 6). By these two events the apostle charges Timothy to fulfill his ministry of the word faithfully. Here it seems that Paul is saying, "Timothy, you must realize that your life and work today have much to do with the Lord's appearing and His kingdom. At His appearing will you be praised by the Lord, or will you receive a rebuke from Him? Will you receive a reward or chastisement? Will you be considered qualified to participate in the divine kingship and reign with Christ for a thousand years, or will you be disqualified from reigning with Him? Timothy, you need to think seriously about these things. Thus, I charge you by the Lord's appearing and kingdom."

It is a matter of great significance to be charged by the Lord's appearing and kingdom. As genuine Christians we are saved for eternity, but how are we living our Christian life, and how well are we fulfilling our Christian duty? Are we taking care of God's New Testament economy? Do we practice the proper church life, the Body life, to express God in Christ through the Spirit? These questions deserve our attention, for the way we answer them may determine our future as far as the Lord's appearing and coming kingdom are concerned. Do not listen to the superstitious and superficial teachings which tell you that as long as you are saved you cannot have any problems with the Lord at His coming. You may have great problems when you meet Him at the judgment seat. Every believer in Christ, every genuinely saved person, must stand before the judgment seat of Christ and be judged by Him not concerning salvation or perdition, but concerning reward or punishment. Because this is a solemn matter, Paul charged Timothy before God and Christ Jesus and by the Lord's appearing and kingdom.

In verse 2 Paul continues his charge: "Preach the word; be ready in season and out of season; reprove, rebuke, exhort, with all longsuffering and teaching." The word Timothy was to preach included what he had learned both of Paul and of the Old Testament (3:14-15). This proves that verses 1 and 2 are a continuation of 3:14-17. In caring for a local church, especially in a time of the church's decline, the preaching of the Word is vital.

Timothy was not merely to preach a word about salvation from hell to heaven. He was to speak a completing word regarding God's revelation concerning Christ and the church. Such a healthy word is the truth, the reality of the contents of God's New Testament economy. Timothy was charged to be ready to preach this word in season and out of season. To preach in season and out of season means to preach whether the situation is opportune or inopportune, whether it is convenient or inconvenient, whether you are welcome or unwelcome. Furthermore, Timothy was to reprove, rebuke, and exhort with all longsuffering and teaching. Reprove here means to convict. The adjective all modifies both longsuffering and teaching. It speaks of teaching in many aspects and directions. The carrying out of such teaching requires longsuffering.

II. THE TIME OF APOSTASY

Verses 3 and 4 say, "For the time will come when they will not tolerate healthy teaching, but according to their own lusts they will heap up to themselves teachers tickling the ear, and they will turn away their ear from the truth, and will be turned aside to fables." The time mentioned in verse 3 refers to the time when the decline of the church becomes worse. At that time many will not tolerate healthy teaching, teaching which is healthy in life and which ministers the supply of life. Instead, they will prefer teachers who tickle the ear. This indicates that those who do not tolerate healthy teaching have an itching ear, an ear which seeks pleasing speaking for its own pleasure. Furthermore, such persons will turn away their ear from the truth and will be turned aside to fables. The itching ear that is turned away is the main factor of the worsening decline in the churches.

Many Christians today do not tolerate the healthy teachings related to God's economy. When we teach that Christ is the God-man, the One who is the embodiment of God as His expression, some accuse us of blasphemy or heresy. Some have even gone so far as to twist our words concerning Christ as the God-man and, in print, to falsely accuse us of teaching that Christ was neither quite God nor quite man. In *The Four Major Steps of Christ* I say, "We know that Christ is God incarnated as a man. Christ is the God-man. He is not only a man of God, He is also a God-man. Therefore, the incarnation of Christ simply means the mingling of God with humanity" (p. 6). Twisting our words and grossly misrepresenting us, certain of our opposers have written, "This incarnate deity was neither quite God nor quite man; He was a third thing, a mingled God-man." We believe that because

Christ is true God and true man, He is the God-man. He is the perfect God and a complete man as well. Both His divine nature and His human nature, each being complete, concur in His one Person—without separation, without confusion, and without being changed into a third nature. Our Lord Jesus Christ, the God-man, one Person with two natures, is worthy to receive our worship and praise forever.

Because many Christians today will not tolerate healthy teaching, they heap up teachers to tickle their itching ears. The teachings in the Lord's recovery are altogether different. Our teachings do not tickle the ear. Instead, they may operate on the ears of those who hear. Unable to bear such an operation, some turn their ears away from the truth.

We have pointed out again and again that in 1 and 2 Timothy truth refers to the reality of the contents of God's New Testament economy. This reality consists primarily of Christ as the embodiment of God and of the church as the Body of Christ. Instead of listening to proper teachings concerning Christ and the church, many Christians have turned aside to other things.

III. TIMOTHY, THE INOCULATOR

In verse 5 Paul says to Timothy, "But you, be sober in all things, suffer evil, do the work of an evangelist, fully accomplish your ministry." For Timothy to fully accomplish his ministry was for him to fill up the full measure of his ministry. This ministry denotes the ministry of the Word to minister Christ in all His riches (Eph. 3:8) to both sinners and believers for the building up of the Body of Christ (Eph. 4:11-12). Such a ministry is desperately needed to counter the declining trend, as prophesied in verses 3 and 4.

IV. PAUL, THE PATTERN

In verses 6 and 7 Paul testifies concerning himself: "For I am already being poured out, and the time of my departure is at hand. I have fought the good fight, I have finished the course, I have kept the faith." In verse 6 Paul indicates that he was already being poured out as a drink offering. The drink offering was additional to the basic offerings revealed in Leviticus 1 through 7 (Num. 15:1-10; 28:7-10). The basic offerings were types of various aspects of Christ. The drink offering was a type of Christ as enjoyed by His offerer, an enjoyment that filled him with Christ as the heavenly wine and even made him wine to God. The Apostle Paul became such a drink offering by so enjoying Christ that he could be poured out by the actual shedding of his blood. To be poured out here means to shed one's blood. "Already being poured out" indicates that the process of being offered as a drink offering had begun.

Paul could say that the time of his departure was at hand. This refers to his departure from the world to be with the Lord (Phil. 1:23) through martyrdom. Paul was imprisoned in Rome twice. The first imprisonment, about A.D. 62-64, was due to the Jews' accusation (Acts 28:17-20). During that time he wrote the Epistles to Colossians, Ephesians, Philippians, and Philemon. After his release (which he expected in Philippians 1:25; 2:24; and Philemon 22) from the first imprisonment, he must have visited Ephesus and Macedonia (1 Tim. 1:3), where he probably wrote the first Epistle to Timothy. Then he visited Crete (Titus 1:5); Nicopolis (Titus 3:12), where he wrote the Epistle to Titus; Troas; and Miletus (2 Tim. 4:13, 20), where he probably wrote the Epistle to the Hebrews. Due to Caesar Nero's sudden persecution, Paul was imprisoned a second time, about A.D. 65. At that time he wrote the second Epistle to Timothy while expecting his imminent martyrdom for his Master.

In verse 7 Paul mentions three items: fighting the good fight, finishing the course, and keeping the faith. A proper Christian life is threefold. It involves fighting the good fight against Satan and his kingdom of darkness for the interests of God's kingdom (1 Tim. 6:12), running the course for the carrying out of God's economy according to His eternal purpose (Heb. 12:1), and keeping the faith for participation in the divine riches in God's dispensation (Gal. 3:22). In this Paul set up an adequate pattern for us.

Paul began to run the course of the heavenly race after he was taken possession of by the Lord, and he continually ran (1 Cor. 9:24-26; Phil. 3:12-14) that he might finish it (Acts 20:24). Now at the end he triumphantly proclaimed, "I have finished the course." For this he will receive from the Lord a reward—the crown of righteousness (v. 8).

Paul could testify that he had kept the faith. This means that he kept God's New Testament economy. To keep the faith is to keep the entire New Testament economy of God—the faith concerning Christ as the embodiment of God and the mystery of God and the church as the Body of Christ and the mystery of Christ.

V. THE REWARD—THE INCENTIVE

Verse 8 says, "Henceforth, there is laid up for me the crown of righteousness, which the Lord, the righteous Judge, will award to me in that day; and not only to me, but also to all those who have loved His appearing." The crown is a symbol of glory given as a prize, in addition to the Lord's salvation, to the triumphant runner of the race (1 Cor. 9:25). This prize is neither of grace nor by faith as salvation is (Eph. 2:5, 8-9), but of righteousness through works (Matt. 16:27; Rev. 22:12; 2 Cor. 5:10). Such a reward will be awarded the believers not according to the grace of the Lord, but according to His righteousness. Hence, it is the crown of righteousness. The One who awards it is the Lord as the righteous Judge, not as the merciful God or the gracious Redeemer. Paul was assured that such a prize was reserved, laid up, for him and would be awarded to him at the day of the Lord's second appearing.

Paul says that such an award will be given to all who love the Lord's appearing. The Lord's appearing, His coming back, is a warning, an encouragement, and an incentive to us. We should love it and look forward to it with earnest expectation and joy. By it, the apostle charged Timothy to fulfill his ministry (vv. 1-2, 5).

The crown of righteousness of which Paul was assured is the incentive to the inoculator. If we are faithful to the healthy word of the truth and if we are faithful inoculators to dispense the ingredients of the divine inoculation into Christians today that they may return to the full knowledge of the truth, this reward will be given to us at the time of the Lord's appearing. This means that if we are faithful to the Lord's ministry, we shall receive the crown of righteousness as our reward.

There is a great deal of talk among Christians today concerning the Lord's second coming. But not many believers realize that when the Lord Jesus comes back, He will not come as the merciful God or as the gracious Savior, but as the righteous Judge. Christians should be warned and encouraged to prepare themselves to stand before this Judge. I hope that many among us will take up the burden in this dark age to bring such a solemn charge to the Lord's people. We all need to receive this charge before God and before the Lord Jesus, the One who will judge the living and the dead. We must declare the fact that when the Lord comes back, He will be the Judge of all, both believers and unbelievers. According to Matthew 25, all of the Lord's servants will have to give an account to Him. The Lord will either say, "Well done, good and faithful slave" (v. 21), or, "Evil and slothful slave" (v. 26). In His righteousness the Lord will decide whether or not we receive a reward.

Because the Lord's coming and His kingdom are solemn matters, Paul gave a serious charge to Timothy in 4:1-8. We should not think that the Lord's appearing will merely be a time of rapture and excitement. It will also be a time of great solemnity for every believer in Christ. This was the reason Paul charged Timothy by the Lord's appearing and His kingdom. May we all give heed to this solemn warning.

LIFE-STUDY OF SECOND TIMOTHY

MESSAGE EIGHT

THE ISSUE OF THE DECLINE

Scripture Reading: 2 Tim. 4:9-22

In this message we shall consider from 4:9-22 the issue of the decline of the church.

I. LOVING THE PRESENT AGE

In 4:9 Paul says to Timothy, "Be diligent to come to me quickly." This is a loving and intimate word. Paul could write such a word only to one who was very close to him. Timothy was close to Paul and intimate with him.

In verse 10 we find the reason Paul charged Timothy to come to him quickly: "For Demas has forsaken me, having loved the present age, and has gone to Thessalonica; Crescens to Galatia, Titus to Dalmatia." Loving the present age, the world now before our eyes, is in contrast to loving the Lord's appearing, mentioned in verse 8. The world, the cosmos, is composed of many ages. It seems that every decade is a different age. The present age is the world which surrounds us, attracts us, and tempts us. Demas was one who loved the present age.

Some believe that Demas came from Thessalonica and that this was the reason he went to Thessalonica after forsaking Paul. But whether or not he was a native of that city, it is certain that he went there because he loved the world and forsook the apostle.

Verse 10 is difficult to understand because the predicate "has gone" governs not only Demas, but also Crescens and Titus. This means that Demas had gone to Thessalonica, Crescens had gone to Galatia, and Titus had gone to Dalmatia. Does this indicate that Titus, like Demas, left Paul in a negative way? If it were not for the fact that the name of Titus is presented positively in the New Testament, I would understand this verse to say that Demas, Crescens, and Titus all left Paul in a negative way. At least, I would take it to mean that Crescens and Titus took their own way. However, I find it difficult to believe that Titus would leave Paul in a negative way, especially after he had received from Paul an epistle addressed to him. After Paul had been arrested and imprisoned the second time, Titus visited him. Although I find it hard to believe that he forsook Paul, it is nonetheless a fact that he is categorized with Demas in verse 10. Did Paul send Crescens to Galatia and Titus to Dalmatia? We do not know for sure if they were sent by Paul or if they went on their own initiative.

In verse 11 Paul says, "Luke alone is with me. Take Mark and bring him with you, for he is useful to me for the ministry." The fact that Paul says that Luke alone is with him may indicate that Titus left either in a negative way or in a neutral way. Demas forsook Paul because he loved the present age; Titus may have left him for some other reason. Because Paul was suffering as a prisoner in Rome, none of his co-workers should have left him for any reason unless they were sent by Paul. They should have remained there with Paul to strengthen him. Paul's word about bringing Mark also indicates that he needed helpers to strengthen him. Ultimately we must leave to the Lord the question of whether Titus was sent by Paul to Dalmatia or went there on his own.

Verse 12 says, "Now Tychicus I have sent to Ephesus." It is difficult to decide how to translate the first word in this sentence. We could use now, but, yet, or and. I prefer to use either but or yet. It seems that Paul is saying, "Although I need helpers and although I need you to come quickly and bring Mark with you, yet I have still sent Tychicus to Ephesus." Although we may have difficulty deciding how to render the Greek word at the beginning of this sentence, we can still praise the Lord that there was a church in Ephesus, that Paul could send a brother there, and that there was a brother willing to be sent. Thank the Lord for such a sending!

I treasure verses 9 through 12 because they reveal that the relationship among Paul and his co-workers was divinely arranged; it was not based on human organization. Paul's co-workers had the freedom to act on their own. Paul did not say, "Titus, don't go to Dalmatia. I need you to stay here with me. If you leave, I shall fire you from the work." But although there was no human organization, there was a divine arrangement in which the leading apostle was the authority. Therefore, Paul could charge Timothy to come to him quickly.

During the years I was with Brother Nee, many co-workers came to him for advice, wanting him to tell them what to do regarding certain matters. Very rarely, if ever, would Brother Nee say anything. However, along with others who knew the situation, I can testify that whenever I asked Brother Nee about something, he always gave me a direct answer. Sometimes when I was in a distant city, he would send me a cable telling me either to come to him or to go to a certain place.

If we compare the books of 2 Timothy and Titus, we shall see that there was greater intimacy between Paul and Timothy than between Paul and Titus. Yes, Paul wrote an epistle to Titus. But he could not say as much to Titus as he could to Timothy. To such an intimate co-worker as Timothy, Paul could issue a command for him to come quickly.

Paul and his co-workers were not related to one another in the way of organization. This means that Paul did not regard himself as a boss who could hire or fire co-workers at his discretion. Likewise, because there is no organization in the Lord's recovery today, there is no hiring or firing.

We have seen that, due to the attraction of the present age, Demas forsook the apostle. In verses 8 and 10 we have a contrast between loving the Lord's appearing and loving the present age. If we love the Lord's appearing, we shall take sides with Him and fight with Him for His interests. But if we love the present age, we shall take sides with the world.

Even though Demas loved the present age and forsook Paul, Paul does not say that he dismissed him from the work. Furthermore, Crescens and Titus may have left Paul without having been sent by him. Perhaps, deep within, Paul wanted Titus to stay with him to help and support him. Whatever the situation may have been, these verses make it clear that Paul did not use his authority according to the way of human organization.

Many of those who have been co-workers for more than thirty years can testify that in the Lord's recovery we do not have a human organization with a boss who exercises authority to hire or fire co-workers. Instead of organization, we have God's coordination with His deputy authority. Because there was also such coordination and authority among Paul and his co-workers, he could tell Timothy to come to him quickly, and he could send Tychicus to Ephesus.

According to Philippians 2, Timothy was one with Paul in a very intimate way. He was one soul with him and was even willing to risk his soul for the work of Christ. Because of this oneness, this intimacy, Paul could command Timothy to come to him. He could also send Tychicus to Ephesus. This, however, is not organization. On the contrary, it is according to the spiritual situation among those in God's coordination. How much the leading ones in God's coordination can say to you depends on the extent to which you are one with the ministry. This is not a matter of organization, but of the degree of oneness.

In verse 13 Paul goes on to say, "The cloak which I left in Troas with Carpus, bring when you come, and the scrolls, especially the parchments." This word also reveals the intimacy between Paul and Timothy. Troas was a seaport in northwest Asia Minor, where Paul received the Macedonian call (Acts 16:8-11). The scrolls and the parchments were materials used for writing in ancient times. The cloak was probably a traveling cloak or traveling case.

II. DOING MANY EVILS

Verse 14 says, "Alexander the coppersmith did many evil

things to me; the Lord will repay him according to his works." Paul did not curse Alexander, but he did utter a word of righteousness, saying that the Lord would repay him according to his works.

In verses 10 and 14 we see two aspects of the issue of the decline. On the one hand, certain of those affected by the decline loved the present age; on the other hand, certain ones did evil things against the apostle. In times of degradation these things occur again and again.

In 1 Timothy 1:20 Paul speaks of Hymenaeus and Alexander. In 2 Timothy 2:17 he again refers to Hymenaeus, and in 4:14, to Alexander. Were Hymenaeus and Alexander genuine believers, or were they impostors? This raises the question concerning the boundary line between the great house (2 Tim. 2:20) and the house of God (1 Tim. 3:15). Only the Lord is able to draw the line with finality. Only He has the full knowledge concerning who is genuine and who is false.

Those who have conducted a scientific study of the difference between the wheat and tares in Matthew 13 point out that in every respect of their appearance, in size, color, and shape, the tares and the wheat are the same until the fruit is brought forth. At that time, the wheat brings forth golden ears and the tares bring forth black ears. Prior to that time, no one can differentiate between the wheat and the tares. This does not mean, however, that we should make no distinction between true believers and false ones. As long as we know that a certain person is not wheat, we should not receive him or accept him as wheat. But if in a particular situation we are not certain, we should receive the person. Such an action is not contrary to our conscience. It is possible that some of those whom we receive may not be genuine believers. It may have been that Hymenaeus was a true believer who became shipwrecked concerning the faith. Some may think that Hymenaeus was not a genuine believer, whereas others may think that he was a genuine believer who later became heretical. Because only the Lord knows for sure, we should not devote too much attention to the case of Hymenaeus.

Concerning ourselves as believers, there should not be any gray areas. This means that it should be easy for others to discern whether we are "black" or "white." Certainly no one doubts that Timothy was a genuine believer. Timothy was not only white, but was white in a bright, shining way. It should also be clearly evident that we are true believers in the Lord.

We have pointed out that it is difficult for us to draw the boundary line between the great house and the house of God. (In the eyes of the world, we are considered part of organized Christianity.) Certain things in the great house may be used by God. However, we should not be used by God in this way. In the great house there are vessels not only of gold and silver, but also of wood and earth. Do you want to be used by God as a wooden or earthen vessel, or as a golden or silver vessel? I want to be used by Him as a golden and silver vessel in the house of God.

Do not spend too much time trying to discern whether or not Alexander was a true believer. Instead, concentrate on those matters which are positive, clear, and nourishing. Whether Alexander was genuine or false, a wheat or a tare, will be decided by the Lord. One thing, however is certain: we should not follow his example. We should be a Timothy, not an Alexander.

Concerning Alexander the coppersmith, Paul advised Timothy, "You also guard against him, for he greatly opposed our words" (v. 15). No doubt, the words opposed by Alexander were the healthy words of God's economy. Today we are facing similar opposition from those who oppose the words of God's economy.

Verse 16 continues, "At my first defense no one came with me, but all forsook me; may it not be counted against them." We do not know whether Demas left Paul before the time of his first defense or after. We know only that all forsook him, that no one came with him.

In verse 17 Paul testifies, "But the Lord stood with me and empowered me, that through me the proclamation might be fully accomplished, and all the nations might hear;

and I was delivered out of the lion's mouth." The expression "the lion's mouth" is a figure of speech referring to an evil matter (v. 18) or an evil person (1 Cor. 15:32). Perhaps at the time of Paul's trial a certain person dealt with him in an extremely cruel manner. Paul may have such a person in mind when he speaks of "the lion's mouth."

In verse 18 Paul says, "The Lord will deliver me from every evil work, and will save me unto His heavenly kingdom, to Whom be the glory forever and ever. Amen." The heavenly kingdom is the kingdom of our Father (Matt. 13:43), the kingdom of the Father (Matt. 26:29), the kingdom of Christ and of God (Eph. 5:5), and the eternal kingdom of our Lord and Savior Jesus Christ (2 Pet. 1:11), which will be a reward to the overcoming saints. It equals the crown of righteousness in verse 8, and it is an incentive to the believers to run the heavenly course. Paul had the assurance to make the triumphant declaration that he would be saved into this heavenly kingdom.

III. THE CONCLUSION

After greeting Prisca and Aquila and the household of Onesiphorus (v. 19), Paul says, "Erastus remained in Corinth, but Trophimus I left at Miletus sick." Miletus is a city in Asia Minor near Ephesus (Acts 20:15, 17). Why did the apostle leave such an intimate one in sickness without exercising healing prayer for him? Why did he not also execute his healing gift (Acts 19:11-12) to cure Timothy of his stomach illness rather than instruct him to take the natural way for healing (1 Tim. 5:23)? The answer to both questions is that both Paul and his co-workers were under the discipline of the inner life in this time of suffering rather than under the power of the outward gift. The former is of grace in life; the latter of gift in power—miraculous power. In the decline of the church and in suffering for the church, the gift of power is not as much needed as the grace in life.

According to the New Testament, miraculous gifts may have a place when the church is first raised up. But for the church to withstand decline or persecution, miraculous gifts or powers are not very helpful. Only the eternal life on which we are to lay hold is prevailing. By this life we can withstand decline and persecution.

It may appear to some that in caring for Timothy's ailment and Trophimus' sickness in a human way Paul acted as if he were an unbeliever. There is no record that he prayed for healing, and he certainly did not exercise the gift of healing. Instead, he encouraged Timothy to take a little wine, and he left Trophimus at Miletus. Paul cared for his co-workers in a very human way. He did not do anything spectacular to make a display. In like manner, in the Lord's recovery we should not seek to make a show. Our emphasis must be on the eternal life by which we can withstand tests, trials, persecution, attack, and opposition. The firm foundation stands. This standing depends not on miracles, but on the eternal life which is the grace within us.

After charging Timothy to be diligent to come before winter and after sending him the greetings of all the brothers with him, Paul concludes, "The Lord be with your spirit. Grace be with you" (v. 22). Here we see that Paul concludes with two of the main elements of his composition of 2 Timothy: a strong spirit and the grace of God. The book of 2 Timothy, which gives instructions concerning how to confront the degradation of the church, strongly stresses our spirit. In the beginning it emphasizes that a strong, loving, and sound spirit has been given to us by which we can fan the gift of God into flame and suffer evil with the gospel according to the power of God and the Lord's life-imparting grace (1:6-10). In the conclusion this book blesses us with the emphasis on the Lord's being with our spirit that we may enjoy Him as grace to stand against the down current of the church's decline and carry out God's economy through His indwelling Spirit (1:14) and equipping word (3:16-17).

In the grievous days during the worsening degradation of the church, what is needed is the eternal grace of God, which was given to us in eternity (1:9) and is appropriated by us in this age. This grace, which is in the indestructible life, is nothing less than Christ the Son of God, who is the embodiment of the divine life, dwelling and living in our spirit. We need to exercise this spirit to enjoy the riches of Christ (Eph. 3:8) as the sufficient grace (2 Cor. 12:9). Thus, we may live Him as our godliness (1 Tim. 4:7-8) for the building up of the church as a testimony of Christ, bearing all the divine realities according to God's economy.

As the saints in the Lord's recovery, we all must know how to contact the Lord in our spirit, realizing that the grace with us is nothing less than the Triune God processed to be the all-inclusive, life-giving, compound, indwelling Spirit. Now our human spirit is one with the Spirit, one with the ultimate consummation of the processed Triune God. Day by day, we may enjoy such a Spirit in our spirit. As long as we know that the Lord is with our spirit and that the processed Triune God is our grace, and as long as we exercise our spirit to enjoy this grace, we shall have the reality of God's New Testament economy. Then in the midst of the degradation of today's Christianity, there will be the testimony of the reality of God's economy.

According to John 1:14, the Word, which is God Himself, became flesh, full of grace and reality. This indicates that as long as we have grace, we shall also have reality. If we exercise our spirit and enjoy this grace, we shall have reality. Then we shall carry out God's New Testament economy.

LIFE-STUDY OF TITUS

MESSAGE ONE

ESTABLISHING THE AUTHORITY IN THE CHURCH

Scripture Reading: Titus 1:1-9

It is helpful to know the sequence in which the four books of 1 and 2 Timothy, Titus, and Philemon were written. Philemon was written first, during Paul's first Roman imprisonment. After his release from prison, Paul wrote 1 Timothy and the Epistle to Titus. Finally, during his second imprisonment, at the time of Nero's persecution, he wrote his last epistle, the Epistle of 2 Timothy.

I. THE SUBJECT OF THE BOOK: THE MAINTENANCE OF THE ORDER OF THE CHURCH

The subject of the book of Titus is the maintenance of the order of the church. During Paul's first imprisonment in Rome, the churches were subject to testing. During this time of testing, certain churches proved not to be so orderly. Thus, after his release from prison, Paul visited various places, including the city of Ephesus and the island of Crete. Realizing the situation of the churches, Paul became burdened to write an epistle to Titus telling him how to maintain the proper order of a local assembly. This was the background and also the reason for the writing of this book. If the order of the church is to be maintained, the authority in the church needs to be established. Therefore, in this message we shall consider from 1:1-9 the establishing of the authority in the church. As we shall see, this has much to do with appointing elders in each city (v. 5).

II. INTRODUCTION

A. Paul, a Slave of God and an Apostle of Jesus Christ

Let us first consider 1:1-9 verse by verse and then consider in more detail certain crucial points.

Titus 1:1 says, "Paul, a slave of God, and an apostle of Jesus Christ, according to the faith of God's chosen ones, and the full knowledge of the truth which is according to godliness." Paul was an apostle according to four things: the command of God (1 Tim. 1:1), the faith of God's chosen ones, the promise of life (2 Tim. 1:1), and the full knowledge of the truth. Command is on God's side, speaking for Him and requiring something of us for Him. Faith is on our side, responding to God's requirements and receiving His grace. It is a proclamation that we are unable to fulfill God's requirements, but that God has done everything for us and that we receive what He has done. The life promised by God is what we have received of Him for the carrying out of His demand. It was in this way that Paul was an apostle to administrate God's New Testament economy.

In 1:1 Paul refers to God's chosen ones. This denotes the believers in Christ, who were chosen by God the Father before the foundation of the world (Eph. 1:4) and selected from mankind for salvation.

Paul was an apostle not only according to the faith of God's chosen ones, but also according to the full knowledge of the truth. Faith is to receive all God has planned for us, all God has done for us, and all God has given to us. Full knowledge of the truth is a thorough apprehension of the truth, a full acknowledgment and appreciation of the reality of all the spiritual and divine things which we have received through faith. Apostleship is according to such an apprehension and appreciation of the reality of God's eternal economy.

In 1:1 Paul indicates that the truth is according to godliness. The truth, the reality, of God's eternal economy is according to godliness, which is God manifested in man.

Apostleship is the dispensing of this reality to God's believing elect and the carrying out of such a godliness among them through preaching, teaching, and administration in the Word and in the Spirit (1 Tim. 6:3).

In verse 2 Paul goes on to say, "In the hope of eternal life, which God, Who cannot lie, promised before times eternal." Paul was an apostle not only according to the faith and the knowledge of the truth, but also in the hope of eternal life, which God, who cannot lie, promised in eternity. This corresponds to "according to the promise of life" in 2 Timothy 1:1. In the hope of eternal life means on the basis of, on the condition of, relying upon the hope of, eternal life. Eternal life, the uncreated life of God, is not only for us to partake of and enjoy today, but also for us to inherit (Matt. 19:29) in its full extent for eternity. Today's experience of eternal life qualifies us to inherit it in the future. Its enjoyment today is a foretaste; the full taste will be the inheritance of it in the coming age and in eternity, which is the hope of eternal life. This is the blessed hope revealed in 2:13, which is comprised of the freedom of the glory of full sonship, the redemption of our body (Rom. 8:21-25), the salvation to be revealed in the last time (1 Pet. 1:5), and the living hope of the incorruptible, undefiled, and unfading inheritance reserved in heaven (1 Pet. 1:3-4). This is the full, spiritual, divine, and heavenly blessing and enjoyment of eternal life, both in the millennium and in the new heaven and new earth (2 Pet. 1:11; 3:13; Rev. 21:6-7), referred to in 1 Timothy 4:8. Paul assumed his apostleship and accomplished his apostolic ministry, not based upon the benefit of the present life, nor on the condition of the privilege of the law, but based upon the condition of this hope, indicating that for his apostleship he relied upon and trusted in the divine life with all its hope, which God promised in eternity and which was brought to us through the gospel (2 Tim. 1:10).

The Epistle to Titus is occupied with the maintenance of order in the churches. For this, the faith of God's chosen ones, the truth according to godliness, and eternal life are indispensable. Hence, in the very opening word these three things are set forth.

Eternal life is the divine life, the uncreated life of God. It is not only everlasting, lasting forever, with respect to time, but in its nature it is also eternal and divine. The eternal life of God is given to all believers in Christ (1 Tim. 1:16) and is the main element of the divine grace given to us (Rom. 5:17, 21). This life has conquered death (Acts 2:24) and will swallow up death (2 Cor. 5:4). It was according to the promise of such a life that Paul was an apostle (2 Tim. 1:1). This life and its consequent incorruption have been brought to light and made visible to men through the preaching of the gospel.

Eternal life was "promised before times eternal." This must be the promise of the Father to the Son in eternity. The Father chose us in the Son and predestinated us unto sonship through Him (Eph. 1:5) before the foundation of the world. It must have been in that eternal epoch that the Father promised the Son that He would give His eternal life to His believers. By receiving this life the believers, who were given to Him in eternity (John 17:2), would become His brothers (Heb. 2:11).

In verse 3 Paul continues, "But in its own times has manifested His word in the proclamation with which I was entrusted, according to the command of our Savior God." The phrase "its own times" refers to the times (not times eternal) of the eternal life mentioned in verse 2. It denotes the proper time for the eternal life to be manifested.

The phrase "His word" in verse 3 is equal to eternal life in verse 2. This corresponds to 1 John 1:1 and 2.

B. To Titus, a Genuine Child according to the Common Faith

In verse 4 Paul says, "To Titus, genuine child according to the common faith: grace and peace from God the Father and Christ Jesus our Savior." Titus, like Timothy (1 Tim. 1:2), was Paul's genuine child not by natural birth, but in faith. He was Paul's child spiritually in the sphere and element of faith. The common faith in this verse is the general faith, which is common to all believers, the like precious faith (2 Pet. 1:1).

III. TO ESTABLISH THE AUTHORITY IN THE CHURCH

A. The Apostle's Charge

Titus 1:5 says, "For this cause I left you in Crete, that you might set in order the things that are lacking, and appoint elders in each city, as I charged you." The words "each city," compared with "in every church" in Acts 14:23, indicate not only that the jurisdiction of a local church is that of the city in which it is located, but also that in one city there should be only one church. The eldership of a local church should cover the entire city where that church is. Such a unique eldership in a city preserves the unique oneness of the Body of Christ from damage. One city should have only one church with one eldership. This practice is illustrated, beyond any question and doubt, by the clear pattern in the New Testament (Acts 8:1; 13:1; Rom. 16:1; 1 Cor. 1:2; Rev. 1:11), and is an absolute prerequisite for the maintenance of proper order in a local church. Because of this, the first thing the apostle charged Titus to do in setting things in order was to appoint elders in each city.

B. The Qualifications of the Elders

In verses 6 through 9 Paul lists many of the qualifications of the elders: unreprovable, the husband of one wife, having believing children, not accused of dissipation, not unruly, being the overseer as a steward of God, not self-willed, not quick-tempered, not an excessive drinker, not a striker, not seeking gain by base means, hospitable, a lover of good, one with a sober mind, righteous, holy, and self-controlled. We have considered many of these qualifications in detail in the message entitled "Overseers and Deacons for the Church's Administration," Message 5 in the Life-study of 1 Timothy.

In verse 9 Paul says, "Holding to the faithful word which is according to the teaching, that he may be able both to exhort by the healthy teaching and to convict those who contradict." The elders are appointed to administrate God's government in a local church that good order may be maintained in the church. To accomplish this, the elders need to hold to the faithful word, which is according to the apostles' teaching, that they may be able to stop troublesome talkers and calm a tumultuous situation (vv. 9-14).

The "faithful word" is the trustworthy, reliable, and true word which was taught in the churches according to the apostles' teaching. The elders in a local church should hold to this kind of healthy word that they may fulfill their duty in teaching (1 Tim. 3:2; 5:17).

The teaching referred to here is the apostles' teaching (Acts 2:42), which eventually became the New Testament. This indicates that the churches were established according to the apostles' teaching and followed their teaching. It also indicates that the order of the churches was maintained by the faithful word, which was given according to the apostles' teaching. The disorder of the church was mainly due to deviation from the apostles' teaching. To counter this, we must hold to the faithful word taught in the churches according to the apostles' teaching. In a darkened and confused situation, we must cleave to the enlightening and ordering word in the New Testament—the apostles' teaching. To maintain the order of the church, the word according to God's revelation is needed in addition to the eldership.

We have seen that "healthy teaching" implies life. Anything that is healthy refers to the health of life. The teaching of the apostles ministers healthy teaching as the supply of life to people, either nourishing them or healing them.

By holding to the faithful word which is according to the teaching, elders can "convict those who contradict." To convict here is to disclose the true character of anything so as to convict and hence reprove by exposing one's fault. The Greek word is translated expose in Ephesians 5:11 and 13.

Let us now go back to verses 1 through 3 and consider certain important points in more detail.

In verse 1 Paul says that he is an apostle of Jesus Christ "according to the faith of God's chosen ones, and the full knowledge of the truth which is according to godliness." Here we see that Paul's apostleship was according to the faith of God's chosen ones and according to the full knowledge of the truth, and that this truth is according to godliness. Three crucial words here are faith, truth, and godliness. Paul was an apostle not directly according to godliness, but according to the faith and to the full knowledge of the truth which is according to godliness. In verse 2 we see that Paul was an apostle also "in the hope of eternal life." The relative pronoun "which" in this verse refers to eternal life. Eternal life implies hope. With temporal life there is no true hope, but with eternal life there is hope. Because eternal life is forever and cannot be terminated, it gives us hope.

The hope of eternal life was "promised before times eternal" by God, who cannot lie. The expression "times eternal" is a special term denoting eternity. In eternity God promised eternal life with its hope. When we go on to verse 3, we see that God not only promised eternal life, but "in its own times has manifested His word in the proclamation" with which Paul was entrusted. In these verses we see that God has done two things: promised eternal life and manifested His word.

In 1 Timothy 1:1 Paul says that he became "an apostle of Christ Jesus, according to the command of God our Savior." However, in 2 Timothy 1:1 he says that he was an apostle "according to the promise of life which is in Christ Jesus." Paul was appointed an apostle by God's command with His requirement. A command requires something of us, but life supplies something to us. Apart from eternal life, Paul would not have had the supply to fulfill God's requirement. In order for Paul to carry out God's command with its extremely high requirements, he needed another life. This life is actually the life of God, the One who issues the command. Furthermore, this life is the very commanding and requiring God Himself. First, God makes a requirement, and then He comes in to supply what is needed to fulfill His own requirement. He requires by command, and He supplies by being life. When Paul received God's command to carry out His New Testament economy, perhaps he said, "Lord, who am I to carry out such a command? I am not able to fulfill this requirement." To this the Lord may have said, "Foolish child, I'll come into you to supply you. If you submit to My requirement, I'll come into you to fulfill it. I will be in you the life which is able to carry out My own requirement."

At this juncture it is worthwhile to compare 1 Corinthians 15:10 with Galatians 2:20. In the former verse Paul says, "But by the grace of God I am what I am: and his grace which was bestowed upon me was not in vain; but I labored more abundantly than they all: yet not I, but the grace of God which was with me." In the latter verse Paul says, "It is no longer I who live, but Christ lives in me." The grace which was with Paul and which enabled him to labor more than others was actually God Himself. God in Paul was eternal life as his supply and support for the carrying out of His New Testament economy. Therefore, the God who commanded is also the God who supplies.

In Titus 1:1 Paul again speaks of his apostleship, but he adds something to what is written in 1 Timothy 1:1 and 2 Timothy 1:1. As we have pointed out, in 1:1 and 2 Paul mentions the faith of God's chosen ones, the truth which is according to godliness, and the hope of eternal life. Although it is wonderful to see that Paul was an apostle according to the command of God and according to the promise of eternal life, we need to ask, in a thoughtful manner, how this eternal life can come into us. It comes into us through faith, through the organic union between us and the Triune God. Therefore, in 1:1 Paul says that he became an apostle not only according to the command of God and not only according to the life of God, but also according to the faith of God's chosen ones, the faith which brought him into an organic union with God. This was the way Paul obtained the life supply and support to fulfill God's command.

In 1:1 Paul is careful to point out that this faith is the faith of "God's chosen ones." We did not choose God; He chose us. Hence, the matter of our believing in Christ depends on God's choice, not on ours. God chose us in Christ before the foundation of the world. We should praise Him and worship Him for choosing us. Today we are in the Lord's recovery because God has chosen us. He was the One who took the initiative. How can you explain the fact that you believe in the Lord Jesus when others, perhaps members of your family, refuse to believe in Him? The only explanation is that God has chosen us. I can testify that I simply must believe in Christ. If I did not believe in Him, I would not have peace. If I did not believe in Christ, I would have no purpose for living. I would not be able to eat or sleep properly. No matter how others may treat me and no matter what my circumstances may be, I have no choice but to believe in the Lord.

In Acts 13 Paul and Barnabas turned to the Gentiles after the Jews rejected the gospel. Verse 46 says, "It was necessary that the word of God should first have been spoken to you: but seeing you put it from you, and judge yourselves unworthy of eternal life, lo, we turn to the Gentiles" (lit.). Verse 48 says, "And when the Gentiles heard this, they were glad, and glorified the word of the Lord: and as many as were ordained to eternal life believed." The reason these Gentiles could receive the word of the Lord and believe is that they were destined, even predestinated, to believe in Christ. Likewise, we who believe in Christ today are God's chosen ones.

In Titus 1:1 Paul does not speak of the faith of the believers, but of the faith of God's chosen ones. By so doing he indicates that the initiative for believing in Christ comes from God, not from us. Because God has chosen us to believe in Christ, we have come to believe in Him. Paul was an apostle according to the faith of God's chosen ones. He had this faith, and we have it also. Through faith Paul was brought into the organic union with the Triune God, and in this way he could receive the supply of eternal life.

Paul could stand against the Roman Empire not because he was strong or capable in himself, but because he had received eternal life. He was an apostle according to this eternal life, the eternal life which he received through the faith which brought him into an organic union with the Triune God.

We have pointed out that Paul also says that he became an apostle according to the full knowledge of the truth. Again and again we have seen that the truth in 1 and 2 Timothy and Titus denotes the reality of the contents of God's New Testament economy. We should have not only the faith of God's chosen ones, but also the full knowledge of the truth. We have the faith to bring us into the organic union, and we have the full knowledge of the truth of God's New Testament economy. This means that we know Christ as the embodiment of God and the church as the Body of Christ.

Actually Paul's apostleship involved four factors: God's command, eternal life, faith, and the full knowledge of the truth. Because of these four elements, Paul was one who troubled religion. He was even called a pestilent fellow, a troublemaker. Of these four elements, two are on God's side—the command and the eternal life—and two are on our side—faith and the full knowledge of the truth. When we first believed in the Lord Jesus, we had faith, but we did not have the full knowledge of the truth. Praise the Lord that in His recovery we have the full knowledge of the truth!

Titus 1:2 says that eternal life was "promised before times eternal." This indicates that the promise was not given directly to the chosen ones. Rather, the promise was made by the Father to the Son in eternity. John 17:2 seems to refer to this: "Even as You gave Him authority over all flesh, that He may give eternal life to all whom You have given Him." By receiving eternal life the believers, who were given to the Son in eternity, become His brothers. Hebrews 2:11 refers to the brothers of Christ: "For both He who sanctifies and those who are being sanctified are all of one, for which cause He is not ashamed to call them brothers." Because the promise of eternal life was made by the Father to the Lord Jesus in eternity, the Bible says that God chose us in Christ. God did not choose us directly; He chose us in Christ. In like manner, the promise of eternal life concerning us was given to Christ. Thus, in the Son we now receive this promise.

According to verse 3, God not only promised eternal life before times eternal, but "in its own times has manifested His word in the proclamation." The eternal life was promised by the Father to the Son; however, what God the Father has manifested is not eternal life, but His word. By reading verses 2 and 3 carefully, we see that the word manifested is the equivalent of the eternal life promised. Paul does not say that God promised eternal life and then manifested this eternal life. He says that God promised eternal life and then manifested His word. Therefore, God's word is eternal life. If His word is not the eternal life directly, it is at least the means of conveying eternal life. In our experience we have eternal life through the word.

The expression "its own times" refers to the times related to eternal life mentioned in verse 2. God promised eternal life through the Son concerning us in eternity, but the proclamation was made in different ages and at different times. God manifested His eternal life in His word by preaching, that is, by proclamation. This proclamation was made in Asia Minor at one time and in Europe at a different time.

Paul here does not say that eternal life was manifested by the preaching of the gospel. Instead, he speaks of times, the word, and the proclamation. The eternal life promised was manifested at different times by proclamation, by the preaching of the gospel. This manifestation first took place on the day of Pentecost in Jerusalem. Later the proclamation went to Antioch, Asia Minor, and Europe. Centuries later this proclamation reached China. Therefore, "its own times" denotes the various times God's word is manifested in the preaching of the gospel. Paul was entrusted with this proclamation according to the command of our Savior God.

LIFE-STUDY OF TITUS

MESSAGE TWO

DEALING WITH THE INFLUENCE OF JUDAISM AND GNOSTICISM

Scripture Reading: Titus 1:10-16

According to 1:10-16, at the time Titus was in Crete two isms were quite prevailing: Judaism and Gnosticism. In this message we shall consider from these verses how Titus was instructed to deal with the influence of Judaism and Gnosticism.

THE INFLUENCE OF JUDAISM

A. Unruly Men, Vain Talkers and Deceivers

In verses 10 and 11, Paul says, "For there are many unruly men, vain talkers and deceivers, especially those of the circumcision, whose mouths must be stopped, who overthrow whole households, teaching things which they ought not for the sake of base gain." Both Paul's word about "those of the circumcision" in verse 10 and his reference to "Jewish myths" in verse 14 point to the influence of Judaism. Those of the circumcision were Jewish believers who were seducers within the church. Paul says that such ones must be stopped. The way to stop them is by severe reproof (v. 13) with the faithful word according to the apostles' teaching (v. 9). These vain talkers and deceivers overthrow whole households, "teaching things which they ought not for the sake of base gain." What they did was similar to what was done by the reprobate prophet, Balaam (2 Pet. 2:15-16; Jude 11).

I would call your attention to the little word "for," at the beginning of verse 10, indicating that this verse is related to the foregoing verse. In verse 9 Paul says that an overseer must hold to "the faithful word which is according to the teaching that he may be able both to exhort by the healthy teaching and to convict those who contradict." Then Paul goes on to explain that there are many unruly men, especially of the circumcision, whose mouths must be stopped. These verses indicate that Paul's charge to Titus concerning the establishment of the eldership is related to the disturbances caused by the influence of Judaism. There was the urgent need for the eldership to be set in order so that those who taught differently could be dealt with. Certain Jewish believers brought their Judaism into the church life and this, with its different teachings, caused a disturbance. Here we have a basic principle related to the eldership: every elder must be a watchman who is on the alert lest some teaching different from that of the apostles' ministry is brought into the church.

B. The True Testimony of a Cretan Prophet

In verses 12 and 13 Paul declares, "One of them, a prophet of their own, said, Cretans are always liars, evil beasts, lazy gluttons. This testimony is true." One of them refers to one of the Cretans. All those mentioned in verses 9b and 10 were such Cretans. The prophet of their own was a heathen prophet, probably Epimenides, a native of Crete who lived about 600 B.C., according to legend.

C. The Apostle's Charge

In verse 13 Paul charges Titus to "reprove them severely, that they may be healthy in the faith." The Greek word rendered reprove here is the same word translated convict in verse 9. It means to disclose the true character of anything so as to convict and hence reprove by exposing one's fault. The Greek word rendered severely may also be rendered sharply. The purpose of such severe reproof was that those receiving it might be healthy in the faith. The gainsayers (v. 9) and vain talkers (v. 10) were infected with doctrinal diseases and became unhealthy in the faith. They needed the inoculation of the healthy teaching and the healthy word (1 Tim. 1:10; 6:3), which the elders should provide for their healing.

As in 1 Timothy 1:19 and 3:9, the faith here is objective. It refers to the things in which we believe. This is to be distinguished from the subjective meaning of faith, which refers to the act of believing.

II. THE INFLUENCE OF GNOSTICISM

A. Jewish Myths— the Seed of Gnostic Mythologies

Verse 14 says, "Not paying attention to Jewish myths." The Greek word for myths is rendered myths here and in 1 Timothy 1:4, tales in 1 Timothy 4:7, and fables in 2 Timothy 4:4. It refers to words, speeches, and conversations concerning such things as rumors, reports, stories, and fictions. It may include Jewish stories of miracles or rabbinical fabrications. These myths were the profane and old-womanish tales. The Jewish myths mentioned here may have been the seed of the Gnostic mythologies.

B. Commandments of Men Who Turn Away from the Truth

In verse 14 Paul also mentions "commandments of men who turn away from the truth." According to the following verse, these commandments of the heretics must have been precepts concerning abstinence from meats and other things ordained by God for man's use (see 1 Tim. 4:3; Col. 2:20-22). These were the commandments of the earlier Gnostics, not the ascetics, who adopted their theosophy from Jewish sources, probably some derivation from the Mosaic law.

The men Paul refers to in this verse are probably those of the circumcision (v. 10). These men turn away from the truth. The truth here and the faith in the preceding verse prove that those who were dealt with here were not unbelievers. There were some in the church who had turned away from the truth concerning God's economy. Most of them might have been Jewish Christians who still held their Jewish myths and traditions and thereby became a great disturbance to the church. They had to be stopped by the word of the truth according to the faith so that the order of the church might be maintained under the established eldership.

In verse 15 Paul continues, "All things are pure to the pure; but to those who are defiled and unbelieving nothing is pure, but both their mind and their conscience have been defiled." The statement, "All things are pure to the pure," must have been a Christian maxim. The apostle quoted it to refute the commandments of men (v. 14), that is, the precepts of abstinence, which forbade certain actions and the eating of certain foods (1 Tim. 4:3-5; Rom. 14:20).

Paul says that to those who are defiled, or polluted, and unbelieving nothing is pure, but both their mind and conscience are defiled. The mind is the leading part of the soul, and the conscience is the main part of our spirit. If our mind is polluted, our soul is spontaneously polluted; and if our conscience is defiled, our spirit is unavoidably defiled. This is all due to unbelief. Our faith purifies us (Acts 15:9).

In verse 16 Paul goes on to say, "They profess to know God, but by their works they deny Him, being abominable and disobedient, and as to every good work disapproved." The Greek word rendered disapproved can also be translated reprobate, worthless, disqualified. It means unable to stand the test.

C. The Apostle's Charge

Paul's charge to Titus is simply not to pay attention to Jewish myths and commandments of men (v. 14).

Just as the elders in the churches in Crete were to watch out for the influence of Judaism and Gnosticism and not permit different teachings to creep into the church life, we also need to watch out for isms today, such as Catholicism and denominationalism. We should also be watchful concerning the hypocrisy and the superficial and superstitious tales circulated among many Christians. If these things are brought into the Lord's recovery, they will cause trouble. The pure church life is built only upon the healthy teaching of the apostles. This is the reason Paul says that elders must hold to the faithful word which is according to the teaching, so that they may be able to exhort by healthy teaching. The teaching in verse 9 refers to that of the apostles (Acts 2:42), which eventually became the New Testament. The apostles' teaching was the healthy teaching. The churches were established according to the apostles' teaching and followed their teaching. Furthermore, the order of the church was maintained by the faithful word given according to this teaching. At the beginning of the church life, when the believers spoke about the teaching, everyone realized that this meant the teaching of the apostles. In Jerusalem those who received the Lord Jesus and were added to the church continued in the teaching and fellowship of the apostles.

In 1:9 Paul does not say "sound teaching" or even "pure teaching"; he speaks of "healthy teaching." Certain teachings may be sound or pure without being healthy. Healthy teaching is always related to life and is able either to nourish us or to heal us. Only something living can be healthy. For example, we do not speak of a table or chair as being healthy. The teachings of the apostles were not only sound and pure, but were healthy, full of life.

The crucial point of the healthy teaching of the apostolic ministry concerns the Triune God processed to dispense Himself as the all-inclusive Spirit into His chosen ones so that they may be brought into an organic union to receive the divine transfusion and thereby become sons of God and members of Christ. As a result, they can be the Body to express Christ, the One in whom the fullness of God dwells. Almost all of this is neglected by Christians today. Even those teachings which are truly sound are for the most part superficial.

Some believers are told nothing more than that if they receive the Lord, they will be saved by grace. They do not even receive an adequate explanation concerning what it is this grace saves them from. According to Ephesians 2:8, a verse often quoted in pointing out that salvation is by grace, to be saved does not mean to be saved from hell. According to the context, to be saved is to be saved from death, or from a deadening situation, that we may be raised up and seated in the heavens in a living way. Furthermore, contrary to the common, superficial understanding, grace in Ephesians 2:8 is not simply unmerited favor. It is the Triune God as everything to us for our enjoyment. Christians who emphasize the preaching of the gospel often quote Ephesians 2:8. However, because they understand this verse very superficially, rarely does anyone touch the reality of it.

In the foregoing message we pointed out that Paul was an apostle according to the command of God, the promise of eternal life, the faith of God's chosen ones, and the full knowledge of the truth. Can the majority of Christian teachers honestly say that they have the full knowledge of the truth? Certainly not. They may be familiar with particular doctrines and consider this doctrinal knowledge the full knowledge of the truth. Some may know all about the seven dispensations and yet not possess the full knowledge of the truth. The Lord Jesus once declared, "I am the truth" (John 14:6). If, as is the practice of many Christians, we interpret truth to mean doctrine, then the Lord Jesus would have been saying, "I am the doctrine." How ridiculous! Many Christians, even Bible teachers, do not know the meaning of truth in the New Testament. Eventually, superficiality can lead to hypocrisy, and hypocrisy, to superstition.

There is a doctrine commonly held among Christians that as long as a person believes in the Lord Jesus, he is saved and he will have no problems at the time of the Lord's coming. According to this view, when the believers are raptured, they will not have any problems with the Lord, and all will reign with Him in the kingdom. There is even a bumper sticker which makes light of the rapture by saying: "Warning—in case of rapture, this car will be unmanned." Many Christians mistakenly believe that simply because they are saved they have a "ticket" which will admit them into the kingdom of the heavens. But as D. M. Panton has pointed out, many will be surprised to realize that this ticket is false and will not admit them into the heavenly kingdom. A great many of today's Christians may have the shocking realization that the ticket which some minister told them would guarantee an entrance into the kingdom will not be accepted at the time of the Lord's coming. Because such superficial and even superstitious teachings are prevalent today, we need to fight against them, just as Paul fought against the hypocrisies of Judaism and Gnosticism.

Another teaching we must oppose is the saying that as long as two or three meet in the name of the Lord, they are the church. According to this erroneous teaching, there can be many different churches in a locality. What falsehood! Two or three believers may meet in the name of the Lord, but that does not necessarily mean that they are the church in that locality.

Although we need to fight against superficial and superstitious teachings, this definitely does not mean that we deliberately cause trouble to our family, relatives, friends, or neighbors. Yes, we must fight for the truth of God. We must be the light of the world and the salt of the earth. However, it is absolutely necessary that we maintain the best relationship with others. The young people must honor their parents, and we all need to have a proper relationship with our family, relatives, and neighbors. We in the Lord's recovery should be the best neighbors and the most peaceable of people. It is an evil rumor and slander to say that we are not human. We aspire to be the most human of people, those who are Jesusly human, divinely human. In all our contact with others, we need to display the highest humanity and the best conduct and behavior. We are not fighting against persons—we are fighting against isms.

Our burden is not simply to oppose superficiality, hypocrisy, and superstition. It is to minister Christ and the church for the fulfillment of God's economy. God our Father certainly has an eternal purpose to fulfill. But Satan has come in with many distractions and falsehoods. Our burden must be to minister the all-inclusive Christ and the church as the Body of Christ to those who love God and seek Christ. We need to help all those who pursue the Lord to come to the full knowledge of the truth. We need to sound the trumpet that those who seek the Lord Jesus may come together as a living Body of Christ to fulfill God's purpose and to hasten the coming of the Lord. Concerning this, we all must be desperate and give ourselves to prayer. On the one hand, we like to maintain a peaceful situation with others. On the other hand, for the sake of God's purpose, we must stand firm for the full knowledge of God's truth and fight the good fight against the evil powers of darkness.

LIFE-STUDY OF TITUS

MESSAGE THREE

BRINGING THE SAINTS OF DIFFERENT AGES INTO AN ORDERLY LIFE

Scripture Reading: Titus 2:1-8

In 2:1-8 the word healthy is used three times. In verse 1 Paul says, "But as for you, speak the things which are fitting to healthy teaching." In verse 2 Paul speaks of being healthy in faith, love, and endurance. In verse 8 Paul refers to "healthy speech that cannot be condemned." Titus was to speak the things which are fitting to healthy teaching and show himself a pattern of healthy words, and the elderly men were to be healthy in faith, love, and endurance. It is significant that in these verses, a portion of Titus in which the saints are charged to live an orderly life in the church, Paul uses the word healthy three times. If we study the verses where this word is used, and especially if we pray-read them, we shall be richly nourished. I would encourage you to pray over Paul's word concerning healthy teaching, being healthy in faith, love, and endurance, and healthy speech. If you do this, you will enjoy an excellent spiritual meal.

I. TO SPEAK THE THINGS WHICH ARE FITTING TO HEALTHY TEACHING

Titus 2:1 says, "But as for you, speak the things which are fitting to healthy teaching." This verse opens with the word "but" to show that it is in contrast to 1:16. In contrast to those who profess to know God, but by their works deny Him, Titus was to speak the things which are fitting to healthy teaching.

The healthy teaching is always according to the truth

(1:14) of the faith (1:13). It is the content of the apostles' teaching, the content of God's New Testament economy. It not only ministers the life supply to the believers and heals the spiritual diseases, but in so doing also brings the church into a sound condition with a good order. Hence, it is very much stressed in these three books, 1 and 2 Timothy and Titus, books dealing with the disorder and decline of the church. In 2:1 Paul charged Titus not to deviate from the healthy teaching, from the apostles' teaching. He should not be like the gainsayers, the vain talkers, those who teach differently and make the church subject to the influence of Judaism and Gnosticism.

We also should be reminded to speak the things which are fitting to healthy teaching. The word healthy points to that which is hygienic and which can both inoculate others against spiritual poison and also supply them with life. Our teachings should not merely pass on knowledge to others, but should supply them with life. Often when I have been tempted to speak about a certain subject, I was stopped. I had the sense that there was not much of the hygienic element in what I planned to say. We need to remind ourselves and be reminded by the Spirit to give forth healthy teaching.

Healthy teachings do not provoke debates or arguments. If we give adequate attention to feeding on the Lord, we shall not care to argue. A dining table is not a place for debate or argument; it is a place for feasting and nourishment. In the church life we should not exchange the dining table for a desk. We all need to learn how to put healthy "dishes" on the dining table to feed the saints.

II. CONCERNING THE AGED MEN

In the foregoing message we pointed out that in fighting the battle for the truth, we need to maintain excellent relationships with others. Our behavior needs to be according to the highest standard and also very human. In every area of our daily life and family life we must be proper.

In the three Epistles of 1 and 2 Timothy and Titus Paul emphasizes the importance of a proper humanity. In 2:2

Paul speaks to the aged men and says, "Aged men are to be temperate, grave, of a sober mind, healthy in faith, in love, in endurance."

A. Temperate

According to this verse, the aged men are to be temperate. To be temperate is to have self-control and to be moderate. It is often easier for an elderly person to be offended or angered than it is for a young person to be bothered in this way. As an elderly person myself, I can testify that in a family it is usually the older ones who become irritated or impatient. Today I can be bothered by certain irritations or nuisances that did not affect me in the least fifty years ago. This indicates that, as an elderly man, I need Paul's charge to be temperate. Of course, temperateness is a virtue needed by everyone in the church life.

B. Grave

Elderly men should also be grave. Gravity is a qualification of human character which is worthy of utmost respect. It implies dignity and it inspires honor and invites it. Gravity is a virtue which invites the respect of others.

C. Of a Sober Mind

In verse 2 Paul charges the aged men to be of a sober mind. He says the same concerning young women (v. 5) and younger men (v. 6). In 1 Timothy 3:2 Paul lists this among the qualifications of an overseer. To be of a sober mind is to be sensible and also discreet in understanding. No matter what our age may be, we all need a sober mind. If we are of a sober mind, we shall avoid the extremes of being too hot or too cold. On the one hand, we need to be burning in spirit; on the other hand, we need to be of a sober mind. If we would be a proper human being, we need this quality.

D. Healthy

1. In Faith

If we would be healthy in faith, we need daily to be under

the transfusion which comes through the organic union between us and the Triune God. The word faith in verse 2 does not refer to the objective faith, to the things we believe, but to our activity of believing. In our daily living we need a faith which keeps us in the organic union. In order to be healthy in faith, we need to come to the Word and contact the Lord by praying in a living way with our spirit. Then we shall have faith, the infusion of the living God into us through our contact with the Word in the spirit. Faith, therefore, is a living Person infused into us. The more we remain in the organic union with this divine Person, the more healthy we shall be in faith.

2. In Love

If we are healthy in faith, we shall automatically be healthy in love. It is possible to love others too much or too little. In either case, our love is not healthy. Instead, we are somewhat sick in our love.

Why do you love a certain brother very much and another brother hardly at all? It is because you love others according to your own taste. In Philippians 2:2 Paul says that we should have the same love. This means that our love for all the saints should be on the same level. To have a different love for different saints is to be unhealthy in love. But to have the same love for all is to be healthy in love.

3. In Endurance

According to Titus 2:2, aged men should also be healthy in endurance. If we have adequate endurance, we shall be able to bear the things which bother us and trouble us. We have pointed out that it is rather easy for an elderly person to be bothered. As one who has many children and grandchildren and who is involved with so many churches and co-workers, I can testify of the need for endurance. For example, I need endurance simply to care for all the mail I receive day by day. I receive so much mail that I have developed a filing system to categorize and arrange it. Even this takes endurance. If I were short of endurance, I would not know what to do with all this mail.

Especially those of us who are elderly need endurance. The older we become, the greater is our need of endurance. In particular, the elders in a church need endurance. For example, sometimes telephone calls come late at night. To take care of such a call in a proper way requires endurance.

Once again I wish to emphasize the fact that in the church life we aspire to live a proper human life, with all the human virtues. We do not want to be angelic. Our desire is to be genuinely human.

III. CONCERNING THE AGED WOMEN

In verses 3 and 4 Paul speaks concerning aged women: "Aged women likewise are to be in demeanor as befits the sacred, not slanderers, nor enslaved by much wine, teachers of what is good, that they may train the young women to be lovers of their husbands, lovers of their children." Paul's use of the word "likewise" indicates that the behavior of the aged women should be similar to that of the aged men. In demeanor they should be as befits the sacred. Demeanor means deportment and includes gesture and habit. The word sacred refers to those who are engaged in sacred things. This may be a special term referring to our service in the church. Any service in the church is sacred, and our demeanor should match this sacred service. Demeanor includes everything we are in our attitude, appearance, and deportment. All this should befit that part of the church service in which we participate. Especially the elderly sisters should have a demeanor which befits the sacred things, the things related to the service of the church.

Paul also says that aged women should not be slanderers. The Devil is a slanderer (Rev. 12:10). To slander is to practice the nature of the evil slanderer. An elderly sister should flee slander, the evil act of the Devil.

In verse 3 Paul also mentions not "enslaved by much wine." This word enslaved can be compared to the word addicted used in 1 Timothy 3:8. To be enslaved may be worse than to be addicted. The aged women certainly should not be slaves of wine.

Paul also says that the aged women should be "teachers of what is good" and train the young women. To be teachers of what is good is to give good instruction.

IV. CONCERNING THE YOUNG WOMEN

In verses 4 and 5 we see that the young women are to be "lovers of their husbands, lovers of their children, of a sober mind, chaste, workers at home, good, subject to their own husbands, that the word of God may not be blasphemed." The aged women should train the young women to love their husbands and their children. In the church life we strongly emphasize the need of a proper married life and family life. According to Paul's word, we desire that the sisters love their husbands and children in an absolute way. Furthermore the young women should be sober, chaste, workers at home, kind, and subject to their own husbands so that the word of God may not be blasphemed. The word of God properly and adequately taught in a local church should be testified to by the sisters' submission to their own husbands. Otherwise, the word of God may be blasphemed, ill spoken of, reproached.

V. CONCERNING THE YOUNGER MEN

Verse 6 says, "The younger men likewise exhort to be of a sober mind." Paul's use of the word likewise indicates that the charge to the younger men is similar to that given to the others. In particular, Paul tells Titus to exhort the younger men to be of a sober mind. We have pointed out that in 1 and 2 Timothy and Titus Paul emphasizes the need for all the saints, young and old, male and female, to be of a sober mind. Everyone in the church life needs a sober mind. This is especially needed during the decline of the church. To guard against any decline, all of us in the local churches need to be of a sober mind.

VI. THE APOSTLE'S CHARGE

In verses 7 and 8 Paul issues a charge directly to Titus: "Concerning all things show yourself a pattern of good works: in teaching with uncorruptness, gravity, healthy speech that cannot be condemned, in order that the opposer may be put to shame, having nothing evil to say about us." The apostle first charged Titus to speak things fitting to healthy teaching (v. 1). Now he further charges him to show himself a pattern of good works. In his teaching, which should be healthy, he should show three things: uncorruptness, nothing corrupted or corrupting, but everything pure, genuine, and sincere in content, presentation, and motive; gravity, dignity worthy of respect; and healthy speech, discourse given with healthy words (1 Tim. 6:3) to minister healthy things, speech which is uncensurable, irreprehensible (v. 8). Such speech will cause the opposers to be put to shame. The Greek word rendered opposer in verse 8 means the one of the opposite, contrary, side; that is, the heathen or Jewish opposer. The healthy teaching with the healthy speech of healthy words is the most effective antidote to the opposer's evil speaking. Such light-shedding and life-imparting teaching of the word of the truth always stops the mouth of doctrinal opinion instigated by the old serpent.

LIFE-STUDY OF TITUS

MESSAGE FOUR

CHARGING SLAVES TO BEHAVE WELL IN THE SOCIAL SYSTEM OF SLAVERY

Scripture Reading: Titus 2:9-15

In the book of Titus Paul gives instructions concerning the church life, the family life, the behavior of slaves in the social system of slavery, and the saints' relationship with the government. Chapter one mainly deals with the church life. Regarding the church life, Paul covers two main points in this chapter: the government of the church and the proper teaching in the church. The church's government is built upon the proper eldership, and the teaching in the church is based on the healthy teaching of the apostles. This healthy teaching swallows up every kind of ism, in particular Judaism and Gnosticism, and every type of differing teaching. If we would have a church life which is healthy and in good order, there must be in the church the proper administration and healthy teaching according to the ministry of the apostles.

In 2:1-8 Paul speaks concerning an orderly human life. In particular, he speaks of the family life. These eight verses give us the foundation of a proper human life in the divine life. We in the Lord's recovery should live such a human life. For the testimony of Jesus we need the highest human life, a life lived out according to the divine life given to us by God. By the divine life we need to have a human life that reaches the highest standard. In our living we should be Jesusly human. We should aspire to have a glorious testimony of the Christ in whom we believe and whom we serve and honor. Then we shall be a shining, golden lampstand. This is our declaration concerning human living.

After speaking of the church and of the family life, Paul goes on to charge the slaves to behave well in the social system of slavery (2:9-15). Certainly Paul did not agree with the system of slavery. However, as a teacher appointed by God and as one with spiritual insight, he did not touch the existing social system. If he had done so, he would have given others the impression that he was a social reformer and not a teacher of God's economy, a herald of the good news. Paul did not involve himself with reformation of the social system. On the contrary, he gave instructions to slaves concerning the need to behave according to the highest standard of human character. The slaves were to have an excellent testimony of the life of Jesus in their human living.

If Paul had advocated the annulment of the system of slavery, he would have been regarded as a social reformer by those who read his Epistles. That would have obscured Paul's teaching concerning the living out of Christ's divine life in our human living in the midst of any kind of social system. In order to guarantee that the light would shine without hindrance, Paul did not say a word about the social system in the way of correcting it or reforming it.

When the Lord Jesus was on earth, He did not touch the social system. Instead, He lived as a typical Jew in a country under the control of the Roman imperialists. The Lord Jesus was born during the time of Caesar Augustus. At the time of His trial, judgment was pronounced upon Him by Pontius Pilate, governor of Judea. The Lord Jesus said to Pilate, "My kingdom is not of this world" (John 18:36). The Lord's kingdom was not earthly; it was heavenly in nature. For this reason, when He was on earth, the Lord Jesus did not deal with the social system or with any earthly government. Paul displayed the same attitude. He did not try to reform the Roman social system.

When the Epistle of Titus was written, a number of slaves had become believers in Christ. According to civil law. a slave had no rights. A master could brand a slave as if he were a horse or a mule. Furthermore, a master could legally put a slave to death. What a dreadful system! To be sure,

God was utterly opposed to such a social system, for it was altogether contrary to the place of man in His creation. Paul certainly did not approve of this evil social system. But instead of trying to reform it, he charged the slaves to behave well in it, to live in it according to the standard of the humanity of the Lord Jesus. Even in the midst of such an unjust social system, Christians could live out a life with the highest standard of humanity. What a testimony this is!

No matter how bad certain social systems may be today, none are as bad as the system of slavery in the Roman Empire. For the saints to live a Jesusly human life in that kind of social system was a marvelous testimony of the divine life. It was God's wisdom that a slave, bought and branded like an animal, could testify of the divine life according to the highest standard.

Some have criticized Paul for not trying to reform the social system. We realize, however, that Paul used the worst social system as an opportunity to charge the believers to live a Jesusly human life in the midst of it. If the saints could live such a human life in the worst social system imaginable, then we should be able to live such a life in any kind of circumstances today. Praise the Lord that by the divine life we can have the highest human living even in the worst social system!

I. THE CHARGE TO THE SLAVES

In verses 9 and 10 Paul says, "Slaves are to be subject to their own masters in all things, to be well pleasing, not contradicting, not pilfering, but showing all good faith that they may adorn the teachings of our Savior God in all things." The slaves here are not servants, but bondslaves bought in the market like oxen and horses. Paul charges them to be subject to their own masters in all things. They had no choice, and there was to be no argument. Moreover, the slaves were not to pilfer. On the contrary, they were to show all good faith. Faith here means fidelity, trustworthiness. In this way they would adorn the teachings of our Savior God. The faithfulness of a bondslave can be the ornament of the teaching of God our Savior. He would even accept adornment from bondslaves!

In 2:5 Paul charges the young women to live in such a way that "the word of God may not be blasphemed." In 2:10 he speaks positively of adorning the teaching of our Savior God. Our daily living should be a beautiful adornment to the teaching we have received. If we live according to the healthy teaching of the apostles, we shall adorn these teachings by our living. If we have a bright testimony of a living which is Jesusly human, our neighbors will realize that we are genuine Christians. They will confess that our living is the adornment of the teachings we have received in the Lord's recovery. We should live not only in a way that is different from that of others, but in a way that is higher and more respectable. Others may even desire to follow us, because they have observed the high standard of our daily life. They may seek to learn how they can have such a life themselves.

In 2:10 Paul speaks of "our Savior God." Our Savior is not only Christ, but God Triune embodied in Christ, as indicated in verse 13. Our Savior God desires not only to save us, but also to teach us the full knowledge of the truth (1 Tim. 2:4). Hence, there is the teaching of our Savior God, which may be adorned, beautified, by the transformed character of the most vile persons saved by His grace.

II. THE GRACE OF GOD

Verse 11 begins with the little word for, indicating that what is to follow explains how it is possible for slaves to have a human living according to God's standard. Verses 11 through 14 give us a remarkable summary of the economy of God's salvation. The apostle uses this as a reason for his exhortations in verses 1 through 10.

Verse 11 says, "For the grace of God has appeared, bringing salvation to all men." The grace of God is actually God Himself in Christ as everything to us for our enjoyment. This grace plays the most important role in the economy of God's salvation. Grace came through Christ (John 1:17). It was given to us in eternity (2 Tim. 1:9), but was hidden in the Old Testament. It appeared in the New Testament through the first appearing of Christ (2 Tim. 1:10), bringing salvation to all men, both Jews and Gentiles.

The eternal grace of God, the saving grace, was destined in Christ to bring to us His salvation, the complete salvation which includes forgiveness, justification, reconciliation, redemption, regeneration, sanctification, transformation, and conformation. The eternal grace of God was also destined to redeem us back to God, to impart His life to us, and to bring us into an organic union with Him for the fulfillment of His eternal purpose.

In verse 12 Paul says that the grace of God is training us that, "denying ungodliness and worldly lusts, we should live soberly and righteously and godly in the present age." Worldly lusts are lusts that find their gratification in this world. Ungodliness is the failure to express God; worldly lusts are the expression of our flesh. Both of these should be denied that we may live a God-expressing and flesh-restricting life. To live soberly is to live discreetly, in a way of self-restriction. Soberly is in regard to ourselves; righteously, to others; and godly, to God.

By the grace of God we are being trained to live soberly, righteously, and godly. This requires that we deny ungodliness and worldly lusts. Ungodliness is a living which does not express God. We should not have anything to do with the life that fails to express God. Furthermore, we should abandon whatever attracts us to earthly things or draws us to them. Forsaking ungodliness and worldly lusts, we should live a life which is sober toward ourselves, righteous toward others, and godly toward God.

In verse 13 Paul continues, "Awaiting the blessed hope, even the appearing of the glory of the great God and our Savior, Christ Jesus." We are to await expectantly what is accepted in faith. According to verse 13, we are awaiting the blessed hope, which is the appearing of Christ in His glory. The appearing of Christ will bring us into full sonship, that is, the redemption of our body, that we may enjoy the freedom of the glory of the children of God for which we have been saved (Rom. 8:21-25). This is the hope of eternal life (Titus 1:2), a hope of eternal blessing, a blessed hope in the eternal life of the Triune God, based upon which Paul became an apostle.

In verse 13 Paul speaks of the glory of the great God; that is the glory of the Father (Matt. 16:27) which has been given to the Son (John 17:24) and into which we, as the many sons of God, will be brought (Heb. 2:10). Unto this glory God by His wisdom has ordained us before the ages (1 Cor. 2:7), and into this eternal glory the God of all grace has called us and saved us (1 Pet. 5:10; 2 Tim. 2:10). The weight of this glory is eternal (2 Cor. 4:17), and with it we shall be glorified (Rom. 8:17, 30). The appearing of this glory of Christ, our great God and Savior, is the blessed hope which we are awaiting.

In verse 13 Paul speaks of "the great God and our Savior, Christ Jesus." Through the centuries there have been two schools of interpretation regarding this remarkable, marvelous, and excellent sacred and divine title. According to one school, two Persons are indicated, God and Christ. According to the other school, there is but one Person, Christ Jesus being the great God and our Savior, thus asserting the deity of Christ. We prefer the second, with a comma after Savior. This corresponds to the two sacred titles revealed at the birth of Christ: Jesus, Jehovah the Savior, and Emmanuel, God with us (Matt. 1:21-23). Our Lord is not only our Savior, but also God, and not merely God, but the great God, the God who is great in nature, in glory, in authority, in power, in deed, in love, in grace, and in every divine attribute. In 1 Timothy 2:5 our Lord is revealed as a man; here, as the great God. He is both man and God. His appearing in His divine glory will be not only for saving His people into the kingdom age, but also for the judgment of the entire world, that He may bring the kingdom of God to this earth. Hence, His appearing in His glory is the blessed hope.

Whether or not we shall be happy at the time of the Lord's appearing depends on our living as Christians today. According to Matthew 25, all the Lord's servants will give an account to Him at His coming. To some the Lord will say, "Well done, good and faithful slave; you were faithful over a few things, I will set you over many things; enter into the joy of your Lord" (Matt. 25:21). But others the Lord will rebuke as evil and slothful slaves (v. 26). The evil and slothful slave is not an unbeliever or a false believer. How could someone who is not a genuine believer in the Lord receive a talent from Him, and how could a false believer meet the Lord at His judgment seat in the air? Such things are impossible. Only genuine believers are spoken of here.

Many of today's Christians will find themselves in a sorrowful situation at the time of the Lord's coming. Instead of being commended by the Lord, they will be rebuked by Him. Oh, the superficiality among Christians today! Many have been drugged by superficial teachings concerning the Lord's coming. They do not have a heart for the healthy teachings regarding God's economy. Because they have been drugged, they imagine that they will have no problems with the Lord at the time of His appearing. They do not seem to realize that, according to Paul's word in 2 Timothy 4:8, the Lord will appear as the righteous Judge. At that time, a great many Christians will hear a very sobering word from the Lord. However, I prefer to hear a sobering word from Him today. In contrast to much of the preaching among Christians today, the ministry in the Lord's recovery does not present sugar-coated teachings. On the contrary, sobering messages are given to the saints.

In verse 14 Paul says that Christ "gave Himself for us, that He might redeem us from all lawlessness and purify to Himself a people for His own possession, zealous of good works." The words "for us" here mean on our behalf. They do not mean instead of us. To redeem means to buy with a price (1 Cor. 6:20; 1 Pet. 1:18-19; 1 Tim. 2:6). Christ gave Himself for us not only that He might redeem us from all lawlessness, but also purify to Himself a people for His own possession. A people for His possession are a peculiar people. This expression is borrowed from the Old Testament (Deut. 7:6; 14:2; 26:18) and denotes a people privately possessed by God as His peculiar treasure (Exo. 19:5), His own possession (1 Pet. 2:9).

III. THE APOSTLE'S CHARGE TO TITUS

In verse 15 we have the apostle's charge to Titus: "These things speak, and exhort and reprove with all authority. Let no one despise you." By "these things" Paul means all the things in verses 1 through 14. Titus was charged to speak these things and to exhort and reprove with all authority. Authority here also means imperativeness. The literal meaning of the Greek word is command. With all authority modifies both exhort and reprove. To exhort and reprove with all authority is to advise and rebuke imperatively with words of authority in every way, as giving command.

Paul's exhortation, "Let no one despise you," is connected with the matter of authority in the preceding sentence. It is the conclusion of all the charges to Titus in this chapter. It mainly concerns his teaching (vv. 1, 7-8, 15). The healthy teaching with the healthy word according to godliness would keep him in gravity and invite the utmost respect.

LIFE-STUDY OF TITUS

MESSAGE FIVE

CHARGING THE SAINTS TO KEEP A GOOD RELATIONSHIP WITH THE GOVERNMENT

Scripture Reading: Titus 3:1-8

When Paul was writing the Epistle of Titus, there were certain basic concepts within him. These concepts were the factors, the elements, of the composition of this book. In writing chapter one of Titus, Paul was deeply concerned for the church. Hence, in this chapter he takes care of the proper order in the church and speaks of establishing the eldership for the administration of a local church, of the termination of the various isms, and of holding to the healthy teaching of the apostles. Paul goes on in chapter two to speak of an orderly human life, which is primarily related to the family life. Then, as we have seen in the foregoing message, he speaks of society, or of the social system. In 3:1-8 Paul speaks of the rulers, that is, the government.

To have an orderly life, we need to take care of four units: the church, the family, the social system, and the government. If we care for these units properly, we shall have an orderly life in every way. When Paul was writing the book of Titus, he had within him a concern for these four units. Unbelievers, of course, care only for family, society, and government. Even the philosophers and thoughtful people throughout the centuries have considered only these three units among mankind. But among us in the Lord's recovery the most important unit is the church. For us, the church is first. We give the church preeminence in our consideration, for the church is the house of the living God, the pillar and base of the truth. Furthermore, the church is the great mystery of godliness, God manifested in the flesh. Paul covered the matter of the church first in this Epistle, and we follow him to give the church the first place among the four basic units covered in this book.

After the church, the most important unit is the family. Some opposers have tried to defame us by spreading the devilish lie that we do not care for the family life. Next to the church, the family is the most important unit in society. Without a proper family life, how could we have a healthy society or country? A nation is constituted of families as the basic factors. We fully realize that without a proper family life it is difficult to have an orderly church life. But we also realize that without a proper church life it is difficult to have a normal and proper family life. We are here for the church and also for the family. Furthermore, we care for society. We respect others, we honor our neighbors, and we care for the existing social system. We are not here as social reformers, and it is not our intention to change the social system. In the Lord's recovery we are here to present to others healthy teachings concerning the all-inclusive Christ and the church as the Body of Christ.

A CHARGE TO THE SAINTS

In this message we are concerned with Paul's charge to the saints to maintain a good relationship with the government. According to the healthy teaching in the New Testament, we must respect the government.

In 3:1 and 2 Paul says, "Remind them to be subject to rulers, to authorities, to be obedient, to be ready unto every good work, to speak evil of no one, to be uncontentious, forbearing, showing all meekness toward all men." To be subject to rulers is to recognize God's authority and respect His government over men (Rom. 13:1-2). To be uncontentious (v. 2) is to be peaceable, not quarrelsome.

Before Paul could teach the saints to respect the government, he himself had to experience a certain amount of transformation. When he was Saul of Tarsus, he was a patriotic Jew and wanted to be free from the yoke of the Roman imperialists. But here he instructs the saints to subject themselves to rulers and to authorities. According to his word in Romans 13, government officials have been appointed by God. Paul recognized that even those officials appointed by Caesar are rulers appointed by God, His deputy authority. If Paul had not been transformed from a natural person into a spiritual person with spiritual understanding, it would have been difficult for him to give such instructions.

GOD'S SUPPLY

To care for the church life, the family life, the social system, and the government, we need a specific supply. In speaking of these four units, Paul also tells us of the divine supply. We have seen that in chapter one Paul speaks concerning the church life. The supply for the church life consists of the faith of God's chosen ones, the full knowledge of the truth which is according to godliness, and the hope of eternal life (1:1-2). Eternal life in particular is the supply which enables us to have the church life. The word of proclamation (1:3) is another aspect of the supply for the proper church life.

Just as there is a supply for the church life, there is also a supply for the family life. The supply for the proper family life includes healthy teaching (2:1), healthy speech (2:8), and being healthy in faith, in love, and in endurance (2:2). For the family unit we need the supply of healthy teaching and healthy speech. The word speech in 2:8 refers to our ordinary daily conversation, such as conversation at the dinner table. If our speech is healthy, it will supply us that we may have a proper family life.

We have seen that in 2:9-15 Paul charges the slaves to behave well in the social system of slavery. This indicates that we need to have the proper attitude toward society. But what is the supply for living in the existing social system? This supply is the grace of God which has appeared, bringing salvation to all men and training us to live soberly, righteously, and godly in the present age as we await the blessed hope, the appearing of the glory of the great God and our Savior, Christ Jesus (2:11-13). By means of this supply we can adorn the teaching of our Savior God in all things.

The supply which enables us to keep a good relationship with the government is wonderful. Paul speaks of this supply in 3:4-7. Prior to this, he says in verse 3, "For we also were once foolish, disobedient, deceived, serving as slaves various lusts and pleasures, spending our life in malice and envy, hateful, hating one another." We should remember that in nature we were once the same as others, living in the fallen condition; therefore, we should sympathize with their pitiful life and pray for their salvation (1 Tim. 2:1, 4). We also once served as slaves various lusts, various desires and gratifications. But now we have a marvelous supply to have a good relationship with the government.

KINDNESS, LOVE, AND MERCY

Verse 4 says, "But when the kindness and love to man of our Savior God appeared." It is the kindness and love of our Savior God that has saved us and made us different from others.

In verse 5 Paul continues, "Not by works in righteousness which we have done but according to His mercy, He saved us, through the washing of regeneration and renewing of the Holy Spirit." Titus 2:11 says that the grace of God brings salvation to man, and 3:7 says that we have been justified by the grace of the Lord. But verse 5 says that according to His mercy He saved us. God's mercy reaches farther than His grace. Our pitiful condition created a wide gap between us and God's grace. It was God's mercy that has bridged this gap and brought us to His salvation of grace.

Notice that in 3:4-5 Paul does not speak of grace, but speaks of kindness, love, and mercy. Love is the source of grace. In the heart of God the Father there is love. But when this love is expressed through the Son, it becomes grace. For this reason, 2 Corinthians 13:14 speaks of the grace of Christ and the love of the Father. In John 1:16 and 17 we have grace; however, in 1 John we touch the love of God the Father as the source of this grace.

What, then, are mercy and kindness? We have pointed out that mercy always reaches farther than grace. When we are in a proper situation, God's love will come to us as grace. However, we were all in a pitiful situation and may still be in such a situation today. Therefore, we need God's mercy to reach us. The mercy of God can come to us even in our pitiful situation.

Kindness is God's attitude in giving grace to us. It is possible to give a gift to a person without having a proper attitude. For example, I may give a valuable gift to a brother but give it in a rather crude, insensitive manner. On the other hand, I may give him a gift in a way that expresses an attitude of kindness. God's attitude in giving us grace is the attitude of kindness.

When we have mercy, love, and kindness, we automatically have grace. Our God and Father has shown us love, mercy, and kindness. It is by this that He saves us.

WASHING AND RENEWING

According to verse 5, God's salvation is also through a certain action: the washing of regeneration and renewing of the Holy Spirit. In Greek, the word for regeneration in verse 5 is different from that for born again (1 Pet. 1:23). The only other place this word is used is in Matthew 19:28 for the restoration in the millennium. Here it refers to a change from one state of things to another. To be born again is the beginning of this change. The washing of regeneration begins with our being born again and continues with the renewing of the Holy Spirit as the process of God's new creation to make us a new man. It is a kind of reconditioning, remaking, remodeling with life. Baptism (Rom. 6:3-5), the putting off of the old man, the putting on of the new man (Eph. 4:22, 24; Col. 3:9-11), and transformation by the renewing of the mind (Rom 12:2; Eph. 4:23) are all related to this wonderful process. The washing of regeneration purges away all the things of the old nature of our old man, and the renewing of the Holy Spirit imparts something new—the divine essence of the new man—into our being. In this is a passage from the old state we were in into a wholly new one, from the old creation into the status of a new creation. Hence, both the washing of regeneration and the renewing of the Holy Spirit are a continual working in us throughout our whole life until the completion of the new creation.

In 1 Timothy the church is stressed (3:15-16), in 2 Timothy the Scripture (3:15-16), and in Titus the Holy Spirit. The church is the house of the living God, expressing God in the flesh, and the pillar and base of the truth, the divine reality of the great mystery—God manifested in the flesh. The Scripture is the breath of God, containing and conveying His divine essence for our nourishment and equipment to make us perfect and complete for His use. The Holy Spirit is the divine Person, washing and renewing us in the divine element to make us a new creation with the divine nature to be heirs of God in His eternal life, inheriting all the riches of the Triune God.

Verse 6 says that the Holy Spirit has been "poured out on us richly through Jesus Christ our Savior." The Holy Spirit, Who is the Triune God reaching man, has not only been given to us, but poured out on us richly through Jesus Christ, our Redeemer and Savior, to bring all the divine riches in Christ to us, including the eternal life of God and His divine nature, for our eternal portion.

HEIRS ACCORDING TO THE HOPE OF ETERNAL LIFE

In verse 7 Paul goes on to say, "That, having been justified by the grace of that One, we might become heirs according to the hope of eternal life." This speaks forth the issue and goal of God's salvation (v. 5) and justification, including the washing of regeneration and renewing of the Holy Spirit. The issue and goal is to make us heirs of God according to the hope of eternal life.

According to verse 7, the believers are not only sons, but also heirs who are qualified to inherit the Father's estate (Rom. 4:14; 8:17; Gal. 3:29; 4:7). We are born of God (John 1:12-13) with His eternal life (John 3:16). This eternal life is for us not only to live and enjoy God in this age, but also to inherit all the riches of what He is to us in the coming age and in eternity. Hence, there is the hope of eternal life. God's eternal life is our enjoyment today and our hope tomorrow. According to this hope we become heirs of God to inherit all His riches for eternity. This is the climax as the eternal goal of His eternal salvation with His eternal life given to us by grace in Christ.

A CHARGE TO TITUS

In verse 8 Paul concludes this section of Titus: "Faithful is the word, and concerning these things I desire you to affirm confidently, so that those who have believed in God may be careful to maintain good works. These things are good and profitable to men." The faithful word here is given in verses 3 through 7, and these things are the things mentioned in verses 1 through 7. To affirm confidently is to affirm consistently, steadfastly, positively, with persistence and thoroughness. It is the same word used in 1 Timothy 1:7.

In speaking concerning the church life, the family life, the social system, and the government, Paul does not give empty instructions. Along with the instructions, he points us to the source of the supply. For the church life, we have the faith of God's chosen ones, the full knowledge of the truth, eternal life with its hope, and the word of proclamation which causes eternal life to be manifested. For the family life, we have healthy words, healthy teaching, and healthy speech. For the social system, we have the grace of God which has saved us and which is now training us to deny ungodliness and worldly lusts and to live soberly, righteously, and godly in the present age. For a good relationship with the government, we have the marvelous supply described in 3:1-8. Therefore, we have the divine supply for a proper church life, family life, social life, and relationship with the government. We have a proper relationship with all these units not by ethical teachings, philosophical instruction, or our natural life and ability. On the contrary, we have a heavenly, divine, and spiritual supply for the church, family, society, and government.

LIFE-STUDY OF TITUS

MESSAGE SIX

DEALING WITH A FACTIOUS ONE

Scripture Reading: Titus 3:9-15

Before we consider 3:9-15, we need a further word on verses 4 through 7. In verse 7 Paul says, "That, having been justified by the grace of that One, we might become heirs according to the hope of eternal life." Becoming heirs of God is the goal of His eternal salvation with His eternal life given to us by grace in Christ. In verses 4 through 6 we see some crucial matters needed to reach God's goal. In verses 4 and 5 we read of certain divine attributes: kindness, love, and mercy. When these attributes are put together, we have grace. God has exercised His love, mercy, kindness, and grace in order to save us. Whenever we are about to do something of great importance, we exercise our whole being. Our mind, will, emotion, heart, and even our disposition are exercised. In like manner, God exercised His being in order to save us. He exercised His love, kindness, mercy, and grace. By means of these divine attributes God has saved us. These attributes, however, are the source; they are not the activity or the process.

In 3:5 and 6 we have activity, an action, constituting the process through which God saved us: "He saved us, through the washing of regeneration and renewing of the Holy Spirit, Whom He poured out on us richly through Jesus Christ our Savior." God's salvation is based upon the exercise of His attributes and through the process of the washing of regeneration and renewing of the Holy Spirit. The goal is that we become God's heirs.

Paul certainly was an excellent writer. Knowing that in verses 4 through 6 he had not written anything concerning justification, he inserts the words "having been justified by the grace of that One." Although justification is somewhat implied by the matters of salvation and washing, Paul mentions it explicitly in verse 7. We have been saved, washed, and justified. The grace by which we are justified is the totality of God's kindness, love, and mercy. These attributes are of God. But when they become a totality in our experience, that is grace. Kindness, love, and mercy are of the Father, whereas grace is of Christ, of "that One." For this reason, in 2 Corinthians 13:14 Paul speaks of the grace of Christ and of the love of God the Father.

In 3:7 Paul says that we become heirs according to the hope of eternal life, whereas in 1:1 and 2 he says that he became an apostle in the hope of eternal life. This eternal life meant a great deal to Paul. It also means a great deal to us as believers. Paul became an apostle in the hope of eternal life, and we become heirs of God according to the hope of eternal life. Why does Paul use the word "in" when speaking of himself and the word "according to" when speaking of us? The fact that he used the word "in" with respect to himself indicates that he was already experiencing the hope of eternal life. But because we have not yet entered into this experience to a very great extent, he says that we are heirs according to the hope of eternal life. As a very matured believer, Paul was experiencing the hope already. He was in it. But, for the most part, this experience lies ahead of us. Therefore, we are heirs according to this hope.

I. THE APOSTLE'S CHARGE

In 3:9 Paul goes on to say, "But avoid foolish questionings and genealogies and strifes and contentions about the law, for they are unprofitable and vain." The questionings here are those aroused by genealogies (1 Tim. 1:4), and the strifes issue out of the questionings and genealogies. Contentions refer to fightings, which are due to different opinions issuing from the deviant and mythological studies of the law. The law in this verse is the law of the Jews used for Gnostic Judaism, which stood in opposition to the simplicity of the gospel. These questionings, genealogies, strifes, and contentions are all vain; that is, they are aimless, without any positive result.

The positive things stressed in verses 4 through 8 should be affirmed strongly and consistently, positive things including our Savior God, Jesus Christ our Savior, the Holy Spirit, God's kindness, love, mercy, grace, and eternal life, with His acts of justifying, saving, washing, regenerating, and renewing. These are the Triune God with His attributes and virtues, plus His divine actions in His eternal salvation: they are things of life, which belong to the tree of life (Gen. 2:9) and produce heirs to inherit all that He is for them. The negative things dealt with in verses 9 through 11 should be avoided. These things include foolish questionings, genealogies, strifes, contentions about the law, and factious, opinionated men. These matters are of the knowledge that is deadening, matters that belong to the tree of knowledge and kill their victims.

Paul's word about avoiding foolish questionings, genealogies, strifes, and contentions corresponds to what he says about teaching differently in 1 Timothy 1. Differing teachings had begun to creep into the church, and Paul charges Titus to avoid them.

The Lord's ministry is not the teaching of any individual. The ministry is the teaching of God's New Testament economy. This means that the Lord's ministry is the healthy teaching which conveys to us the New Testament economy. Unfortunately, most of today's Christian teachers have missed the mark of God's economy. God's economy may be likened to a kernel or a grain. Most Christian teachers pay attention not to the kernel, but to the stem, the leaves, and even to the husks. They may argue and debate over husks and neglect the kernel.

In Colossians 1:25 Paul says, "I became a minister according to the stewardship of God, which was given to me for you, to complete the word of God." To complete the word of God means to complete the divine revelation. This completion of the word of God is the mystery of Christ. This expression refers both to Christ and to His mystery. The mystery of Christ is the church. The content of the teaching of the New Testament economy is the all-inclusive Christ and the church as the Body of Christ.

Any teaching which deviates from this central focus should be regarded as a differing teaching. For example, suppose a certain Christian teacher insists that we baptize people in the name of Jesus Christ, not in the name of the Father, Son, and Holy Spirit and not even in the name of Christ Jesus. Although such a teaching may be presented in a way which sounds fundamental and scriptural, it is actually a differing teaching because it emphasizes something other than the focus of God's economy and distracts the saints from the proper church life. Yes, the Bible commands us to be baptized. But we should not be influenced by differing teachings related to the name in which the believers are baptized. To pay too much attention to such matters will cause us to be distracted from God's economy.

It is not the goal of the Lord's recovery to recover doctrinal truths. The goal of the recovery is to bring us back to God's New Testament economy, which is Christ and the church. What the Lord desires of us, and what we ourselves need, is to have our entire being focused on God's economy. In the Lord's recovery we must pay our full attention to Christ and the church.

As we direct our attention to God's economy concerning Christ and the church, we must avoid differing teachings. These teachings may be scriptural, and certain preachers may speak of them in an eloquent, attractive manner. However, we must discern whether or not such speaking is focused on Christ and the church, whether or not it strengthens the believers to live Christ and practice the church life. A person may deliver an excellent message on love from 1 Corinthians 13. However, if he has not seen the vision of the New Testament economy concerning Christ and the church, even his inspiring message on love may be a distraction. The more he expounds 1 Corinthians 13, the more those who listen to him are distracted from Christ and from the church life. Instead, they pay their attention to love.

Many seeking Christians have been distracted not by heresies, but by good teachings on certain favorite portions of the Bible. Many Christians are impressed by 1 Corinthians 13, and they appreciate messages on this chapter. But although they may talk a great deal about love and about the need to love one another, they neglect the church life.

Christians today appreciate the book of Psalms. For many, Psalms is their favorite book in the Bible. Paying our full attention to the Psalms, however, may distract us from living Christ and may encourage and strengthen us to be merely believers who emphasize the devotional life. Furthermore, some may be distracted from the church life and even completely neglect it. They may even criticize certain ones in the church for not emphasizing the devotional time the way they do.

How are we to discern which messages to receive and which to avoid? Although we must oppose heresy, we should not oppose teachings which are not heretical. But we should not pay attention to teachings that are not focused on God's economy, even though they are sound. We need to avoid differing teachings and concentrate on God's economy concerning Christ and the church.

II. DEALING WITH A FACTIOUS MAN

Titus 3:10 and 11 say, "A factious man after a first and second admonition refuse, knowing that such a one has been perverted and sins, being self-condemned." A factious man is a heretical, sectarian man who causes divisions by forming parties in the church according to his own opinions. The Gnostic Judaism referred to in the preceding verse must be related to this. The divisiveness is based on differing teachings. This is the reason that verse 10 comes after verse 9. Certain believers may have insisted on the teaching of the law and in so doing became divisive.

In verse 10 Paul charges Titus to refuse a factious man after a first and second admonition. In order to maintain good order in the church, a factious, divisive person, after a first and second admonition, should be refused, rejected.

Because such divisiveness is contagious, this rejection is for the church's profit that contact with the divisive one be stopped.

In verse 11 Paul speaks a severe word, saying that a factious man has been perverted, that he sins, and that he is self-condemned. Literally, the Greek words rendered "has been perverted" mean turned out of the way. It is more than being turned away from the right path (Titus 1:14). One who has been perverted in this way is spoiled, damaged, destroyed, with respect to God's New Testament economy.

Paul tells us that factious persons are self-condemned. When a factious person is alone, deep within he may become conscious of a feeling of condemnation. He knows that he does not have genuine peace. With his tongue he may say that he is not condemned, but deep in his heart he has questions and a sense of uneasiness. Some of those who left the Lord's recovery argued strongly about various things. But deep within they did not have true peace. Instead, they were self-condemned. If they did not have a feeling of condemnation within, they would not struggle to vindicate themselves and to convince others they are right. Their efforts at self-vindication are a sign of their self-condemnation.

III. THE CONCLUSION OF THE BOOK

A. The Apostle's Fellowship

In verses 12 and 13 Paul says, "When I send Artemas to you or Tychicus, be diligent to come to me to Nicopolis, for I have decided to spend the winter there. Zenas the lawyer and Apollos send forward diligently that nothing may be lacking to them." Nicopolis was a city in the southwestern corner of Macedonia, where this Epistle was written. Artemas and Tychicus were intimate fellow-workers of Paul; Zenas and Apollos worked independently of him. Yet Paul still charged Titus to care for them, showing there was no jealousy between the two groups of co-workers.

Paul's word in verse 14 is related to what he says in verse 13: "And let those also who are ours learn to maintain good works for necessary needs, that they may not be unfruitful." They were to take care of the needs of the Lord's servants and to help them on their way.

B. Greetings

In verse 15 Paul concludes, "All who are with me greet you. Greet those who love us in faith. Grace be with you all." The faith here is subjective and denotes our believing act which brings us into organic union with the Lord (John 3:15; Gal. 3:26) and operates through love (Gal. 5:6). It is in the element and operation of this faith that the saints who were one with the Lord in His concern loved the suffering and faithful apostle.

LIFE-STUDY OF PHILEMON

MESSAGE ONE

A SLAVE REBORN TO BE A BROTHER

Scripture Reading: Philem. 1-16

I. THE SUBJECT OF THE BOOK

The subject of the book of Philemon is an illustration of the believers' equal status in the new man. In the new man all the believers, whether masters such as Philemon or slaves such as Onesimus, have the same status.

II. INTRODUCTION

The book of Philemon opens with the words, "Paul, a prisoner of Christ Jesus, and Timothy the brother, to Philemon the beloved and our fellow-worker." In verse 2 Paul refers to Apphia the sister and to Archippus and to the church in Philemon's house. According to the family nature of this Epistle, Apphia must be Philemon's wife, and Archippus, his son. Philemon lived in Colosse (v. 2, see Col. 4:17; v. 10, see Col. 1:2; 4:9). According to history, he was an elder of the church in Colosse. It should be that the church in Colosse met in his house. Hence, it was the church in his house.

The introduction to this Epistle concludes with Paul's word in verse 3: "Grace to you and peace from God our Father and the Lord Jesus Christ."

III. A SLAVE REBORN TO BE A BROTHER

In verses 4 and 5 Paul goes on to say, "I thank my God always, making mention of you in my prayers, hearing of your love and the faith which you have toward the Lord Jesus and to all the saints." Notice that in verse 5 Paul speaks first of love and then of faith. In the initial stage faith came first, and then love was produced by faith (Gal. 5:6; Eph. 1:15; Col. 1:4). But here love is referred to first and then faith, because what is dealt with in this Epistle concerning the equal status of believers is a matter of love, which comes out of faith. In the new man the members love one another in faith (Titus 3:15). The relationship is of love through faith. The apostle appreciates the fellowship of Philemon's faith (v. 6) and is encouraged by his love (v. 7); thus he entreats him to receive Onesimus because of this love (v. 9). These two virtues are referred to in a combined way. Philemon has both of them, not only toward the Lord, but also toward all the saints.

In verse 6 Paul continues, "That the fellowship of your faith may become operative in the full knowledge of every good thing which is in us for Christ." This verse is actually the continuation of verse 4. Full knowledge here means full acknowledgment, entire appreciation, and experiential recognition. By "every good thing" Paul does not mean natural things (see Rom. 7:18), but spiritual and divinely good things, such as eternal life, the divine nature, and spiritual gifts, which are in us, the regenerated believers, not in natural men.

The Greek word rendered "for" in the phrase "for Christ" literally means unto, toward. All the spiritual and divinely good things in us are unto Christ, toward Christ, for Christ. The apostle prays that the fellowship, the communication, the sharing, of Philemon's faith toward all the saints may operate in them in the element and sphere of the full knowledge, the full realization, of all the good things in us for Christ, causing them to acknowledge, appreciate, and recognize all the spiritual and divinely good things which are in the believers for Christ.

In verse 7 Paul says, "For I had much joy and encouragement over your love, because the inward parts of the saints have been refreshed through you, brother." The word "for" introduces the reason the apostle prays for Philemon's faith to operate in the saints (v. 6). It is because his love has refreshed the inward parts of the saints and has hence rendered the apostle much joy and encouragement. The Greek word rendered refreshed also means soothed, cheered.

Verses 8 and 9 continue, "Wherefore, having much boldness in Christ to charge you what is fitting, because of love I rather entreat, being such a one as Paul the aged, and now also a prisoner of Christ Jesus." The Greek word for aged here may also be translated an ambassador (Eph. 6:20). Prisoner here and in verse 23, and bonds in verse 13, indicate that this Epistle was written during imprisonment, the apostle's first imprisonment in Rome.

In verses 10 and 11 Paul says, "I entreat you concerning my child whom I have begotten in my bonds, Onesimus, who formerly was useless to you, but now is useful both to you and to me." During his imprisonment, Paul begot Onesimus through the Spirit with the eternal life of God (John 3:3; 1:13). In Greek the name Onesimus means profitable, useful, helpful; it was a common name for slaves. He was Philemon's purchased bondslave, who, according to Roman law, had no human rights. He ran away from his master, committing a crime which could bring the death penalty. While he was in prison at Rome with the apostle, he was saved through him. Now the apostle sends him back with this Epistle to his master.

The word useless in verse 11 also means not of service, profitless. This refers to Onesimus's running away from Philemon. The word useful also means of service, profitable. Onesimus became of service because he had been converted and was willing to return to Philemon.

Verse 12 continues, "Whom I have sent back to you—him, that is, my very heart." Literally, the Greek word for heart means bowels, as in verses 7 and 20; Philippians 1:8; 2:1; and Colossians 3:12. It signifies inward affection, tenderheartedness, compassions. Paul's inward affection and compassions went with Onesimus to Philemon.

Verses 13 and 14 say, "Whom I resolved to keep with myself, that on your behalf he might minister to me in the bonds of the gospel, but without your mind I did not want to do anything, that your goodness should not be as of necessity, but voluntary." Just as the Lord would not do anything without our consent, Paul would not keep Onesimus with him without Philemon's consent.

In verses 15 and 16 Paul says, "For perhaps therefore he was separated from you for an hour that you might fully have him forever, no longer as a slave, but above a slave, a beloved brother, especially to me, and how much more to you, both in the flesh and in the Lord." The word "for" in verse 15 introduces the reason for the sending in verse 12. The word perhaps here is not only an expression of humility, but also one which shows no prejudice.

This short Epistle serves the special purpose of showing us the equality in eternal life and divine love of all the members in the Body of Christ. In the age of Paul the life of Christ had annulled, among the believers, the strong institution of slavery. Since the sentiment of the love of the Christian fellowship was so powerful and prevailing that the evil social order among fallen mankind was spontaneously ignored, any need for institutional emancipation was obviated. Because of the divine birth and living by the divine life, all the believers in Christ had equal status in the church, which was the new man in Christ, with no discrimination between free and bond (Col. 3:10-11). This is based on three facts. First, Christ's death on the cross has abolished the ordinances of the different ways of life for the creation of the one new man (Eph. 2:15). Second, we all have been baptized into Christ and made one in Him without any difference (Gal. 3:27-28). Third, in the new man Christ is all and in all (Col. 3:11). Such a life with such a love in equal fellowship is well able to maintain good order in the church (in Titus), carry out God's economy concerning the church (in 1 Timothy), and stand against the tide of the church's decline (in 2 Timothy). It is of the Lord's sovereignty that this Epistle was positioned after the three preceding books in the arrangement of the New Testament.

According to Paul's word in verse 16, Onesimus was above a slave, or more than a slave. He was even more than a free man; he was a beloved brother.

There are a number of intimate terms in this Epistle: a beloved brother, the sister (v. 2), the beloved and our fellow-worker (v. 1), our fellow-soldier (v. 2), my fellow-workers (v. 24), my fellow-prisoner (v. 23), and a partner (v. 17). These terms indicate the intimate sentiment in the apostle concerning his relationship with the fellow members in the new man.

The expression "both in the flesh and in the Lord" means in the flesh as a slave and in the Lord as a brother; in the flesh a brother for a slave, and in the Lord a slave for a brother.

The title of this message is "A Slave Reborn to Be a Brother." Only through the preaching of the gospel could a slave like Onesimus be reborn to be a brother. Paul did not preach the gospel to Onesimus in an ordinary way or in a careless, superficial way. Paul preached the gospel to him while he was a prisoner in Rome. This indicates that no matter what kind of situation Paul was in, he was always exercised to carry on the preaching of the gospel. He says, "Now I want you to know, brothers, that the things concerning me have turned out rather to the advancement of the gospel, so that my bonds have become manifest in Christ in the whole praetorium and to all the rest." Nero's royal guard heard Paul preaching the gospel and even saw him preaching the gospel. Philippians 4:22 indicates that certain members of Caesar's household were saved: "All the saints greet you, and especially those of Caesar's household." Now we know from the Epistle to Philemon that the slave Onesimus was saved through Paul.

Paul did not preach the gospel to Onesimus in the way practiced by most Christians today. Paul regarded his gospel preaching as an act of begetting. For this reason, Paul refers to Onesimus as his child begotten in his bonds. Paul's preaching involved a process of begetting and giving birth to a child. This indicates that in his preaching of the gospel Paul ministered the divine life into others. The eternal life of God imparted into Onesimus caused him to be reborn as Paul's spiritual child and brother in Christ. When we preach the gospel today, we also must preach in the way of begetting, in the way of imparting Christ as the divine life into those to whom we preach the gospel.

Furthermore, after begetting this child, Paul did not neglect him or leave him as an orphan in the care of others. Because this child was so dear to him, Paul kept him and loved him. He even referred to him as “my very heart.” Mothers often feel this way toward their child. If the child were taken away from them, it would seem as if the mother’s heart had been snatched away. Do you have this kind of feeling concerning one whom you have brought to the Lord? Probably we do not have much of this kind of feeling. However, Paul considered Onesimus not only his child, but also his heart. For Paul to send his child to Philemon meant that he also sent his heart to him. What concern we see here!

There are some parents who do not regard their children in the flesh as their own heart. They may say within themselves, “God has given me this child, and it is my duty to take care of him. In this matter I have no choice.” Often Christians who bring others to the Lord have a similar attitude. In contrast to Paul, they lack a deep parental concern for the one saved through them.

Although Paul had such a loving concern for his child, he realized that he was not the right person to keep him. Because Onesimus was a slave who had escaped from his master, he had to return. It is possible that Onesimus had stolen something from Philemon. Verse 18 may indicate this: “And if he has wronged you in anything or owes anything, charge that to my account.” Onesimus may not merely have pilfered things from Philemon; he may have stolen something precious.

Here we see that Paul’s concern was that the human relationship between Onesimus and Philemon would be rectified. After we have brought a sinner to the Lord, we should first regard him as our spiritual child and then help him to rectify his relationships. For example, if one has wronged his parents, we should help him to be reconciled to his parents. If a wife is wrong with her husband, or a husband with his wife, we should help the wife or husband to restore the proper relationship with the spouse. This is an important principle.

In sending back this escaped slave to his master, Paul, an excellent writer, appealed to Philemon's love. In verses 5 and 6 Paul says, "Hearing of your love and faith which you have toward the Lord Jesus and to all the saints, that the fellowship of your faith may become operative in the full knowledge of every good thing which is in us for Christ." Because in this Epistle Paul is appealing to Philemon's love, he puts love before faith in verse 5.

Verse 6 is difficult to understand. Here Paul seems to be saying, "When the brothers in different localities learn of what you did in love through faith and have fellowship regarding your faith, your faith will work in them. It will become operative in them in the full knowledge of every good thing which is in us for Christ, because all believers have the same good things within them." These good things include the divine life, the divine nature, and the divine gifts. A full record of these things is found in the three books of 1 and 2 Timothy and Titus. All these good things in us are for Christ. The fellowship of Philemon's faith may be likened to a fan with which we fan into flame for Christ all the good things within us (2 Tim. 1:6). When the saints hear what Philemon did in love, the good deposit within them will be stirred up. This is the operation of the faith of a certain saint through the fellowship among the believers.

In the book of Philemon we have an excellent pattern and example of bringing a sinner to the Lord through begetting him with the divine life; regarding him as a child, even as our heart; and helping him to rectify all the human relationships. In the churches in the Lord's recovery it is our practice to send back the escaped one and the divorced or separated wife or husband. We want to help rectify all human relationships. In doing this, we must have a loving concern and appeal to the love of the other party. Finally, in keeping with Paul's example in this Epistle, we must help the newly saved one to come into the church life. Paul's desire was to bring Onesimus into the church life. Having been begotten by Paul, Onesimus was now a slave reborn to be a brother. As the one who had begotten him, Paul bore the responsibility to bring Onesimus into the church life, into the fellowship among the members of the Body.

LIFE-STUDY OF PHILEMON

MESSAGE TWO

A BROTHER RECOMMENDED FOR THE ACCEPTANCE OF THE NEW MAN

Scripture Reading: Philem. 17-25

The subject of the book of Philemon is an illustration of the believers' equal status in the new man. Apparently this Epistle does not say anything concerning the status of the believers. Actually, this book touches the heart of this matter.

When Paul wrote to Philemon, Philemon was in Colosse and Paul was far away, a prisoner in Rome. One of his co-prisoners, Onesimus, was brought to the Lord and begotten by Paul in the Spirit to become not only a believer in Christ and a child of God, but also a dear child to Paul himself. Since there was a church in Rome, why did Paul not recommend this newly saved one to the local church there? Paul did not do this, because Onesimus was a runaway slave and his master, Philemon, lived in Colosse.

The fact that there were churches in Rome and in Colosse indicates that the churches as the expression of the Body of Christ are universal. This was true in ancient times just as it is true today. The first church, the church in Jerusalem, came into existence approximately A.D. 34 or 35. The Epistle to Philemon was written about thirty years later. Even during the comparatively short time of thirty years, churches had been established not only in Judea, but also in the Gentile world. Thus, the church was universal. This was according to the Lord's sovereignty to carry out the commission He had given to Paul. It also was the fulfillment of Paul's desire to see a new man on earth.

By the spreading of the Roman Empire the various nations and peoples around the Mediterranean Sea were brought into contact with one another and were even unified politically. There was a great deal of traffic and communication between people in various parts of the empire. This communication was altogether related to the old man. But at the time Paul wrote to Philemon, another man had come into existence on earth. In the midst of the old man, the new man had come into being. This is fully revealed in Colossians 3:10 and 11: "And having put on the new man, which is being renewed unto full knowledge according to the image of Him Who created him; where there cannot be Greek and Jew, circumcision and uncircumcision, barbarian, Scythian, slave, freeman, but Christ is all and in all." Philemon was an elder of the church in Colosse. In the Epistle to the Colossians Paul emphasized that all the believers are part of the new man. Furthermore, in the new man there cannot be Greek and Jew, slave and freeman. Philemon was a freeman, and Onesimus was his bondservant. But in the new man they were of equal status.

In Colossians 4 we have a record of the fellowship of the new man. Colossians 4:9 speaks of Onesimus, and verse 17, of Archippus, the son of Philemon. A freeman and a slave who were members of the same household were also part of the church as the new man.

The Epistle to Philemon should be regarded as a continuation of Colossians 4 and considered an illustration of how in the new man all social rank is put aside. In the previous message we pointed out that this short Epistle serves the special purpose of showing us the equality in eternal life and divine love of all the members in the Body of Christ. The distinction of social rank and status among the believers is nullified not by an outward legal act, but by an inward change of constitution. Ranks have been abolished because the believers have been constituted of Christ's life. Christ's life had been constituted into Philemon, and the same life with the same divine element had been constituted into his slave, Onesimus. According to the flesh, Philemon was a master and was free, and Onesimus was a slave and was not free. But according to the inner constitution, both were the same. Because of the divine birth and a living by the divine life, all the believers in Christ have equal status in the church, which is the new man in Christ, with no discrimination between free and bond.

In Titus 2:9-15 Paul charges the slaves to behave well in the social system of slavery. He instructed them to live a Jesusly human life in the midst of such a social system. But in the Epistle to Philemon he gives the churches an illustration of how slaves and masters alike have been reconstituted of the life of Christ. As a result, they all are part of the new man. In the old social system, which belongs to the living of the old man, the distinction between master and slave exists. Paul did not touch this social system in the way of trying to reform it. On the contrary, on the one hand he instructed the slaves to live a Jesusly human life under this social system; on the other hand, he illustrated how both slaves and masters are brothers in the Lord and, as members of the new man, share the same status.

Philemon 16 makes this relationship very clear. Concerning Onesimus Paul says, "No longer as a slave, but above a slave, a beloved brother, especially to me, and how much more to you, both in the flesh and in the Lord." Through regeneration Onesimus had become more than a slave and even more than a free man, for he had become a beloved brother. Now Onesimus had a relationship with Philemon "both in the flesh and in the Lord": in the flesh as a slave and in the Lord as a brother. In the flesh Onesimus was a brother as a slave, and in the Lord he was a slave as a brother. Philemon, therefore, had to receive Onesimus and embrace him in a loving, intimate way. Of course, he was to receive him not in the old man, the old social system, but in Christ and in the new man. Although Onesimus was still Philemon's slave, in Christ he had become Philemon's brother. Now, in the new man, Philemon had to receive Onesimus as a brother and one of equal status. Here we see Paul's recommendation of a brother for acceptance in the new man.

In the book of Philemon there is no mention of the

expression "the new man." But as we examine the situation portrayed in this book, we see that Paul was recommending a brother not to a local church in the city where he was at the time, but to a local church in a remote city. This indicates that Paul's recommendation took place within the sphere of the new man. As we have already indicated, this can be proved by Colossians 3:11, where we are told that in the new man there is no bond or free. As Paul was writing to Philemon, he may have been thinking something like this: "Onesimus has become a dear brother in the Lord. Now I wish to recommend him, a slave, to a brother who is a free man. I want to help them both realize that as brothers they are equal. One should be received, and the other must be willing to receive him." This is what I mean in saying that the Epistle to Philemon is an illustration of the equal status of the believers in the new man.

As long as we see that the believers have an equal status in the new man, there will be no problems among us concerning social rank, nationality, or race. We shall have no problems with different peoples. Those who discriminate among people in any way do not practice the proper church life. If we would have the genuine church life, we must receive all the saints regardless of race, nationality, or social rank. It is a fact that in many places believers are not willing to do this. As a result, they cannot have the proper church life.

We should never speak of a church according to race or color—there is no white church, yellow church, black church, or brown church. The church has only one color, and that color is heavenly blue. After you come into the church life, there must not be deep in your being any discrimination between believers on the basis of race or color. As long as such a discrimination exists within you, as far as you are concerned, you are nullifying the church life. The colors which represent the different races have already been nullified by the cross. Now we must be willing to pay the price to have them nullified in the real and genuine church life.

In society distinctions are still made on the basis of color, nationality, or social status. But no such distinctions can exist in the church, in the new man. The old man has been divided by these distinctions. But in the new man distinctions on the basis of color have been nullified. Paul strongly taught this, and we must consider it part of the full knowledge of the truth.

Again and again we have pointed out that in 1 and 2 Timothy and Titus the full knowledge of the truth concerns the content of God's New Testament economy concerning Christ and the church. If we still make distinctions on the basis of color, race, or nationality, in this matter we are reprobate concerning the truth. We do not hold the full knowledge of the truth.

As a Jew, it was not easy for Paul to say that in the new man there cannot be any Jews. But because this was part of the full knowledge of the truth, he declared it plainly and taught it clearly. According to the full knowledge of the truth, in the universe there is one new man, one Body of Christ, and one church of God. Furthermore, there should be only one local church in a locality. We all need to realize this aspect of the truth.

According to the Lord's sovereignty, the Epistle to Philemon was written before the Epistles to Timothy and Titus. But in the arrangement of the books in the New Testament, Philemon was placed at the end of this group of four books. These books reveal the practice of God's New Testament economy, and Philemon shows us a particular aspect of that practice.

In the practice of the economy of God, it is crucial that all social ranks and differences among races and nations are swallowed up. If these ranks and distinctions are allowed to exist in the church life, the new man will be nullified, and the proper church life will be destroyed. How wonderful that in the New Testament there is a little book which tells us about a slave who was brought to the Lord and brought into the church life! If this book had told us that Caesar Nero had been saved, I would not appreciate it as much. But this book tells that a slave, one regarded by the Roman social system as little more than an animal with no legal rights, was saved. Some may think that it was not worthwhile for Paul to even write about him. Others may say that it is sufficient for a slave to be saved and to have the assurance of heaven. Paul, however, exercised great wisdom in writing this Epistle. Never has there been another letter written in this way.

Why did Paul exercise such a loving concern over a slave who had been saved? He did so because he was burdened to illustrate that among all the saints and all the local churches, the believers are equal in the new man. Onesimus and Philemon are a good illustration of this equality. Surely it was sovereign of God that Onesimus was saved in prison through Paul. It was the salvation of Onesimus that afforded Paul the opportunity to give such a marvelous illustration concerning the life of the new man. He could point out that a slave, then in Rome, and his master, far away in Colosse, were equal as believers in the new man.

Paul knew that, for the sake of his conscience, he had to care for Onesimus in a proper way. Paul knew Philemon and his family very well. Perhaps Paul said to himself, "Now Philemon's slave has been saved through me. What shall I do with him? Shall I send him back to his master? And what shall I say to Philemon about Onesimus?" Actually, this was a very important matter, arranged sovereignly by the Lord. No other illustration could better portray the nullification of the difference of status in the new man. The case of Onesimus and Philemon illustrates to the uttermost that in the new man all the believers have an equal status. Oh, it is crucial that we see this! Praise the Lord for the salvation of Onesimus, and praise the Lord for this illustration of our equal status in the new man!

I. THE APOSTLE'S RECOMMENDATION

In verse 17 Paul says to Philemon regarding Onesimus, "If then you hold me as a partner, receive him as myself." The use of the word partner here indicates the deep relationship of fellowship in the Lord. Paul appealed to Philemon to receive Onesimus as if he were Paul himself. A local church with its elders is in partnership with the Lord, and the Lord entrusts the newly saved ones to them just as the good Samaritan entrusted the one he had rescued to the innkeeper (Luke 10:33-35).

II. THE APOSTLE'S PROMISE

In verses 18 and 19 Paul continues, "And if he has wronged you in anything or owes anything, charge that to my account; I Paul have written with my own hand, I will repay; not to say to you that you owe me even your own self besides." The phrase, "if he has wronged you in anything or owes anything," indicates that Onesimus may have defrauded his master. Concerning this, Paul says, "Charge that to my account." In caring for Onesimus, Paul did exactly what the Lord does for us. In verse 19 Paul says, "I will repay," just as the Lord pays everything for His redeemed.

In verse 19 Paul also reminds Philemon, "You owe me even your own self besides." This indicates that Philemon had been saved through Paul himself.

III. THE APOSTLE'S REQUEST AND CONFIDENCE

In verse 20 Paul goes on to say, "Yes, brother, may I have profit from you in the Lord; refresh my inward parts in Christ." The Greek word for profit here, *onaimen,* is an allusion to the name Onesimus. This is a play on words, implying that since Philemon owed Paul even himself, he was an Onesimus to Paul. Hence, Philemon should be profitable to Paul in the Lord.

In this verse Paul also asks Philemon to refresh his inward parts in Christ. The word for refresh means soothe, cheer. Literally, the Greek word rendered inward parts means bowels, as in verse 7. Since Philemon refreshed the inward parts of the saints, his partner asks him now to do the same for him in the Lord.

In verses 21 and 22 Paul says, "Having confidence in

your obedience, I wrote to you, knowing that you will do even beyond what I say. And at the same time also prepare me a lodging; for I hope that through your prayers I shall be graciously given to you." Paul's expectation that he would be liberated from his imprisonment and visit the churches again is also expressed in Philippians 1:25 and 2:24. Paul considered his visit a gracious gift to the church.

IV. THE CONCLUSION

In verses 23 through 25 we have the conclusion of this Epistle: "Epaphras, my fellow-prisoner in Christ Jesus, greets you; as do Mark, Aristarchus, Demas, Luke, my fellow-workers. The grace of the Lord Jesus Christ be with your spirit." The apostle always greeted the recipients of his Epistles, both in the opening and in the conclusion, with the grace of the Lord. This shows that he trusted in the Lord's grace for them, as well as for himself (1 Cor. 15:10), to accomplish what he wrote to them. No human effort avails for the accomplishment of such a high revelation as the completing revelation of the Apostle Paul.